THE WILL WENG OMNIBUS, VOLUME **2**

Selected and edited by Will Weng

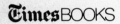

There is a certain fascination about an omnibus of any kind, whether of poetry, short stories or crossword puzzles. The newness may not be there, but the quality and bulk are.

And just as a good story or poem is worth a new reading, a good puzzle is worth a new solving. Even though an occasional word combination or phrase might seem vaguely familiar, most puzzles are as satisfactory for solving the second time around as is a rereading of "The Gold Bug," if you happen to like cryptography.

If that theory is wrong, there probably is no need to provide any answers in the back of the book. But they are there, just in case.

Will Weng

1 American Lit. by William Lutwiniak

This course concentrates on one author.

ACROSS

1. City on the Donau
5. ____-pie
9. Urbanites
13. Ringleader's offering
17. Feverish chill
18. Moves quickly
19. Environs
20. Toga or stola
21. Novel about a civil war
25. Figures of speech
26. Athirst
27. Pad
28. Neighbor of Wash.
29. Hymn-ender
30. Go for
31. Trunk item
34. Encumbrance
35. Takes a chance, at bridge
39. Hay or choir place
40. See 69 Across
42. Greek letter
43. Wave, in Spain
44. Bit of sculpture
46. College pursuit
47. Literary hand-me-down
48. Straw in the wind
50. Ardent
52. Old-fashioned
53. Writer of works named herein
57. Lapwing
59. Dame Myra
60. Reflux
63. Grocery purchase
64. Unfailing
66. P.T.A. people
67. Neighbor of Ore.
68. Neighbor of Ind.
69. Novel about a loser, with 40 Across
72. Actor Devine
73. Autonomy
75. Long times
76. Attire
77. Appraise
78. Miss Baxter
79. Knightly title
80. Approach and speak to
83. Deputy: Abbr.
84. See 33 Down
88. Novel about a sport
92. Plate
93. Maui goose
94. Tide stage
95. Departed
96. Overwhelm
97. Plug-ugly
98. Ifs, ____ or buts
99. Diminutive ending

DOWN

1. Slight breeze
2. Stravinsky
3. Kind of dollar
4. R.I. resort
5. Opted
6. Draw a bead
7. Teacher's ____
8. Feeling unworthy
9. Plane area
10. Incensed
11. ____ Aviv
12. Crackers
13. Delves deeply
14. Take it easy
15. Up to
16. "____-ce pas?"
22. Now's partner
23. Happening
24. ____ chance (risk)
29. "____ Misbehavin'"
30. Itemize
31. ____ over (spill)
32. Marco or water
33. Novel about W.W. I, with 84 Across
34. Endures
35. Noted nuclear physicist
36. Writer's framework
37. Merit
38. Kind of Chinese chop
41. Damages
44. Gave way
45. French article
47. Half of this is acceptable
49. Proverbial crowd
50. Fifth or cart
51. Roman bronze
52. Hundred-weights: Abbr.
54. Pang
55. Lunchtimes
56. Base of Wrigley's fortune
57. French peas
58. La femme
61. Las Vegas numbers
62. Routes
64. Closing
65. Ubangi feeder
66. Leonine feature
69. Contents of a certain bag
70. Compact
71. Treasure State
72. Settle
74. Insubstantial
76. Famed couturier
78. Pale
79. Flight units
80. Puts with
81. Plaster over
82. Hacienda
83. ____ time (never)
85. Cheer on
86. Blanc, e.g.
87. Snick and ____
89. Modernist
90. Marshy place
91. Shaver

2 Campus V.I.P.'s by Mary Russ

They rank just behind the cheerleaders.

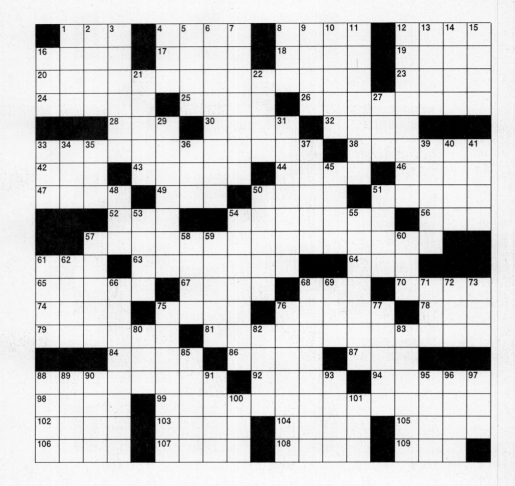

ACROSS

1. Private eye
4. Snare
8. Big name in whaling
12. Cry of woe
16. Poet Teasdale
17. Pueblo Indian
18. Saxhorn's relative
19. See 24 Across
20. Nassau's pride
23. First name in spydom
24. W.W. II broadcaster, with 19 Across
25. Tennis pro
26. Jack-of-all-trades
28. Explorer Johnson
30. Related
32. Thank-you-____ (road bump)
33. Baker Field celebrity
38. U.C.L.A. wildlife
42. Surface measure
43. Declaim
44. Miss Tyler Moore
46. Quite mad
47. Row or gravy
49. Wind direction
50. Mosquito memento
51. Wyoming range
52. Go on the cuff
54. Unavailable fruit of song
56. Onager
57. Tucson creatures
61. Bushy clump
63. Figaro's city
64. Swiss canton
65. What Garbo wanted to be
67. "How sweet ____!"
68. Made a lap
70. Make dull
74. Money in Venice
75. O.T. book
76. Golfers' cries
78. Shade of green
79. Like a magnifying glass
81. Eastern bowl users
84. Leap or light
86. Doctrines
87. Chinese aborigine
88. Squirmed
92. "Toodle-oo"
94. High-hat
98. Saarinen
99. Cattle in Austin
102. Portico
103. What the three monkeys shun
104. Lake or canal
105. Respiratory sound
106. Desert accommodation
107. Hindu mother goddess
108. West German island
109. Cunning

DOWN

1. Edible root
2. Ben Hecht's Dorn
3. "____ beat that?"
4. Article
5. Roster
6. Renegade
7. Small opening
8. Panay native
9. Actor O'Brian
10. At right angles, on a ship
11. Dickens's ____ Rudge
12. Honorary West Pointer
13. Rich soil
14. Dog star
15. Playwright O'Casey
16. N.Y.C., for one
21. "Topper" character
22. Low-caste Hindu
27. Women's org.
29. "It's ____" (nothing to it)
31. Dutch church pastor
33. Calloway
34. Spanish gold
35. Meadow
36. Author Fleming
37. South African province
39. Whits
40. Sgts., e.g.
41. Family members
45. Pull apart
48. Rocky hill
50. Weeps noisily
51. Ivan or Nicholas
53. Discerning
54. "South Pacific" island
55. In a severe manner
57. Decorate
58. Sheep genus
59. Gritty's partner
60. Dinner-check extra
61. Soft mineral
62. Stew
66. Annapolis denizen
68. Certain sister's writing
69. Indonesian island group
71. G.I.'s address
72. Miniskirt's revelation
73. ____ Vegas
75. Of high station
76. Women, e.g.
77. Cut
80. Brain test: Abbr.
82. Landing vessels
83. Those who give
85. Female ruff
88. Mae or Rebecca
89. Network
90. Golf club
91. 514, to Caesar
93. Indigo
95. Spoken
96. Exclusively
97. Literary initials
100. Muhammad
101. Obtain

3 I.Q. Readings by Martha J. DeWitt

But not exactly in Binet-Simon terminology.

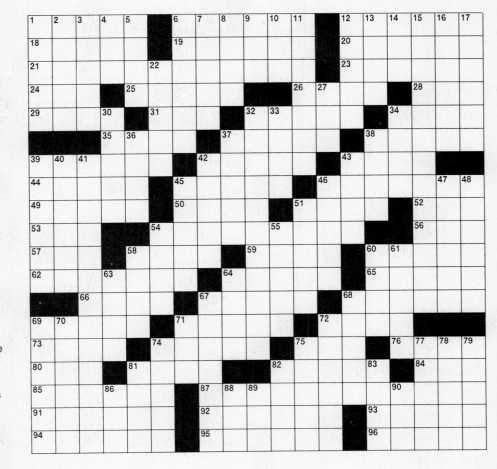

ACROSS

1. Miss Bow
6. Ten-_____ hat
12. Figaro, for one
18. Bode
19. One-celled animal
20. Earhart
21. Frivolous one
23. Shade of blue
24. Townsman
25. Gen. Jubal ___
26. Ids' offspring
28. Asian holiday
29. Neisse tributary
31. Whiz leader
32. He lies awaitin', in song
34. Quaker pronoun
35. Jack of old Westerns
37. Concord
38. Direction
39. Bad-mouth
42. Vintage plane
43. 1899–1902 war
44. Antelope
45. Glove groups
46. Miss Holm
49. D'Azur and others
50. Plant blight
51. Reared
52. Largo or West
53. Condo or co-op
54. Know-it-alls
56. Wrath
57. Ott or Allen
58. Evanesce
59. Clark Kent's friend
60. Nut that's chewed
62. Get ready
64. Pulitzer poet
65. Mountain ridge
66. Verge
67. Lead car in an auto race
68. Household catchall
69. Oral declaration
71. Dowdy
72. One of the Scotts
73. Symbol of heaviness
74. Sassy
75. Tiny
76. Biblical country
80. Silkworm
81. Mackerel's cousin
82. Woman's robe
84. Nigerian
85. Josh
87. Like Simon
91. Forever, to poets
92. Upstate N.Y. lake
93. Homely deer
94. Calm down
95. Meager, as fare
96. Flop now worth a fortune

DOWN

1. Bay in Maine
2. Clear
3. Small type
4. Dull routine
5. Johnson
6. Artist's hangout
7. Mosey
8. Pacific parrot
9. Meadow
10. Japanese sash
11. "No, No" girl
12. Club-sandwich filling
13. Hebrew prophet
14. Johnny _____
15. Loudmouthed ones
16. Well-known sister
17. Told on
22. Quarter décor
27. Sprightly
30. Mainz's river
32. Conceited
33. River isles
34. Orchard component
36. Betting factors
37. Get up
38. Narrated
39. Vanish in a hurry
40. Gretna Green user
41. Lacking concentration
42. Effect's associate
43. Apiarist's charges
45. Self-respect
46. Flood stage
47. Cylindrical
48. Grommet
51. Kind of patch
54. "Very _____ for May"
55. Island of amusement parks
58. Kind of safe
60. Burden in "Ol' Man River"
61. Eat
63. Egg on
64. "_____ to the basics"
67. Lady's accessory at Ascot
68. Clobber
69. First-year midshipmen
70. Make soda water
71. Commandment total
72. Behave
74. Thick soup
75. Lady Windermere's creator
77. Antics
78. Potbellied
79. Paradigm
81. Kind of caterpillar
82. Kind of fire
83. Frost
86. Refrain syllable
88. Feminine suffix
89. Valets
90. Lose attentiveness

4 Dozing Off by William H. Ford

No prescription needed for this tranquilizer.

ACROSS

1. Nautical position
6. Heat unit
11. Greek letters
15. Like the Paris tango
19. Brazilian dance
20. Far East capital
21. Lily plant
22. Lake near Maggiore
23. Bear's extended nap
25. Electric blanket's predecessor
27. "____ Three Lives"
28. Too wonderful for words
30. Interlude in a Mexican day
31. Always, to poets
32. Wall St. purchases: Abbr.
33. Scout units
35. After JKL
36. Positions again
38. Garden tools
39. ". . . tails ____ lose"
41. N.C.O.'s
44. Trace
45. Month: Abbr.
46. Becky
48. Household need
49. Be considerate
52. Enjoys
53. What the voice told Macbeth
56. Norwegian king
57. Enchanted
58. Take ____ (snooze)
59. One of the Mels
60. "Certainly not!"
62. Music from a Boston orchestra
65. Organic compound
66. Bara
67. Reacts to pain
70. Places for guest appearances
72. Like the Pacific off the Marianas
73. Fitted with footwear
75. "____ take arms against . . ."
76. Vegetable
78. Ely's river
79. Jehovah
82. "____ Gang"
83. Gets out of bed
84. Amish verb
85. Defective
86. Swan genus
88. "____ appétit"
89. Moonlight and Biscay
91. Reply: Abbr.
92. D.C. officer
93. Even-money wager
97. Agency of the 1930's
99. Paper sizes
101. Word with stool
102. "The stag at ____"
103. Dulcet
106. Belittling ones
108. Tennis term
109. Place for dreams
111. Place for dreams
113. Miss Sommer
114. Actress d'Orsay
115. Bolt
116. Extract
117. Heraldic band
118. Kind of grass
119. Checks
120. "And so ____"

DOWN

1. More livid
2. Holder of property in trust
3. Fireplace logs at the end
4. Retired
5. Blemish
6. Kind of giving
7. Dislikes
8. Star in Pegasus
9. Santa's airstrip
10. Iraqi turrets
11. Casals
12. One given to nodding
13. Prefix for an antiseptic
14. Does basting
15. Sophia and family
16. Place for 12 Down
17. Printer's instruction
18. "G.W.T.W." locale
24. Partner of gritty
26. Draw a bead on
29. Cattle genus
32. Fly
34. Cleaner
37. Kind of stock
38. Command, to Shakespeare
40. Container
42. Plant bulb
43. Graf ____
45. Dopy one
46. Medicinal herb
47. Chicken dish
49. Mountain gaps
50. Came to earth
51. Enjoy a catnap
52. At close quarters
54. Compliments
55. Case in question
57. Downfall
61. "If music be the ____ love . . ."
62. Photograph
63. Poet's word
64. Ridge on a guitar
66. Hotsy-____
68. Basic character
69. Holy women: Abbr.
71. Napped
73. Hunk
74. Israeli dance
76. Kind of companion
77. Continent: Abbr.
80. Neighbor of Ala.
81. English county
83. Kind of map
87. Explorer of the Midwest
88. World-weary
90. Famed potters
92. Captain's boat
93. Captor of Fort Duquesne
94. Smudge
95. Demonstrate
96. Worked at the bar
98. Kyushu volcano
100. TV et al.
101. Invite
103. Hebrew letter
104. Chest sound
105. Like water ____ duck's back
107. Couples
108. Orchestra leader Ray
110. Of no value
112. Steep

5 Another Language by Sophie Fierman

It's understood only by the dashboard set.

ACROSS

1. U-boat
4. Grumble
8. Greek letter
13. Woman's garment
16. Direction: Abbr.
17. "Celeste Aïda," for one
18. Noncitizen
19. Bishops' seats
20. Kind of wind
21. Police everywhere, in CB lingo
24. Buddies
26. TV adjunct
27. _____ Antoinette
28. Where pupils say "présent"
30. Printed
31. Spanish bigwig
33. Return trip, CB style
35. Coal scuttle
36. Ark builder
37. Intuitiveness: Abbr.
38. Multiple bet
40. Dancer's garment
42. Short haircut
45. Bender
46. Meadow
47. Local movie houses, for short
50. Like Jupiter, as a planet
52. Scorches
54. Dedicated group
55. Confused
56. Outdoes
59. Icelandic poetry
60. _____ the whirlwind
61. Strainer
62. Gray's ploughman, for one
64. Sand ridge
66. Relative of golly
67. April accompaniment
68. Time units: Abbr.
69. Built
72. Obtains a new tenant
74. Favoring
76. Earth
77. Moccasin
78. Pudding additive
82. Lacking eyes
84. Word with lop or one
86. Choice
87. Richthofen, for one
88. Faulty development of an organ
90. Family branch
91. Zip past another car, CB style
95. Mobster's gun
96. Fraternal people
97. On the ball
98. Noble, in Germany
99. House addition
100. Use a hair rinse
101. Ships' spars
102. Blood component: Prefix
103. River in Scotland

DOWN

1. Radar trap, CB style
2. Loosen a shoestring
3. Roar
4. Engineer's spot
5. Locality
6. Cheerful
7. Lights showing on a police car, CB style
8. Came the light
9. Antelope of Africa
10. Girl's name
11. Wire: Abbr.
12. Picnic intruder
13. Lurking police, to a CB user
14. Depends
15. Unalert
19. _____ song (farewell)
22. Soldier of India in colonial days
23. Native of a Midwest city
25. Err
29. Growing out
31. Sticky stuff
32. Stool pigeon
34. Waste matter
36. Approaches
39. Flower of forgetfulness
40. New _____ on life
41. Competed at Le Mans
42. Proclaim loudly
43. Garden spots
44. Request to use a channel on CB
46. Depart
48. Church official
49. Top-billed ones
51. One who stares
52. Break a traffic law
53. Flower part
57. Bluish star
58. Craftier
63. At hand
65. Take umbrage
67. Legislative timeouts
70. Lettuce
71. "My country, _____ . . ."
72. Bane of speeders
73. "Dear _____"
74. Swindled, with "off"
75. How some vaccines are taken
77. TV previews
79. Blockaded
80. Pierce
81. Irk
83. Highs and _____
84. Frolic
85. Electron tube
88. Fruit drinks
89. Southwest wind
92. Poor actor
93. High note
94. Ziegfeld

6 Dimensions by Evelyn Benshoof

Looking into the general scope of things.

ACROSS

1. Kind of money or aleck
6. Bedouin
10. Assemble
15. Ma Bell patron
16. Attain status
17. Philippine port
18. Shoe part
19. Turkish title
20. Bumbling
21. Completely
24. Philippine native
25. Ship salvagers' quest
29. Gone
32. Monks' titles
34. Stray
35. Easy gait
36. Rat's fare at Jack's house
38. Name for a señorita
40. Jet plane
42. Letter
43. Petitions
45. Roof part
47. Rouse
49. Realistic
52. Sounded a horn
54. Irish Gaelic
55. Florida bowl
58. Suffix for drunk
59. Diamond cup
61. Subject
63. Fix up
64. Malicious look
66. Tease
68. Urgent
70. Moisture
71. Does crystal gazing
74. Favorable time, in Britain
76. As an extra
81. Arrested
84. ___ of thumb
85. ___-toe
86. Unique
87. "The frost ___ the punkin . . ."
88. Feature of the heart or spade jack
89. Handled rudely
90. Hodgepodge
91. Independently

DOWN

1. ___-Japanese War
2. Pole
3. Maui greeting
4. Trusted
5. Eastern U.S. capital
6. River to the Caspian Sea
7. Conservative's direction
8. On land
9. Safari workers
10. Farewell
11. Resolute
12. ___ Maria
13. Syrup source
14. Toper
15. Hullabaloo
22. More malodorous
23. Of the ankle
26. Gained instant prominence
27. Rapier
28. Beheld
29. Elec. unit
30. Dame
31. Flowering shrub
33. Kind of whisper
37. Assignment
39. Prevent
41. Offshoot
44. Toboggan
46. Reduced
48. At a distance
50. Idolizer
51. Discrimination against women
52. Football-game unit
53. Breeze, in Spain
56. Literary work
57. Ruckus
60. Miles Standish, for one
62. Rock-a-bye baby's place
65. Make more precise
67. Shirtwaist
69. Arthurian maiden
72. Subdued, with "down"
73. Certain flights
75. Chemical compound
77. Secluded places
78. Shoshoneans
79. Comedienne Martha
80. Summer, in France
81. Clout
82. ___ bonne heure
83. "___ is the hour . . ."

7 Turnabouts by Jordan S. Lasher

Some familiar combinations seem to work both ways.

ACROSS

1. Kind of pudding
8. Package
14. Mat. times
18. "... ____, a ten o'clock scholar"
19. Toots one's own horn
20. Magnetite product
21. Promote Broadway fare
23. ____-Lenape
24. Id follower
25. Plant shoot
26. Movies, Variety style
27. Prepare to kick off
28. Replay a Lou Brock feat
32. Knobbed
33. Baler intake
34. Buster Brown's dog
35. "____ Frankenstein"
36. Table fowl
39. Overhaul
40. Quarter horse, e.g.
43. Hog plum
44. Odometer unit
45. Fencing foil
46. "Pygmalion" author
47. ____ G. Carroll, TV's Topper
48. Up-to-date
49. Winter vehicle
51. Greek vowel
52. Rio de ____
53. Draw even with 'Bama
56. ____ Yutang
57. Moroccan range
58. Lustrous
59. Soft shoe, for short
60. Conjunction
61. "____ Rhythm"
63. Opposite of dele
64. Highway radio buff
66. Broadway org.
67. Math term
69. Pork cut
70. ____ a sad note

71. City near Orléans
72. Fordham team
73. 1051, to Seneca
74. Of ancient France: Var.
76. Capture diptera specimens
81. March follower
82. Straggle
83. Yves St. Laurent's birthplace
84. ____ pro nobis
85. Word with shoppe
86. Heroic grasshopper
90. Lascivious look
91. Cling

92. A word to ____
93. Thesaurus wds.
94. Double dagger
95. More placid

DOWN

1. Breaks horses
2. "Add ____ of bitters"
3. ____ Alegre, Brazil
4. Kind
5. Miss or Bull
6. Hard to forget
7. A Shaw
8. Dusk
9. Pile
10. Legal acts of negligence
11. "For want of ____ ..."

12. Charon's river
13. Sigmoid
14. Plane-wing parts
15. Unencumbered by property
16. Muscle readiness
17. Attack slyly
22. Inn
27. Tennille
29. Order to Dobbin
30. Ecru
31. Amour propre
32. Bullfighter on horseback
35. Representative sample
36. Adjective for dieters
37. Vespucci
38. Camel's last straw, in a way

39. Old public entertainments
40. Lady Macbeth's stigma
41. Erode
42. Kigali resident
44. Austere
45. Chemical ending
48. German coins: Abbr.
49. Circumspect
50. Shamus
54. Stratum
55. Demolition compound
62. Bridge-score adders
64. Fruit desserts
65. Cafe
66. Indigo
68. Helix
69. Pathet ____

70. North Pole aid
72. Kind of gallery
73. Crème de ____
74. British lockups
75. Marquand's late hero
76. Hiding place
77. Ax handles
78. Antiseptic tincture: Var.
79. Take out
80. Word with nay or sooth
82. Lombardy city
86. Shaver
87. ____ Lanka
88. Part of H.R.H.
89. Sheep

8 Light Reading by Maura B. Jacobson

A test of one's penchant for wasting time.

ACROSS

1. Digging remark
5. Omits
10. Comics prince, for short
13. Angler's come-on
17. Virginia dance
18. Yearly account
19. Yoko ____
20. time ____ half
21. Pisa's river
22. Bulgarian capital
23. Dogpatch denizen
25. Trudeau strip
27. Caveman character
28. Kind of rot
29. Musical pause
31. Hurok
32. African gullies
35. Hans or Fritz Katzenjammer
36. Grampus
39. Bedouin
43. Author Wiesel
44. Cote call
45. Sun Valley's state
47. Thurmond of the N.B.A.
48. "____ transit gloria . . ."
49. Comics duo
52. Cellular matter: Abbr.
53. Hire
55. Gull's acquaintance
56. "That's the ____ my life"
58. Do lacework
59. Is ambitious
62. Like a cocktail oyster
63. Kind of law
66. Teachers' org.
67. Peking sight
70. Wood sorrel
71. Adventure hero
75. Compeer of a Sen.
76. Certain lights
78. D'Artagnan's friend
79. Negligent
80. School gps.
81. Actor Peter
83. Slithery one
84. Thesaurus entry: Abbr.
85. Giggle
86. After zeta
88. Dillon
90. Guidonian note
91. "____ ld"
96. Rube Goldberg's amiable dope
101. Popeye's girl
102. Autograph book
103. Addict
104. Cattle, old style
105. Apiary resident
106. Tuscany city
107. Mah-jongg piece
108. Parts of mins.
109. ____ long (soon)
110. Norse epics
111. Polio researcher

DOWN

1. Kind of nail
2. Before sol or space
3. Italian river
4. Well-known wife of the comics
5. Impudent
6. Door handle
7. Angers
8. In twos
9. Assassinates
10. Sole of the foot
11. Indigo
12. Lazes about
13. Nebuchadnezzar's city
14. ____ Domini
15. Notion: Prefix
16. Infield covering
24. Long time
26. Hesitant sounds
30. Mrs. Lincoln, once
32. Young man's direction
33. Inter ____
34. Tess Trueheart's love
35. Krazy ____
37. Nickname for Hornsby of baseball
38. Fischer's forte
40. Do-gooder of the comics
41. ____ time (never)
42. Unhearing
44. Bakery buy
45. Baseball nine
46. Frequent, in odes
49. Main theme
50. French artist
51. "An eye ____ eye"
54. Nibble
57. Maid's do-it-all
59. Winged
60. Defunct auto
61. Ben Franklin advice
63. Biblical kingdom
64. Height: Prefix
65. Words before king
67. Small or chicken
68. Goddesses: Lat.
69. Church area
72. Haggard title
73. Actress Celeste
74. Rather of TV news
77. Silk threads
80. Schulz's strip
82. Raison d' ____
84. Impassive
85. Compassionate regard: Abbr.
87. Hacienda brick
89. Demean
90. Lazarus and Bovary
91. Oriental pans
92. Nastase
93. ____ oxide
94. ____ and terminer
95. Run off
97. Synthetic rubber
98. Info org.
99. Tattle
100. Journey

9 In a Rut by Henry Hook

Presenting a puzzle with a consistent border.

ACROSS

1. Group of workers
5. Kind of shell or wagon
9. Legwear for a test bird
13. _____ together (join forces)
17. Prefix for tenant
18. Completed
19. Skunk's protection
20. Matty, Felipe or Jesus
21. "_____ Clock Jump"
22. Unlucky Roman number
23. Variety of pistol
25. Deli offering
27. Elec. unit
28. Magnet:iron: :serge: _____
29. It was made of gopherwood
30. Pro _____
32. "Ship of Fools" director
34. Railroad workers
38. Have standing
39. "It's _____, it's a plane . . ."
44. Shed
45. Ditto
46. Setting
47. _____ account
48. Continue
51. Leader of an Indian uprising
52. Beam of a ship
54. Not masc. or fem.
55. Prefix for meter or tude
56. Sort
57. "Be brief, be sincere, be _____"
59. Weight-conscious one
61. Garment, for short
64. Nastase
65. Theda of silents
66. Sore
70. African nation
72. Most dreadful
74. Pizarro's conquest
75. Short-order dish
76. Zane Grey's was purple
77. Part of A.E.C.
79. Perry Como sang with his band
80. Lyricist Harbach
81. Poor Richard's writing
83. Least loony
85. Fish-eating bird
86. Bridge call
89. "If _____ I Would Leave You"
90. Stomach
91. Needed liniment
96. Purchase of note
99. Düsseldorf donkey
101. Seen again: Fr.
102. Buck heroine
103. Greek letters
104. Will Rogers country: Abbr.
105. Board-room V.I.P.
106. Sign on a street corner
107. Constitutional
108. BB, on a box score
109. Board or side

DOWN

1. Take a powder
2. Japanese aborigine
3. _____-do-well
4. Simon and Garfunkel et al.
5. Kind of car or office
6. Fly
7. Marcus' partner
8. Reason for calling a plumber
9. Neckwear
10. Lay it on thick
11. "_____ for Sergeants"
12. Hive dweller
13. Whiffenpoof word
14. Can. province
15. Black, in Burgundy
16. Canvaslike fabric
24. It's 14,408 feet high
26. Type of allowance
31. Rampaging
32. Hot-dog additive
33. Lead-in to a cloverleaf
34. _____ hot and cold
35. Painter Guido
36. Texas _____ M.
37. Sea-speed units
40. Luncheonette order, for short
41. Calendar listing for Veteran's Day
42. Word for McCoy
43. Evade
45. Potato
46. Suffragist Lucretia
49. Abstract beings
50. Shoe width
51. Excuses
53. Patty Hearst and Doris Duke
55. River of Yorkshire
58. Landed
59. Challenge
60. Wisconsin city
61. Use a handkerchief
62. Hoarfrost
63. Busy as _____
65. Racist
67. Former golfer Tony
68. Writer Hoffer
69. Dead or lame
71. Endangered tree
72. Grammar cases: Abbr.
73. _____-shanter
76. Of the breastbone
78. Lake in Ethiopia
80. _____ time
81. Bargain buy from Russia
82. Poet who wrote "Lilacs"
84. "_____ from the Bridge"
86. Squander
87. City in Kansas
88. Like a Jekyll-Hyde personality
90. Tabby talk
92. Work gang
93. Numerical prefix
94. Knievel
95. Daffy or Donald
97. Liquid in a well
98. "_____ not what your country . . ."
100. "Mighty _____ a Rose"

10 Field Trip by Catharine Probst

Featuring some items for the nature lover.

ACROSS

1. Certain votes
5. Poultry disease
9. Co-op units: abbr.
13. Southern holly
17. Infrequent
18. Sea eagle
19. Riding whip
20. Bit part in a play, often
21. King or Alda
22. Florida county
23. Flowery heroine of Italian comedy
25. "Pinafore" girl
27. Town in Bolivia
28. Direction: Abbr.
29. Porter of music
30. Shack
31. Command to Tabby
33. Goal
37. See 74 Down
39. "It's ____"
42. Athletic bird
43. Offsetting things
45. Arm bone
46. Resolve, as a traffic jam
47. Horse colors
48. He always rings twice
50. Ribbon: Prefix
51. Artery
52. Laetrile sources
53. Talks impudently to
55. Scabbard
56. See 32 down
59. Duel aftermaths
60. Partner
64. W.W. I soldier's legwear
65. British guns
66. Former Turkish title
67. River of France
68. Cyrano's creator
70. Witty teasing
71. High nest
73. Goddess of spring beauty
74. Kind of bomb
75. Code words for N
77. Printing measures
78. Covers with turf
79. Shooter ammo
81. Make amends
83. Actor Vincent and family
88. Vine named for a Swiss naturalist
90. Theater section
91. Formerly, old style
92. Valley on the moon
93. "Shake____!"
94. Something unique
95. Word after like
96. Beams
97. Nineveh's partner
98. Hoses down
99. Nicholas or Peter

DOWN

1. Steed
2. Korean border river
3. Common Latin word
4. Heaven-____
5. What Burns' luve was like
6. Delphian ____
7. Immoderate
8. Glance
9. Chargers' needs
10. Campus official
11. Balsam of S.A.
12. Goads
13. Diplomat: Abbr.
14. Patron of sailors
15. ____ Fein
16. French notion
24. Isinglass
26. School, in Paris
30. Hair dye
32. An item in Frans Hals' apparel, with 56 Across
33. Peevish look
34. Pitcher: Lat.
35. Ceremony
36. Plant named for a diplomat
37. Castle protections
38. Morse code senders
40. Med. course
41. Swedish districts
43. Hearts
44. Marsh birds
47. ____ Sharon (flowers)
49. Be in session
51. Son of Jacob
52. Lend ____ (help)
54. Prized bridge holding
55. Part of an Italian opera
56. Fraternal initials
57. Vallee
58. Constantly
59. They fell on Alabama
61. Italian city
62. Relative of Ted
63. Merit
65. Prehistoric period
66. Outmoded
69. Like most models
70. Bridge players, at times
72. Hindu land grant
74. Flowery request, with 37 Across
76. German political unit
78. River in France
79. Young salmon
80. Essayist
82. "____ pennies a day"
83. Kind of worm
84. Triton
85. Rainbow goddess
86. Town in southern Morocco
87. Silver: Abbr.
89. Jolson et al.

11 Sales Patter by Marie West

Hucksters love to use shorthand.

ACROSS

1. Minus
5. Respond to stimuli
10. Band
15. Aswan and Hoover
19. Can. province
20. Indian court staff
21. Emigré
22. Precinct
23. Layer
24. Two on the _____
25. Last edition
26. Headliner
27. Manual for a do-it-yourselfer
31. Neckwear
32. Ingredients of a certain bed
33. Catchall abbr.
34. Sooner than
35. Bronx cheers
37. _____-Saud
39. _____ Constitution
42. Weight-watcher's guidebook
49. Chicago's Mich. et al.
50. Sign gas
51. Firebug's crime
52. Swiss river
53. Converged
54. Davis or Midler
56. Rocker
57. Up _____ (Cornered)
58. Rampaging
60. Jack-in-the-pulpit
61. Babylonian sky god
62. Investment company's sales talk
69. In medias _____
70. Pile up
71. Prickling
72. Lonesome George
75. Annoying insects
76. Fountain orders
78. Long John Silver's creator
79. Duck genus
80. Coronet
81. "_____ Camera"
82. Banquette
83. Apparel ad
88. "Mighty _____ a Rose"
89. Nabokov novel
90. Despot
91. Call _____ day
92. Defeat at bridge
94. Must
97. Wagers
100. Box-top directions
107. Bagnold
108. Zeal
109. Brussels suburb
110. Pedro's coin
111. Roller coaster
112. Colombian poncho
113. "_____ is an island"
114. Caliph
115. Appian Way, for one
116. Regaled
117. Parts of the deck
118. Mah-jongg piece

DOWN

1. Overdue
2. "Pygmalion" girl
3. Ragouts
4. Moslems hostile to the Crusaders
5. Like some peanuts
6. Gives forth
7. Besides
8. Young seal
9. "They wanted a home of _____"
10. Bistros
11. Miss Oyl
12. Collieries
13. Yogi or Papa
14. Part of S.R.O.
15. _____-i-Lut, Iranian desert
16. Of a joint
17. Average
18. Noted puppeteer
28. City in Honduras
29. Bantu language
30. Sheik of Araby's digs
35. Borscht vegetable
36. Siouan Indian
37. Stravinsky
38. Hecht or Hogan
40. Foal's father
41. Pintail duck
42. Happening
43. Greek letters
44. Foreword, for short
45. Rowdies
46. Endangered transport
47. Chemical suffix
48. Planet
49. Mine, in Paris
54. Face of a cut gem
55. Devours
56. Salad green
57. The opposition
59. Miss Brewer
60. Incarnation of Vishnu
61. Film dog
63. Philippine Moro
64. Japanese porcelain
65. Yugoslav port
66. Heron's kin
67. Raines and Fitzgerald
68. Dry run
72. Highlander
73. Spanish ounce
74. Relapse into error
75. Lollobrigida
76. Heroic account
77. "Jug of Wine" poet
80. Knight or Williams
81. Brazen
82. Slipshod mental asylum
84. Appraise
85. Preminger
86. Kittens' loss
87. Greenland base
93. Graybeard
94. Attacked
95. Have _____ to pick
96. Fine fiddle
97. Lost sheep
98. Fragrant oleoresin
99. Rope fiber
100. Persian elf
101. Monad
102. Levantine cup holder
103. Quiz answer
104. Novello
105. Wife, in law
106. Teapot _____

12 In Good Time by Adelyn Lewis

It's largely a matter of when.

ACROSS

1. College grad's aspiration
7. Put flower seeds in place
12. Supplicates
18. Become visible
19. Course of travel
20. London's ____ Row
21. F.D.R.'s time
24. Hair
25. Hebrew measures
26. Priest's robe
27. Ram's mate
28. Bring into agreement
29. Peter or dish
31. Play time
35. Restrict
36. One hundred, in old Rome
39. Semiprecious stone
40. John ____ Garner
41. Time for Gainsborough's walk
42. Disappeared
43. Old newspaper section
44. Does a thorough burgling job
45. Social science: Abbr.
46. Par ____
48. Et ____
49. Debussy's time
56. Evergreen
57. Stingless bee
58. Stone: Suffix
59. Will additions
63. Declare to be true
64. Of a poetic form
65. Simple wind instrument
66. Hotel postings
68. Musical Lawrence
69. Malayan knife
70. Less believable, as an excuse
71. Civet's kin
73. Bulk-beer holder
74. Portrayers of Aïda

75. Suffix for cash or cloth
76. Depot: Abbr.
78. Lube for a violin bow
79. Literary masterpiece
84. Tennessee's time
89. Take umbrage
90. Take a powder
91. Stacked, as wood
92. Geishas' adornments
93. Short daggers
94. React to pollen

DOWN

1. "____ la vie!"
2. Asian river
3. Coty of France
4. Is inaccurate
5. Protections
6. Stitches again
7. Pitching-stat initials
8. Witticism
9. Rustic
10. Loosely woven cloth
11. Deranged person
12. Cons' partners
13. Tennis stroke
14. Juillet's season
15. Gambling city's frontage
16. Glen
17. Social climber
22. Compass point

23. Grand ____, Evangeline's home
28. See 61 Down
29. Cyrus the Great's domain
30. Mrs. Leonowens
31. Synonym expert
32. Historical period
33. Paddled boat
34. Victor Emmanuel III's wife
35. Lampoons
36. Pine or spruce
37. Not ascertained: Abbr.
38. Metric weights: Abbr.
40. Short narrative
41. Molly's family

43. Stool pigeon's specialty
44. Rehearsed casually
47. Signify assent
50. Word for an opposite page
51. Gives a speech
52. Scapa and others
53. Helpers
54. Practical
55. Bottle parts
59. ____ out (renege)
60. Wood sorrel
61. Koestler time, with 28 Down
62. Dies ____
66. Trattoria offering
67. "____ All Seasons"

70. On the Big Board
71. Mementos
72. Catherine of ____
74. First scale tone: Var.
75. Bag or cube
76. Ships: Abbr.
77. Tea plant genus
78. Mil. groups
80. Positive
81. Marquis de ____
82. Mother of Don Juan
83. Suffix for motor
85. O.T. book
86. Feminine suffix
87. Toll road: Abbr.
88. "____ my man"

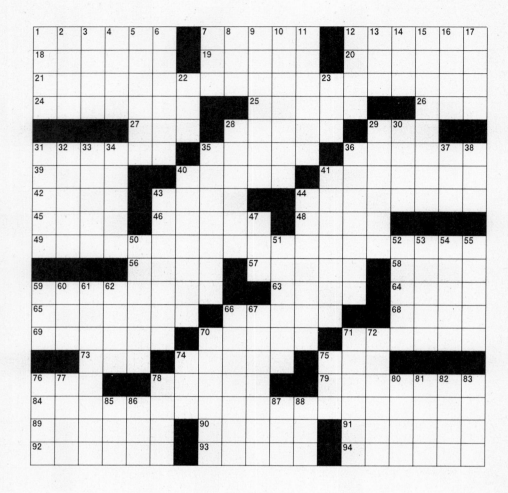

13 Body of Literature by Elaine D. Schorr

Titles that have something in common.

ACROSS

1. Old Hebrew month
5. Culinary artist
9. Autumn pear
13. ___ away (stored)
17. Memo
18. Knit
19. Official proceedings
20. Preposition
21. Graham Greene title
25. Neighbor of Turkey
26. Art colony of New Mexico
27. Magistrates of Sparta
28. Assamese people
29. Chinese dynasty
30. Outlander
31. Oceans
34. Something shed
35. Hassles
36. "___ said it!"
39. Widow's mite
40. G. B. Shaw title
43. ___ Dolorosa
44. Flowerless plant
46. Senior citizens, early style
47. Landing craft of W.W. II
48. Involves
50. Military bloc of the 30's
51. Lake Mead feature
53. Penny pincher
55. Dullards
60. Command to an ox
61. Biblical king
63. Do a plantation job
64. Kind of foot in the park
67. Dies ___
68. Biblical kingdom
69. Kind of lock
70. Aldous Huxley novel
74. Rayburn of TV
75. Neighbor of Md.
76. Ohio city
77. Perdition
78. QE2, for one
79. Indigo plants
81. Pedestal section
82. Roman 1004
83. Bristlelike
85. Moslem judge
86. Greek goddess of the soil
90. Thomas Hardy work
93. Atmosphere: Prefix
94. Hairdo
95. Give the gate
96. Ethereal
97. Show lack of use
98. Like a moray
99. Early Lisbon coins
100. Fish delicacies

DOWN

1. Theatrical org.
2. Physicist Niels H.
3. Series component
4. Executes, in a way
5. Preside over
6. Juno's counterpart
7. Have a bite
8. Drifting logs, etc.
9. Zubin Mehta' implement
10. N.Y. Times publisher
11. Hallowed one: Abbr.
12. Burton musical
13. Willowy
14. Top-bottom, Love-hate, etc.
15. Roman road
16. English actress Diana
22. Son of Seth
23. Ladies in general
24. Mischievous
29. Sea bird
30. Sums up
31. Goalies' achievements
32. The pokey
33. Fine fiddle
34. Leg bones
35. "___ it goes"
37. Grass variety
38. Us, in Berlin
41. Suspect's out
42. Rice or Fudd
44. "Spirit of '76" instrument
45. French pronoun
49. Gabriel, e.g.
50. Hindu principle of life
51. Buddhist divine being
52. Attention-getter
54. Water wheel
56. Actress Jeannette
57. Forest trembler
58. Fund-raiser of Revolutionary days
59. Occasion for matzoh eating
62. Rank the students again
64. Trundle ___
65. Oral vote
66. Tellers of tales
67. Beliefs
68. Pinza
71. Girl's name
72. Taciturnity
73. Examiner of a sort
74. Heed
78. Thing to be out on
80. Kind of game for a pitcher
81. Foolish
82. Thaws
83. Kind of board or chamber
84. Irish exclamation
85. Snaky formation
86. Lucy's first
87. Musical combo
88. Being: Fr.
89. Flat sea fish
91. John or Jane
92. Vietnamese port

14 Mixed Drinks by Anthony B. Canning

Some dubious advice on how topers should ply their talents.

ACROSS

1. Mountain crests
7. Jerkwater train
12. Makes "it" in a game
16. Cork sound
19. The home, figuratively
20. Have done with
21. Navigation aid
22. Scottish explorer
23. To-do
24. ____-air (kind of refueling)
25. High-wrought
27. Start of an old ditty about drinking
30. German river
31. Monday froth
34. Diving bird
35. Blood carrier: Prefix
36. Quakers
37. D.D.E.
38. Yokel
39. Fish-eating bird
40. Word for Adenauer
41. Capek play
42. Parking lot hazard
43. Down provider
44. Cherry workers, at times
48. Dropped a vowel
50. Czech city
51. Begin
52. Part 2 of ditty
53. Part 3 of ditty
55. Put ____ on (pressure)
57. Highway sign
58. Power source: Abbr.
59. Toledo stewpot
60. ____ out (exclude)
61. Landing place
62. Longing for
64. Clergyman
66. Ready
67. Part 4 of ditty
71. Hail
74. Uses one's stationery
75. Most vociferous
79. Waves' motion
80. "Woe ____" (alas)
81. "____ Rhythm"
82. Western alliance
83. Camel's-hair fabric
84. Dumas's Monte ____
87. Classified-ad heading
88. Kind of throat
89. Add power of a kind
91. Galway islands
93. Car-group member
94. Ineffective
95. Cut down
97. Card game
99. Argentine native
100. The sweetsop
101. Voice
102. Unique thing
103. Board
104. Broke
107. Three, in Munich
108. California wine area
109. Gaelic
110. Moslem ruler
111. End of ditty
115. November hopeful
117. "For want of ____ . . ."
118. Recorded part of Ivan Denisovich's life
122. N.Y. time
123. Garter or Bath, e.g.
124. Chemical salt
125. Old-movie Baby and namesakes
126. Wind direction
127. U.S. humorist and family
128. Equerry's charge
129. Sonnet finale

DOWN

1. Asian gazelle
2. Agent: Abbr.
3. Musical sense
4. Believes, old style
5. Polar departure point
6. Made piercing noises
7. Escape, as a secret
8. Adjust
9. Mr. Grant
10. About
11. Da Vinci
12. Realty sign
13. Sandarac tree
14. Gift of a sort
15. Melodrama backdrop
16. Green chalcedony
17. Type of cake
18. Titled ones
21. Villain, often
26. Revival word
28. In good season
29. Something to pick
31. Having an alarm device
32. Guitar's little brother
33. Infers
36. Maiden's mecca
39. German article
40. Nick and Nora's dog
42. Word coming from another: Abbr.
43. Drop a fly
45. Red dye
46. Had sway over
47. Floor
49. Measure of noise
50. Bleater's word
51. Scenes
53. Make a botch of
54. Under other conditions
55. Muscles
56. Kind of puppy
59. Away, in Scotland
60. Math ratio
61. Make a fund contribution
63. Tedious iteration
64. Heavyweight Carnera
65. Surf sound
66. ". . . ____ a jolly good fellow"
68. Word before while
69. Santa's clothes cover
70. Small violin
71. Metric weights
72. Feature of 41 Across
73. Happify
76. Farther back
77. As ____ a cliff
78. A-one
81. Electrified particle
84. Measure
85. Annoyed
86. Causes to be: Suffix
87. Young boy
88. Toper
90. Demosthenes did this
91. Ones with skills
92. Maxwell competitor
93. Deflectors of a sort
95. Certain user of a meter
96. Sheltered
97. Complicated
98. Military cap
102. Burning
104. Gaits
105. Collect
106. Income, in Dijon
107. History-exam entries
109. Watchers
111. Created
112. Kind of political rule
113. Overfill
114. Some athletes' weak spot
116. Abstainer
119. Morse click
120. Word of agreement
121. Most recently born: Abbr.

15 Sound Observation by A. J. Santora

Made by a beloved late leader in the Mideast.

ACROSS

1. Former Israeli V.I.P.
5. São ____
10. Censure
16. Sicilian city
17. Thrusting sword
18. Opera singer Jan
19. Start of a quotation by 1 Across
22. Silkworm
23. "Bridge of San Luis ____"
24. Baylor of basketball
25. Newt
26. Loafs on the job
28. Storage bins
29. Breeding-ranch animal
30. Part 2 of quote
32. More irritated
33. Trudges
36. Spanish wave
37. Rhythmic beats
39. The old ____
40. Anklebones
42. Kind of squash
43. Eagerly expecting
45. Of birth
47. Clinches a chess game
50. Part 3 of quote
53. Daub
54. Terror
55. Slaughter of baseball
57. Ecological series
59. "The ____ the limit"
61. It's for its own sake
62. Musical interval
65. Scurry
66. Perplexed
68. "____ were the days"
69. Part 4 of quote
72. Latin or Eastern
73. Butter trees
74. Stays stationary, as a ship
78. Typing spaces
79. Beatles' "____ Day's Night"
80. Kind of Lizzie
81. From A ____
82. End of quote
86. Rusted away
87. Uncle's favorite
88. Dutch or brick
89. Chummy couple
90. Agitated moods
91. Apportion

DOWN

1. Made a catty sound
2. January, in Juárez
3. ____ time (speedily)
4. Comedienne Charlotte
5. Spanish money
6. Wan
7. Miss Hagen
8. ____-mist (garden flower)
9. Eyelike spots
10. Orbital points
11. Witnessed
12. Part of a min.
13. Overdue debt
14. Like some Arctic ports
15. Correspondence
20. Most contorted
21. Having no angle
27. Stitched: Abbr.
28. Privacy
29. R.C.M.P. member
31. Kind of bear
32. No. 1 pig's building material
33. O.T. book
34. Aquatic plant
35. Dishonor
38. Slapstick
41. Belfast's county
42. Perceptions of pain
44. Definite
46. Farming: Abbr.
48. Lab burners
49. Dinah or sea
51. Mud volcano
52. Los Angeles basketeer
56. R.R. depot
58. Patriot Hale
60. Texas border river
62. Scattered
63. Fanciful dream
64. Whiz
65. Bowler's target
67. Lao-____
70. Long-legged birds
71. "____ Restaurant"
73. Hangars
75. Kitchen range
76. Play hard
77. Atmosphere
79. Declare
80. Delicacy
83. Cool drink
84. Hilo garland
85. Thumb or cat

16 Forwarding Addresses by Alfio Micci

Postal changes for some people if they got restless.

ACROSS

1. Wife of Abraham
6. French cleric
10. Current unit
16. Calm
17. Signs up
19. Did fingerpainting
20. Fascinate
21. Noxious emanation
22. Portico
23. Displaced Greek misanthrope
25. Reference book: Abbr.
26. Landed
27. Eye part
28. Mold
32. Compass point
33. Miss Kelly
34. In the center of
36. Austrian psychiatrist
38. Takes a powder
39. Restraint
40. Rock bottom
41. Communication
45. Displaced Grecian beauty
50. Shoe-buckling numbers
51. Upper part of a dress
52. Crazy as ____
53. Of a certain lung part
54. Ames man
55. Arabic letter
56. Displaced suitors of Silvia
64. Retreat
65. Diving bird
66. Tin, in Toulouse
67. Enlarged: Prefix
69. Señorita's watchdog
71. Burns or Gobel
72. Displaced British colonial
75. Melancholy
76. Loggers' contest
77. Wine: Prefix
78. Slippery fish
79. Neckpiece
80. Two-master
81. Ulnae and tibiae
83. Ruler: Abbr.
86. Meantime
88. "Step ____!"
89. Tidy
91. "The ____ Game"
92. Displaced insurance firm
97. Fashionable
101. Throw off the tracks
102. Thin layer
103. Breastwork
104. British novelist Laurence
105. Kitchen device
106. Cuts short
107. French wave
108. Port Columbus sailed from

DOWN

1. Infirm
2. Musketeer
3. Distant
4. Presently
5. Sandwich
6. Cations' opposites
7. Insolent
8. Pear
9. Pollster Roper
10. Prayer endings
11. Displaced Antonio
12. Accepted standard
13. Christian or Roman
14. Kind of room
15. Dutch city
16. Caterpillar's hair
17. Ants
18. Adage
19. Lieu
24. Moth attracter
28. Canine name
29. Potato country
30. Of days gone by
31. German denial
33. Half a Samoan port
34. Guinness
35. Excavation
37. Certain carriers: Abbr.
38. Displaced English soldier-writer
41. Shed
42. Plenty, to poets
43. Grease: Prefix
44. For men only
45. Inventor Elias
46. Cheese
47. Certain football players
48. Out of tune
49. Inter ____
51. Nut's partner
54. "____ no consequence" (forget it)
55. Entertainers' org.
57. Noted fiddler
58. Now, to Caesar
59. Caen's river
60. Jacket or collar
61. Thin
62. Revokes, for short
63. Singles
67. La Scala locale
68. Prevent
69. Before vier
70. Rhinoceros beetle
71. The fair sex
72. Student's concern: Abbr.
73. Places
74. Shape
75. Take care of
78. Maroon
80. French psychologist Alfred
81. Russian aristocrat
82. Pale green
83. Glossy coating
84. Sheep
85. "Common Sense" author's family
87. Irritates
90. Ivan the Terrible
92. Parliament members: Abbr.
93. Mother of Apollo
94. Descendant of Judah
95. Dud
96. Hemingway or Haydn
97. World news org.
98. Collar
99. Hit sign
100. Mariner

17 On Edge by Sidney L. Robbins

A few items to whet one's curiosity.

ACROSS

1. In front
6. Puts together
10. Vote into office
15. Fake
19. Straight: Prefix
20. Big-toe complaint
21. Big shot
22. Refrain syllables
23. Buenos ___
24. Platinum wire loop
25. ___ of a coin
26. Isfahan's country
27. Common murder weapon
30. Latin 1909
31. Air-raid warners
32. Optimistic
33. Edgar Allan
34. Miss Lillie
37. Place for ski autographs
38. Bakery item
39. "___, ergo propter hoc"
43. Mr. Rackstraw
45. Own, in Scotland
46. Florida's come-on
47. Flat plinth
48. Get money the easy way
53. Arthurian lady
54. Thine, in Paris
55. Speeds
56. Half a prison
57. Type of steak
58. Wall Street word
60. The, in France
61. Lassoed
62. Golf mound
63. Wall Street complaint
67. ___ to the good
68. Elk's pride
71. S.F. hill
72. ___ lightly
77. More acute
78. It's usually accompli
80. Type of beaver
82. Vidal
83. Does a hatchet job
84. Snide remark
86. Ship of 1492
87. Debark
89. "But ___ on forever"
90. Chemical compound
91. Race-track listings
92. Morse-code sounds
94. French composer
97. Letters
98. Graduate degree
99. Whirring sound
100. Diamond features
102. Gooey stuff
105. Office-stampede time
110. Musical finale
111. Violinist's need
112. Speck
113. Ace or king
114. Declare
115. Wear out
116. Opposite of profit
117. "Only ___ a customer"
118. Type of job
119. Sand mounds, in England
120. Angers
121. French heads

DOWN

1. Kuwaiti native
2. Hitler greeting
3. Light color
4. Sun disks
5. Poetic couplet
6. Greek contests
7. Common contraction
8. Does a maid's job
9. Suffix for gang
10. Inflame with love
11. Most recent
12. Hard wood
13. Kind of accountant
14. Cooking measure: Abbr.
15. Do a deli job
16. Injure
17. Soviet range
18. Breed of cat
28. Gershwin
29. Heaven: Prefix
30. Mr. Hart
33. Soprano Lily
34. Kind of cast or way
35. Keep an ___ the ground
36. Permit
38. Nervous spasms
39. Sleigh
40. Trees of N.Z.
41. Cat-___-tails
42. Yielded
44. Inane observation
45. Friend of Tarzan
46. Offspring
48. Town ___ (early newsy)
49. Boy
50. Chilled
51. Consumed
52. Tower city
57. Enameled ware
59. Prescient one
60. Legal degree
61. Mother-of-pearl
64. Division
65. Novelist Pierre
66. Bear or Berra
68. Saying
69. Ex-President
70. Trick's alternative
73. Bird's beak
74. Sheer fabric
75. Tennessee ___ Ford
76. Peruses
78. Source of Astor's wealth
79. Consumed
80. Chicken fruit
81. Past
84. College girl
85. Part of TNT
88. ___ and seek
90. Big blower
92. Do arithmetic
93. Good-night girls
94. Chinese philosopher
95. Entry
96. Albanian coin
99. Animal of the West
100. Type of walker
101. Displayed brilliance
102. Atlantic fish
103. Zero, to Connors
104. Roman date
105. Golf warning
106. Roman 951
107. Dill
108. Kyle Sr. or Jr.
109. Ones favoring
111. Ink for losers

18 Drawing the Shades by Hugh McElroy

They come in all forms.

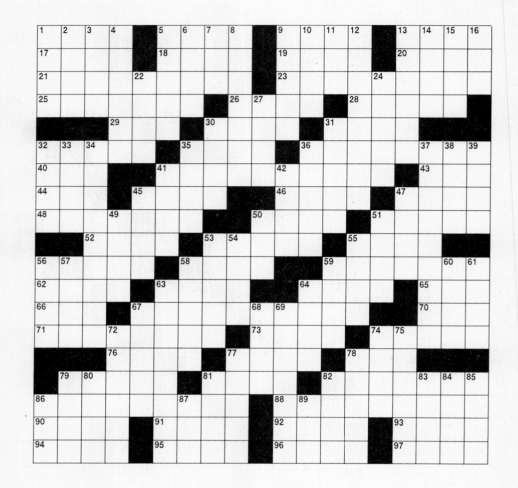

ACROSS

1. Cowardly Lion actor
5. Black fish
9. Italian host
13. Lhasa ____
17. Thought: Prefix
18. "Was it ____ I saw?"
19. Damage
20. Art colony near Santa Fe
21. Unsullied
23. Gown shade of song
25. Lends
26. Taj Mahal site
28. Actor Tom
29. ____ Palmas
30. Nazimova
31. Waikiki welcomes
32. Famed Dublin theater
35. Food size
36. Draws a bead on
40. Coolidge
41. Fish deception
43. Lamb's mother
44. Miss Farrow
45. Adriatic wind
46. Tell all to the D.A.
47. Brooks and Torme
48. Kind of artwork
50. City routes: Abbr.
51. Daring bank withdrawal
52. Nut with caffeine
53. Bends out of shape
55. Mend
56. Halloween scarer
58. Human-kindness product
59. Welshed
62. Praise
63. Regretted
64. Full or running
65. Milland
66. Carney
67. Play about microbe hunters
70. A Gabor
71. Like Victorian drapes
73. Calhoun
74. Forest in "As You Like It"
76. You love, to Ovid
77. Chow or lo
78. "Many ____ called, but few . . ."
79. V.P. Barkley
81. German city
82. Lands and property
86. "The ____" (O'Casey work)
88. Well and happy
90. Leap, for one
91. Bronte's Jane
92. Western alliance
93. "Rheingold" goddess
94. U.F.O. takeoff place
95. Scout's good thing
96. Insect
97. Take it easy

DOWN

1. Actress Damita
2. Take ____ view of
3. Beatles film
4. Ian Fleming's "Casino____"
5. Thai coins
6. Galatea's friend
7. Posed
8. Furtive action
9. Surname of Kipling's Kim
10. Room in a casa
11. Prefix with angle
12. Doing a TV host's job
13. Maximally
14. Aura of gloom
15. Kind of searching
16. Ending with verb or comat
22. Fay of "King Kong"
24. Stevenson's middle name
27. Hilarity
30. Verdi heroine
31. Meat cuts
32. Top
33. Lure
34. Some staged sketches
35. Arctic hazard
36. Levers
37. In a rage
38. Cobblers' items
39. Acid or road
41. Reporter Barrett
42. Inviting initials
45. Swindle
47. No more than
49. Riding or Robin
50. Houseboat of yore
51. Fonda, to friends
53. Use with force
54. Actor Ray
55. Poop, for one
56. Strip of wood
57. Prefix with graph or mour
58. Boudoir slippers
59. Naughty, as a novel
60. Roof part
61. Miss Cannon of films
63. Cut a boil again
64. Farm adjunct
67. Arabian nation
68. British architect
69. Welding
72. Items often rattled
74. Johnson of TV
75. Grim figure
77. Cut hay
78. "____ in the Dark"
79. Kind of code
80. Regan's father
81. Use an auger
82. Miss Kett
83. Retreadable item
84. Book holders
85. Star in Aqarius
86. Fitness H.Q.
87. Bread or whisky
89. Form of Anna

19 Classics by Herb Risteen

All good reading, in spite of Mark Twain.

ACROSS

1. Du Maurier's Ibbetson
6. Biblical pool
12. Cracker's target
16. Range crest
17. Punish by a fine
18. Nice-Nelly
19. Dickens' outlook
22. Long periods
23. Writer Herman and family
24. Oil land
25. Kind or rot or wit
26. Arab abodes
27. Handles a banquet
29. Farm animal
30. Author of "The Stranger"
31. Looks at closely
33. Trojan-War instigator
34. Hill dweller
37. Dusky, to poets
38. Milton or Beverly
39. Plumlike fruit
40. J. F. Cooper's remnant
44. Out of the wind
45. Highways
46. Short messages
47. Old Tunisian ruler
48. Backyard additions
49. Stable occupants
50. Italan poet
51. Flat on one's face
53. Flashy people
55. Irish county
56. Retainer
59. Affectations
60. Over and top items
61. Epochs
62. Grist for George Eliot
66. Ceremony
67. Pump up
68. Bien ____ (French darling)
69. Building beam
70. Stingier
71. Highlanders

DOWN

1. Called via loudspeaker
2. Goof
3. Very small
4. Greek letters
5. On a pension: Abbr.
6. Early Englishmen
7. Put the blame on
8. Garlic relatives
9. Grampuses
10. Statute
11. ____ culpa
12. Village high points
13. Noisy
14. Sibelius and Nurmi
15. German river
20. Pitchers
21. Roman emperor
26. Lone Ranger's friend
27. Monte ____
28. Religious sect
29. "Roaring Camp" writer
30. Tranquilizes
31. Low place
32. Famous nonhitter
33. Feet, in Paris
34. Winglike
35. Roman period
36. D'Urbervilles' servant
37. Pitcher's support
38. Thin rock
39. Cross the goal line
41. Kind of page or door
42. Plays the piccolo
43. Senseless
48. Fire worshiper
49. Man with a code
50. Type of window
51. Missouri tributary
52. Newscaster Dan
53. Master, in Madras
54. Michelangelo work
55. Between Arthur and Doyle
56. "Ethan ____"
57. Canvas holder
58. Curves
60. African gazelle
61. Essay name
62. Numerical prefix
63. Thrash
64. Radziwill
65. Weary

20 Stakeouts by Burt Kruse

Presenting varied pieces of turf.

ACROSS

1. Platoon, e.g.
5. Rude awakeners
10. Attempt
14. Small quaff
17. Beautiful woman
18. ____ firma
19. ____-Jones, English artist
20. Soccer immortal
21. Befuddlement
24. Severn feeder
25. Cultivation of the soil
26. Oscar Wilde's Mr. Gray
27. Tendency
28. Dramatic parts
30. Turned rapidly
31. Greek port
32. Gave a hard look
33. It precedes iota
34. Woody or Steve
35. Swiss river
36. Platonic book
39. W.W. II area
42. Encircle
43. Othello, for one
44. Nothing, in France
45. Without end
46. Some
47. Imagination
51. What some machines do
52. Parade-ground command
54. Hostess name
55. Pithy
56. Fresh horse
58. Three, in Rome
59. More savage
61. Revival words
62. Pitti-Sing, Peep-Bo, and Yum-Yum
64. Plans
65. Facial spot
66. He was not "to be" long
69. Service stencil
72. Elevator man
73. Large room
74. Kind of edge
75. Chemical compound
76. Educational org.
77. Ho-hum places
81. Normandy battle site
82. Loop
84. Between Pisces and Taurus
85. Decision from the bench
87. Thin
89. Curve cutter
91. Current times
92. Abstractor's concern
93. New Orleans university
94. Hall-of-____
95. Medley
96. Biological branch
101. Walk site
102. Lacked
103. Unfamiliar
104. Mrs. Chaplin
105. Mass. cape
106. ____ down (faded)
107. Untrue
108. Acne age

DOWN

1. Boom periods
2. Lepidopterist's need
3. Gershwin
4. Giggled
5. Wearing a fur
6. Boxing jabs
7. Bridge section
8. Kind of team
9. More gritty
10. Girl of Cantor song
11. Musical chord
12. Presently
13. Franklin
14. Illusory existence
15. Miss Massey
16. Is hanging
19. Sackcloth
20. Ex ____
22. German article
23. Strong point
27. Soapstone
28. Color, as a wood surface
29. Saloon wrecker
30. Heat unit
31. Roman writer
32. Long tale
33. Rower's need
34. Templeton
36. Hoist a glass
37. River at Orsk
38. Twining stem
40. Future, for instance
41. What a waiter waits for
43. Base
45. Net star
47. Defendant, in law
48. Special nerve
49. Composer Grofé
50. Impertinent
53. Tints
55. Try
56. Novarro
57. Do strenuous acting
59. Satisfies
60. "____ a man with . . ."
62. English philosopher
63. Mallard genus
64. Parisian friends
66. Hesitate
67. Golden item
68. Metal tag
70. Shoe parts
71. Succulent plant
75. Edible snail
77. Minister to, in a way
78. Kind of facial expression
79. Mideasterner
80. Guard or tackle
83. Acrylic fiber
85. Global-reaction theory
86. British statesman
87. Leaf opening
88. Retailer's bonus
89. Leather
90. Oxlike antelope
91. Seizes
93. Bangkok native
94. Emulate a butterfly
96. Religious degree
97. Angel's wear, to a cockney
98. Buck's partner
99. Number
100. British isle

21 Pertinent People by Mel Taub

The names may not be familiar but their linkages should be.

ACROSS

1. Kilted bag man
6. Playwright Connelly
10. Lady knight
14. Sign on a road
18. Bouquet
19. Baseball brothers' surname
20. Original victim
21. Tuscany city
22. Biblical maker of a well-known product
24. Farmer's busy daughter
26. Frolics
27. Shadowy figure
29. Comedian Myron et al.
30. Scrape off
33. Light gas
34. Stung
36. Film star of the West Indies
40. Iowa college town
41. Poe's taciturn visitor
42. Irregularly notched
43. Weasel's aquatic cousin
45. _____ loss
48. Pre-event periods
49. Blister
50. Fruit of the blackthorn
51. Smeltery dross
52. Wriggler
53. What a conservative gal says
58. Foundation
59. Court decree
60. They put on hands
61. Pure
63. Olé or rah
64. A.L. team
65. Puzzling problem
66. Relative of won't
67. Linksman Palmer
68. Disney World guide
71. With it
74. Bearing

75. Mah-jongg position
76. Small whirlpool
77. Hood's gal
78. Inflate expenses
79. Sheet metal
81. Gay _____
83. Magna _____
84. Carson's "Tonight" predecessor
85. W.W. II invader from Kansas
88. Autocratic rule
91. Fruitless
92. Pressing
93. Region of Spain
94. Swelling disease
96. Radar's aquatic relative
98. Leonardo's smiling landlady
100. Virtuous castle dweller
105. Suppose
106. Type of type: Abbr.
107. Extol
108. Cheat the I.R.S.
109. Prepares a table
110. Not a few
111. To be, in Cannes
112. Pretend

DOWN

1. Thumbs-down review
2. Author Levin
3. Exclamation
4. Rivals successfully
5. Moslem holy month
6. Teacher's grade
7. "Wellaway!"
8. Reagan, familiarly
9. Shillelaghs
10. Singer Vic
11. Down with: French
12. Runs across
13. B.P.O.E. member
14. Tourist attractions
15. Tittering sound
16. _____ on (continually)
17. Settles up
21. Nocturnal woodsman
23. L.A.'s La _____ tar pits
25. Caesar's "veni"
28. Ace place
30. Shake hands on it
31. Sioux warrior
32. Make merry
33. Daughter of Tantalus
35. Mother of Leeds
37. Miss Bly
38. Deodar, banyan, etc.
39. Metal bond
44. Short blast
45. Mr. Hiss
46. Wild goats
47. Insurance salesmen: Abbr.
49. Small nightclub
50. France's Scotland Yard
51. Ending for yes and no
53. Reduces strain
54. Resort town near Boston
55. Purposeful course
56. Stable sound
57. Unyielding
58. Washbowl
61. Ben Jonson girl
62. Dragged before a judge
63. Korea, in Tokyo
64. Dealt in securities
65. Pack down tobacco
66. Go after flies
67. Priscilla Mullens' married name
69. Draws nigh
70. Showed old movies
71. Big crowd
72. Rock star John
73. Assembly-line site
77. Swamp tree
79. Con's goal
80. Singer Frankie
81. Nanny's buggy
82. Good-natured
83. Chewy candy
84. Polytheists
86. Excessively
87. Debussy's "Claire de _____"
88. Figure of speech
89. Waste disposal: Abbr.
90. Noted D.C. hostess
93. Prophet after Joel
95. College official
96. Aspersion
97. Merrie _____ England
99. Point the blunderbuss
101. Have a bite
102. Turn stool pigeon
103. Brouhaha
104. Quarterback Dawson

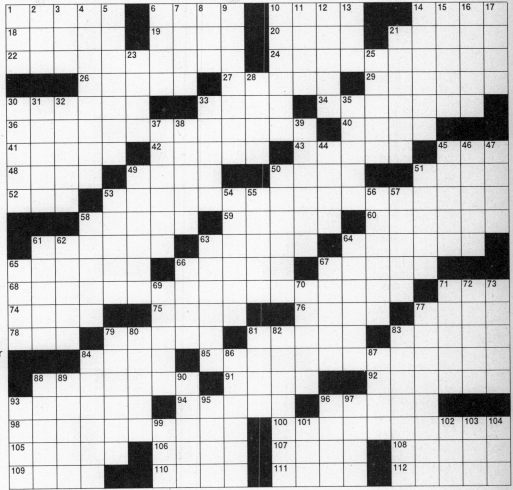

22 Play it Again, Sam by Jack L. Steinhardt

Even if Humphrey Bogart never said it.

ACROSS

1. Examined the layout
6. Minor canard
9. Skimmer
12. Southern side dish
17. Independently
18. V.I.P. in Ankara
19. _____ de vie
20. Summarize
21. Parthenon's supports
24. Miss Massey
25. Relieve
26. With the anchor free
27. Recording sessions
29. Israeli plain
31. Blasting explosives
34. Mat. day
35. Tout egotistically
40. Electrical spark
43. Survived
45. Rival
46. Seals one's fate
48. Explorer Johnson
49. Recent: Prefix
51. Golf vet
53. Ganges garment
54. "O death, where is thy _____?"
56. Utter
58. Free and clear
63. Perfume alcohol
64. Fevers
65. Fence
67. Arctic explorer
69. Teacup handle
72. Beverage
73. Buddhist aphorisms
74. Flub
75. Reaction
78. Cinch, with "up"
79. Accepts the consequences
84. Law's appendage
86. Natural gas fuel
87. Safari aide
91. Hodgepodge
94. Riveter of W.W. II
98. Fairy or tall
99. The bounding main
100. Foment
104. Monkeyshine
105. Long time
106. Passing grade
107. City near Marseilles
108. Intermediate, in law
109. Gull or horse
110. Haw's other half
111. New Hampshire city

DOWN

1. Bistros
2. God of Islam
3. March master
4. Inserts
5. Scottish river
6. Fiction's alternative
7. Borodin's prince
8. Island east of Java
9. Lunar-landing vehicle
10. Scottish John
11. Farnum or Hoffman
12. Bellyaches
13. Hot-dog additive
14. Scared effigy
15. Zest
16. Health haunts
22. Alighieri
23. Author Sinclair
28. Goddess of vengeance
30. Bireme blades
32. Novelist Wister
33. Orbital intersection
35. Saar, e.g.
36. Old chinese weight
37. Gorges
38. Estuary's relative
39. Rorem
40. Commercial layouts
41. Bookbinding leather
42. Of a heart feeder
44. Capable of shifting
47. Spendthrift's counterpoint
50. Pitcher Claude
51. Champagne designation
52. Short-lived men's jacket
54. Sign that angels love
55. Youth org.
57. Is endowed with
59. Assay
60. Yawning
61. House for Henry VIII
62. Calamitous
66. Kind of breaker
67. Ginger
68. Baseball stat
70. Italian harp
71. Control
73. Desiccated
76. Type of whale
77. Military sword
80. Minor athletic injury
81. State for a medium
82. High on the _____
83. Lyric poems
85. Develop
88. Set aside
89. Burstyn
90. Famed shortstop
91. Kind of rubber
92. Dermal affliction
93. Exposes to moisture
95. Pained outcry
96. Well-known graf
97. Particular
101. Fish spawn
102. O'Connor or Merkel
103. Bucket wood

23 Dirty Work by Louis Baron

Whodunits with a bit of literary license.

ACROSS

1. ____ for knowledge
7. Fear
12. Jacks of clubs
16. Winged
21. Cores
22. Betel palm
23. Shahless nation
24. Of the cheek
25. Phyllis Murder Case
27. Annie Murder Case
29. ____ standstill
30. Corn unit
31. Pass on
33. Fold
34. Fibs
35. Fathers
36. Reward, in olden days
37. Foot or soap
40. Give ear
41. Sundered
42. Twists
46. Unity
48. Tierra del ____
49. Civil War V.I.P.
50. River in Greece
51. Parking props
52. "G.W.T.W." Murder Case
54. Porn
55. Correct
56. "____ be the breeze . . . ?"
57. Bugbear
58. Clue for 52 Across
59. Pipped cubes
60. Mends
61. Baby wear
63. Samisen player
64. Corrode
65. House Dick Murder Case
67. Parks and Adler
68. Can
70. Hostelry
71. Hair color
72. Turns inside out
73. Nick Charles Murder Case
77. P.D. report
80. Shoe grippers
81. React in a maidenly way
82. Bury
83. Vibrate, in Dundee
84. Metric unit
85. Storm
86. Append
87. Transfer design
88. Cadmus's daughter et al.
89. Abel Murder Case
92. Royal digs
93. ____ 'easter
94. Bundled
95. ____ winner (bet well)
96. In an implied way
97. What lawyers do
99. Millionths of meters
100. Sound
101. Scottish eyes
102. Like Etna's leavings
103. Spruce genus
104. Had obligations
105. Answer choice
107. Elegance
108. "Roses ____ . . ."
110. Coarse wool
113. Dirty Dozen Murder Case
115. Love-Thief Murder Case
118. I.Q. name
119. Author O'Flaherty
120. Hill nymph
121. Immanent
122. Shirt ornaments
123. Met production
124. What the worm does
125. Induced

DOWN

1. Pop-singer Paul
2. Abandon
3. Calif. campus
4. Limey's underworld
5. Hide's partner
6. Unflagging
7. Kind of look
8. Van Gogh milieu
9. Dickens girl
10. Fence's loot
11. Bearing
12. Sty newcomer
13. Ranges
14. Indian servant
15. Plank curve
16. Charms
17. Rio Grande city
18. Pond plant
19. Stretched
20. Ocean bird
26. Dehydrates
28. Request to a doorman
32. Trial's mate
35. Wheat variety
36. Kind of critic
37. Hair cosmetic
38. Lack of vigor
39. Peter Wimsey Murder Case
40. Buffalo quorum
41. Fantasy state
42. Basic group
43. Hoary Gang Murder Case
44. Verities
45. Nuthatch genus
47. River in England
48. Kind of bone or business
49. Work earnestly
52. Vermont city
53. Bird Murder Case
54. Bake eggs
56. Hubbell and Reiner
58. TV feature
60. Old bills
61. Song of the 20's
62. "Say it ____ so"
63. Zoroastrian of Mideast
65. Ex ____ (one-sided)
66. River isles
67. Light unit
69. Cauterizes
71. Bruckner or Dvořák
72. Writer Glyn
73. Chilly
74. Port Said locale
75. Honshu town
76. Rubber or ink
78. Sibyl
79. Cat hangouts
80. Eastwood
81. College in Maine
83. Knishery
85. Life of ____
86. Ghana's capital
87. Pond carp
89. Gesundheit nut, perhaps
90. Most films, to ad writers
91. Bull's-Eye Murder Case
92. The flu, often
94. Long-eared dogs
96. "____ is human . . ."
98. Cooled off
99. Marsh vapor
100. Outdoorsy fabrics
103. Implore
104. Bach's favorite
105. Glassmaking ingredient
106. Hokkaido native
107. Caesar's 107
108. Caesar's field
109. Danube, to Hungarians
110. Titled Turks
111. ____ noir
112. Well or ill
113. Playwright's initials
114. ____ carte
116. Neighbor of Arg.
117. Wildebeest

24 Occupied by Alice H. Kaufman

Presenting various phases of the working world.

ACROSS

1. What to do about the diem
6. Long, wide scarf
11. Passport endorsements
16. Approximately
17. White statuary marble
19. Not completely
20. Reptile eater of Africa
22. Rainy season in India
23. Actress Sommer
24. Jason's ship
25. One who makes springs
27. Egg drink
28. Some: French
29. Add zest to
30. Waltz by Strauss
33. Healthy
34. City transit lines
35. "____ seat belts"
36. City of central Spain
39. Liquid measure: Abbr.
41. Possessive pronoun
42. Stormed
45. Evasive one
46. Fleets of warships
49. Author of "The Virginian"
50. Groom's need
51. Swing about
53. Cyst
54. Daniel Webster's art
55. Small particle
56. Relating to touch
58. Tizzy
59. Denials
60. Wraps in bandages
62. Braided
65. Wee, to a Scot
68. Resound
69. Distillation
71. Encourage
75. Symbol of flatness
77. River in Yorkshire
78. Swerve
79. Lasso
80. John Jacob and Mary
81. Fills the bill
83. One with a happy expression
85. Allen
86. Become rigid
87. Knack
88. Horse gait
89. Waxy ointment
91. Body of soldiers: Abbr.
93. Square-rigged vessel
94. Area in Westminster Abbey
97. At right angles, at sea
99. Musical notes
102. Type of postal service: Abbr.
103. Precarious
104. Topsoil
105. Arrange
106. Go over again
109. Service area off a dining room
112. Strip
113. Show contempt
114. Bottom-line figure
115. ____ nous
116. Indolence
117. Kind of steak

DOWN

1. Looked a joint over
2. White poplar
3. Plymouth and Inchcape
4. Simon-____
5. French season
6. "Beetle Bailey" heavy
7. Test a garment for size
8. Sphere
9. Not of the clergy
10. Box-score listings
11. Forefront
12. Tax org.
13. Early shipbuilding center in Conn.
14. Distant
15. Irish dramatist
17. Do the honors on Thanksgiving
18. Mine entrance
19. Said and Salut
21. Basting stitches
22. Flat-topped hills
26. Stoppers at London storeys
29. Put on cargo
31. Mark with lines
32. Slightest
33. Protects a doubtful bet
34. Shade tree
36. Period
37. Hodgepodge
38. Alfred of stage
39. Cowboy of the pampas
40. Mountain ridge
41. Rhodesia's Smith
43. Architect Saarinen
44. Prohibitionists
47. Piercing tool
48. Abysses
49. Steno's ailment
52. Shaping machine
54. In reserve
57. French river
58. Most level-headed
61. Ones with clothes on
63. Crowbar
64. Fearless
65. Healthful water holes
66. Sailboat feature
67. Predecessor
70. Galilee, for one
72. Alice's friend Ben
73. Dueling sword
74. Subdivision of a country: Abbr.
76. Desire
77. Previous month: Abbr.
81. Nobles
82. Weekday: Abbr.
84. Cripple
86. Ingredient of a hard heart
90. Kind of indigestion
91. Films on a new go-around
92. Fairy-tale baker of a witch
93. Animal
94. Self-esteem
95. Frequently
96. Kernels
97. Watchful
98. Late Senator from Idaho
99. Game of chance
100. Scottish island
101. Fashion
105. One who feels superior
107. Play by Capek
108. Drink
110. Sign of the zodiac
111. Thai coin

25 Onward and Upward by Cornelia Warriner

Some phrases to stir one's inner soul.

ACROSS

1. Chutzpah
5. Leaflet
10. Marquis of note
14. ____ song (cheaply)
18. Needle case
19. Purple Sage frequenter
20. Pleasant spot
21. Early fiddle
22. Observation by Donne
25. Put up
26. Lacking validation
27. U.S.A. total
28. Canyon in Utah
29. Cut of beef, in Scotland
30. Half a score
31. Karloff
32. Expected
34. Bookie's concern
35. Tapestry
36. Tiny bit
37. Shield borders
40. Check an opposing force
42. Arab cloak
45. Reward
46. Genus of sea birds
47. U.S. poet Allen
48. Halt
49. "Go to the ____, thou . . ."
50. Advice from T.R.
54. Field crossing
55. Backs away
57. Vibrate
58. Disgraced
59. Frightening
60. George Ade piece
61. Scene of Las Vegas action
62. "Tristram Shandy" author
64. Deranged
65. Accelerations
68. Thick soup
69. Keep a sailboat on course
71. Kind of sided or eared
72. Sheltered
73. Old coins of Riga
74. Strange: Prefix
75. African fox
76. Arrest
77. Constitution V.I.P.'s
81. Avarice
82. Wipes out
84. Rotation: Abbr.
85. Snoop
86. Like Alan Paton's country
88. "Who ____?" (ho-hum)
89. ____-la-la
90. Corp. officials
93. Abridge
94. Biblical Mount
95. Stirrer
97. William Blake's animal
98. Antiwar slogan
100. Group character
101. Leisure
102. Stir up
103. Feel in need of liniment
104. Rents
105. Drinks
106. Parking-place sentry
107. Pitcher Johnny Vander ____

DOWN

1. Class
2. Expiate
3. Like hastily mashed potatoes
4. False witness
5. Hot-dish holder
6. Up
7. Coarse fiber
8. 100 years: Abbr.
9. Cocked-hat shape
10. Niggardly
11. Islamic codes
12. Withhold
13. Tag or bitter
14. Containing iron
15. Slogan for old Life magazine
16. Air survey, for short
17. Performed
21. Discount
23. Observes
24. Moslem bridge to paradise
31. Opportunity
32. Accord
33. Kind of eyed
34. Flower-garden unit
35. Famous Titan
36. Delay
37. Khayyám
38. Friend of Pierre
39. Speedily obeyed order of God
40. Containing fat
41. Intend, in Scotland
43. Tree trunk
44. Copied
46. Thin
48. Sedate
50. Fish net
51. Taboret
52. Range of activity
53. Swipe
54. Wisp
56. Peep show
58. Office worker
60. Like some eyelashes
61. Backbone
62. Bridge length
63. City south of Moscow
64. Wool consumers
65. Super!
66. Model
67. Hurried
69. Abhorred
70. Osaka and Montreal events
73. ____ majesty
75. Place: Suffix
77. Vacillates
78. Swaggers
79. Uncanny
80. Certain pitch
81. Clutch
83. Bronco shows
85. Not a ____ (no chance)
86. Asian palm
87. Type size
88. Halt
89. Present or past
90. Express
91. Place for a mouchoir
92. Scoff
94. Ratify
95. Uptight
96. Carriage
98. ____ soup
99. Shoe cap

26 Tattling by Ruth W. Smith

Lack of privacy always seems to be a problem.

ACROSS

1. Metrical foot
8. Newman and Muni
13. He's in charge
17. Gets again
18. Coin of India
19. Conceptions
21. Juicy target in "Peyton Place"
23. ____ incognita
24. Consumed
25. Laughs, in Cannes
26. Geological division
28. Trojan war hero
29. Kind of truck
30. Hurry
32. Compass direction
33. Moslem faith
36. Stone or light
38. Wave, in Madrid
40. ____ Mater (Roman goddess)
41. Truckers' hauls
43. Easing of strained relations
46. Middle: Prefix
47. Rose city
49. Buffalo or chestnut
50. Hindu philosophy
52. Ancient Greek contest
53. Out of favor
54. Twitching
56. "Black Narcissus" author
61. Uncle Sam
62. "For want of ____ the horse . . ."
64. Venezuela copper center
65. Capital of Moselle
67. Beauty's friend
68. Validates a will
72. At a distance
75. Patio pieces
77. Goes on the lam
78. Lop off
79. "The ____ -tale Heart"
80. Time periods
81. Italian beach of W.W. II
82. Affirmative vote
84. Sizing
88. Brings up
90. Ibsen character
92. Astaire
93. Spanish stitch
94. Adjective suffix
97. Improvise
99. Newspaper features
102. Shabby
103. Exceptional people
104. Component
105. Chemical suffix
106. Psalms expression
107. Calms

DOWN

1. Madrid miss: Abbr.
2. Kind of fuel
3. Eye
4. Mango part
5. Three-dimensional exhibit
6. At last, in Lille
7. Star, in Avila
8. White House V.I.P.
9. Self: Prefix
10. Samoan island
11. "Arrowsmith" author
12. French legislative body
13. Kind of part
14. Ancient Greek theaters
15. Glib pleader in "Pickwick Papers"
16. Plastic wrapping
20. ____-Coburg
22. Sun god
27. Kind of eyes or gin
29. House recreation spot
30. Ibsen play
31. Interweave
33. Doctrine
34. Marie or Thérése: Abbr.
35. She had a lover
37. Sheep sound
39. Martin or Acheson
42. Lily
43. British fop, for short
44. Pekoe and oolong
45. Wagnerian goddess
47. French resort
48. Wynken and Blynken's partner
51. Hansel's sister and others
54. Checks
55. Understanding words
57. Plans
58. Be mistaken
59. Certain fiddler's locale
60. Letters
63. Bone: Prefix
66. Mountain lakes
69. Atmosphere: Prefix
70. Use a shredder
71. Perfumes
73. Cuckoo
74. Old car
76. Hebrew letter
78. Freed, with strings
82. Groups of sayings
83. Alpine sound
85. Rival of Athens and Sparta
86. Sierra ____
87. One of the Fords
89. Corn meal
91. Helps
93. Word of disdain
94. "Haven't ____ you before?"
95. Actress Bancroft
96. Landing vessels
98. Tournament-pairing draw
100. Spanish Mrs.
101. Lizard genus

27 Word Signs by Henry Hook

If you can draw, you can unlock some of the answers.

ACROSS

1. Tease
5. "If ____ Million"
10. Dog's offering
13. Fiber cluster
16. Subtraction word
20. Palo ____
21. Absorb
22. Pronoun
23. Shoulder: Prefix
24. Start from scratch
25. Yankee Hall-of-Famer
27. Madison Sq. Garden events
30. One of the leagues
31. Ibsen's "____ House"
32. First-rate
33. Measuring standards
34. Poetic word
35. Parrot's kin
36. Unisex wear
39. Plays charades
41. Dumbo's wings
42. Paled
45. "____ Blue?"
46. Scales of the Zodiac
48. Bogart-Bacall film
49. "____ look now . . ."
51. Unaltered
55. Renowned cardiologist
56. "Peerage" compiler
57. Albee's "The ____ Story"
58. Pack away
59. ____ years (elderly)
60. Blacksmiths, at times
62. Circus employee
65. Twenty, to Lincoln
66. Cain's exile site
67. Unseaworthy
68. Hosiery
69. Great Lakes mnemonic
70. Utah city
72. Make
73. Shop-window sign
74. Do newsroom work
76. Aloof
78. Knights of the turntable
82. Harmonious
86. Dozes
88. Yepremian of football
89. Circus climax, for short
91. Economist John Maynard
92. Gin-lime mixtures
95. Wilkes of "G.W.T.W."
97. Heavyweight champ in 1932
98. Kin of dese, dose and dem
99. At ____ for words
100. Please, in Germany
101. Activity
102. Kind of loser
103. Kind of gin
104. "Wherefore ____ thou?"
105. Place for a spare
106. Poisons
107. Matter, in philosophy
108. New, Fair or big
110. Gander of rhyme
111. Hopeless case
112. Barnyard sound
114. Does a pitching job
116. One place to spend liras
117. Russian vehicle
120. Jacques' world
121. One's face, familiarly
122. Bushy clump
125. Lend ____ (help)
126. Special-interest group
128. Grandfather, in Madrid
130. Big bird
131. Allan Jones song
135. Late-November fare
137. Saharalike
138. Ludwig ____ Beethoven
139. Blockhead
140. Platitudinous
141. "Othello" heavy
142. Not stereo
143. Opposite of odi
144. Portion: Abbr.
145. Protection
146. Dickens topic

DOWN

1. "M*A*S*H" actor Farr
2. Peaceful branch
2. Ecdysiast Lili
4. Ersatz
5. Dancer Duncan
6. Aces through tens
7. Suitably
8. Like dishwater
9. Tarzan's cronies
10. Greek letter
11. Nuclear org.
12. December door décor
13. Short-shadow time
14. Host on T.V.
15. Hoosegow
16. His words can be stood for
17. Send money
18. "Waiting for Lefty" author
19. Kind of back or rose
26. Hogwash
28. Rinsed the car
29. Largest of the Marianas
36. TV host Bert
37. French heavenly being
38. Army member: Abbr.
40. Defense org.
41. Israeli statesman
42. Joseph Wambaugh novel, with "The"
43. A Stooge
44. Old baker's number
46. Poe's radiant maiden
47. In the same place
48. Piano's 88
50. Believers in Odin
52. Kind of bomb
53. Writer Sir Thomas
54. Farmyard animals
55. One end of a transfusion
60. "A gentle thing," said Coleridge
61. Babylonian deity
62. Misprint, for short
63. Guinness
64. Shenanigans
65. Tibia locale
68. What Casey gave Mudville
71. Phrase of non-originality
75. Pseudo shirtfronts
77. Russian agency
79. Siberian output
80. American Indian
81. McFarland of "Our Gang"
83. Destroyed
84. "____, My God, to Thee"
85. Kefauver
87. Cavalry weapon
90. Work unit
92. Reckless
93. In a deplorable way
94. Air-conditioner setting
96. String instrument
97. Elbow bender
101. Started a golf hole
102. Evangelist Ira David ____
104. Aleutian island
105. Pigeon-
106. Russian wolfhound
109. Globetrotter Meadowlark
110. Card-table cry
111. Money in Amsterdam
113. Gives a boost to
115. Union units
116. Get ____ the city (be honored)
117. Complete, for short
118. Arrested
119. Garfield's middle name
121. Feast of Lots
122. Mid-morning
123. End
124. Spanish dollars
125. He "had 'em," in short verse
127. Soft fabric
128. "____ boy!"
129. Puppeteer Tillstrom
132. Zsa Zsa's sister
133. Expected
134. "Wall Street Lays an ____"
136. "No way!"

28 Paging M. Rodin by William Lutwiniak

Things that might apply to one of his statues.

ACROSS

1. Rx info.
5. Stadium seating
9. Summary
13. U.K. business center
16. Albion's neighbor
17. Dueling gear
18. Theater org.
19. Social affair
22. Intellectual muscle
25. Region of France
26. Gob's insigna
27. Zero
28. Skin layer
29. Italian painter
30. Caviar
31. _____ out (make do)
32. Horse pill
33. Split
34. Credited
36. French writer
37. Semiprecious stone
39. Roll of bills
40. Brainstorm
42. Monastic brother
44. In fitting style
47. Kitchenware
48. Insects
49. _____ impasse
50. Deadly pale
51. Corrida star
52. Musical skip
54. Ladybug's prey
55. Greek letter
56. Wear for a scholar
58. Gift
59. Artist's milieu
61. King, in Portugal
62. Outcome
64. Fit of shivering
65. Mood
71. Nursery word
72. Execrate
73. Tracking gear
74. Paintings
75. Food fish
76. Back-road features
77. Tempo
78. Unspeakable
79. Beat
80. Mt. Blanc, for one
81. Offspring of a sort
84. Biol. or chem.
85. Wardrobe
87. Alençon
88. Stool pigeon
92. Green places
93. Long bone
94. Labor grp.
95. Miss Arden
96. Gem features
98. Wheat, e.g.
99. Live _____ (enjoy)
100. Pump sign
101. "We _____ amused"
102. Mood
105. Herb infusion
106. Together, musically
107. Leer
108. Sign
109. Brit. money
110. Snoozes
111. Shoe tips
112. Irker

DOWN

1. Coy
2. Prayer
3. Went wrong
4. Aim
5. Made a bridge error
6. Began
7. Existed
8. Educ. institution
9. Kind of table
10. Verily
11. Arrests
12. Scarlett's milieu
13. Itemized
14. Mental carrier
15. Numerical prefix
19. Swiftian works
20. Miss de Havilland
21. Poetic word
23. Street sign
24. Aphrodite's love
32. Composer Béla
33. Lawn grass
35. Starey-eyed
37. Caravel of 1492
38. Rail-shipment quantity
40. "_____ Yesterday"
41. Dusting powder
43. Plus
44. P.G.A. standards
45. Port of Lake Erie
46. Mental activity
47. Luau staple
49. G.I. mail drops
51. Asian native
52. Villainous hallmark
53. Currency exchange
54. Not up yet
56. Stadium feature
57. La Douce
60. Braces
62. T.L.C. dispensers
63. Uproar
65. Certain mendicants
66. Cordage fiber
67. Arabian Sea gulf
68. One who frustrates
69. Temperate
70. Oléron, e.g.
72. Parseghian
75. Please
77. Adriatic port
78. Andes denizen
79. Well-armed sea denizens
81. Bruins' home
82. Finishing touch
83. African Moslems
84. Greets
86. Bacchante
88. Scintilla
89. Pea or bean
90. Bypasses
91. Feel annoyed
93. Girl's name
96. Jack Sprat eschewed it
97. Seed covering
98. Fed
99. Shakespearean villain
103. Realty unit
104. Kind of banana

29 The Long of It by Mary Russ

Many of these entries are better known in shortened form.

ACROSS

1. Shade of green
5. Italian artist Giulio
10. Part of Latin-class trio
14. Bearing
18. Political league
19. Oak tree fallout
20. Kentucky college
22. Wheel shaft
23. Part of T.L.C.
24. Rumania's Comaneci
25. A Walton et al.
26. Bravo and Grande
27. "For Pete's sake, say yes or no"
31. In ___ quo
32. Where gamblers gamble
33. What oglers do
34. Weems or Knight
35. Shank's mare, to a playgoer
42. Gaseous element
44. U.S. satellite
45. Lion, for one
47. Common, to Miss Loren
50. Alley or fraidy
51. Colorado Indian
53. Agnus ___
54. Mast
57. Lobster claw
59. Aunt's relative
61. Ceremonial heap
62. Stubborn
64. Located
66. Lover, usually old
68. Where the buck begins
74. Soap plant
75. Wear away
76. Talked back
77. Dash
80. Alerts
82. Night, in Bonn
84. Virginia willow
85. "My ___ Sal"
86. Picnic visitor
87. Dined
89. Mans the tiller
91. "For amber waves of ___"
93. ___-terre
95. Sibling
99. Mayday
104. Explorer Johnson
105. Presiding spirit
106. Hat brim, in Italy
107. M.I.T., etc.: Abbr.
109. One-time banana-republic words
116. Persian poet
117. Having a fixed gaze
118. Word with farm or home
119. Pickle additive
121. River to the Seine
122. Unearthly
123. Put into circulation
124. She, in Paris
125. Astaire
126. Certain recitations: Abbr.
127. Like some sleeves
128. Do ushering

DOWN

1. Rudiments
2. Kind of back or horse
3. Like Ethelred II
4. Skilled
5. Bulbous mug
6. U.S.M.A. or U.S.N.A.
7. Like Chaplin's times
8. Valued highly
9. Agitated
10. Actor Walter
11. T.V.'s Griffin
12. Musical passages
13. Holding a tone, in music
14. Miss Dietrich
15. Corn lily
16. Artists' patron saint
17. Love or bird's ___
21. Indian state
28. Ejects
29. Type of column
30. Investigate
31. Wall St. item
36. Football score
37. Esau family name
38. Laurance, to John D.
39. French menu word
40. Astor or Bountiful
41. River to the North Sea
43. John Alden was one
46. Old-school item
48. Jeeter of "Tobacco Road"
49. Lamb
51. California campus
52. Part of I.B.T.C.W.H.
54. Dallas campus
55. Witty offering
56. Muhammad
58. Certified
60. Cause's consequence
61. Continue stubbornly
63. Rel. of a college
65. Poetic contraction
67. ___ culpa
69. Part of a blind
70. Harem rooms
71. Adherent
72. Bee follower
73. Nabokov novel
77. Kind of nog
78. Porsena
79. Jai ___
81. Ingenuous
83. Goddess of youth
86. Abrogate
88. Blue-pencils
90. Violinist's need
92. Snubbed
93. Dagger
94. Germ-free state
96. Antagonistic
97. "Great Expectations" heroine
98. Headland
100. Entertain
101. Athlete's award
102. African fly
103. Most unusual
108. People in X-rated films
109. What revelers raise
110. Arab prince
111. Flower holder
112. First: Abbr.
113. Humorist Bill et al.
114. Hawaiian island
115. Character in "Henry VI"
120. Tennis call

30 Weightlifting by W.W.

In this case, it really isn't an effort.

ACROSS

1. Spanish metropolis
7. Unexpected defeat
12. Soak
15. Famous lioness
19. "Somewhere ___ Is Calling"
20. Dreamy
21. Mine product
22. Household jewel
23. Breakthrough on the girdle front
25. Spanish castanet dance
27. Bacchanalian cry
28. Easily angered
29. Partner of illegal or immoral
30. Squander, in Scotland
31. Spanish room
33. This, in Spain
34. Seconds that count, caloriewise
38. Desensitizes
40. Upper-space region
44. Italian poet
45. Game played in hotel rooms
47. Novelist Graham
48. Name for Clemenceau
49. Grain container
50. Western Indian
52. Weekdays: Abbr.
53. Blood of the gods
54. Kind of mortem
55. "I will ___ evil"
58. Animal doc
59. Turner and Pendleton
60. Mooring post on a ship
61. Tossed around
62. Time periods: Abbr.
63. Common affliction of office workers
67. Five-spot
69. Nonstudio T.V. relays
70. Bothers
71. Insect stage
74. Sky Altar
75. Sewed together
76. Key-shaped
77. Locations
78. Diplomat's forte
80. Football units: Abbr.
81. Era
82. Things often split
83. Old liquid measures
85. Wavering
89. Natives of an Italian town
91. Hosiery thread
92. It rains here
93. Slams the door again
94. Tibetan priest
96. Suitcase
98. Vicinity
99. These should be tipped sparingly
103. Hospital section
105. In present condition
109. Kinship
110. What an indiscreet eater is
112. Seed covering
113. Lincoln Park or Bronx
114. French military group
115. ___ the altar
116. Ring out
117. Letters
118. Look scornfully
119. Like the ultra martini

DOWN

1. Famous auntie
2. Tel ___
3. Extinct bird
4. Laugh, in France
5. Here, in France
6. Rebellious
7. Deep browns
8. Whiff, as of smoke
9. Alone on stage
10. Albion
11. Nautical rope
12. Furniture item
13. Speechifies
14. Men, for short
15. Comes out from
16. Wool: Prefix
17. Omen
18. Sick as ___
24. Chilled meat, to a poilu
26. Inhibit
29. Eclat
30. Sadder but ___
32. Drag
34. ___ hand (abjectly)
35. Heath genus
36. They make one heavy
37. Full of holes: Var.
39. Salvo to the hips
41. Chores, to nondieters
42. Go in
43. Pauses
45. Like the N.Y.–N.J. Port Authority
46. Insect
47. People who have had it
49. Toast for a nondieter
51. Baseball hit
54. Simple Simon's friend
55. U.S. air agency
56. Blow up a photo
57. Poem
60. Nurtures
61. Twice, in music
64. Black-ink abbreviations
65. Holzman or Grange
66. As brawny as ___ mover
67. Deadly
68. Teheran resident
72. Intrinsically
73. Lunkheads
76. Former Mideast org.
77. Fine Indian silk
79. Keeps no secrets
84. Respond to
86. Slow horses
87. Title
88. Fabled animal
89. Slanting stroke on a letter
90. Thoroughly chilled
92. Oasis of the old West
93. Worker on shoe soles
95. Indian corn
97. Egret's pride
99. Snare
100. On hand
101. Literary pseudonym
102. Son of Seth
104. Arrow poison
105. Turkish regiment
106. Flank
107. Adherents: Suffix
108. Drink, as of liquor
110. Dads
111. Poetic contraction

31 Nursery Folk by Tap Osborn

Memory course in basic reading.

ACROSS

1. Rice dish
6. Dismay
11. Smith or Bede
15. Emir's tongue
21. Chemical prefix
22. Olivelike fruit
23. London gallery
24. Montana city
25. She had an arachnid problem
28. Shooters
29. Giant of fame
30. Alcove
31. Mother of this puzzle
32. Comic Johnson et al.
33. Bad: Prefix
34. N.Y. Governor
35. Printer's mark
36. Like a pleasant day
38. Gobbled up
39. Iowa State U. locale
40. Sloping surface
41. Brook
42. Halter's relative
45. Deducted from a bill
47. He loved sugar candy
50. Yutang
51. City on the Oka
52. Prancer's driver
53. Latin dance
54. Mutual or trust
55. Issuer of a check
57. Rivera painting
58. Hepburn, to friends
59. Poetic paean
60. Corsica's neighbor
61. He lacked dessert money
63. Time
64. Add-on
65. U.S. chief justice
66. Sun disk
67. Understood
71. Studio-audience sign
73. Sophia
75. Drive one's horse to a win
76. Actress Norma
77. Prod
78. Old Italian coin
79. Women's ___
80. Four-poster
81. He had a lively trio
84. Miss Cinders
85. Words on a marquee
88. Bananas
89. Sheik's land
90. Word with sooth or nay
91. Woodwind
92. Kind of hog
93. Mime's forte
94. Beach noisemaker
95. Grand Coulee, e.g.
96. She lies in bed until 9:30 A.M.
99. Trounce
102. Scrap
103. Phooey!
104. Like a parabola
105. Move slowly
106. Gershwin
107. Customary practice
109. ___ a fiddle
110. Depart
111. Chigger
112. Data
114. Bandleader Lester
115. Throw the shot
116. Month: Abbr.
117. Maintenance
119. "___, Betsy, Bess" (girl of rhyme)
123. Madre or Nevada
124. Nora's terrier
125. One who prods
126. Writer Bret
127. Driest
128. Hammer part
129. Sea bird: Var.
130. Goose genus

DOWN

1. Western observatory
2. Copy
3. He slept under a haystack
4. Insect
5. Subsequent: Abbr.
6. Esteemed
7. Does comparison shopping
8. Aggressive
9. Church area
10. Moon vehicle
11. "Life Begins ___"
12. Mrs. Dionne's doctor
13. Nuclear trial
14. Parcel out
15. Cry of surprise
16. With great pomp
17. False ___
18. She lost her holiday shoe
19. Arrow poison
20. Late Miss Elliot
26. Kind of paint
27. Where Idi ruled
34. Minister to
35. Saddle part
36. Tippler's toot
37. Actor Ray
40. Erie, e.g.
41. Arrested
43. Corona
44. Hardy or Griffith
46. Vicinity
47. Predatory person
48. Flower part
49. Writer Alan
52. "___ is icumen in"
54. Blue streak
55. Fruit covers
56. God, to many
57. U.M.W. member
58. High flier
59. Poetic Muse
61. Stuffed
62. N.Y.C. restaurateur
63. Eat away
65. Troika makeup
67. "Gee whiz!"
68. She sat among the cinders
69. Zola
70. Forbid
72. Clark
73. Polish city
74. Like certain trees
75. Prize or hatch
77. Clearing in the woods
78. Like a Dracula film
81. Birdlife of a region
82. Pompeii's neighbor
83. Avarice
84. Justice Warren
85. Hassle
86. Steel beam
87. He sings for his supper
88. Social layer
90. Glove material
92. Dross
93. Mysteries
94. Snowstorm aid
96. Rubber tips
97. Bangor native
98. Craftsman: Var.
99. Abolitionist's target
100. Short solo: Var.
101. He was in the rye
105. Fowl
108. Metric unit
109. True's partner
110. Release
112. Bother
113. ". . . baked in ___"
114. Pole vault
115. Protagonist
118. Kind of poker hand
120. Drive up a wall
121. Asian sheep
122. Young Peter

32 Who's Who by David A. Scully

Presenting a few meaningful people.

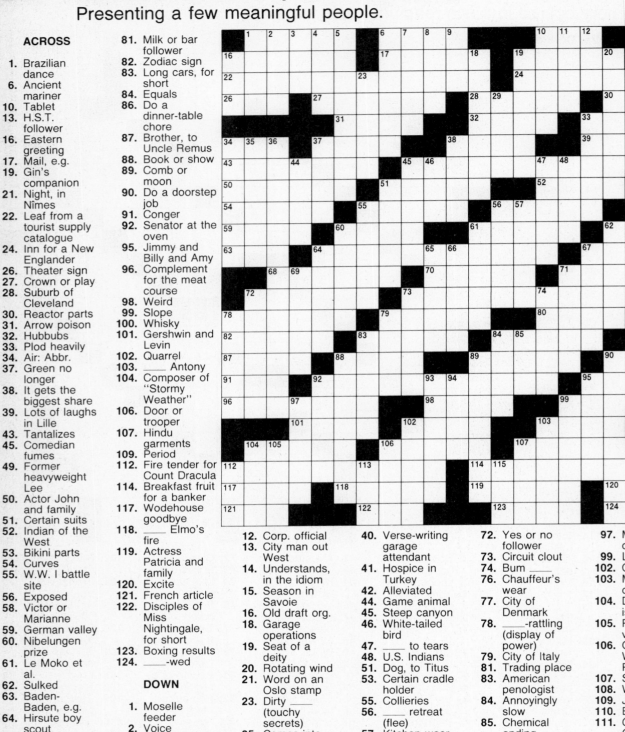

ACROSS

1. Brazilian dance
6. Ancient mariner
10. Tablet
13. H.S.T. follower
16. Eastern greeting
17. Mail, e.g.
19. Gin's companion
21. Night, in Nimes
22. Leaf from a tourist supply catalogue
24. Inn for a New Englander
26. Theater sign
27. Crown or play
28. Suburb of Cleveland
30. Reactor parts
31. Arrow poison
32. Hubbubs
33. Plod heavily
34. Air: Abbr.
37. Green no longer
38. It gets the biggest share
39. Lots of laughs in Lille
43. Tantalizes
45. Comedian fumes
49. Former heavyweight Lee
50. Actor John and family
51. Certain suits
52. Indian of the West
53. Bikini parts
54. Curves
55. W.W. I battle site
56. Exposed
58. Victor or Marianne
59. German valley
60. Nibelungen prize
61. Le Moko et al.
62. Sulked
63. Baden-Baden, e.g.
64. Hirsute boy scout
67. Did battle
68. ". . . five ____ and two fishes"
70. Remain still, as a ship
71. Like winter streets
72. Lists of politicos
73. Jewel for a jurist's wife
75. Arafat's org.
78. Screened
79. Walden et al.
80. Pigeon-____

81. Milk or bar follower
82. Zodiac sign
83. Long cars, for short
84. Equals
86. Do a dinner-table chore
87. Brother, to Uncle Remus
88. Book or show
89. Comb or moon
90. Do a doorstep job
91. Conger
92. Senator at the oven
95. Jimmy and Billy and Amy
96. Complement for the meat course
98. Weird
99. Slope
100. Whisky
101. Gershwin and Levin
102. Quarrel
103. ____ Antony
104. Composer of "Stormy Weather"
106. Door or trooper
107. Hindu garments
109. Period
112. Fire tender for Count Dracula
114. Breakfast fruit for a banker
117. Wodehouse goodbye
118. ____ Elmo's fire
119. Actress Patricia and family
120. Excite
121. French article
122. Disciples of Miss Nightingale, for short
123. Boxing results
124. ____-wed

DOWN

1. Moselle feeder
2. Voice
3. Scottish prefix
4. Item for a Thai's purse
5. Vespucci's namesakes
6. Took 40 winks
7. Priestly vestment
8. French acquaintance
9. Farm animal
10. Products of fools like Kilmer
11. Siam visitor

12. Corp. official
13. City man out West
14. Understands, in the idiom
15. Season in Savoie
16. Old draft org.
18. Garage operations
19. Seat of a deity
20. Rotating wind
21. Word on an Oslo stamp
23. Dirty ____ (touchy secrets)
25. Comes into view
29. "Dies like ____ . . ."
33. Fish on a Boston menu
34. Trees
35. Gets ready to drive
36. Chicago merchant's stadium
37. Sets a price
38. Prospector's dream

40. Verse-writing garage attendant
41. Hospice in Turkey
42. Alleviated
44. Game animal
45. Steep canyon
46. White-tailed bird
47. ____ to tears
48. U.S. Indians
51. Dog, to Titus
53. Certain cradle holder
55. Collieries
56. ____ retreat (flee)
57. Kitchen wear
58. Non-stirrer on Xmas eve
60. Ranted
61. Orange leavings
62. Ezra or Roscoe
64. Ides and nones, e.g.
65. Treeless plain
66. Fliers
67. Sheets of ice
69. Horse opera
71. Fib

72. Yes or no follower
73. Circuit clout
74. Bum ____
76. Chauffeur's wear
77. City of Denmark
78. ____-rattling (display of power)
79. City of Italy
81. Trading place
83. American penologist
84. Annoyingly slow
85. Chemical ending
86. Haul
88. Ex-Harvard president and family
89. Mary of late TV
90. Song-and-____ (Cohan, e.g.)
92. Employs
93. Banish
94. Doomsayer on Wall Street
95. Rod of baseball

97. Miss Rudolph of track
99. Light stroke
102. Carbines
103. Miss Thomas of films
104. Donegal island
105. Reckoned value
106. Onion or Washington Red
107. State: Abbr.
108. Withered
109. Jewish month
110. Blooming
111. One, in the Orkneys
112. Heat meas.
113. Paddle
115. Seine
116. Kind of tide or blow

33 Two for the Price of One by William H. Ford

Some extra definitions that may or may not help.

ACROSS

1. Range, or a viewing device
6. Jam, as a drain
12. Cleanses
17. Resplendent
19. Give a new image, or do a letter again
20. Conductor Previn
21. ____ hand (close)
22. Luzon native
23. Embankment
24. Wins customers, or is scolded
27. Nations' flying arms: Abbr.
28. German admiral
29. Matterhorn, for one
30. Suffix for north or south
31. Growl
32. Beauty-shop offering
35. Like a flooded carburetor
37. "____ homo!"
38. Neighbor of Iran: Abbr.
41. French honker
42. Times of day: Abbr.
43. Charger
44. Got angry, or enlarged
46. Decisive
48. South American sloths
49. Small quantity
50. French lace
51. Sets free, or speaks out
56. Part of Q.E.D.
57. "Look Homeward, Angel" hero
58. Carnival wild man
59. Glass bottle
60. Understand, or grab
62. Relative of aloha
63. Miss Sommer
64. Gen. Arnold
65. Femme's friend
67. Piece of tableware
69. Latin American soup
72. Letters
73. Famed railroad initials
74. Basic nucleic acid
75. "____, Brute"
76. Eban et al.
78. On the watch
80. At the drop of ____
81. Beetle
82. Miss Hagen
83. Old English moneys
87. Part of a millennium: Abbr.
88. Vanished, or book title
93. "When I Grow Too ____ Dream"
95. Like Santa's laugh
96. Have ____ on (be tipsy)
97. Kind of peach
98. Islamic angel of death
99. Hidden
100. Bantu tribesman
101. Length units
102. Pentagon wear

DOWN

1. Lyrics, or small sums
2. Obnoxious one
3. Colonizer of New Mexico
4. Analyzer of a kind
5. "L'____, c'est . . ."
6. Dotted, in engraving
7. Give a ____ (help)
8. Sioux
9. Brain ridges
10. Where to put a card, or laugh
11. Singer Roberta
12. My Gal et al.
13. Pronoun
14. Prepayment
15. Introduction
16. Gets furious
18. Old English letter
25. Relieve
26. Bend of a ship's plank
31. Finishes, or recovers
33. Chit
34. Tuck's companion
35. Channel
36. Blend
38. One of David's men
39. Fauna's companion
40. Do injury to
43. "____ vous plaît"
45. Be on guard, or care for
46. Miss a pitch, or gab
47. Pennsylvania city
48. Inquire
50. Mover
52. ____ off (begin)
53. Caller at Kuwait
54. Kind of Godfor
55. Miss Verdugo
57. Pol. party
61. Linden or Holbrook
66. Papyrus writings: Abbr.
67. Between bi and quadri
68. Ode holder
69. Vainglorious one
70. Famous Moor
71. Substitute
73. Magpie: Var.
76. ____ Annie, in "Oklahoma"
77. City of Texas
78. Alcohol bases
79. Advice to a young man
82. Absolute
84. "____ cockhorse . . ."
85. Pique
86. Anthony and Barbara
88. Discothèque dancer
89. Kind of hog
90. Dies ____
91. Tropical fiber tree
92. River to the Danube
94. Learning regimen: Abbr.

34 Reunion by Raymond F. Eisner
Time for a gathering of the clan.

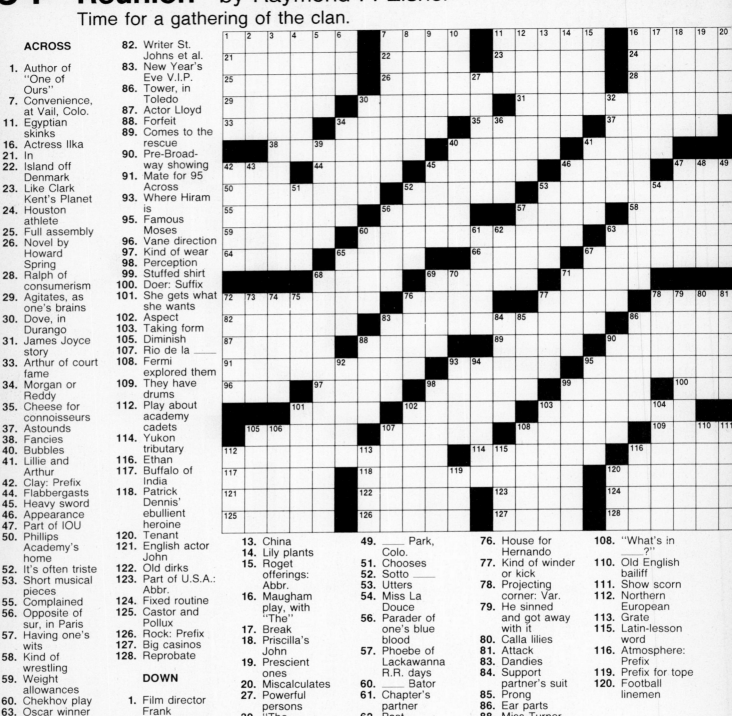

ACROSS

1. Author of "One of Ours"
7. Convenience, at Vail, Colo.
11. Egyptian skinks
16. Actress Ilka
21. In
22. Island off Denmark
23. Like Clark Kent's Planet
24. Houston athlete
25. Full assembly
26. Novel by Howard Spring
28. Ralph of consumerism
29. Agitates, as one's brains
30. Dove, in Durango
31. James Joyce story
33. Arthur of court fame
34. Morgan or Reddy
35. Cheese for connoisseurs
37. Astounds
38. Fancies
40. Bubbles
41. Lillie and Arthur
42. Clay: Prefix
44. Flabbergasts
45. Heavy sword
46. Appearance
47. Part of IOU
50. Phillips Academy's home
52. It's often triste
53. Short musical pieces
55. Complained
56. Opposite of sur, in Paris
57. Having one's wits
58. Kind of wrestling
59. Weight allowances
60. Chekhov play
63. Oscar winner Signoret
64. Wash. legislators
65. Blackthorn fruit
66. Concerns of psychiatrists
67. Toddlers-to-be
68. Type of bag
69. Antelope of Asia
71. Writer Wiesel
72. Pope's church in Rome
76. Siamese and alley
77. Skirt feature
78. Auditors: Abbr.
82. Writer St. Johns et al.
83. New Year's Eve V.I.P.
86. Tower, in Toledo
87. Actor Lloyd
88. Forfeit
89. Comes to the rescue
90. Pre-Broadway showing
91. Mate for 95 Across
93. Where Hiram is
95. Famous Moses
96. Vane direction
97. Kind of wear
98. Perception
99. Stuffed shirt
100. Doer: Suffix
101. She gets what she wants
102. Aspect
103. Taking form
105. Diminish
107. Rio de la ___
108. Fermi explored them
109. They have drums
112. Play about academy cadets
114. Yukon tributary
116. Ethan
117. Buffalo of India
118. Patrick Dennis' ebullient heroine
120. Tenant
121. English actor John
122. Old dirks
123. Part of U.S.A.: Abbr.
124. Fixed routine
125. Castor and Pollux
126. Rock: Prefix
127. Big casinos
128. Reprobate

DOWN

1. Film director Frank
2. North African chain
3. Edith Wharton novel
4. Sounded the horn
5. Big birds
6. Radiation dosage
7. Hot fare
8. Stendhal and family
9. Often-fatal crime
10. There's this at the top
11. Navy V.I.P.
12. When soap operas are seen
13. China
14. Lily plants
15. Roget offerings: Abbr.
16. Maugham play, with "The"
17. Break
18. Priscilla's John
19. Prescient ones
20. Miscalculates
27. Powerful persons
30. "The ___ Principle"
32. "___ man in your future"
34. Talked falteringly
36. Uncommon
39. Rainspout feeders
40. Dishonest
41. Twining stem
42. Agreements
43. Lake in Finland
45. King of Israel
46. Louvre name
47. Gibson garnish
48. Common contraction
49. ___ Park, Colo.
51. Chooses
52. Sotto ___
53. Utters
54. Miss La Douce
56. Parader of one's blue blood
57. Phoebe of Lackawanna R.R. days
60. ___ Bator
61. Chapter's partner
62. Past
63. Tizzy
65. Ladies of Spain: Abbr.
67. Nastase
68. Glenway Wescott novel, with "The"
69. Fill up
70. Old English letter
71. Place for O'Neill's desire
72. Actress Hope
73. Bedeck
74. Tissue layers
75. Ardor
76. House for Hernando
77. Kind of winder or kick
78. Projecting corner: Var.
79. He sinned and got away with it
80. Calla lilies
81. Attack
83. Dandies
84. Support partner's suit
85. Prong
86. Ear parts
88. Miss Turner
90. One-way and round
92. Martinique volcano
93. Gist
94. Having a handle
95. Pasture grass
98. Destroy
99. People who make calls
101. Triangular sail
102. Space traveler
103. Flower part
104. Wrestler's half
105. Pointer
106. Beulah of films
107. Kind of danish
108. "What's in ___?"
110. Old English bailiff
111. Show scorn
112. Northern European
113. Grate
115. Latin-lesson word
116. Atmosphere: Prefix
119. Prefix for tope
120. Football linemen

35 Who, What or How by Anthony B. Canning

A mélange of trivia about people.

ACROSS

1. Hebrew measures
6. Small nails
11. Quench
18. Scene of Evangeline's exodus
19. China piece
20. Swizzle stick
21. Dr. Johnson or Noah Webster
23. Processing, as a pelt
24. Type of type
25. Word after black or check
26. A dash of spirits
28. Sign of success
29. Yoko ___
30. Carry on
31. Earl in "Macbeth"
32. Symbol of redness
33. Lawn with a view
35. Inventor Nikola
36. Chinese truth
38. Desiccated
39. Seneca, Octavia and Antonia
44. A case of thou
45. Emoter
46. ___ King Cole
47. Took a dice bet
48. Seethe
49. Part of N.J.: Abbr.
50. First name of a U.N. official
52. Customarily
54. Pond fish
55. Dead ___ (empty bottle)
57. Spumante locale
58. Prepare TV laughter
59. Esthetic field
60. Thoreau, Whitman or Clara Barton, for a while
62. Old Siamese coins
63. Where, to Cicero
64. Tilt
65. Disciple
66. To ___ (exactly)
67. Well-known Pittsburgh family
69. Word with diem
70. Dime-novelist Buntline
71. Winged figure
72. ___ et retour (round trip, in France)
73. Total measurement: Abbr.
75. Phone-book abbr.
76. Jewish month
77. Like H. H. Munro, Spartacus or Zebulon Pike
81. Legal claim
82. Waterfall: Var.
83. People who look
84. Strong disapproval
87. Singer Gluck
90. Strident
92. In the midst of, for short
93. Smorgasbord fish
94. Wrong: Prefix
95. Butter ingredient
96. Popular presidential birthplace
97. Trap
99. Board a local
101. Mazarin, Salazar or Pitt
104. Tom Brown's ordeal
105. Big pocket watch
106. Waters from a French spa
107. Settle
108. Walking ___ (ecstatic)
109. Italian poet

DOWN

1. American cat
2. Miss Elliot of stage
3. Job held by Watterson or Morley
4. Wedding missiles
5. ___ Paulo
6. Beauty's companion
7. Transported
8. Fräulein's cry of dismay
9. Pushkin or Hamilton
10. Like unplanned metropolises
11. At one's business
12. ___ lose it all (be vulnerable)
13. Half of Warden Lawes's place
14. Place for an ode
15. Originate
16. Literary style
17. Rye fungus
18. Toby's contents
19. Group of three
22. Iced
27. Hartebeest
30. Seldom seen
31. Cutting line: Abbr.
32. ___ Law of Britain
34. Movie unit
35. Conway
37. Business
39. Norwegian port
40. Hid away
41. Mann or Conant
42. One doing narration
43. Danish city
44. Mexican staple
45. Spartan menial
48. Gym apparatus
49. Boswell's fixation
50. Hinder
51. Zone
53. Brit. money
54. High fevers, in medicine
55. Give the once-over
56. That, in old Rome
57. Teenagers' woes
60. Showing contempt
61. Water buffalo
66. Rudolf Hess or Della Street
68. Fairy in "Iolanthe"
69. Uses flattery
71. Drink-stand items
74. Without ___ (broke)
75. "Treasure Island" initials
76. Japanese indigene
78. Existent
79. Shakedown cruise
80. Attempt
81. "Vive ___!"
84. Zoo swinger
85. Gaucho ropes
86. City in Oklahoma
87. Microscopic animal
88. Cruise-captain's command
89. Spectral type
91. Pronghorn's habitat
92. Possessive
95. Anodyne's target
96. Kind of potent
97. Polynesian dance
98. Bitter vetch
100. International business deal: Abbr.
102. Novelist Wolfert
103. Balloon rigging

36 Town Meetings by Adelyn Lewis

Some likely get-togethers for civic bodies.

ACROSS

1. Washington city
7. Latium city
11. Heart
14. Georgia town
20. Evolutionary figure
21. Moslem priest
22. Shoe part
23. Musical movements
24. Sea nymph
25. Waterproof canvas
26. In the center of
27. Like ships in poetically calm waters
28. Places in N.H., Ind. and N.C.
32. Prophet
33. Aloft's opposite
34. Moves quickly
35. Recipe abbr.
38. Bit of info.
40. Spanish gentleman
42. Catchall words
46. Honeybee genus
48. Thy, in France
50. Russian city
52. Bean of India
53. Mover's need
54. Ida., Tex. and Fla. towns
60. Walk restlessly
61. Small space
62. Having an intention
63. Hebrew letters
65. Ben or men
66. De ____ (superfluous)
67. Diving-bell inventor
69. Extract forcefully
70. Lawyer: Abbr.
71. Be wrong
73. Arizona town
76. Peter Pan's creator
78. La., Ariz. and Ga. towns
85. Christmas, in Italy
86. Vega's constellation
87. Woodworking tool
88. Times of day: Abbr.
90. Armada's home
93. Whole or half, e.g.
95. "____ each life some rain . . ."
98. Pub dispenser
100. Harangue
102. Dairy device
105. Waxy ointment
106. Dismounted
107. Wyo. and Conn. towns
110. Cattle genus
111. Wood sorrel
112. Early bard
113. Earth: Prefix
114. Pay, in Scotland
115. Small star, to a Roman
118. Span's partner
121. Terza ____
124. Certain carriers: Abbr.
125. Tankers
127. Hindu merchant caste
128. River bank: Lat.
130. S.C., N.J. and Pa. towns
137. Wrinkled grape
138. Fencing sword
139. Warm-sea fish
140. Mild cigars
142. Acquiesce
143. Some votes
144. Owl genus
145. Author Glyn
146. Alaskan town
147. Financial offs.
148. N.Y. town
149. Calif. town

DOWN

1. Work on leather
2. Imitated
3. Parrot's bill area
4. Hebrew measures
5. French city officials
6. On the other hand
7. Miss Moreno
8. Gen. Bradley
9. Author Mannes and namesakes
10. Pierce: Var.
11. Naval off.
12. Medleys
13. Go on a diet
14. Powerful rich person
15. Covered with woolly hair
16. Picasso, for one
17. Stravinsky
18. Inquisitive
19. Fast plane
22. "For ____ of all ____ of tongue . . ."
29. Persona ____
30. Emphatic negative
31. Abed
35. Aleutian island
36. "He that ____ his rod . . ."
37. Olive stuffing
39. Attract
41. Fasten again
43. Get around
44. Revs up an engine
45. "____ of robins . . ."
47. Detect
49. Goad
51. Wash basin
55. German, to a Frenchman
56. Look closely
57. Characteristic quality
58. Word with sex or snob
59. Sumatran town
60. Polynesian skirt
64. Drink stick
68. Daughter of 40 Across: Abbr.
72. Actor O'Neal
74. Plank's curve on a ship
75. Michigan town
77. High heart or diamond
79. Eastern church member
80. Full of: Suffix
81. Rhythms
82. Devilfish
83. Bullring V.I.P.
84. Nonpro
89. Uses one's money
90. Attempts
91. Helmsman
92. Rebel
94. "Iliad" and "Odyssey," e.g.
96. Secret group
97. Working state
99. Goddess of discord
101. Edibles such as vegetables
103. Orphans, sometimes
104. Light sword
108. More robust
109. Dancer Shearer
111. Green gemstone
116. Relax
117. Passionate
119. Noisy demand
120. Motion: Prefix
122. Hashes
123. Handsome youth
126. Deep sleep
129. Make ____ attempt (try futilely)
130. ____ Grande, Ariz.
131. Actress Virna
132. Flight formations
133. Bass or snare
134. Fireman's burden
135. Musician Rapee
136. Board's partner
137. Cheer
141. Wife of 40 Across: Abbr.

37 Togetherness by Hugh McElroy

Presenting a gathering of the clan.

ACROSS

1. Health resort
4. Severe
9. Recipe abbr.
13. Tarkenton or Allison
17. Greet
18. Large snake
19. Prefix for distant or poise
20. Kind of tender
22. "Tar Baby" narrator
24. Rosalind Russell role
26. Poet Sara
27. Adriatic wind
29. Used a sickle or sythe
30. Earthen building material
31. Dormouse
32. Like hotel-lobby palms
33. Stage awards
35. Bundle of grain
36. Early slaves
37. Green area of Paris
38. Kind of clock
40. Frank Buchman's org.
43. Western Indian
44. Snake and scarf
45. London cleaning woman
46. _____ in the wool
47. L.A. time
48. Lanchester and Maxwell
50. Limn
51. Prepared
52. Poor abode
55. Word before Jane or sailing
57. _____ Tuesday
58. Fully attended
60. Fair
61. More severe
62. Opposition to dogma
63. Pencil tip
64. Rebound
65. Home on a high tor
66. Kindly trait
67. Dazzling success
70. To date
73. Laurel or Musial
74. Son of Adam
75. Stir up
76. Greek letters
77. Boston time
78. Carroll O'Connor's all
82. Excellent
83. Works a trade
84. Mariner's cry
85. River of France
87. _____ play (soft job)
89. Fiction writers' concerns
90. Arabian judge
91. Worley of TV
92. Lab burner
93. Urbane
97. Shimmy expert of song
100. Guardians of Cub Scouts
102. Helps with the dishes
103. Affirm
104. Ancient theater
105. Therefore
106. Ocean vessels: Abbr.
107. Storm-country girl
108. Stir to action
109. Relative of Mayday

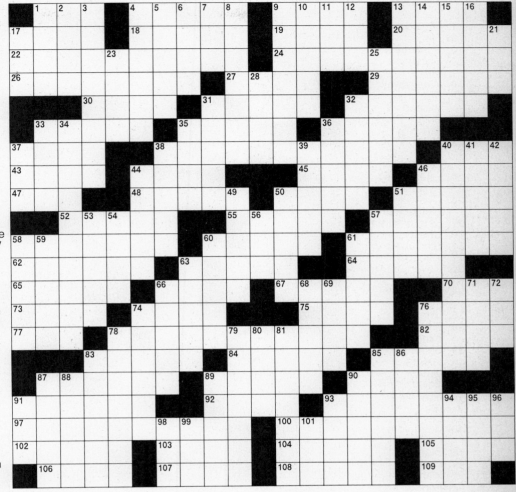

DOWN

1. Having one's reason
2. Kind of type
3. Condiment
4. Annoy
5. White poplar
6. "When in _____, do . . ."
7. Dallas campus
8. Fallen idol
9. Rip away
10. Settle on public land
11. Bit of wit
12. Command to Fido
13. Faster on foot
14. Adds new mounting
15. Open-mouthed
16. Identified
17. Relative of 52 Across
21. _____ Zeppelin (rock group)
23. Miss Adams
25. Laundry worker
28. Toward the mouth
31. _____ apso
32. Relative of "Bosh!"
33. Feel one's
34. Play and movie about V.M.I.
35. Women of Juárez: Abbr.
36. Frome of fiction
37. Cork noise
38. Relative of "Gosh!"
39. Bitter
40. Howard Spring novel
41. Pass a rope through
42. Viper
44. Dressler co-star
46. Frankie _____, boy actor of the 1930's
49. Go separate ways
50. Admirer of Beatrice
51. Chastity's mother
53. "_____ a million"
54. Flower holder
56. Chaney
57. Keystone or Empire
58. Period between changes
59. Old English courts
60. German, in W.W. I argot
61. Like fish
63. Primrose and bridle
66. Heads: Fr.
68. _____ cross
69. Lively tune
71. One in Frankfurt
72. Half an African fly
74. Duke of baseball
76. Districts of Louisiana
78. Malady
79. Hesitates
80. Bard's river
81. Manolete, for one
83. Playwright Harold
85. Molly or Dorothy
86. Mine entrance
87. Coconut fibers
88. _____ made (is on easy street)
89. Rose and Fountain
90. Perry and family
91. Juridical degree
93. Tire, in Paris
94. Male lead, usually
95. Work units
96. Honor medal
98. Krazy _____
99. "_____ Maria"
101. Old name for Tokyo

38 De Senectute   by Sidney L. Robbins
And about other times of life as well.

ACROSS

1. Exclude
6. Fly
10. Strikebreaker
14. Showman Mike
18. Wear away
19. Frozen dessert
20. Sulfur: Prefix
21. Eternally
22. Heart: Prefix
23. Street urchins
24. Like olives
25. Assam native
26. Like Methuselah
29. Kind of throat
30. Unaspirate
31. Stadium in Queens
32. Cover
33. Adult
34. Office machine
36. Uttered
38. Frug-type dance
39. Suffix for acoust or dynam
42. Voice or clef
43. New Deal org.
44. Fleming
45. What your boots may be
46. Sum
48. Ratio
51. Dishonors
53. Parent
54. Gram. case
55. Aid
58. Hillock, in Spain
59. Orbital position
62. Gershwin
63. Indonesian isle
64. Place for a mavourneen
65. Hitting 18, votewise
68. Firecracker sound
70. London dandy
72. Mutuel-window sign
73. Early theologian
74. Words of compre-hension
75. Social climber
76. Life force
77. Part of a royal flush
78. Ipecac product
80. What Grandma Moses reached
84. Stage whisper
85. Eastern V.I.P.
87. Connectives
88. Zoo creature
89. Newspaper notice
92. Time zone
93. New York, once
95. Olive leftovers
96. Roman date
98. Surmounted
99. These, in France
100. Kyser and others
101. Gremlins
105. Pivotal
106. People who last
110. Source: Abbr.
111. Richard or Yorick
112. Villain's forte
113. Magazine run
114. ____ fixe
115. Gaelic
116. Hebrew months
117. Hard age
118. C.P.A. entry
119. Require
120. Length units
121. Wiser

DOWN

1. Transfer design, for short
2. Wipe out
3. Chemical
4. Scrambled
5. Diplomat Whitelaw
6. Classifiers
7. Triple Crown horse
8. French cleric
9. Hebrew letter
10. Impassive
11. Julia of cookery
12. Sickens
13. Kind of young hood
14. Reproductive novelties
15. Resort to excessively
16. Boy Scout setback
17. Fold
19. Bops
27. Movie dog
28. Of the pelvis
29. Convened
33. Polynesian force
35. Fit
36. Home, to Ingmar
37. After Mar.
38. Light-bulb capacity
39. Words of identification
40. Colleagues
41. Depot
44. Furious
47. St. Valentine, perhaps
48. Like an index reference
49. Structure
50. Irish gift
52. U.S. Indian
53. Game pieces
56. Stretchy item
57. Clothes moths
60. Like some skiing snow
61. Self
66. Storms in Grasse
67. Direction
69. Civet's relative
71. Investigative org.
79. Final chess move
81. Would-be lake
82. Type of chain
83. Fitting
85. Italian agreement
86. Hockey last-ditchers
89. Wild asses
90. Nobles in old Russia
91. Mass. ____ of Tech.
94. Finished, poetically
95. Squinted
97. Nap
98. Raise a brat
99. Selected
100. Massage
102. Dixon's friend
103. Fruit for stewing
104. Beef on the hoof
106. Ripped
107. Sandy ridges
108. Ruin
109. Alger
111. Pig pad

39 Sing-along   by Mel Taub

With some prompting needed on the titles.

ACROSS

1. "Everything ____ Is Yours"
6. "____ your sunny side up"
10. Pequod's skipper
14. Tchaikovsky ballet roles
19. "West Side Story" girl
20. Latin pronoun
21. Dashiki
22. Evangelist McPherson
23. "Borstal Boy" ballad
27. N.F.L. team
28. Trial impression
29. Vendor
30. Succeed to the throne
33. "I ____ a song coming on"
34. They reckon
36. Ballad about a Chinese Scandinavian
40. Ballads
41. Ending with auto or pluto
42. Horatius' bridge opponent
43. Composer Khachaturian
45. Sliding wheel projection
48. ____ up (excited)
49. Palmer specialty
50. Overfeed
51. Lombardy city
52. Roster headed by Sophie Tucker
59. At ease, cutely
60. Hollows
61. Early epoch
62. Corroded
65. Like Carolina in the morning
66. Fumigating device
67. Lounged about
68. Boo-boo
69. Son of Jacob
70. Ballad of salad days at the beach
75. Pasha and Baba
76. French river
77. Verb ending
78. ____ Kippur
80. "She didn't say ____"
81. Loose's partner
82. La ____ tar pits of L.A.
83. Singer Gluck
84. Rx item
86. Korean love song
91. Confidence
95. Just the way you see it
96. King in "The Tempest"
97. "We aim to ____"
98. Ex ____ (one-sided)
100. Kind of code
102. Ballad of Galahad's moonshining
108. Traveler
109. Fitzgerald
110. Satanic
111. Feeble light
112. Call to a bellhop
113. Solicit an encore
114. One-time "What's My Line" host
115. Like a winter day in Buffalo

DOWN

1. "____ stranger in paradise"
2. Bandleader Kemp
3. Stock up on materiel
4. Ready for a straitjacket
5. Lessening tension
6. Furnace
7. Whiffenpoof singers
8. Wapiti
9. Prying persons
10. Space between leaf veins
11. Santa's exclamation
12. Sternward
13. Maestro Bernie
14. In a rational way
15. Reed of Knick fame
16. Soap plant
17. "____ in a million years"
18. Onlookers
24. Hubbub
25. Begin to form
26. Sunnite's faith
30. He wrote "The Nazarene"
31. Stendhal hero
32. Long-snouted animal
33. Word before with or right
35. 1836 fight site
37. Like well-dried washables
38. Trim and smart
39. Logging engine
44. Olés up north
45. Large body with a tail
46. Hersey town
47. Niggardly one
49. Hair ointment
50. Noisy French vegetable
51. The face, in Spain
53. Justice's appurtenance
54. Symbol of ring defeat
55. Show plainly
56. Queen in Jaipur
57. Titter
58. "____ the pity"
62. Put fear to rest
63. Actor Peter O'____
64. Famous name in rock
65. July date
66. Destroyer's antisub missile
68. Units of heat: Abbr.
69. Bewildered
71. Small wild ducks
72. Relative of "Nuts!"
73. Parachute material
74. House: Lat.
79. Saint-____, Channel port
81. Takes to the hills
82. Coached thoroughly
83. Of the wind
84. Pheasant's female relative
85. Introduce
87. Cold-weather headgear
88. Concerning
89. Disagreeably damp
90. Points of view
91. Spruce up
92. Of a forearm bone
93. Space rocket, for short
94. Divulge
99. Miss Nazimova
100. Bandleader Spitalny
101. Slithery
103. Sleuth
104. Power monogram
105. Postal initials
106. Hack
107. "____ a little tenderness"

And into the puzzle.

ACROSS

1. Quantity, as of cookies
6. Mildew
10. Objectionable child
14. Confound
19. Pontiff's vestment
20. Extent
21. Function
22. Indian coin
23. Seeker of 21 Across
24. Type of test
25. Small quantity
26. Aquatic mammal
27. Locale for Duke Mantee
31. Goddess of healing
32. Towel monogram
33. Until now
34. Gypped
38. Greenish-yellow color
41. Swedish coin
43. Sumac genus
45. Underdone
46. Ersatz mouthful
49. Eye, in France
50. Small finch
51. It hung in the well
55. Poet's atelier
56. Old car
57. Empresses
58. Rower's need
59. ____ onto (be a pest)
61. Detail
62. Kind of bridge
68. Finished
69. Hindrances
72. Musial
73. Like show dogs
75. Hindu deity
76. Reiner and Sandburg
77. Betrayer
78. Originate
81. Promise to pay
82. Keep
86. Sinclair Lewis husband
89. Correct
90. Broadway and TV comedienne

91. Makes certain
92. Latin verb
93. Judge's seat
94. Psychic parts
95. Off the straight and narrow
99. Applies cosmetics
101. Steal
103. Venomous snake
105. Bravo!
106. O'Neill emotion
112. Brilliant parrot
115. Bushy clumps
116. Persuade
117. Columbus' takeoff port
118. Do spellbinding
119. ____ were
120. Miss White
121. Sheeplike
122. Recorded
123. Permits
124. Asian festivals
125. Remits

DOWN

1. Stiff hat
2. Bunker or Moore
3. Spuds
4. Noise of a city horse
5. Where the gang is
6. New Zealand native
7. Fragrant root
8. Riffle through a book
9. Spanish artist
10. Newlywed
11. Ridgepole
12. Choir member
13. Weepy
14. Got up
15. Grumbling one
16. Suitable
17. Tappan or Zuider
18. Poetic contraction
28. Predecessor of "You're welcome"
29. Ogle

30. Transit lines
35. John Dickson of mysteries
36. Pennsylvania city
37. New-car-owner's dread
39. Old name for Tokyo
40. Bored to ____
41. Traveled à la John Glenn
42. Got together
44. Popular play
47. Beverage
48. Green
49. Approves
50. Indian garment
51. Lowest deck of a vessel
52. Withdraw
53. Adored
54. Light, loose shirts
55. Friends of guys
58. Choose
60. Dernier ____
62. Prepares shrimp
63. Deprives of weapons
64. Foe of the North: Abbr.
65. Entrance halls
66. Claw
67. Follow
69. Oil country
70. N.Y. athlete
71. Coined
74. Network
76. Goddess of agriculture

78. Young people's org.
79. ____ Simbel, Nile landmark
80. Ancient Semitic image
82. Enlarge an opening
83. Anarchist Goldman
84. Durable wood
85. Precede in time
86. Deceive
87. Certify
88. Naval vessel: Abbr.
90. Promoter's need
93. Vehicle
94. ____-Saud
96. Go to bed

97. Kind of nut
98. Affirmations
100. Stitched
102. Ejects
103. Dialect
104. Does a slow burn
107. Tralee bloom
108. Sprinkle with powder
109. Eagle
110. Body of poetry
111. Projecting edge
112. Witty saying
113. Parrot genus
114. Surpass

41 Move Over by Elaine D. Schorr

It's all a matter of getting under way.

ACROSS

1. Parks of TV
5. Sweden's gift to tennis
9. _____ parmigiana
13. Not reg.
17. Lab-dish substance
18. Of the cheek
19. Tamarisk trees
21. Injure
22. Take a spin
24. Circulates
26. Marathon entry
28. Certain link to Moscow
31. Melville's captain
32. Yemen cover-up
33. Waters or Kennedy
34. Position: Prefix
35. Plant pouch
37. Ladies of Seville: Abbr.
41. Good Samaritans
42. Incapacitate
43. _____ Dame
45. Give _____ whirl
46. Eugene of early labor movement
47. Hawaiian city
48. _____ the cup (tipple)
49. What the nose knows
50. "_____ was going . . ."
51. P.T.A. member
53. Frying aid
54. Actor George
55. Small woods
57. Haley opus
59. Jurist on the missing list
60. Anti
62. Do a chef's work
63. On _____ (exactly)
64. Restless one
65. Noble of France
66. Former British P.M.
67. Begot
68. Unload
69. Like Santa Claus

72. Vapor, in Scotland
75. Old money in England
76. Mah-jongg pieces
77. Importune
78. Regulate
79. Land of _____
80. Upset
81. Depots: Abbr.
82. Hair coloring
83. Check
85. _____ in hand (abjectly)
86. Industrial shows, for short
88. Church dignitary
89. Writer George
91. Hebrew letter
92. Russian body of water
94. Music makers on the go
101. Like some uneatable fruit
102. Reactivates
106. Branches
107. Time of deepest depression
108. Fearful
109. Kind of ball or brand
110. Electrical force
111. "_____ Fall in Love"
112. Survey results: Abbr.
113. Bold stroke

DOWN

1. Catch
2. Conceit
3. U.K. airmen
4. Some fishermen
5. Cleopatra's vessel
6. Like a miasma
7. A-bomb hazard
8. Creator of a bad-money law
9. Macho of Rudy Vallee song
10. City on the Thames
11. Templeton
12. _____ majesty

13. Rhodesian natives
14. Betel leaf
15. Sea bird
16. Naval V.I.P.
18. "Magic Mountain" author
20. Thorn in the Crusaders' side
23. Makes an eddy
25. "Ay, there's the _____"
27. Work on lace
28. Miss Hopper
29. Western red men
30. John Gilbert classic
34. Emporium event
35. Rigel and Spica

36. Like the Kara-Kum
38. Follow the fox
39. Makes up for
40. Philosopher Jean-Paul
42. Stuck
44. Emulate Robert Ingersoll
47. Actress June
49. Praying figure
51. Attitudinized
52. Oceangoing nomads
54. Kind of line
56. Apples for baking
58. Crumb
59. Oak, in Orléans
60. Welles and Bean

61. Agatha Christie sleuth
62. One headed for success
63. Rod toters
65. Armor plate
68. Marilyn Horne, for one
70. Failing to conform
71. Pewter coins
73. Twelve months, in Paris
74. Stiller's other half
76. Troubled city of 1979
78. Gives one what for
81. "Faerie Queene" creator

82. Forms a scar
84. Prado's home
87. Roman 41
90. Political party: Abbr.
92. Molding ridge
93. Network
94. Sported
95. Grandparental
96. Jules Verne captain
97. Kind of type: Abbr.
98. "September Morn" figure
99. "True _____"
100. Caustic
103. Rival
104. Period
105. Soak

42 Items of Interest by Manny Miller

At least for those concerned with making bread.

ACROSS

1. Mouths
4. Bryant or Loos
9. Spat
13. Wooden shoe
18. Circumference
20. Imitative ones
22. "It's more ____ bargained for"
23. Absorbed
24. Gay place
25. Storms
26. Favorites
27. Security
30. Savings acct. item
31. Goat antelope
32. Make trouble
33. Take in the view
34. Vouched for
37. Name, in Nantes
39. Endearing word
40. Subordinate: Abbr.
41. Sundial number
42. Cable ____
43. Oriental inns
45. Barry and Raymond
47. Start of a thrifty aphorism
51. Barber's call
52. Marker of a sort
53. Punt non-returner's call
57. Cry of astonishment
59. Basics
61. Roman 1,051
62. Miss Kirk
63. Heavies in prison riots
67. Rulers
70. Blank spaces
72. Outside: Prefix
73. Religious degree
75. Lew, the comedian
77. One, two, etc.: Abbr.
78. "And ____ was one"
81. Costello
82. Recording equipment
85. Middle of aphorism
91. Pontiac, for one
93. Fictional giant
94. Rum, below the border
95. Ike's domain
96. Open space
97. Torah repository
99. Slippery ____
100. Board constituents
102. ____ man (everybody)
103. Fox and turkey
105. Loose fabrics
107. One of twelve: Abbr.
108. End of aphorism
111. Rule
113. Cruising
114. Bow down: Var.
115. Dreamer's source of income
118. Guitarlike instrument
119. Bland
120. Implored
121. Germany and Lynne
122. ____ off
123. Leavings
124. Draft letters

DOWN

1. Undo, poetically
2. Performance
3. Silver
4. ____ patriae
5. Much-probed loch
6. Common contraction
7. Was prolific
8. Warmth
9. Parasite
10. "____ as I go"
11. Spanish festival
12. Stitching that conceals edges
13. ____ throat
14. King of Israel
15. Sugar residue
16. Unity
17. "A ____, a Tasket"
19. Wrathful
21. Fight
28. Paragon
29. Rhapsody or goulash
31. Blood liquids
34. Direct
35. Farm tool
36. To, to MacDougall
38. Chinese name
40. Region of Spain
43. Pretenders to gentility
44. Service branch: Abbr.
46. Abbr. on a letter
48. Branch of dentistry
49. Estuary
50. Ale, in Scottish pubs
54. Bolivian export
55. Jeff Davis' domain
56. ____-been
58. "How Ya Gonna Keep 'em Down ____?"
60. Pitcher Maglie
63. Word with blanket or wash
64. Hans' exclamation
65. Hwy.
66. Son of Noah
68. Pilots
69. Chases away
71. Myron and Octavus Roy
74. Food fish
76. Flow
79. Article
80. Casey Jones' job: Abbr.
83. Areas exempt from customs
84. Confined aliens
86. Poetic word
87. Like many old manuscripts
88. Goofs
89. "____ said it!"
90. Maritime signal
91. Zagreb is its capital
92. W. R. and Patty
96. Relaxed
98. Defrauds
100. Evergreen shrubs
101. City north of Cairo
103. Rulers
104. Slender spines
106. Panhellenic festival scene
109. Dapper
110. Make a chess play
111. Bird's waxy area
112. Pro votes
116. Degree
117. Giacomin and Mathews

Liquid Assets by Herb Risteen

Enough to keep one afloat for a while.

ACROSS

. Dry, as wine
. Tapestry city
. Shindig
. Christmas bounty
. Miss Rehan
. Winter haven
. Coveted award
. Bright bird
. John Barth novel
. Disowns
. Lahore nobles
. Word with whiz
. Awkward
. Tavern stock
. Have origin
. Predecessor of tem
. Kind of nest
. Short-order dish
. Place or welcome
. Effrontery
. Possessive
. Fly's host
. Cuddles
. Item of interest
. Cubic meter
. Caesar
. Playing card
. Hook part
. Lucky chance
. Mediocre
. Pampered
. Went into second base
3. Animal life
4. Shooting iron
5. Exams
6. "The Marble ____"
7. Tiny insects
8. Hesitate
9. Suffix for marion
70. ____ witness (testify)
71. Artificial rubber
72. "The Good ____"
73. Stadium sound
74. Reveler's song
78. Salamander
81. Wall climbers
83. Fly high
84. Miss Stevens
85. Global region
86. Ocean pliers
88. Sewing-basket item
90. Headquarters
91. Is aware of
92. Incited

93. Endure
94. Wickerwork material
95. Deep pinks
96. Cribbage cards
97. Climb
98. ____ out (quit operating)
99. South Seas isle
100. Exist
101. Miss Bailey
102. Chair part
103. Most aloof
106. Garden blooms
108. Contemptible one
109. Halloween figure
111. Kind of tent
113. Dixie's Green Wave
114. Forgoes food
116. Tennis stroke
117. Club for Geronimo
119. No. 2 star in a constellation
120. Mends
122. Finnish port
124. Oklahoman
125. Supposed
128. City near the Thousand Islands
132. Bailey of comics
133. Be theatrical
134. Keep a subscription alive
135. "____ live and breathe!"
136. Elia's forte
137. Gaelic
138. Pastures or tea
139. Writer Deighton

DOWN

1. Desert dweller
2. Light-colored metal
3. Eateries
4. Biblical book
5. Narrow inlet
6. Pack ____
7. Sonoran's friends
8. Math ratio
9. Scare word
10. Minor-pain cure-all
11. Locales
12. Field rodents
13. Zeus or Thor

14. Wrath
15. Windup
16. Victor Hugo novel
17. Weather outlook
21. Talk
23. Letter
24. Mine car
25. Singer Peggy
26. Precious thing
31. City in Kansas
34. Quarry
35. Ethiopian title
37. Whale chaser
39. Fenny tract
40. Dutch town
42. Extorted
43. Done away with
45. Stupefies
47. Shortcut between fields
48. Very, to Pierre
50. California fort
51. Pivot

53. ____ of Pines
54. Active one
56. Book-jacket puff
57. Deadly
58. River deposit
59. Mafeking fighter
60. Grecian gulf
61. Some beach visitors
62. Moselle tributary
63. More subtle
64. ____ avis
66. Charges
67. Unframable painting
68. Charlatan
70. Homey gatherings
71. Ponder moodily
72. Different
74. Feeder visitor
75. Unanimously
76. Playful trick
77. French river
79. Occupy

80. Moscow agency
82. Churchill letters
85. High abode
86. Miss Horne
87. Operatic prince
88. Sight for a kayoed boxer
89. Mall's partner
90. Décor for Mamie
91. Fail, as a play
93. Frightened
94. Study
95. Horseshoe part
97. Witnessed
98. Rudely brief
99. Mr. McNutt
101. School auxiliary
102. Winter apples
103. Bird call
104. Armed with quills
105. Potato protein

107. Slopes
108. Eddie or Ida
110. Farmer, in the spring
112. ____ up (become lively)
113. Squaw's H.Q.
114. ____ of mind
115. Weekday: Abbr.
117. Pull
118. Kind of flush
119. Hair style
121. Impress deeply
123. Tennis star
124. Fastened
126. High note
127. Moslem ruler
129. Western red man
130. Compass point
131. Born, in France

44 Assembly Line by Bert Kruse

Some possible ways to refer to special groups.

ACROSS

1. Explosion
6. Brazilian tree
9. La-____ (affected gentility)
14. Miss Lane
18. Soil
19. Bench, in France
21. Tomato swelling
22. Back
23. Harden
24. Wall Street group
27. Fictional uncle
28. Hover
29. Moon: Prefix
30. Zero
32. Variety of iris
34. Parasitic worm
39. Drama-judging groups
44. Foul-ups
45. ____ mode
46. Miss Chase et al.
47. One of the Stooges
48. Shipping company
49. "Stabat Mater" composer
52. Watery places
53. More forward
55. Socialize well
56. La's predecessor
59. Feeling below par
60. Indian buffalo
61. Greek trading areas
63. Overdo on the boards
65. Asperse
68. Army div.
69. ____ dealers (auto sales group)
73. Kentucky bluegrass
74. Old Italian coin
76. Arbuckle of silents
77. Make a lunge for
79. Salmon
80. Came to rest
81. Querying word
83. Spiritless, to Shakespeare
84. Bridal-wreath bloom
86. Speed
87. Stretched-out circle
89. Glance
90. Miss Arden
91. Alike, in Paris
94. Irish sea god
95. Take in
98. Assembly of wet blankets
102. Unfaithful
104. Grain bundle
105. Connective
106. Singer Guthrie et al.
108. Chorus member
109. Workshop unit
113. Assembly of stewers
119. Additional
120. Opera offering
121. Relative
122. Finger or toe, in Spain
123. Approximates
124. Sentence part
125. ____ the line (last stop)
126. Time inits.
127. Brewing malt

DOWN

1. Foamer
2. Lola or Priscilla
3. Cuckoopint
4. Co-author of "Elements of Style"
5. Doctoral paper
6. Australian native
7. Barn-door need
8. Pyrenees republic
9. Investigator: Abbr.
10. Words heard often in June
11. Fortifications
12. Stroll
13. Zenanas
14. Floating zoo
15. Drone
16. Prevent
17. Stuttering sounds
20. Miss Leachman
25. Fail to mention
26. Judah's son
31. Choice cut
33. Most uncomplicated
35. More unbelievable, as a tale
36. Tankful ____ (thinkers' group)
37. Beach sight
38. Danish weights
39. Frozen dessert
40. Distant, in Dijon
41. Assembly at Stowe or Aspen
42. Fly lightly
43. Iron-horse fodder
50. Francis Drake, for one
51. Having trouble
52. Give a place to
53. Modern money
54. Being judged
57. Good name, for short
58. First-year Latin word
60. Military staff off.
62. "Flying Dutchman" girl
64. Captains, majors, etc.
66. More unrefined
67. Rags
70. Roman bronze
71. Biblical verb ending
72. Tint
75. Writer Studs
78. Gen. Marshall's alma mater
80. Volcanic matter
82. Succor
84. W.W. I plane
85. Prefix for scope
86. Prepared to plant
88. Uris
91. Winker
92. Having a beard
93. Furnishes
96. Provided that
97. Actor Power
99. "____ she blows!"
100. Tea variety
101. Vienna's famed park
103. Original bishop in chess
107. Brazilian heron
110. Oriental
111. Possessive
112. One-time, at one time
113. Often-broken item
114. Gold, in Granada
115. Hang on the clothesline
116. Parent
117. Ump's relative
118. Drunkard

45 Calculating by Jack L. Steinhardt

But not in the sense of being crafty.

ACROSS

1. Turkish city
7. Kingfisher's feature
12. Sahl
16. Surviving trace
21. Did a garden job
22. Montague's son
23. Ben Adhem
24. Skin blight
25. Casals, at the time of his death
27. Mirror-breaker's span of bad luck
29. First poker bettor
30. "____ were the days!"
32. Idled
33. Liquidates
37. Swarm
38. Miss Keaton
39. ____ Yat-sen
40. Struts the boards
42. Bear or eater
43. Literary analysis
48. Discharges violently: Var.
49. Bookkeeping systems
55. Lunch-counter dispenser
56. Type of renewal
57. Sheer linens
58. Exams
59. "Yond Cassius ____ lean . . ."
60. Soft, in Salerno
61. Karenina and Christie
62. Beguile
63. Cut a film
64. Festive times
65. Petty peeves
66. ____ and blood
67. Chili con ____
68. Society tyro
69. Geometric solids
71. Musicals
72. White poplar
74. On top of, poetically
75. Sea anemone
76. Horse color
78. Containing four planes
83. ____ Cruces
86. Gold lace
87. Refuge, in Regensburg
88. Like college walls
89. Prehistoric ax
90. Petroleum cartel
91. The devil
92. Of ____ (similar in dimensions)
93. European capital
94. Aswan crossing
95. Town west of Barcelona
96. ____ down the hatches
97. Master suit at cards
98. Compass point
99. Social Security applicants
101. Gabriel, for one
102. Any U.S.S.R. member
104. Spanish gold
105. Three in one
106. Globe
107. Androcles' target
109. Popocatepetl pouring
112. Beauty-parlor jobs
113. Astronomy muse
116. Get the dice ready
117. Vestments
119. Resembling the U.S. defense H.Q.
121. Versatile football back
127. Coup
128. Bombast
129. Stretched tight
130. Actress Piper
131. River to the Missouri
132. Stores in casks
133. Chemical compound
134. Unbroken

DOWN

1. Bristle
2. Prefix for Platonism or lithic
3. Awareness
4. Miss Huxtable
5. ____ Park, N.Y.
6. Skilled ones
7. Stretch the neck
8. American composer
9. Moslem title
10. Farer or horse
11. Survival annuities
12. Type of jar
13. Plump
14. Thick cord
15. "For shame!"
16. Acts of abandonment
17. Verdi opera
18. Ericsson
19. Familial suffix
20. Type of fish
26. Maiden-name intro
28. Dinsmore and Janis
31. Antipathy
33. Started anew
34. Upgrade
35. Like some shotguns
36. Bargain purchases
38. Valleys
41. Anglo-Saxon hireling
43. Toweling fabric
44. Nettle
45. Polyphonic musical form
46. Bruinlike
47. Distaff relatives
49. Attitude
50. Ancient Greek colony
51. Final inning, usually
52. Shiny silk, in Spain
53. Roman appellation
54. Bind up
59. Villain
62. Spanish city
65. Hard or soft
66. "____ Jacques"
67. San Quentin digs
69. Letters
70. Eccentric
71. Type of block
73. "Funny Girl"
75. Dresses up
76. Earlier
77. Perennial herb
78. What a relief map shows: Abbr.
79. Blot out
80. Tissue: Prefix
81. ____ Perón
82. Adorn gaudily, old style
84. Sustenance
85. Basic items
87. Goddesses of the seasons
89. "The ____ Green"
91. Schoolbook
92. Hank of the homers
93. Israeli symbol
95. Sailor's luggage
96. Hair clasp
99. Marked with lines
100. Cranny's partner
103. Writer Susan
105. Kind of tale
107. Title for Macbeth
108. Discontinues
109. Memory failure
110. More qualified
111. Rival
113. Hair style
114. Female ruffs
115. Wall column
116. Stumbling block
117. Soupçon
118. Southeastern Asian
120. "____ pro nobis"
122. Legal thing
123. Path to nowhere
124. Cap'n ____ of fiction
125. Tune
126. Driver's spot

46 Bonus by Dorothea E. Shipp

Two diagonal entries are added to the regular acrosses and downs.

ACROSS

1. Item often checked
4. Fish's armor
9. Pick-me-up
14. Barfly
19. Opposite of yep
20. Siberian native
21. Minneapolis suburb
22. Elbows
24. This, literally
27. Crystal or Cow
28. Columnist Hopper
30. Provided a computer with data
31. Neighbors on
33. U.S. painter
34. Garden flower
36. Doorways: Abbr.
38. Remove: Abbr.
39. 1946 Bikini event
40. Italian wine center
43. Ibex, for one
46. Think, to Shakespeare
48. Time periods: Abbr.
49. Detective Mickey
51. New Deal org.
52. Gothic arch
54. Break a commandment
55. Dill herbs
57. God of agriculture
60. Became uptight
64. Aconcagua's range
66. "____ bad!"
68. ____ Manuel or Miguel
69. Old English official
70. Old-time reward
71. Furrier's stock
73. Like the ragged rascal's rock
77. Gull
78. Rail braking device
81. Sinew
84. Judas, for one
86. Raccoon's relatives
88. Part of a vowel sequence
89. Swift's forte
90. Secretive
92. Word with wanted or yourself
94. International easing of tension

97. Click beetle
98. Butt
100. Anklebone
102. Bit of weather info.
104. Norway's Tryggvesson
106. ____ mater
108. Juliette Low's org.
109. Muscle condition: Suffix
110. Vocation
112. Habits
115. Upstate N.Y. city
118. Antiquity
119. Burned to a ____
121. Brewery product
122. Well up on things
124. Charity or peeve
126. Mrs. Truman
128. Simple flute
131. Suburb of Paris
132. Jewel
134. Bankruptcy
136. Writer Gardner
137. Swan genus
139. Unique people
141. City of France
143. Detroit white elephant
145. Fifth wheel
149. More delicate
151. Discover the truth
154. Intestine: Prefix
155. Sign up
156. Proverb
157. "The ____ of all evil"
158. Talkative
159. Grand or Custer's last
160. Songstress Tucker
161. Actor Conway

DOWN

1. Elias or Julia Ward
2. Imitated
3. Stray piece of hair
4. Porcine compound
5. It can keep one awake
6. Stub ____
7. Praised
8. Certain kind of ways
9. Mystery character, for short
10. River of Croatia
11. Weepy wife of Amphion
12. Affront
13. Like some stomachs
14. Medicine dosage: Abbr.
15. Writer of "Butterfield 8"
16. Thermoplastic: Var.
17. Tax deadbeat
18. Senate's time off
19. ____ degree
23. Spanish painter
25. Truth, in Confucianism
26. Rubinstein and others
29. (Diag. down to No. 145A) Mother's words to child drinking milk
32. Industrial hazard
35. Ballet lake
37. Poet Teasdale
40. Indian state
41. Small piano
42. Type of box
44. Handwriting process
45. Makes lace edging
47. Expert on quips
50. ____ Palmas

53. Greenness
56. Impresario Hurok
58. Old Mideast initials
59. Puts to flight
61. Dotted, in heraldry
62. ". . . happily ____ after"
63. Moisture
65. Proclamation
67. Hall-of-Famer Mel
71. Nero or Pan
72. Former Iranian V.I.P.
74. Like some necklace pearls
75. They're ajar, on high
76. Make corrections
79. Film actor Sidney
80. S.A. rodent
82. Shoe size
83. Droop
85. Musical patchwork
87. Stile units
90. Part
91. Part of Q.E.D.

93. Opera-bill partner of Cav.
95. Beliefs
96. Gaboriau and Zola
97. Comedian DeLuise
99. Tante's Spanish relative
101. Baton Rouge campus
103. Kind of wagon
105. Celebrated happenings
107. Culture medium
109. Tic-____-toe
111. Eve's beginning
112. Stock market booms
113. Robert ____
114. "I've Got a ____"
116. Abstract theorizing
117. Play a certain ice game
120. Wheys
123. Dulles or Kennedy
124. Betel palm

125. Volcano outpourings
127. "____ Night"
129. Corny
130. Shade of green
132. Reddish clay
133. Addicts
135. Girl's name
138. Kiln
140. (Diag. up to No. 33A) Annoys
142. Carbine
144. Israeli name
146. Mine: French
147. Space
148. Newt
150. Horseman Rogers
152. California fort
153. Kind of garden or pot

47 Sounding Off by Alfio Micci
Or maybe alike, or whatever.

ACROSS

1. Dim
6. Class division
11. "Put the blame on ____"
15. Of time past, to poets
20. Come to mind
21. Thespian
22. Sacred image
23. Kind, in Caen
24. Palestinian fish delicacies
27. Ponderous delays
29. Craggy hill
30. Company lover
31. Kind of seal
33. It flies, at times, for Caesar
34. City trains
35. Equilibrium
36. Thick carpets
37. Panhandle
38. Sea bird
39. Modified leaf
40. ____ contendere
41. Shake
44. Kinsmen
48. Epitaph for a moth
52. Possess
53. Emulates Daniel Webster
55. Miss Adoree
56. Inter ____
57. Wallet items
58. Household gods
59. Kind of race
60. Neighbor of Egypt
62. Work on shrubbery
63. Swelling disease
64. Animal husbandry of a kind
67. O'Hara's "____ to Live"
68. Not a Rep.
69. Shelter
70. Sailors' saint
71. Put away
72. Ontario city
75. "The Greatest"
76. Cat's target
78. Snowstorm's start
80. Adjective ending
81. Tiber tributary
82. Family member
85. Hawaiian veranda
86. Fell victim to a broken gum machine
90. Restraint
92. Those against
93. Brainstorms
94. Ten-percenters: Abbr.
95. City of Spain
96. Chinese porcelain
97. Samoan port
98. Pliny the ____
100. Purloined
101. Protection
102. Household quartet in an embassy
106. Italian family
107. Spanish nobleman
108. Actor Pickens
109. ____ Dame
110. Mine find
112. Hippie's digs
113. Doze
114. Arrested
116. Subjoin
119. "Madam, ____"
123. Family of American artists
124. Group of five
125. Man: Lat.
126. Words to a conductress
128. Birth of a son
131. Start of a Dickens title
132. "Picnic" playwright
133. Changes one's address
134. Wisps of precipitation
135. Fragment
136. Boilermaker component
137. What "i.e." means
138. Made comfortable

DOWN

1. Strong point
2. Nathanael West's "____ Million"
3. Champagne buckets
4. Greek letters
5. ____ l'oeil
6. Designer Oleg
7. Flu symptoms
8. Gape
9. Conservative
10. Cockney idol
11. Settle in another region
12. Farmland
13. Temper
14. Letters
15. N.Y. city
16. Loose-textured soil
17. Plumbing problem
18. Famous last words
19. Cape
25. Norwegian sights
26. Deny
28. Miss Dallas
32. London's Marble
36. British composer
37. Voicing disapproval
39. Spree
40. Actor Lloyd
41. Winter cruises
42. Exact punishment
43. Do a lawn job
44. Worked on shoes
45. Moslem decree
46. Defoliated elevation
47. Halt
49. Mistakes
50. "Wreck of the Mary ____"
51. Valley, in North Africa
52. Kind of movie
54. That, in Spain
59. Arabian vessel
60. Figure of speech
61. W.W. II org.
62. ____-cake
65. Shows response
66. Islam's God
69. Coastal reef
71. Scottish snow
73. Vanishing carriers
74. Speaker of Cooperstown
76. Middle: Prefix
77. Liberal or fine
78. Chipped
79. Downy growth
80. Call ____ day
81. Israeli desert
83. Atoll
84. Ladd movie
86. Fatlike substance
87. Hatred
88. Char
89. Nucleus
90. Geographical abbr.
91. Cry at an orgy
97. Burning
98. Regard
99. Eucalyptus secretion
100. Pearl White medium
103. Internal sheathing
104. Coward or Harrison
105. Conflict
108. Showed mercy
111. Salad item
113. Marsh plant
114. Bailiff
115. Incas' milieu
116. Declares
117. Lament
118. Forest nymph
119. "____ corny as Kansas"
120. Handed-down story
121. Distant
122. Valley
123. Window unit
124. Trudge
127. Pol. party
129. French chum
130. By way of

48 Forked Tongues by Louis Baron

In this case, some branching out of expressions.

ACROSS

1. Balsa product
5. Pueblo Indian
9. "Once ____ time . . ."
14. Columbia River city
21. Certain duckling
22. Merit
23. Tycoon
24. Raising Cain
25. Weather report
26. "Well done!"
28. Bay of Bengal islands
29. Tumult
31. Breaks fast
32. Fallow
34. Poe forte
35. Unyielding
36. Bellini "sleeper"
40. Subdues
42. Futile
43. Like bone
44. Forbidding
46. Imogene
49. Prison inmate: Abbr.
51. Madrid matrons
53. "____ longa, vita brevis"
56. Mennonites
58. Pollinators
60. African fox
61. Juggled word
63. P.O. item
65. "Streetcar" star
67. Baylor U.'s site
69. "____ homo"
70. Follower of 26 Across
71. One was Great, one Terrible
72. Attila, for one
73. Word after hang or hob
74. Tokyo money
76. Blue Nile source
77. Old land tenure
79. Cuba's V.I.P.
80. Finds 26 Across, etc., baffling
86. Rude
87. Brio
88. Bucket, in France
89. "Vive le____!"
90. Shirley MacLaine role
91. ____ de deux
92. Connery and O'Casey
93. Chaste
98. Earth pull: Abbr.
99. Kind of code
101. Built-for-two
103. Omitting nothing
104. Couturière
106. ____ of the earth
108. W.W. II alliance
110. Wild dog of Australia
111. Milkfish
112. Autumn apple
114. Alg. or trig.
116. City of France
117. Czech river
118. Hat
122. Swiss river
124. Some girders
128. Boneyard quadrille
131. Have a bite
134. Thing from the blue
135. Pitcher
137. Church levy
138. Statue base
140. View killer
142. A priori or a ____
146. ____ Hari
147. Sweet thoughts
148. Pallid
149. Vane readings
150. Son of Zeus
151. Footed the tab
152. Exploits
153. ____ D.A.
154. No more than

DOWN

1. Lawyer Choate
2. Yawning
3. Coquette
4. Beginner
5. Of a Biblical language
6. Trireme need
7. Madrid's "Louvre"
8. 100 (lie) proof
9. Oust
10. Player's words to a blackjack dealer
11. Kimono must
12. ____ de guerre
13. Seething
14. U.S.S.R. sea
15. Indispensable thing
16. Clump of ivy
17. Basket grass
18. Fissured
19. Altogether
20. Miss DeMille
27. Travel stops
30. Neighbor of Tenn.
33. Pedestal part
37. Hoity-toity one
38. Chaliapin et al.
39. Caucho trees
41. Constellation
42. ____ da Gama
45. Forecasting
46. Magician's garb
47. Its capital is Muscat
48. Ring: Abbr.
50. Beak
52. Kind of moon
53. Arched mart
54. More risqué
55. ____ a rat
57. "The Wall" author
59. Wise one
60. Up to here
62. Aladdin encounters
64. Dregs
66. Da ____, Vietnam
68. Whale hater
75. Sholem Asch character
77. Amin's old bailiwick
78. Cliffhanger rescuer
79. Damon or Pythias
80. Groove
81. Drake's "hit"
82. Rank stripes, in Rome
83. ____ majesty
84. Adjective suffix
85. Gad about
86. Athenian S
91. Place for petits fours
92. Buddhist mounds
94. Rural steps
95. Diminutive
96. Jason's ship
97. Trotsky
100. Mount for Balaam
102. "Mamma ____!"
105. Take a dip
107. Bos'n's boss
109. Knife
113. Mahler's "Das Lied von der ____"
115. Angel, proverbially
119. Caught
120. City on the Somme
121. Mother: Prefix
123. Appomattox initials
124. Composer Jacques
125. Actor of Casbah fame
126. Ecole student
127. Befuddled
129. Hungarian hero
130. Eternities
131. Pitfall
132. Absolute
133. Cycle stage
136. Garden villain
139. Moslem title
141. Scrap
143. Sugar
144. Haggard book
145. ____ judicata

49 Riddles by Jordan S. Lasher

Some likely answers to unlikely questions.

ACROSS

1. Antislavery author
6. Statesman Eban
10. Door part
14. Obtuse
19. Every 60 minutes
20. Grasped
21. Spread
22. McKinley's powerful backer
23. Lyric Muse
24. How do you make antifreeze?
27. Crème de ____
29. Wankel or Diesel
30. Yorkshire district
31. Venus de ____
33. Writer Anaïs
34. Mortgage
35. Misdo
36. What did one dandelion say to the other?
43. "Thanks ____!"
44. Marksman's forte
45. Viewed
46. Famed soloist's nickname
50. Stock-market gamble
52. Warmly ensconced
55. Messy places
58. Grass genus
59. Burrowing mammal of Madagascar
61. Why is the nose in the middle of the face?
64. Fitted closely together
66. Amour propre
67. Divert
68. Norwegian king
70. Unfavorable
72. "A ____ clock scholar"
73. Particle accelerator
78. As well
80. One of the Hoods
84. What does a 200-lb. mouse say?
87. Breakfast staple
89. Wife of Bragi
90. Lobster claw
91. Sudden pain
93. First Earl of Bristol
94. Like phosgene
96. Bell sound
98. Card game
100. Opposite of stet
101. What did the ocean say to the beach?
107. Calendar abbr.
110. Film-actor James
111. Wild sheep
112. Smart elegance
113. Segregate mail in advance
115. Crushed apple pulp
118. Woman adviser
122. Why do birds fly south?
125. On one's way
126. Belong
127. Gram or dram, e.g.
128. ". . . were Paradise ____"
129. Sudden thrust
130. Trepidations
131. ____ di Como
132. Rather and Blocker
133. Gravel ridge

DOWN

1. Noah's eldest son
2. Made confetti
3. Algerian port
4. Recorders of electrical usage
5. God, in Hebrew scriptures
6. Patients' expressions
7. It's often noire, in Paris
8. Small scaleless fish
9. Ballet duet
10. Wayne or Payne
11. Toward shelter
12. Debussy's "La ____"
13. London policeman: Var.
14. French-English divider
15. Phoned
16. Shallow-depth measurer
17. Show contempt
18. Attendant to Bacchus
25. "Peanuts" character
26. Told tales
28. Zeno of ____
32. Amos of baseball
34. Permissive
36. President after T.R.
37. Ethan or Fred
38. Language of the Hellenistic period
39. Atlanta arena
40. Take ten
41. "____ people . . ."
42. All smiles
47. Girl of song
48. Between zwei and vier
49. Tabby's plaything
51. Captured anew
53. Salt Lake City collegian
54. Leslie Caron role
56. Ethyl acetate, e.g.
57. Picturesque
60. Boston cager
62. Conductor Georg
63. Undermined
65. Vader of "Star Wars"
69. Elected
71. Oodles
73. Voucher
74. Tokyo, once
75. Heart of the matter
76. Red Square name
77. Hose material
79. N.Y. Giant slugger
81. Like a certain flower
82. Israeli region
83. Roof projection
85. Chinese sleeping platform
86. Asian border river
88. Treated with a caustic
92. Pear variety
95. Winter homes of a sort
97. Thingumabob
99. Will-____-wisp
102. Poi source
103. "A ____ of Rain"
104. Liquefied, in a way
105. Coastal marsh bird
106. Shimmy
107. Spruce up
108. A Shaw
109. Seed integument
114. Hoosegow
115. Overly decorous one
116. Bismarck
117. N.C. college
119. Gordie Howe's milieu
120. Famous dean of St. Paul's
121. Roman field
123. Santa ____
124. Electrical units: Abbr.

50 Escapism by Frances Hansen

For reasons outlined by means of verse.

ACROSS

1. Desert plants
6. Gluck's namesakes
11. "____ beaucoup!"
16. Highlander
20. Ethan
21. New York's Abe
22. Make a strong effort
23. Spy for Moses
25. Entreaties
26. Fiber for caulking
27. Wrinkles
28. January, in Juárez
29. Start of a limerick
33. Where Caesar was stabbed
34. Compass point
35. Fraternal member
36. Magpie: Var.
37. Crude salt
40. Rocky peak
41. Subtract
43. Lamb's call to mother
46. Ottoman sultan
48. He herds reindeer
51. Pain-measuring unit
52. Rudiments
56. Brilliance
58. Friends, to Titus
60. Goal
62. Cartoonist Gardner
64. "Ten thousand saw ____ a glance"
65. More of limerick
70. Red light
71. Poets Allen and Nahum
72. Casterbridge official
73. When lapels say "I gave"
74. Convened
75. Dogpatch creator
77. Collar
79. Actress Nita
80. More of limerick
88. Rajah's wife
89. Owing
90. "I could ____ horse"
91. Golfer's pou sto
92. Actor Edward and family
94. La Scala city
96. Jai-alai basket

99. H. M. Pulham et al.
103. More of limerick
107. Red or Dead
108. ____ Paulo
109. Sault ____ Marie
110. Slipped
111. "Blue ____ Shoes"
112. Whirlpool
114. Capek play
116. A code we live by
118. Decree
120. It's in the sky
121. Special Sunday
124. About-to-be grads
126. Anoint, old style
128. "What news on the ____?"
131. Fine paper: Abbr.
133. From ____ Z
134. Artists' garbs
138. End of limerick
144. Gymnast Comaneci
145. Confirmation slap
146. Storehouse
147. River to the Caspian
148. Verdon and others
149. Flower part
150. Admit
151. Boy in Rousseau story
152. Advantage
153. In ____ (stupefied)
154. Out on a limb, in a way
155. Shylock's collections

DOWN

1. Matadors' cloaks
2. "For ____ Know"
3. Athenian general
4. Dealer in hyson or bohea
5. Greedy
6. "Baby, Take ____"
7. Jacob's wife
8. Powerful shark
9. Talisman
10. Jelly or gelatin, e.g.
11. Simple
12. Diffuse, as charm
13. Do a new job on the lily

14. Started a tin lizzie
15. Hot news for Rona Barrett
16. Like the Amalfi Drive
17. Musical piece
18. City southeast of Buffalo
19. Coat with an alloy
24. Vessel for gravy
30. Holland: Abbr.
31. Miles or Vague
32. Sumptuous
38. Gave forth, as fragrance
39. Word on a bill
42. Dumb girl
43. British back streets
44. One-____ (child's game)
45. In addition
47. Wine's partner
49. Protective wall
50. "What a ____!" (too bad)
53. Hobo's bedroll

54. Where some bacon comes from
55. Remain at home
57. Cleo's way out
59. Bay of Maine
61. "____ and Only"
63. Tripping the light fantastic
66. Greenland base
67. Instill
68. Slender nail
69. Cord around a kaffiyeh
74. Metric units
76. ". . . people may require ____"
78. Interfered rudely
80. Hogfish
81. ____ over (reminisced)
82. Group of nine
83. Want
84. Arizona city
85. Whodunit suspects, often

86. Le Mans entrant
87. Closefisted
93. "The ____ others should teach us caution"
95. "____ Smile Be Your Umbrella"
97. Brontë's Jane
98. Ekberg or Bergman
99. Large bird
100. Ooze
101. Moslem judge
102. Snick's partner
104. Oaf
105. Sincere
106. Did some calculation
113. Cheer-leaders' activity
115. Used scathing words
117. Birthright seller
119. Blackjack, in Birmingham

122. Welcome words during a drill
123. Tebaldi
125. Not so harsh
127. "____ or Leave Me"
128. Pealed
129. ____ of (daunted)
130. Totted up
132. Bolivian hub
135. South American Indian
136. Prepared to be dubbed
137. "____ alive!"
139. Bark cloth
140. Fit as a fiddle
141. Kismet
142. English painter John
143. Pull at one's heartstrings

51 Word-tampering by Mel Taub
A few liberties taken just for the fun of it.

ACROSS

1. Rabelais's forte
7. Stint
11. Used the casino tables
16. City on the Moselle
17. Vegetable spread
18. Opposite of apogee
20. Marshals
21. Have second thoughts about communism
23. High lake
24. Jack-in-the-pulpit's relative
26. Mata ____
27. Ablaze
28. Señor's one
29. New Year word
30. Belfast official's assistant
33. N.C.O. insignia
35. Good for Fidel
36. Tommy's weapon
37. Joe Louis victim in 1937
38. Leave alone
39. Clergyman
41. Pedro's lady friends
43. Aphrodite's son
44. Well-known Ibn
45. Kingly first name
46. Egotist's concern
47. Broken-down
51. Use a gunsight
52. Soothing drinks for sore throats
54. Actor Erwin
55. Widen one's lead, in a race
58. Leo's digs
59. Yucatán native
61. Palm leaf: Var.
62. Enticement
63. Brawn
64. Primitive lip ornament
67. Like timeworn hands
68. Rainfall unit
69. Currier's cohort
70. In that
71. And aweigh they go
74. WAC disciplinarian
77. Whilom Eastern ruler
78. "____ it there!"
79. N.Y.C. transit initials
80. Not masc. or fem.
81. Mendacious one
82. ". . . in them ____ hills"
83. Prehistoric Albanian creature
87. Fuel gas
89. Mountaineers
90. Jokebook entries
91. Drifts
92. Sheiks' relatives
93. Black
94. Clara, Catalina et al.

DOWN

1. Prestige
2. Out-and-out
3. Mafia acreage
4. John of Odessa
5. Philip of Spain
6. They try
7. Small round hat
8. Baking-powder ingredient
9. Get the picture
10. Birthplace of Hippocrates
11. Conductor Solti
12. Clubman Palmer
13. Arabic letter
14. Catchword of 1789
15. Makes fun of
18. Grand, e.g.
19. Breadth
22. ____ of Cawdor
25. Hosp. people
29. Use an atomizer
30. Inappropriate sign in a fish store
31. C.S.A. people
32. In reserve
34. Defamer of Desdemona
35. Uncle Miltie
38. Suspicious
39. High waterproof boots
40. Capek play
41. "When I was ____"
42. Late Israeli leader
44. Cauterize
46. Delay an execution
47. What an atheist renounces
48. Demented toady
49. Type type, for short
50. Adjust the ivories
52. Emulate Ruth
53. French philosopher-critic
56. In the ____ way (desperately)
57. Taproom order
59. Chew steadily
60. Author of "The Nazarene"
62. Proclivity
63. Muezzin's towers
64. City and speed
65. Cupidity
66. Count in "All's Well . . ."
67. Streak, in biology
70. Young readers' Doctor
71. "Eureka!"
72. ____-Urundi (former African area)
73. Importance
75. Kind of circle or tube
76. Is getting there
77. Milksop
81. Stupid kind of head
82. Accordingly
84. Muhammad
85. News-service initials
86. Enter a primary
88. Refrain syllable

52 Of Importance by Henry Hook

Some people who carry weight.

ACROSS

1. Saw
6. Piper or Annie
12. Nevertheless
18. Shaw's Miss Undershaft
20. A Brewer not from Milwaukee
21. Egotist from G. & S.
23. Beginning of time
24. She has kids
25. Galvanize
26. Draw
27. Separators of E and I
28. Three sheets to the wind
31. Roman 250
34. "____ never!"
36. Kind of sequitur
37. One of four, in a game
39. Campanella
40. Actress Joanne
43. Michigan, in Chicago
47. Kiwi
49. November shooting star
51. Rooftop décor
52. Mackerel's relative
53. Timeouts
55. Verb-adjective word: Abbr.
56. As an Angel, her name was this
60. Pseudonym initials
61. Sardonic people
62. Recital unit
63. Response to "Shall we?"
65. ____ "An Enemy of the People"
66. Accomplish
69. About 60% of all earthlings
71. Soho flock
72. Whence oranges: Abbr.
73. Thumbs-down votes
74. Bed, in Rouen
75. Cather
77. Direction: Abbr.
78. Family hand-me-down
82. Beiderbecke
83. "Ca ____" (French rallying cry)
85. Ahs' friends
86. White House architect
88. Antimacassar soiler
92. Ginger Rogers film
97. ____ surprise
98. Ueberroth's command
99. Office people
100. As ____ molasses
101. Dame of fame

DOWN

1. "It's ____ . . . World"
2. Gazelle of Africa
3. ". . . is ____ forever"
4. Beckett no-show character
5. Heretofore
6. Czech measure
7. One place for a shot
8. African river
9. Rogers Hornsby, to his fans
10. Material for a famed French mask
11. Makes
12. Consumed
13. QB Dawson
14. Ex-Red head
15. Spooky
16. "Dot the ____ cross the t's"
17. Boudoir powder
19. Where Laverne and Shirley work
22. Place for a horse and rings
27. Ointment spoiler
29. Garland
30. Ruler: Abbr.
31. Grant's foes: Abbr.
32. Baker's wares
33. Scholarly people
35. Bagel topper
38. Part of N.W.T.: Abbr.
40. Complete an Alpine venture
41. Steve and Elmo
42. Dollars and cents, e.g.
44. Once-able exile
45. Groundless
46. Evasive ones
48. One led to Zanzibar
49. Less chaste in thought
50. Abbr. on a stock ticker
53. Sign of a boss's approval
54. Belt's relative
56. F.D.R. pet
57. Bank jobs
58. U.S. banking org.
59. Become a member
64. Willy Loman was one
66. The whole shootin' match
67. Part of a turtle shell
68. Native: Suffix
70. What forceps do
72. Rig, as a race
75. Burglar's usual entree
76. "Butchered to make holiday!"
78. Not ____ (so-so)
79. Kind of song
80. Exclamation
81. QB's Snead and Van Brocklin
82. Instrument for a Mummer
84. Mexican friend
85. Mel et al.
87. Semitic deity
89. ". . . some kind of ____?"
90. Busy one
91. Gaelic language
93. From ____ Z
94. March and Stafford
95. La-la preceder
96. Mencken et al.

53 Welcome Mats by William Lutwiniak

Places to wipe one's feet.

ACROSS

1. Queen of Rumania
6. Winged
11. Word of helplessness
15. Like divorced people
16. Watch
17. Sea detecting device
18. Dig in, as a guest
21. On the rocks
22. _____ nous
23. Carolina river
24. M.I.T. grads
25. Swamis
26. Lose one's cool
27. Took on
28. Chili con _____
29. North Star
32. _____ slipper (orchid)
33. N.Y.C. or Balto
36. Up
37. Fluids
38. "Scat!"
39. Like dutiful chickens
43. French writer
44. Stately trees
45. Knotty
46. Relative of Mayday
47. Cheer for a diva
49. Emissaries
50. Crossbeam
51. _____ noires
52. Compete
54. Egg white
55. Fuse abbr.
58. Wise goddess
59. Earthquake
60. Parents and a child
61. Go over big
64. Sets down on the runway
65. Workshop tool
66. French clerics
67. Up-tight
68. Church parts
69. Lachrymose

DOWN

1. Mrs. Eisenhower
2. Quickly
3. Hoes' relatives
4. Angered
5. Ike's arena
6. Gets even
7. On the Big Board
8. Teen-_____
9. Flooring
10. Wee one
11. Stick together
12. Battery part
13. Designated
14. Arbor Day planting
17. Dutch painter and family
19. Approaching
20. Foolish doings
25. Lorelei
26. Cairo name
27. _____ made (succeeds)
28. Gives a darn
29. S.A. rodents
30. U. of Maine site
31. Citrus fruits
32. Auxiliary proposition
33. Take a picture
34. Oater group
35. Carries
37. Figure out
38. Fountain orders
40. Word before ho
41. Former
42. Jolly badge of piracy
47. Produces
48. Gave an ecstatic review
49. Dog-walkers' aids
50. Up-to-date
51. Carefree
52. Costly fiddle
53. Object
54. Fellows
55. Oranjestad's island
56. Acquisitive one
57. Ballads and odes
58. Like Napoleon before Elba
59. Exchange
60. Bride-_____
62. Palm leaf: Var.
63. Toque

54 Fatherly Words by Martha J. DeWitt

A reminder or so of our early history.

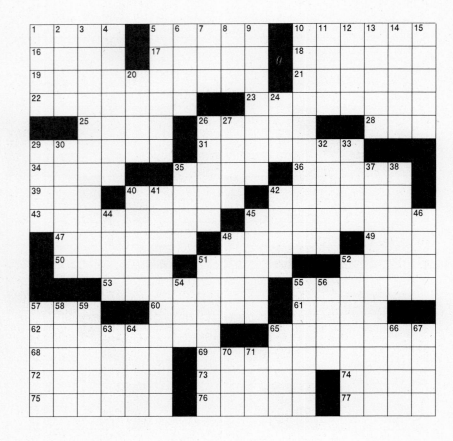

ACROSS

1. Yield
5. Long for
10. Payola figure
16. One of the Aleutians
17. Refuge
18. Pan
19. Endowed with ESP
21. Met offerings
22. Seals a leaky pot
23. Spangle
25. Time periods
26. ____ once
28. "____ Kapital"
29. Cowpoke's horse
31. Samovars' relatives
34. Weight
35. Operate a glider
36. Roasted game dish
39. Gone by
40. Makes a deal
42. The Swamp Fox
43. Grand Central, e.g.
45. Grouch
47. I.C.C. or F.A.A.
48. Old ____
49. Cambodia's Lon ____
50. Staircase pillar
51. Burn
52. Manche's capital
53. Pounced
55. Common hedge
57. Homily: Abbr.
60. Glove material
61. Prime
62. ". . . the ____ of your company"
65. Visual teaching aid
68. More steady
69. Washington wanted an "in" before this
72. Renter
73. Live
74. Routine
75. Tire parts
76. Smells
77. State of agitation

DOWN

1. Gang rods
2. Beginning of logical or graph
3. Washington's HQ
4. Made do
5. Like burlap
6. "Darn it!"
7. Residue
8. Clock number
9. Rough-scaled fish
10. Prehistoric vegetarian
11. Clothing, in Spain
12. Entry
13. Showed
14. Babylonian hero
15. Takes a break
20. Play and bull
24. Knock
26. Kwajalein or Wake
27. Grasslands
29. French feline
30. Sea off Greece
32. Stay around
33. Boo-boo
35. Do in
37. Retirement HQ for G.W.
38. Shoe part
40. Muscle
41. Items in envelopes
42. Othello, for one
44. Stables
45. English hillside
46. Place for a token
48. Turned right
51. One reaching 65
52. Gorme and Lawrence, e.g.
54. First word of a common prayer
55. Does art work
56. ____ to ruin
57. Wheat
58. Young lamprey
59. Pee Wee
63. Celestial handle
64. Pit
65. Kind of job
66. Beginning of a play
67. Athletic event
70. Devonshire river
71. Sky food

55 Taking a Flier by Alice H. Kaufman

But not the Amtrak kind.

ACROSS

1. Flat-topped hill
5. Became slightly overcast
10. Pacific Coast port
16. Relatives of Reos and Maxwells
18. Relating to birds
19. Shout of triumph
20. Manor
21. Becomes fuzzy
22. Netherlands house
23. Nursery mystery
26. Norse goddess of healing
27. Minstrel's offering
28. Poetic contraction
29. Beverage
31. Inactive
34. "Of Thee ___"
37. Thai moneys
39. Craggy hill
40. Browbeaten
41. Having branches
42. Filled
45. Large moths
46. Of a noble
47. Choice thing
48. Actress ___ O'Brien Moore
49. Marx Brothers movie
52. Gas-station offering
53. Artists' easels, in a way
56. Wildebeest
57. Remove
59. Farmyard sound
60. Shaw, Wilde et al.
61. Pixies
62. Dental filling
63. Mexican sandwiches
64. Models' showings
66. Sub-par score
67. Apiece
68. Relaxes
69. Bitter-tasting herb
70. Imply
74. Old English letter
75. Small island
76. ___ Lanka
77. Bull ___
78. Pulitzer novel
86. Kay Thompson brat
87. Abzug
88. Seat of authority
89. One using a seine
90. On the level
91. Soared
92. Declare
93. Storehouse
94. Positioned a ball

DOWN

1. Golf club
2. Subject to blackmail
3. Overcharge
4. Not pro
5. Tin Woodman portrayer
6. Greedy
7. Bluish-white metal
8. Within: Prefix
9. Approach the airport
10. Androcles's extraction
11. Gold: Prefix
12. Complainer
13. Of the study of birds
14. Attractions
15. Yes
16. Popular hide-out in Paris
17. Mutuel-window employee
24. Youth
25. Small barrel
30. Peer Gynt's mother
32. Detail
33. McKuen or Serling
34. Ancient district of Asia Minor
35. Certain finales
36. Plural endings
37. Hump and running
38. Common Latin verb
40. Like mountain streams
41. In the ___ (among the also-rans)
42. Quarrel
43. Inter ___
44. Marks-manship contests
45. Miss Horne and others
46. "Swell!"
49. Mother of Perseus
50. "Do ___ others . . .''
51. Follower of sour
53. Spelunkers' obsessions
54. Inspires dread
55. Mr. Eckstein
58. French pronoun
60. Put on guard
62. Author Fleming
63. Half a score
64. Observe
65. Tells secrets
66. Something to consume
67. Tapering ends
69. Sesame
70. Dernier ___
71. A.L. player
72. Twisted, as an ankle
73. Finished
75. Watchful
76. Roller or good
79. Type of hawk
80. Czech river
81. Come together
82. Miss Korbut
83. Cut short
84. Mountain pass
85. French cheese
86. Spanish queen

56 In-Flight Operations by Tap Osborn

The birds will never be the same again.

ACROSS

1. Shovel's partner
5. "Seven ___ a-swimming . . ."
10. Fraternal order, for short
14. Dec. 24 night noises
19. Together, in music
20. May, for one
21. Frying need
22. "Manon" or "Orfeo"
23. Sausage-loving bird
26. Star in Boötes
27. Michael Arlen's was green
28. Ore deposit
29. Kite's home
30. Indicate
31. Cambodia's Angkor ___
32. High-spirited horses
33. More calm
34. Birds having investments ___
39. Starve
40. Intimate
41. Donkey, in Liverpool
42. Kind of apple acid
43. Crewman
46. Church corner
47. Driving spot
48. Lively dance: Var.
49. Salad item, familiarly
50. Proceed
51. Will's English sparrow
54. Birdlife
55. Biblical kingdom
57. More like a day in June
58. Too ___ be true
59. Stash
62. Be compatible
63. Nodded off
64. Al of baseball note
65. Gets together
66. Name given to Esau
67. Ten-percenter
68. Flower-loving birds
71. Hole makers
75. Type of play: Abbr.
76. Old wall hanging
77. Mauna ___
78. Canter, for one
79. Poetic contraction
80. Showed affection
81. Caliph's relative
83. Infirm
84. Person with a foil
86. Income of a complaining bird
88. Like a room freshener
90. Barely audible
91. Roost occupant
92. Billfold
93. Got the lay of the land
94. Work for
96. Nonflying bird
99. Crazy as ___
100. Food for Yiddish avifauna
103. Lord it over
104. Formerly
105. Heavy Tyrolean cloth
106. Hungary's Nagy
107. Jockey Earl
108. Red-flannel hash ingredient
109. Poetic Muse
110. One on the move

DOWN

1. Primrose route
2. Concept
3. Abrupt
4. Knowledge
5. ___ as silk
6. ___ of mouth
7. Feed the pot
8. Great degree
9. Did sheep-farm work
10. Ad testimonials
11. Where Dior made his name
12. Cockney's steed
13. N.Y. summer time
14. Of epic proportions
15. Thinks
16. Outdoor sport for birds
17. Give a speech
18. European falcon
24. Eccentric
25. Dog-tired
30. Resign
31. Audubon art representation
32. Extra
33. Art gallery
34. Irwin or G. B.
35. Volume
36. Foretoken
37. Prompt
38. Ogle
39. Prefer
42. Amateur connoisseur
44. High as ___
45. Do a lawn job
48. Gaudy
49. Early early-bird
51. Lessen
52. Projecting windows
53. Like some meat
54. Goose eggs
56. Fasting period
58. Coffee blends: Abbr.
59. Emulate John Curry
60. Tidal wave
61. Frighten off a diving bird
62. Member of the cat family
63. Metric unit of area: Var.
65. Moody one
68. Despised
69. Northern native
70. Tribulations
72. Gamin
73. Miss Damita
74. Printer's mark
76. Rental sign
80. International thaw
81. Zodiac sign
82. Reagan's 1984 opponent
83. Sports center
85. Dump
86. Piston packing
87. Mind: Prefix
88. Pirates' booties
89. Variety of lily
90. Bedroom ___
93. Sugar source
94. Norse saga
95. Lend a shady hand
96. Sea saint
97. Sole
98. One with a habit
100. Maneuver for Borg
101. Conjunction
102. Actor Young

57 Stag Party by Ruth W. Smith

An assortment of qualified guests.

ACROSS

1. Ancient Roman port
6. Sad, in Lyons
12. Poet Ezra and family
18. Inclines
19. Borne by the wind
20. Scorecard listing
21. Home for a musical lad
23. Andean boy
24. Singer Berger
25. Land of the ex-shah
26. Sidewalk users: Abbr.
28. Chimpanzees
29. Guarded
31. Surface measure
33. Small case
35. Headland
38. Religious splinter group
40. Love-letter boy
45. Christie and Held
47. Places
49. Emerald Isle
50. Direction
51. Mr. Pierloader
53. Kind of house or bag
54. Kind of chair
56. Pierrette's partner
57. "Hark! hark! the ____ . . ."
59. Hokkaido, formerly
60. Restless longing
61. Wreath
62. Symbol of peace
65. Common Latin abbr.
68. Kind of crasher or keeper
69. Aperture
73. Red or Blue
75. Needlefish
76. Boy from a Canadian port
78. Container
79. Hammer, for instance
81. "____ Kampf"
82. Grassy plain
83. Manicurist's boy
86. Musical instrument
88. French possessive
89. Rubber trees
90. ____ of the line
92. Second in a series
94. Beverages
97. Sediments
99. Course, in Lille
101. Prefix for graph or technic
105. Japanese dwarfed tree
107. Boys with silly behavior
110. Actor Delon et al.
111. Direction in music
112. Moon crater
113. Table linen
114. Blue ____ (constant stream of words)
115. Gibe

DOWN

1. Wine pitcher
2. Very, in Bonn
3. Tin plate
4. Acquired relative
5. Tree
6. Words on a boy's towel
7. City of Italia
8. Actress Massey
9. Transgress
10. Capital of Taiwan
11. Ending for differ or depend
12. ____ of paris
13. Painting
14. Like some bills
15. Tide
16. Mussolini title
17. Resorts
22. Yorkshire river
27. Fleur-____
30. Avow
32. Baseball stat
34. North American Indians
35. Grate
36. Prefix for trust
37. Old weapon
39. Rocky pinnacle
41. Give out news on the Q.T.
42. Wave, in Nice
43. Actress Merkel et al.
44. Alien: Prefix
46. French months
48. Place for wine
52. "What's up, ____?"
53. Mourn
55. A beauty
58. At the age of: Abbr.
62. Free-for-all boy
63. Whale
64. Kind of ray
65. "____ homo"
66. Mine car
67. First-class
68. Festive
70. Marsh elders
71. Recent: Suffix
72. God of love
74. Pillar: Prefix
75. It hangs high
77. Suffer
80. Tapering shaft of stone
81. Of the middle: Abbr.
84. Borscht's home
85. Monte Carlo, for one
87. Virginia ____
91. Creator of Friday
93. ____ strings
94. ". . . a good war or ____ peace"
95. "Damn Yankees" character
96. Palestine city
98. Greek letters
100. Bonheur
102. River to the Seine
103. ____ majesty
104. River to the North Sea
106. Reply: Abbr.
108. Russian commune
109. Hesitation words

58 Looking Back   by Hugh McElroy

All the way to when we made the world safe for democracy.

ACROSS

1. John's last name
4. Sphere
7. Word with soft or no
11. Alphabet vanguard
15. Kind of suggestion
16. Locality
17. Kind of seaman
18. Chicago athlete
19. What it was in 1914
23. Spread by hearsay
24. Prefix with angle or cycle
25. Climax of a distance run
26. Strength, to Caesar
27. Assets
29. It's often bitter
30. ___ in the right direction
33. Overcook and then some
34. It's 24 karats
39. Cowardly Lion actor
40. Piper of myth
41. Blue or Lyon
42. Continually
43. Before
44. Girl "underneath the lamp-post"
49. Compass heading
50. Mother ___ (American saint)
52. Jewish month
53. Worshiped
55. At the drop of ___
56. British guns
57. Insect
58. Power of films
60. Laugh, in Paris
61. Christie and Crumm
64. Old Mideast initials
65. Mademoiselle's W.W. I home
68. High note
69. Pub stock
71. Yoko
72. Travel idly
73. Sketched

74. Aged agreeably
77. Role for Oland
79. Spring color
80. One of a suit
81. Steve or Fred
83. After avril
84. Seed coverings
87. "___ the ramparts we . . ."
88. Very hot day
92. Counterpart of the shores of Tripoli
95. Captive of Hercules
96. Harold of vintage funnies
97. Landed
98. Café au ___
99. Jumble
100. Lamarr
101. Ledger word

102. Across the ocean from Amer.

DOWN

1. Miss Bett of fiction
2. Kind of bomb
3. Achieved by persuasion
4. To the mouth
5. King, in Madrid
6. Flapjack mixture
7. Smooth fabric
8. Sash
9. Slalom site
10. Salt's companion
11. "___ Too Far"
12. Orson or Roy

13. Wagon
14. Prohibitionist
15. Swiss river
16. Amazes
20. Sound-stage worker
21. Algerian city
22. River in northern Ireland
27. "Scarface" star
28. Competes in a bee
30. Guinness
31. Teasdale
32. It's often rolled out
33. Exotic isle
35. French article
36. Where the word was sent in 1918
37. Unaspirated
38. ___ Scott
40. "Caretaker" playwright
41. Borneo sultanate

44. Wild grapevine
45. Breed of sheep
46. "Red ___"
47. Pestered
48. Actress Best and others
51. Greek letter
54. Feed-bag unit
56. Miss Starr
58. Town near Galway
59. Kind of lock
61. Flaherty's "Man of ___"
62. Sailing word
63. Cut into planks
66. Larry, Curly and ___
67. Actor Richard
70. Reduces drastically
73. Light rain
75. Eight: Prefix
76. Riches
77. Music sign

78. Babe or Woody
79. Look upon
82. Zany
83. Catcher's glove
84. "___ shalt not . . ."
85. Slithery creatures
86. Robt. ___
88. In a ___ (upset)
89. Hilo feast
90. Potentate
91. Tattletale
92. Holt of old westerns
93. But: Lat.
94. Bullring shout

59 Getting Literal by Maura B. Jacobson

Presenting what some people really are or do.

ACROSS

1. Miss Kett and family
6. Mitchum
12. Idolater
17. Going nowhere
18. Botanical sheaths
19. "____ ho!"
20. Bicycle manufacturer
22. Girded
23. That, to Juanita
24. Reamer's leavings
25. Dirk of yore
27. Hesitant sounds
28. Go one better
31. Slack
33. Actor Max Von ____
35. Dentists
39. Type of knight
42. Expires
43. Scissors sound
45. Be congruent
46. Impulse
47. Boxing middlemen
50. Give off
52. Mideast gulf
53. Factory owners' org.
55. Same old routine
57. Saucy quality
59. Part of AWOL: Abbr.
62. Crackerjack farmer
65. Maiden-named
66. Cross
68. Make a gaffe
69. Queen of the fairies
71. Biography
72. Car or winder
74. "Money ____ object"
76. ____ Shah Pahlavi
80. In re
82. Progeny
84. Acid salts
86. Musical transitions
88. Driving instructors
91. "What's the ____ worrying?"
93. River landing
94. Female ruff
95. Altar constellation
97. Chaste, in Madrid
99. Kind of ante
101. Santha Rama ____
104. Start at tennis
106. Shoe salesmen
110. "____ Was a Lady"
111. Hornswoggle
112. One of Arthur's men
113. Parts of basilicas
114. Podium bore
115. Lagoon site

DOWN

1. Old English letters
2. Picking up the tab
3. Deadlock
4. Labor initials
5. Kind of ladder
6. Calgary events
7. Jaguar's kin
8. Trumpet, tuba, etc.
9. Adult elver
10. Scottish explorer's family
11. Sea birds
12. Daughter of Minos
13. Atmospheric prefix
14. Umpire
15. Declare
16. Rorem and Sparks
17. Wonder
21. Spin a yarn
26. Hurricane center
29. Johnson's partner
30. Arafat's org.
32. Sea gull's acquaintance
34. Pipe or barrel
35. Actress Joanne
36. Capek classic
37. Talks in undertones
38. Silly smiles
40. Georgia ____ Clark
41. Uptight
44. Like spilled type
48. Let this ring
49. Big ____, Calif.
51. Vibrato effect
54. Chemical suffix
56. Between Mao and tung
58. Sing-along syllable
59. Armchair traveler's book
60. Pickling solution
61. Bank watchmen
63. Before omegas
64. Joseph C. Lincoln's Cap'n
67. Brilliant planet
70. Prop up
73. Chemical compound
75. Injurious, old style
77. Unsubstantial
78. Zuider or Tappan
79. Onager
81. Squaws' domains
83. Go gallivanting
85. Sense of pitch
87. French pittance
89. Cook too long
90. Hand over
92. Tolkien character
95. On the deep
96. Do a harvest chore
98. Cattle-stopping hedge
100. Ascetic discipline
102. Seed covering
103. Defense arm: Abbr.
105. Be a contestant
107. Neighbor of Ga.
108. Feed-bag bit
109. Deuce

60 XYZ Affair by Herb Risteen

Without any real international intrigue.

ACROSS

1. Mrs. Truman
5. Deadly crawler
8. Phosgene or neon
11. Egyptian goddess
15. Speed up
17. Sweat gland
19. Sensational headline
20. Involuntary actions
21. Toe, in Glasgow
22. Common gull
23. College degrees
24. Mil. base supermarkets
25. Large container
27. Harvest goddess
31. Plain-weave fabric
32. Speed-trap gear
34. Mason's colleague
35. Math ratios
37. Makes up for
39. Edge
40. Small carriage
41. Item on a bank counter
42. Take a _____ (insult)
44. Chicago's white wear
45. Greek letter
46. Beasts of burden
47. Ancient Greek portico
48. French soul
51. Western Indian
52. Stingy with words
53. Wildly gay
56. East German region
58. Guinea pigs' home
59. Pump up
61. Followed a Broadway pursuit
62. Music makers
64. White House man
65. Part of H.R.H.
66. Kind of jumping bean
68. Headlight setting
69. Manager: Abbr.
70. Head part
71. Energy
73. Wire measure
75. Involving connected words
78. Glorify
80. Like bread
81. Baker's unit
82. _____ of Pines
83. Compass point
84. Liquid measures: Abbr.
85. "Bird thou never _____"

DOWN

1. Defeat
2. Do an archeology job
3. Apply lavishly
4. Comprehend
5. Sighted
6. Like some prunes
7. _____ diem
8. Neighbor of Pol.
9. Woodcutters
10. Up to now
11. Wrath
12. Maugham's partner of the moon
13. Unskilled
14. Soap-frame bar
16. Flood-control unit
18. Store workers: Abbr.
26. Beige color
28. Italian city
29. Theater sign
30. Kind of notch or secret
31. Narrow inlet
32. Sentence, often bum
33. Have an effect on
35. Sweet age
36. Vast amount
38. "_____ Minutes"
40. Bone cavity
43. "_____ whiz!"
44. Neighbor of Isr.
47. Old Mediterranean ship
48. _____ rule
49. Flying and slot
50. Superficial
52. Vehicle
53. Make the most of
54. Perfume dispenser
55. Residence room
57. Above, in poems
58. Remiss
60. Unburden
62. Brings on the dinner
63. Learned one
66. Where Casco Bay is
67. Athletic teams
69. Spanish painter
70. English river
72. Clothing style
74. Spring period
76. Miss Arden
77. Dutch town
78. _____ out (renege)
79. At once

61 Word Doings by Lois Hillis

An assortment of general entries.

ACROSS

1. Tap
7. Tap's tap-tap
11. Butcher's follower
16. Disregard
17. Nobleman
18. Dressmaker's style
19. Writer George Jean
20. Father, in Eastern names
21. Collector's item
22. Wall climbers
23. Hard-to-slice peaches
25. Seaweed
26. Prophet
27. Dived into second
28. Vending-machine offering
30. Printers' measures
31. Devoured
33. Certain voter
35. Variety of corn
38. Town
39. As ____
40. Up from ____ (like Alger heroes)
42. Horticul-turist's trellis
46. "That's ____ trick!"
47. Incline
48. Walden Pond's offering
52. Silk ____
55. Brown pigment
56. Dissolute one
57. Perform
58. Never a land for him
61. Blow one's horn
63. Poet's work
64. Nevertheless
65. Come upon
66. Fleer from the hounds
70. Trevi fountain input
72. Turn
74. Potato
75. Types of print: Abbr.
77. Do a van job
78. What a dancer should be
79. Sheep sheds
80. Stravinsky
81. Palm off
82. Having a notched margin
83. Assembly-line items
84. Kind of interest

DOWN

1. The end
2. Fiber plant
3. Take out a knot
4. Stick together
5. Christian and Paleozoic
6. Little Indians, at the start
7. Business doings
8. Fanatical
9. Cast or flat
10. Book-blurb writers
11. Martini maker's station
12. Name for Athena
13. Kind of whale
14. Riddle
15. Change an acting lineup
23. Hotel-desk worker
24. Recapitulate
27. Daze
29. Pancake spread
32. Part of an electron-tube circuit
33. Do, in Scotland
34. Ancient temple area
35. School orgs.
36. "Heaven forbid!"
37. Banana protector
41. ____ the roof
43. Minimal thing
44. Homer's style
45. Landlord's due
49. Like the senators' house
50. Having two molecular units
51. Resembling: Suffix
52. Judges
53. "____ but you"
54. Pair
58. Kind of state
59. Lou Grant, for one
60. Monster: Prefix
62. Dull sounds
65. Good turn
67. Superior in a monastery
68. Singer Della
69. Made a mistake
71. Drinks
73. Robe of office
74. It marches on
76. Direction: Abbr.
78. Miss Ullmann

62 Title Revisions by Elaine D. Schorr

Sometimes an extra word is appropriate to a literary listing.

ACROSS

1. Kind of back
5. Sailor's call
10. In the van
15. Lambeth or side
19. Eight: Prefix
20. Eudora Welty's "____ Wedding"
21. "West Side Story" girl
22. Helm position
23. Employee for H. G. Wells
27. ____-la
28. ____ wintergreen
29. Roberts
30. Looks like
31. Psalm pauses
33. "Oliver Twist" villain
35. Inlet
36. Fr. companies
38. Novelist Ambler
39. Augur
40. Marie: Abbr.
43. Medical study for E. C. Bentley
49. ____ of exchange
50. Deed, in Dijon
51. Patricia of films
52. River to the Baltic
53. Guido's note
54. Prefix for caine
56. Evangelist's kind of again
57. "Thus ____ Zarathustra"
58. One who sanctions
60. Henry VIII's last
62. Bee: Prefix
63. Man-about-town for Hall Caine
70. Chaney
71. Overfill
72. Evaluate
73. Washbowl
76. La-di-da
78. Draw a blank
79. Atlas abbr.
80. "____, poor Yorick"
81. Swan genus
82. Choir voice
84. Uncles, in Uruguay

85. Rural diversion for Henry James
91. Fleur-de-____
92. Kind of ticket
93. Musical creation
94. In a ____ (agitated)
95. Church area
96. ____ it out (agonize)
97. Allergic eruptions
101. Japanese-American
104. Thai money
105. Snitch
108. Germ cells
109. Busybody for Arnold Bennett
113. Barnyard sound
114. Unit, in Oberhausen
115. Like-minded
116. Wrench
117. Kind of way
118. Stage, in St. Lo
119. Assembles
120. Coup de ____ (rash action)

DOWN

1. Reformer Lucretia and family
2. Palette pigment
3. ____ away (decamp)
4. Long-tailed monkey
5. Acts the mentor
6. Prop for Salome
7. Kind of ran
8. Most severe
9. Actor Hunter
10. Vespucci's turf
11. Biblical plotter
12. Of a time
13. Hebrew letter
14. Spring bloomer
15. Forgo
16. Mr. Ray
17. King or Norman
18. Florida ____
24. Good game for a pitcher

25. Good reasoning
26. Declaims
32. Teen-ager's problem
34. Johnson
35. He sent his regards to Broadway
37. "Roots" ship
39. Part of a boilermaker
40. Drink mix
41. Migration
42. Edward Rochester's Jane
43. Deal with
44. Meeker or Rackstraw
45. Stopping place for troops
46. Squirrel's find
47. Horse sound

48. Blunder, in Bologna
54. "____ your life!"
55. Place for Gretel's witch
56. Cheese selection
57. Tower tip
59. Appetizer
60. Dissemble, with 61 Down
61. See 60 Down
62. Locale of Mont Blanc
64. Dome athlete
65. 1945 conference site
66. Animal tracks
67. Chinese province
68. Renaissance sword
69. Pee Wee of baseball

73. ____ out (scold)
74. Kirghiz range
75. Be fresh to
76. Aquatic plants
77. Moslem weight
81. Partisan
82. ____ fortis (nitric acid)
83. Purify ceremonially
84. Works on lace
86. Motivate
87. Hobo's usual destination
88. Barracudas
89. Dons royal attire
90. Miss Keaton
95. King of Magadha
96. Frugal one

98. Goddesses of the seasons
99. Thing that comes to pass
100. Noncom
101. Portico
102. Indian caste member
103. Hawaiian bird
104. Kind of cherry
106. Bitter-drug plant
107. Camp unit
110. How, in Bonn
111. Perky head cover
112. Likely

63 Small Talk by William H. Ford

A few phrases that are handy in conversation.

ACROSS

1. _____ gown
7. Waste matter
12. _____ hand (humbly)
17. Orbital point
18. Adoree of films
19. Swiftian
21. Army-tank part
22. Basket fiber
23. Missile from the gallery
24. Algonquian
25. Nevertheless
28. F.D.R. agency
29. Tradition
31. Akin in a certain way
32. Line, as a roof
33. Tattled
34. Oasis in Egypt
35. Mel and family
36. Despises
39. Grape syrup
41. Neat
44. Whitelaw and Ogden
45. Affect
46. Like some anchors
50. U.S. holly
51. Coin of old England
52. Memorable African leader
54. Let a chance slip by
56. Münchhausen offering
57. One with high aims
58. Sweet wine
59. O.T. book
60. Grasslike plants
61. College in Maine
62. Gaze
63. Old World deer
65. _____ out (makes do)
66. German name for Moravia
67. Opposite of aweather
70. Commedia dell' _____
72. Russell College
73. Take out
74. Entices
75. Somewhat brittle
79. One of Shakespeare's seven
80. Press on
82. Odor: Prefix
83. Galoot
85. Judge's call
86. Phonograph inventor
88. Forsaker of a homeland
89. Practical
90. _____ speak of (very few)
91. Curves
92. Pith helmets
93. Role for a grandparent

DOWN

1. Good marital prospect
2. River to the Orinoco
3. Intent reader
4. Acknowledge a stalemate
5. Born
6. Minutiae
7. In a dull manner: Var.
8. "God _____ you merry, gentlemen . . ."
9. Like a certain Johnny
10. Of the moon
11. Playground item
12. Blackjack player's request
13. Islands off New Guinea
14. Piper's offspring
15. Sulky
16. Boob
20. Rake over the _____
26. Inc., in London
27. Rat-_____
30. Actress Diana
32. Calls a spade a spade
36. Musketeer
37. _____ oneself (upset)
38. Greeted Cleo at her final moment
39. Use a child's vehicle
40. _____ impasse
42. Tennis activity
43. "When _____ one-and-twenty . . ."
45. Garfunkel and Carney
47. Line on a weather map
48. Revolve, in Milan
49. Dutch painter Jan van der _____
51. Outward show
52. "_____ alive!"
53. High notes
55. Companion of jam and jelly
56. Carry
58. Goes swimming
61. "'Tis _____ have loved and . . ."
62. Droops
64. German basin
66. "Twenty love-sick _____ we . . .:"
67. Allan-_____
68. Soybean, e.g.
69. Resins for perfumes
71. Equip, as a sailboat
72. Muchacha after marriage: Abbr.
74. Works out with Ali
75. Goddess of agriculture
76. Stands ready to start
77. Whacked
78. Certain bridge card
80. Golfing cry
81. Sun: Prefix
84. Gatling, Sten, etc.: Abbr.
87. "_____ Hear a Waltz?"

64 Tuning Up by Louise Earnest

And getting things to harmonize.

ACROSS

1. Tricky
5. Eerie wind sound
9. M.D.'s diagnostic aids
13. Exchange fee
17. Purse item in Naples
18. Doubleday
20. Xanthippe
22. Joker holder
23. Combined: Abbr.
24. Kind of rocket
25. Home of the Tut treasures
26. Highways: Abbr.
27. Combo for River City
31. Peak periods
32. "Red as ___ is she"
33. "___ my wits' end"
35. Showery mo.
36. Do ___ (don't wait)
38. Elected ones
39. Mauna ___
41. Meredith Willson musical
45. Do-it-yourself recital
48. Commotion
49. Inch or mile, e.g.: Abbr.
50. Kind of song
51. Aware of
52. Mature
53. Done to ___
55. Pretense
56. Gog's partner
57. Roadside havens of a sort
59. ". . . as ___ to the slaughter"
60. ___ it out (stayed)
61. Line from "King Henry VIII"
68. City of Yugoslavia
69. As hard as ___
70. Thing that sticks
71. Miss d'Orsay and namesakes
74. Swindle
75. Harebrained
77. Where, in old Rome
78. Egyptian god: Var.
79. Pay attention to
80. Vex, in Scotland
81. Tucker's partner
82. Sound familiar
85. Go after business
89. High place: Abbr.
90. Fold
91. He wrote "The Old Wives' Tale"
92. After pi
93. Actress Thorndike
95. Froth
97. Joins forces
101. Stop fooling around
105. Square's partner
107. Zodiac sign
108. Plains Indians
109. Gershwin and Wolfert
110. Out of kilter
111. Port du ___
112. Sidestep
113. Cozy place
114. Apple shooter
115. Popeye's saint
116. Swiss-cheese holes
117. Cote dwellers

DOWN

1. Lack of harmony
2. Actress Anouk
3. Kind of boat or train
4. Lewis River, Wash., installation
5. Joan of Arc and St. Valentine
6. Follows orders
7. Opposites of syns.
8. St. Philip ___
9. Fund held in trust
10. Opposite of order
11. Sooty accumulation
12. Man from Belgrade
13. Relevant
14. Makes out
15. Bar rocks
16. Gives approval
19. Wife of Alexander the Great, and others
21. Courting
28. Small Asian deer
29. Ending for cyclo or iso
30. Skylab's creator
34. Indian of note
36. Bakery worker
37. Govt. agent
38. Hospice
40. On tiptoe
41. Ear protuberances
42. Home to a Navajo
43. Wide-mouthed pitchers
44. "___ down to the seas again"
45. Pundit
46. Metrical feet
47. Detest
50. Hovel
53. ". . . my ___ as a lusty winter"
54. Certain ball-holders
55. Oil-spill result
56. Warfare: Suffix
58. Outdoor window décor
59. ___ as the hills
60. Vegetation on the Nile
62. Miss Normand of silents
63. One of the archangels
64. Hindu ascetic
65. Curaçao's neighbor
66. Make a new offer
67. Sachem's group
71. Orwell's "Animal ___"
72. Opposites of origs.
73. Name for Fanny Brice
75. Caesar's conquest
76. "Woe ___!"
79. With it
80. One on the house
83. Landed
84. As ___ a billiard ball
85. TV program sample
86. Renews trouser creases
87. "___ Old Black Magic"
88. Salad green
91. ___ rights (fixes)
94. Aquamarine
95. Hog fare
96. Lung: Prefix
97. Hebrew letter
98. Kind of ball or driver
99. Edict
100. Attention-getting sounds
102. Edges, to Caesar
103. Wander
104. Team-schedule heading
105. Jack Sprat's hang-up
106. Reverence

65 In Transit by Evelyn Benshoof

Time for getting a move on.

ACROSS

1. Hindu bigwig
6. Play the siren
12. Chest for valuables
18. City near Minneapolis
19. Undo
20. Loath
21. Wind up in the discard
23. Mean
24. Saperstein of Globetrotter note
25. Not-so-sweet home
26. Central European river
28. ____ de mer
29. In case
31. Comedian Brooks
32. Jaunty headwear
34. Diminutive suffix
35. Port of Yemen
37. Boorish
38. Additional
39. John Hancock role
42. Start the day
43. Crutch's relative
44. Battery terminal
45. Viewpoint
46. The one that ____ (biggest fish)
49. Pigeon material
50. Imitating
51. "____ Spake Zarathustra"
52. She-bear, in Spain
53. Artificial languages
54. Intermediary
56. Start of a movie dog's name
57. Condition: Suffix
58. "The King ____"
59. Praying figure
60. Aleutian island
61. Visual inspection
63. German president
64. Watchmaking gauge
65. Mexican ones

66. Glorify
67. Sullen
68. Crust or berth
70. Go ____ for
71. Speck
72. Karnak's waterway
73. ____ City, N.C.
74. Murmuring sound
75. Perfume unit
79. Brew
80. Normandy town
81. ____ Coeur
83. "But ____ on forever"
84. Peek
86. Degenerate
90. Reduce tension
91. Extreme disgust
92. Miss Astaire

93. Sleepers' scripts
94. Bowers
95. Parcels out

DOWN

1. Majestic
2. Western brick
3. Alters a course at sea
4. Some
5. Biblical verb
6. Football team
7. Prestigious prize
8. Cat's-paw
9. "There ____ tavern in . . ."
10. Wax: Prefix
11. Sign a check
12. Middy

13. Word at the bottom of a page
14. Marsh
15. All the way
16. Holdings
17. Two-____ (old movie)
22. "Iliad" creator
27. ____ Moines
30. Actress Jessica
32. Put to use
33. Direction
34. Volcano
36. Scottish river
37. Do some neck-stretching
38. Farm crop
39. Of the pelvis
40. ____ parentis
41. Casual
42. Excuse
43. Dracula, for one

45. English china
46. Belgian treaty city
47. Korean and Chinese
48. "____ go home"
50. Actress Moorehead
51. Sprees
55. Gain forcibly
58. Hebrew zither
60. Broadcast
62. Kind of deep or jerk
63. Czech river
64. Share
66. Sandwich filling
67. Comedian Garry
68. Like new wine
69. ____ of society

70. "____ we meet again"
71. Coffees
73. Degrees
74. Kind of corner
76. Fasten tightly
77. Lithe
78. Burrowers
80. Pond covering
81. Tolerably
82. Cheese
85. Educational org.
87. Rower's need
88. Place for three men
89. Netherlands city

66 Specialties by Hume R. Craft

Presenting a few appropriate menu items.

ACROSS

1. Washington hospital name
5. British women fliers
10. Tibetan priest
14. Smeltery leavings
19. Shah Jahan's city
20. Word on a ticket
21. Sacred image
22. Prehistoric: Prefix
23. Cheese for a French novelist
25. Dessert for Kukla's friend
27. Toy-pistol ammo
28. Formal procedures
30. One promoting joint action
31. Lidos
34. Quahogs
35. Lunacy
36. Melodious
37. King Arthur's was Perilous
38. Competes at logrolling
39. Upton Sinclair's Lanny ___
40. Confection for a Puritan clergyman
42. Haight-Ashbury lodging
45. Tennis serves
46. "Your Majesty"
47. Makes an inquiry
48. Tractor-trailer rig
49. Philippine peasant
50. Pastries for honest George
54. Discover by chance
55. In a lavish manner
57. Wins
58. H. L. Mencken's forte
59. Jason Jr. of films
61. Erie Canal user
62. Ariel and others
63. Marbles
64. Political unoriginality
65. Scottish tots
66. Strides
67. Entree for the Friars Club
69. Whodunit atmosphere
72. Stravinsky
73. Young salmon
74. "The Bad ___"
75. Palm tree
76. Daniel's milieu
77. Snacks for L.A. fans
81. Kind of mat
82. Canapé spreads
83. Folkways
84. ___ with the same brush
86. Coleridge subject
89. Zane Grey settings
90. Removes, as a spar
91. Charlotte ___
92. William Godwin's ___ Williams
93. Grant's first name
94. Dressing for Minnesota brothers
96. Food for a sad snack-lover
101. Hit the deck
102. Place of learning: Abbr.
103. Craggy abode
104. City on the Rhone
105. Loudness units
106. Joey and Ruby
107. Stand-in host
108. "___ no money"

DOWN

1. Kind of time
2. Capital "I"
3. Fluff
4. Sandwiches for a Peace Nobelist
5. "I ___ be alone"
6. Woodworking tools
7. Cupid
8. Iraqi coin
9. Movie fledgling
10. London elevator operators
11. Boyle's Thirty ___
12. Extinct birds
13. Raggedy doll
14. Like Ichabod Crane's figure
15. Rabbit furs
16. Having wings
17. Rayburn and Lockhart
18. Paris evenings
24. Shell occupants
26. Tackles' neighbors
29. Cassio's rival
31. Capital of Morocco
32. Caterpillar larva
33. Aspect of an English philosopher
34. Process server
35. Fur animals
37. Word before "wrong number"
38. Mat fibers
40. Light blues
41. Chili con ___
42. Cakes at a bridge table
43. Love, in Italy
44. Has a repast
46. Lean-tos
48. Popular protest of the 60's
50. Largest asteroid
51. Rhymers' Club member
52. Arcane card
53. Jargon
54. Man to be wild about
56. Second-___
58. Worked with John André
59. Like some transit
60. Model-track size
61. B.S.A. founder
62. "___ alive!"
64. "September" et al.
65. Fox and rabbit
67. More unusual
68. Beneficiaries of a suit
70. Chamber-music group
71. Merchandise
73. Irish bootleg whisky
75. Candies for Ott and Torme
77. Benji, Lassie, etc.
78. Western and Spanish
79. Amount taken
80. Catchall prize dispenser
82. Hairy
84. Three-line rhyme
85. Oriental servant
86. Family members
87. Bitter, in Naples
88. Synthetic fiber
89. Billiard stroke
90. "The ___ cast" (too late to change)
92. Movie: Prefix
93. Animal head
95. It's first, at times
97. Rumanian coin
98. Private ___
99. Gun's offspring
100. Football player

67 Forgettable Songs by Jordan S. Lasher

But their titles deserve a place in musical history.

ACROSS

1. Make ___ for (promote)
7. Escalates, as an auction price
13. Spanish sherry city
18. Second person
21. Like a sand bar
22. Embarrassing textbook addition
23. ___ a customer
24. Militarize
25. Line from a W.W. I song
28. Undercover org.
29. Abrasives
30. They contain veritas
31. Youngsters
33. Faces the pitcher
36. Denouement
37. Commoners
39. Same old things
40. ___ as a kite
43. River ending at Lyons
44. "... for ___ is the kingdom of God"
46. Sian's province
47. 1880 lilt
52. According to
53. Transferrer of property
55. Physical-exam exclamations
56. Claw
57. Research centers
59. Many relatives
60. Overshoe
63. Ibn-
64. Fire or sand
65. Squiffed
66. Suffix with super or infer
67. Town on Lake Geneva
69. Part of H.R.H.
70. Pinkie, for one
72. Rigged event at a track
76. Mirage vision
78. Miss Miles
79. Jimmie Rodgers hit, 1958
80. Vincent of the chillers
81. Agora change
82. Unencumbered
83. "... secluded place"
84. Bien ___, city near Saigon
85. Inter ___

87. Paul Newman role
88. Fish story
89. Hardy fish
92. "Wearin' ___ Green"
94. Bony
96. ___ the point (irrelevant)
99. Opposite of da
100. Sum of the parts
102. Men's org.
103. City on San Francisco Bay
105. Genetic compound
106. Song from "To Beat the Band"
111. Make blunt
113. Morale, for short
114. Bradley and Sharif
115. Leopardlike cat
116. Gale of football
118. John Paul and predecessors
119. Article
122. Leonine feature
123. "I ___ saw, I conquered"
124. Game of chance
126. Closes tightly
129. World relief org.
130. 1959 rock hit
137. Eggs ___ yong
138. Devour
139. E.E.C. area
140. Put a new value on
141. Hostelry
142. "___ Latin from Manhattan"
143. Dramatizes
144. Dancer Duncan's brother, maybe

DOWN

1. Hockey-stick wood
2. Greek letter
3. Charged atom
4. Absorbs
5. "Return of the Native" hero
6. Stevenson character
7. Nigerian river
8. Peeved
9. Prohibitionists
10. Dunderhead
11. Miss Hagen
12. Rich upstart
13. Blondell and Crawford
14. War goddess
15. Guns the engine

16. D.D.E.'s command
17. Baggy wear of yore
18. Song popularized by Al Jolson
19. Protruding window
20. New England campus
26. Dander
27. Calumny
32. State flowers of New Mexico
33. Lava rock
34. Squared stone
35. 1914 song about monkeys
37. Couples
38. ___ cit.
39. Service branch: Abbr.
41. Brownies' parent org.
42. Theme song for Leslie Caron
43. Video annoyance
44. "A Taste ___"

45. Persnickety
47. Hat material
48. Miss Merkel
49. Suffix with professor or janitor
50. Lake in the Canadian Rockies
51. Kin of ifs
54. "What's ___ for me?"
58. Agnew
60. Lawrence's singing partner
61. Mecca natives
62. 1950 song popularized by Como
66. "___ you so!"
68. Honshu city
71. Big party
72. Kind of rhythm
73. Corn Belt metropolis
74. "___ Abulbul Ameer"
75. These: Fr.
77. Lurer
78. Palliate
79. Obtrusive
83. Staffer

84. Sewing-machine pioneer
86. U.S. Japanese
88. Airport transport, for short
90. One of the Beatles
91. Towns: Ger.
93. French president's home
95. Suffix with rook or cook
96. Max and Buddy
97. Culbertson et al.
98. Well-known Hill
101. Knightly prowesses
104. Something easy
107. Bitter vetch
108. Listless
109. Foists upon
110. Dundee denial
112. "O ___! O mores!"
116. "Star Trek" genre
117. Homer king

118. Argentine plain
119. Phoenix suburb
120. Nineteenth President
121. Wapiti
124. Take the bait
125. Large birds
126. L.A. problem
127. Spore clusters
128. Luau music makers
131. Exclamation
132. Quarter-back's shout
133. Ethan Allen's brother
134. Ems or Nauhein
135. Siouan
136. Part of r.p.m.

68 For the Patient by Jack Luzzatto

A subject that requires intensive care.

ACROSS

1. Sky blazers
7. One ____ time (gradually)
14. Empty talk
20. None too red-blooded
21. Tapestries
22. Morning juice
23. New doctors' acquisitions
25. Doing a lawn job
26. Dismounted
27. Western entertainments
28. Suffered a penalty
30. Oil-land baron
31. Pouch
32. End-all's partner
33. Yellowstone attraction
35. Western Indian
36. Bandage to immobilize a limb
38. Fast buck
40. Can of movie film
41. Something of value
43. Caricaturist of Tweed
45. Set the scene
47. Plant poison
49. W. R. Hearst's friend
51. Get in a stew
53. Summer hat
56. Skunks
58. Water animal
60. Regret one's ways
62. African warrior group
63. Caffeine nut
65. Bawled out
67. Social org.
68. Oven
69. Reasons for ambulance calls
71. Quick snack
72. Varied information
73. Enjoy night life
74. Creeds

75. "Three acres and ____"
76. Poem, often about love
78. Strike hard
80. Cultured wisecracks
82. Pilfers
84. On guard
86. Too
87. Dreamland
89. Sag
91. Goddess of discord
92. Mental error
95. Summon by loudspeaker
97. Slider
99. Taunts
102. Building wing
103. Lion, at times
105. Jackets
107. Chop
108. Cabbage dish
110. Highland group
111. A martial art
113. Marsh rail
114. Capitol group
116. Doctor's reading matter
119. Woman adviser
120. Dined too well
121. Key hockey player
122. Tennis players
123. Word for a beloved late relative
124. Played rowdily, with "around"

DOWN

1. Lily with an edible bulb
2. Single time around the track
3. Aloe or foxglove, e.g.
4. Issue
5. Nervous twitch
6. Frighten
7. Burdens with
8. Saplings
9. Therefore
10. Good golf scores
11. Chemical ending
12. Skin tent
13. One who tests ore
14. Crowd, Mongol style
15. Mouths
16. Capture
17. Ill will
18. Set afire
19. Sorrowful retrospect
24. Get the camera ready
29. L.I. resort town
32. Fundamental
33. Enlarge
34. Showered
37. Yield under pressure
39. Plane-booster system: Abbr.
42. Sinecure
44. Kitchen vessel
46. Regain health
48. With a loving touch
49. Chain-reaction pieces
50. Plant pore
52. "Thanks, m'sieu'"
54. Johns Hopkins, etc.
55. Topic at 54 Down
56. Rabbits' relatives
57. Weavers' reeds
59. Pay-envelope surprise
61. Tartan trousers
64. Enticing scent
66. Musical pace
70. Dutch money
71. Spanish section of a city
73. Fur hunter
77. Tourist loch
79. Cupid
81. Antiseptics' targets
83. Flower part
85. Endure
88. Andes plateaus
90. Having leaves
92. Diminish
93. Assert
94. Orbiting body
96. Conference city
98. "How ____ the little busy bee . . ."
100. African shillelagh
101. Moved in rhythm
104. Wide water
106. Whinny
109. Friendly
111. Harvest home in Scotland
112. Quick as ____
113. ____ Night light
115. Connect
117. Gods, to Livy
118. Great Lakes canals

69 On the Wing by Marion Moeser

Some offerings on the feathery side.

ACROSS

1. Foreman's milieu
5. Plains state: Abbr.
9. Take an athletic runaround
12. Chemist's glass
17. Bernese Alps river
18. Hand over
19. Miss Stowe's brainchild
20. Sans sense
21. Wheeler-dealer bird
24. Strict-speaker Newman
25. Old Egyptian V.I.P.
26. Clever one
27. Fixes sheaves
28. Old Mideast org.
29. Destroy documents
30. Long Island Harbor
31. Military caps
34. Made efforts
35. Father Damien's island
39. Isfahan's country
40. Brahma show
41. Worker
42. ____-Saud
43. Ford-era button
44. Alley of comics
45. Scoffs nastily
47. Shock deeply
48. Suspend for a time
51. "____ Dorn," Hecht novel
52. Two English Williams
53. King Zog's land
55. Marksman's sport
57. Shopping places
59. W.W. II wheels
61. Slovenly
64. Selves
65. Breaks up a sentence
67. TV spots
68. Mailing initials
69. "Caught you!"
70. Bargains
71. ____ nous
73. Perform in a fishbowl
74. Spoiled self-indulgers
76. Halloween visitor
77. Some exercise machines
78. Decrepit cabin
79. Blouse's companion
80. Marie Dressler role
81. Dis-tressed, à la Samson
84. Drab job
85. Pleasant punch
89. Greek column style
90. Cooing language
92. Utah national park
93. Yore
94. Archie Goodwin's boss
95. Miss Fitzgerald
96. Big-band items
97. Isle in Cambridge-shire
98. Verdon
99. Solid portion

DOWN

1. Give the boot to
2. Mata ____
3. Algerian city
4. Bird dressed for dinner
5. Do the sink
6. Interior or H.E.W.
7. Indiana humorist
8. Neckline accessory
9. Took an SST
10. Like Humpty
11. Du Nord, e.g.
12. Tie-dyed horse, possibly
13. Musical mood
14. Chess piece
15. Site of Phillips Univ.
16. Common bills
22. Greek letters
23. Halo that sounds like a bird
29. Left port: Abbr.
30. Jacob had many of these
31. Down Under bird
32. Sligo's land
33. Lean and slippered old bird
34. Fine-feathered fops
35. U.S. general of W.W. II
36. Wright flight site
37. Stand next to
38. Hospices
40. Miss Loren's city
41. Those who receive
44. Spheres
46. Significant time
47. Arthur's men
49. Building wings
50. Stadium areas
52. Livens, with "up"
54. Loser to D.D.E.
56. Cover up
57. Tomcat's plaint
58. Titled Turk
60. Like a Tom
62. English painter
63. DeLuise and others
65. Fourth-down ritual
66. Making horsy sounds
70. How the ball goes
72. Royal Navy drink
73. Kind of bar or tennis game
75. Trebly
76. Like icy roads
77. Crosby
79. Moonshine gear
80. Massenet girl
81. Brothers or sisters
82. Israeli stomp
83. Cuff-link material
84. Graf
85. Not green
86. Small waterway
87. ____ Verde
88. Obsessed whaler
91. Brand-____

70 Out of Place by Cornelia Warriner

Some creatures in basically unusual situations.

ACROSS

1. Syria of yore
5. Watch holder
10. Rainbow goddess
14. Polio-vaccine developer
19. Reminder
20. Wife of Polynices
21. One of three in 1492
22. U.S. painter
23. Like ___ (restless)
26. Soviet co-op
27. Most rational
28. Stamp collectors' quests
29. Twangy
30. Health resort
31. Opp. of a local
33. Mention again
34. Dido
35. Echo-ranging device
37. Kind of bag or party
38. Dutch artist
39. Old English coins
42. Cause of Cinderella's calluses
46. ___-la-la
49. Styles
51. Chemical suffix
52. Zilch, in Paris
53. Hindu caste member
54. Hubbub
55. A dubious purchase
60. Upright
61. Entertains
63. Solitary
64. Dwellings of the Southwest
65. Agave fiber
66. Prudish person
67. Al Capone's field
68. Fireplace shelf
70. Spikes the punch
71. Remembers
74. Change
75. Be annoying
78. Dandy
79. Actor Bert
80. Girl in "South Pacific"
81. Cries of pain
82. Tennis offering
84. Compass point
85. A spider was Miss ___
90. Like some hair
91. Sinai or Rainier
93. Goddess of healing
94. Care for
96. Bring about
97. Hindu destinies
100. Teacher's ___
101. Friend, in Vichy
104. Sam made them too long
105. How some paintings are sold
107. Chinese news medium
109. Point of view
110. Alice heard a ___
112. Gary shipment
113. Steven's partner
114. Outmoded kind of suit
115. Sheltered
116. Civil wrongs
117. Dry
118. Tartan patterns
119. Felt pain

DOWN

1. Pile up
2. Summary
3. Iowa community
4. Speck
5. In need
6. Salt mixture in Indian soil
7. Stravinsky
8. Hindu guitar
9. Small drums
10. Handkerchief décor
11. Castor-bean poison
12. Like a stamp pad
13. Back talk
14. Wrench, in England
15. Ventilate
16. What a kook has
17. Of the intestine
18. Dickens's little girl
24. Olaf's capital
25. Icy coatings
32. Uneasiness
34. "Have you two fives for ___?"
35. Perceive
36. Phoned
38. Graf ___
39. Khayyám
40. Took Dobbin out
41. An unfair intruder
43. "Gott ___ dank!"
44. Fetters
45. Turn or walleyed
47. Oriental staple
48. Skills
50. Fish-cannery worker
53. Fragrance
56. ___-mell
57. Stupor: Prefix
58. Strange
59. Chaser of a sort
60. Decrees
62. Daisy's relative
64. Neighborhood
66. Paw, in France
67. Thwart
68. "The ___ Animal"
69. Word of regret
70. Table section
72. Passion
73. Hurried
75. Gab, for one
76. Trifle
77. Miss Verdon
80. Crescent
83. Dutch town
85. Clams' cousins
86. Worldly
87. Flowing robe of old
88. Killer whale
89. Quarrying drills
92. Retail store
95. Safekeeping: Abbr.
96. Division of a poem
97. Rascal
98. Following
99. Fishnet
101. In any way
102. Brawl
103. Displeased
104. Gone by
105. Chills
106. Cut apart
108. Attempt
111. Fate

71 Bonuses by Sidney L. Robbins

Buy one, get one free, in a way.

ACROSS

1. Jars
6. Get rid of
10. Cut wood
15. Animation
19. Alto or bass
20. Fruit
21. Not fitting
22. Aware of
23. Decorate
24. Unusual
25. Large packages
26. Etats-____
27. Authoritative hit
30. Flanged beams
31. "Gentlemen, be ____"
32. Wagon
33. Solidify
34. Taxi
37. Certain breads
38. Old watch attachments
39. Brisk, in music
43. Educ. institutions
45. Poetic word
46. "Cruel kindness," for one
47. Gambling game
48. Chang or Eng
53. Part
54. "____ Brute!"
55. Edible mushrooms
56. War god
57. Organic compounds
58. Unkind bridge opponents
60. Southern campus
61. Small things
62. Writer Yutang
63. Properties
67. Soak
68. Poplar tree
70. Child's toy
71. Most severe
76. "____ lost" (it's hopeless)
77. Fix salad eggs
79. Gleamed
81. Preposition
82. Shock
83. Certain spy
85. Bar-sign ingredient
86. Least prompt
88. Picnic intruder
89. Capital of Guam

90. Goddess of the hunt
91. Actual being
93. Young salmon
96. French salt
97. Opp. of civilian
98. Arctic hazard
99. Usher
101. Type of opera
104. London street sight
109. Places
110. Swarm
111. Quinine's target
112. Drunk
113. Section
114. Kind of ego
115. Roots: Abbr.
116. Piano ____
117. Mary Baker or Nelson
118. Vehicles
119. Golf V.I.P.'s
120. Commence

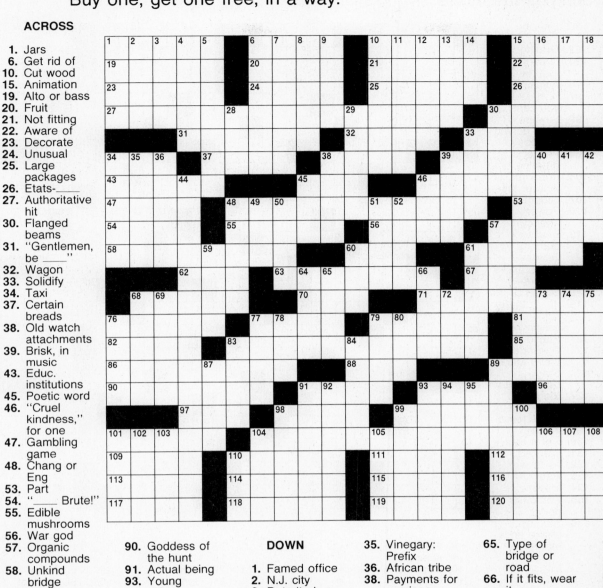

DOWN

1. Famed office
2. N.J. city
3. Detroit player
4. Lands
5. Shippers
6. Imp
7. Strains at
8. Dog-____
9. ____ Scott
10. Commuter's home
11. Climbing-fish genus
12. Cox of TV
13. Sword
14. Drunk's woes
15. Gambling choice
16. Siam visitor
17. Hoosegow
18. Cowpoke's mount
28. Beta or X
29. Scents
30. Place of control
33. Author Elinor
34. Coated
35. Vinegary: Prefix
36. African tribe
38. Payments for services
39. W.W. II group
40. Bride's need
41. Turns over
42. Change for a five
44. Insurance provision
45. Scottish uncle
46. Be obligated
48. Play part
49. Doer: Suffix
50. Church area
51. Bridge position
52. Verified
57. French seasons
59. Diamond girl and namesakes
60. It disappears on standing
61. Court decree
64. Sandpiper

65. Type of bridge or road
66. If it fits, wear it
68. Wedding milieu
69. ____ out (say impulsively)
72. ____ Arbor
73. Trojan hero: Var.
74. Early age
75. Having harmony
76. Movie dog
77. Political V.I.P.
78. Three strikes and ____
79. Intelligent
80. Altitude: Abbr.
83. Satan, to Scots
84. Artist's aid
87. Chemical prefix
89. Does a cop's job
91. Avoided

92. Becomes subdued
93. False: Prefix
94. Entry
95. Korean mil. man
98. Strong point
99. Poe
100. Lake or brook
101. Sticky application
102. French circle
103. Type of indigestion
104. Occupant of a child's buggy
105. Wyatt
106. Synthetic rubber
107. Consumer
108. Spanish painter
110. Owns

72 Cap-a-pie by Stephanie Spadaccini

Covering all the bases.

ACROSS

1. Type
4. Pouch
7. Plants
12. Dalai ____
16. Siamese, today
17. Questionable
19. Room at the top
20. Gershwin and Levin
21. Specially selected
23. Lively songs
25. More equally distributed
26. In disorder
28. French town
29. Era
30. Affirmatives
31. What a lady says to a mouse
32. Handel specialty: Abbr.
34. Resists
36. Wail
38. Greek letter
40. Tied securely
42. Greek letters
45. Ample space
48. Serviceable
52. Pledge
53. Gander's due
54. Writer Sinclair
56. Reasonable
57. Have ____ (be kind)
59. Wear for Halloween
61. Weekend days: Abbr.
63. Joker
64. Florida city
65. Cleaning solution
66. Nabokov book
68. Exhortation to sinners
70. Alpine phenomenon
72. Mr. John
74. Silkworm
75. Make beloved
77. Range of knowledge
78. Like 3, 5 or 7
80. Swap
84. "____ Sharkey"
85. Miss Merrill
87. Hangman's prop
89. Teaching unit
90. Like the Piper
92. Grating
94. "I cannot ____ lie"
96. Await
97. "On ____ day you can . . ."
99. Sincere
101. Falls behind
102. Dodges
104. Part of a greeting
105. Prefix for john or tasse
107. Gloom
110. Power agency
112. English author's initials
114. Clear, as an anchor
118. Stamp or riot
119. "____ three ships come sailing . . ."
121. Stupid
123. Caesar's friend Mark
124. Stage equipment
127. Menu distributor
129. Large piece of ice
130. Not a soul
131. Hideous
132. Neck part
133. Rant
134. Insects
135. Compass point
136. ____ by (make ends meet)

DOWN

1. "____ often walked down this street . . ."
2. Lois and lovers'
3. Like some swimming pools
4. Thus, usually in parentheses
5. "____ no questions, and I'll . . ."
6. Dancing method
7. Pan, for one
8. W.W. II area
9. French seasons
10. Repeats
11. Certain businessman or Indian
12. Guff
13. Regions
14. Gower's ex
15. Fools
16. People in general
17. Evergreen
18. QB's gains
22. Cádiz coin
24. John and Paul, e.g.
27. Bitter
31. Ex-Gov. Grasso
33. Off balance
35. Poetic works
37. Author Rebecca
39. Bide-____
41. Quantities: Abbr.
42. Application of paint
43. Laugh
44. Thing
46. Kind of signal
47. Better
49. Grovel
50. Element
51. ____ go (free)
55. Sculled
58. Ran the 440
60. "Jack Sprat could ____ . . ."
62. Malice
65. Doone or Luft
67. What a reporter needs
69. Cacophonous
71. Terrifying
73. Actress Lotte
75. Saga
76. Mr. Coward
79. Editor's mark
81. Confused
82. Bell sound
83. Comes to a close
84. Acct.
86. "Racketeer" Arthur
88. Palindromic man
89. Like the ten o'clock scholar
91. Benchley's "The ____"
93. Buttinsky
95. Legal degrees
98. Use
100. O'Neal of films
103. Terry's Lady
106. Prestige, in Hawaii
107. Mr. Duck
108. Tulle school
109. Kind of pigeon
111. Grippers
113. ____ through (skims)
115. Wheels, to Cicero
116. Awkward
117. Funeral ____
120. Stop!
122. Cry of discovery
123. Carpenter's tool
125. Wire: Abbr.
126. Blast producer
128. Rightful

Heady Thoughts by Louis Baron

Presented in a do-it-yourself fashion.

ACROSS

1. Foot bones
6. Bow or Schumann
11. Indian butters
15. Monthly pub.
18. Hill nymph
19. Boar heads
20. A Muse
21. _____ nerves
23. By failing, the exorcist _____
27. Essay name
28. Stage villain
29. Absorb, as knowledge
30. Frequent aftermath of applause
31. Direct
32. Painter Edouard
33. D'Oyly or à la
34. Hoax
35. Bombast
36. Interrogate
37. Be nepotic
38. Does liquidating mean _____?
46. Slide troughs
47. Cancel
48. Baker's aid
49. Bar order
50. Boiled
51. Verdon and namesakes
52. Made crow sounds
54. Suttee climax
55. Siamangs
56. Vague amount
57. Kind of surgeon
58. Arrowroot
59. Buying nylon seconds is _____
66. Negotiate a corner
67. White: Prefix
68. Cheerless
69. Using a broom is like _____
79. Name to remember
80. Connectives
81. Berserk
82. Tennis pro
83. Easy victory
84. Concord
86. Vacuum coffee maker
88. Local ordinance
89. Guevara
90. Resorts
91. Chinese province
92. What jingoists rattle
93. He who gets bad colds _____
99. Old Irish frocks
100. Barks
101. Actor Ray
102. Eateries
104. Not scantily
105. Chayefsky
107. O.S.S. successor
110. Filmed again
111. Sacred mount
112. Flat plinth
113. "Death in Venice" author
114. A calendar is mortal because _____
119. Royal headwear
120. Raises
121. Simulate
122. Writer Horatio
123. Writer Rand
124. Paris suburb
125. Take _____ (look)
126. Brant

DOWN

1. Babel's fiasco
2. Babylonian Hades
3. Balsam yield
4. Heroic tale
5. Amin
6. Red wine
7. Epee gambit
8. Lingo
9. On a pension: Abbr.
10. Gray color
11. Very much
12. Le _____, French port
13. Keep _____ mind
14. Alchemy gold
15. Eyelash beautifier
16. Spirit
17. Calabash
20. Channel swimmer of 1926
21. Sift
22. Charge
24. Provisions
25. Astolat lady
26. Where halos abound
32. Like a lion
33. Iron or double
34. Encrusted
35. Repeat tryout
36. Fed.
37. Cocktail hour
38. Sculpt
39. Seattle sound
40. Actor Paul and family
41. Garson
42. Humble
43. Have a fitting
44. Eagle's pad
45. Slender
46. Steep rock
51. Ganges tributary
52. Spring flowers
53. Burr
54. Word with tem or forma
56. Close-fitting
57. A life _____ and downs
58. Both: Prefix
60. Pay _____ mind (ignore)
61. Ending with fraud or flat
62. Ready for charity
63. Remnant
64. Extinct German bison
65. Torquemada prop
69. Kind of hare
70. Oahu "hi"
71. Glacial ridges
72. Mischief-maker
73. Wasp's pride
74. Australian cockatoo
75. Didn't _____ (was mum)
76. Man and Wight
77. Chicago hub
78. Reporter's offering
84. Armadillos
85. Willie of baseball
86. Like some fog
87. Noun-forming suffixes
88. Exchange, as words
90. Athens's old rival, to Greeks
91. Section of Queens, N.Y.
92. Rarely
94. Showy but cheap
95. _____ kind (unique)
96. Gospel songbook
97. Gets even
98. Won steadily
102. Old festival of Apollo
103. One of the Hebrides
104. Met roles
105. French verse piece
106. Palmer of golf
107. Hold's contents
108. Curare relatives
109. Previn or Maurois
110. Stoolie
111. Compass pts.
113. Kind of drama
115. Three: Prefix
116. Doctors' org.
117. Mr. Van Winkle
118. Santa's load

74 Who's What by Anthony B. Canning

Presenting double samples to be pinned down.

ACROSS

1. Harvey was one
7. Eye part
11. Insect feeler
15. Trim a photo
19. Miss Stritch
20. Song of joy
21. Arab chief
22. Verdi spectacular
23. Horror-movie reaction
24. Kublai Khan or Arpad
27. Bread-winner's verb
28. Defendant's answer
30. Stagger
31. Headgear for a horse
32. Cakes' partner
33. Roger Williams or Horatio Alger
35. Own up, for short
36. Strong brown papers
38. Orient
39. Soprano Frances
40. Golf-card listing
43. Tight overcoat
45. She, in Berlin
46. Big continent, to French
47. Concealment place
48. Marco Polo and Plutarch
53. Government
56. Kind of drum
57. Treat badly
58. Arab cloak
60. Observes
62. Relative of golly
63. Had a fitting
64. "For better ____ come"
67. City of East Germany
69. ____ of nowhere (appear suddenly)
70. Foe of "The Virginian"
71. Mr. Baba
72. Labor
74. P.M. periods
75. Site of an Octavian victory
76. ____-out
78. Gyroscope pioneer
81. Menuhin and Mozart

84. Aug. 31 or Sept. 30
85. Hitler's fly-away aide
86. At all
87. Novelist France
90. Boston summer time: Abbr.
91. "The ____ Animal"
93. Negative contraction
95. "Was it ____, or a waking dream?"
99. Wash
100. Like Marlowe or Nietzsche
102. Roosevelt-era initials
103. Clothing
106. Half of a Louvre name
107. Was sorry
108. G. & S. princess and others
109. Schliemann or J. J. Astor
112. Norse playwright and family
114. Teen-____
115. Yen
116. Kind of bearer
117. Make charges
118. Lawn need in the fall
119. Electric force
120. Star in Serpentis
121. One having wants

DOWN

1. Repair one's sewing
2. ____ la Real, Spanish city
3. Devoid of interest
4. Très ____
5. ____ jam (beset)
6. Charteris sleuth
7. Subordinate
8. Northwest fur-trade traveler
9. Poetic time of day
10. Morning rousers
11. Church plate

12. Chemical constituent
13. Mythical Norse survivor
14. Did investigative work
15. Sky Dog
16. Doone in-law
17. Early Danish family land
18. Reduce
25. Put in office
26. Sky Bear
29. "____ we forget . . ."
33. Cohered
34. Robert ____, jurist of 1700's
35. Dog biter
37. "____ a man in your future"
39. Terrier's native dale
40. Sax Rohmer or Nellie Bly

41. Freshens a room
42. Holds against
44. Curved molding
45. Fleet or Wall
46. Formal mall
47. Plautus or Sabatini
49. Going after fish
50. Asian weight
51. Macho
52. Early home of the Olympic games
54. ". . . under my feet ____ thy hat"
55. Asian aborigines
58. Case for papers, lunch, etc.
59. Flogged
61. Sterne's Tristram
63. Journey

65. Jannings and Ludwig
66. Potato
68. Turkish regiment
73. Greek peak
76. Bulwer-Lytton heroine
77. Miss Keaton of films
79. Leftover from yore
80. Hinds
82. Breathing sound
83. Fully
88. London gallery
89. Of a Roman poet's works
91. Japanese ship name
92. Glorified street
93. "____ long, long way . . ."
94. California peak
96. "Naturally!"

97. One-time stocking stuffer
98. Late Mideast leader
99. Metric measure
100. Used a gunsight
101. "____ little bit of heaven . . ."
103. "It's ____ cry"
104. Academic gown
105. Wagon-train journey
106. ____ Maggiore
108. Capri, for one
110. "That's ____, brother" (Wilson sign-off)
111. Pitcher Maglie
113. French wheat

75 Tourist's Nonguide by Bert Kruse

Some places one would be unlikely to visit.

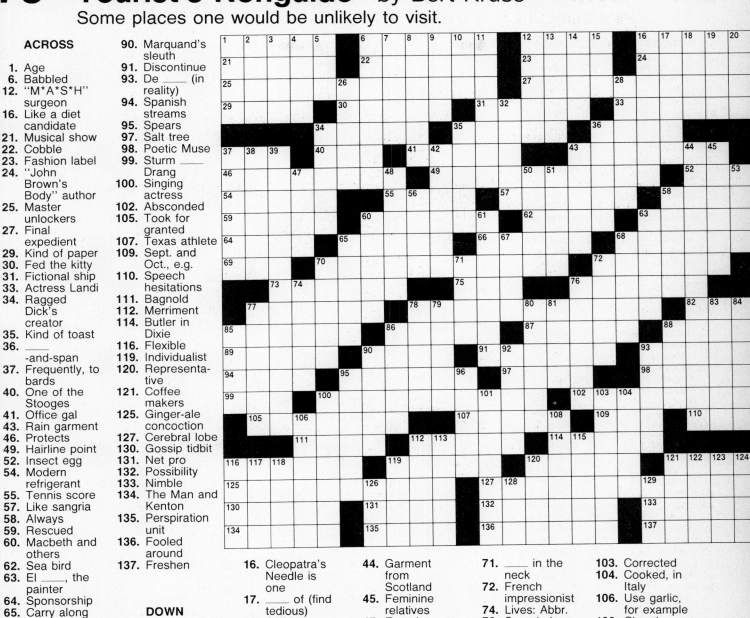

ACROSS

1. Age
6. Babbled
12. "M*A*S*H" surgeon
16. Like a diet candidate
21. Musical show
22. Cobble
23. Fashion label
24. "John Brown's Body" author
25. Master unlockers
27. Final expedient
29. Kind of paper
30. Fed the kitty
31. Fictional ship
33. Actress Landi
34. Ragged Dick's creator
35. Kind of toast
36. ____ -and-span
37. Frequently, to bards
40. One of the Stooges
41. Office gal
43. Rain garment
46. Protects
49. Hairline point
52. Insect egg
54. Modern refrigerant
55. Tennis score
57. Like sangria
58. Always
59. Rescued
60. Macbeth and others
62. Sea bird
63. El ____, the painter
64. Sponsorship
65. Carry along
66. Irritate
68. Addressed with respect
69. Bill
70. Obstructs a traffic flow
72. Ones of low mentality
73. Old French coins
75. Exist
76. Balzac
77. Stage speeches
78. Watch parts
82. Aves.
85. Mr. Dowd
86. Pooh's creator
87. Ameliorates
88. Chinese dynasty
89. Dams up

90. Marquand's sleuth
91. Discontinue
93. De ____ (in reality)
94. Spanish streams
95. Spears
97. Salt tree
98. Poetic Muse
99. Sturm ____ Drang
100. Singing actress
102. Absconded
105. Took for granted
107. Texas athlete
109. Sept. and Oct., e.g.
110. Speech hesitations
111. Bagnold
112. Merriment
114. Butler in Dixie
116. Flexible
119. Individualist
120. Representa- tive
121. Coffee makers
125. Ginger-ale concoction
127. Cerebral lobe
130. Gossip tidbit
131. Net pro
132. Possibility
133. Nimble
134. The Man and Kenton
135. Perspiration unit
136. Fooled around
137. Freshen

DOWN

1. Heretofore, heretofore
2. Dog breed, for short
3. Done's companion
4. Grass stem
5. Half a laugh
6. Having antlers
7. French income
8. Inquirers
9. Drove slantingly, as a nail
10. English isle
11. Come down
12. Off the cuff
13. Tropical vine
14. Medicate
15. Carney
16. Cleopatra's Needle is one
17. ____ of (find tedious)
18. Seth's son
19. Words from pulpits: Abbr.
20. Miss Kett
26. Eagle's weapon
28. Instant TV item
32. Uppity
34. Tack on
35. My, in Munich
36. After seis
37. Kind of printing
38. Cattle feed
39. Clubs in a certain golfer's bag
42. Conscience unit
43. Put in two cents worth

44. Garment from Scotland
45. Feminine relatives
47. Enemies
48. Former Indian titles
50. Cause, as havoc
51. Makes sport of waves
53. Walked heavily
56. Lion's-den visitor: Abbr.
58. Mistake
60. Lines up
61. Disfigured
63. Choppers
65. Having a trunk, as a tree
67. Capitol Hill opinion: Abbr.
68. Airs
70. Long-gone birds

71. ____ in the neck
72. French impressionist
74. Lives: Abbr.
76. Sounded reptilian
77. ____ day's work (routine)
78. Unexpected snag
79. Tonic plants
80. Annoy
81. Fence piece
83. Giggle
84. Headdresses
85. Beige
86. Organic unit
88. Injure
90. Like horses or lions
92. Planet
93. Banquet
95. City and speed ____
96. Be unselfish
100. Bill collectors
101. Large, fast bird

103. Corrected
104. Cooked, in Italy
106. Use garlic, for example
108. Church instruments
112. Morning quaff
113. Signed
115. From now on
116. Groups of words: Abbr.
117. Boor
118. "____ la Douce"
119. ____ majesty
120. Winged
121. Prod
122. Curb
123. Shade of green
124. Oodles
126. Seize
128. "____ 'nuf!"
129. Distant

76 Prosit by Brook H. Sandel

What some thespians might take at the happy hour.

ACROSS

1. One hooked on a habit
7. Light containers
12. Quantity of paper
16. Possess
19. One who gathers fuel logs
20. Of bees
21. Spanish river
22. Greek letter
23. Kind of goat or cat
24. Shakespearean pub actor
27. Radiation quantity
28. Miss Wray
30. Ardent
31. Grassland
32. Cocktail-hour entertainer
36. Harrison
38. South American rubber
42. City linked to St. Joan
43. Plague
44. Church recesses
45. Bay of Jamaica
48. He declined to drink to an Oscar
51. Soviet range
52. Drink
54. Cedar Rapids college
55. Charge with gas
56. Victim of a post-Saturday night hangover
60. Member of Cong.
62. Suffix for cyclo
63. Relative of "Occupied"
64. Eggs
65. Kind of phone or lith
66. Famous friend
67. Kind of row
68. Fair
69. Orgs.
74. Tournament drawings
75. French donkey
76. Arrested
77. Leaf holder
81. Aim
82. He likes it cool
86. Not too much or too little
88. Poetic contraction
89. Roman 56
90. Singer Petina
91. The spirit of a godfather
96. Empowered
98. "In ___ Spanish garden"
99. Like the musical Yankees
100. Come up anew
102. Tanager
103. Irish exclamation
104. Shake for an actor
108. Orchestra section: Abbr.
110. Empty, in Soho
112. Thou, in Nice
113. In the past
114. He likes his tonic
119. Gentle breeze
122. American cartoonist
123. Stead
124. Eatery
125. Bars, in law
126. Range of sight
127. Sand hill, in Brighton
128. Edible starches
129. ___ the occasion (came through)

DOWN

1. Medal or citation
2. Receiver of a gift
3. Doctrine
4. Swearing-in words
5. Wax: Prefix
6. Scene of a Nelson victory
7. Mineral compound
8. Wire-service initials
9. Auto's ID
10. Iranian religion
11. Obstacle
12. House of Lancaster's flower
13. Fade away
14. Holder for a hot dog
15. Grimace
16. Emblem of sovereignty
17. "You and ___ else?"
18. Kind of support often sued over
25. Go back on one's word
26. Harmony
29. Small space
33. ___ many words (less prolix)
34. Theological degree
35. Verb suffix
37. All-inclusive abbr.
39. What you wish upon
40. Right-hand page
41. Pale
43. South Pacific boat
44. Sleeve card
45. Spider crab
46. Milan's river
47. Biblical prophet
49. Suffix for hill
50. Grape-juice syrup
53. Drew forth
57. KO number
58. Sheep genus
59. June hero
60. Put on the market again
61. Something super, personally
65. Monastery resident
67. Dict. entry
68. U.S. air group
69. Nigerian native
70. Florida shell island
71. Tangle
72. Kol ___
73. Golfer Sam
74. Old World herb
77. Curtis ___, W.W. II air general
78. Stupid
79. One of low I.Q.
80. Optimistic
82. Hersholt of films
83. Scottish alder
84. "Thanks ___ much"
85. One who belittles
87. Kind of child or awful
88. Imitation gold
92. Transmitter: Abbr.
93. Extravagantly ornamented
94. Lottery highlight
95. Suffix with law or saw
97. Botanist Gray
101. Does a job on a coat
103. Palmer
104. Turkish rug
105. Western resort
106. Little dancer at the Chicago fair
107. Back of a body: Prefix
109. Narrated
111. Jar parts
114. Kind of boat
115. Formerly
116. Sunburn
117. Craving
118. Nontraditionalist
120. Within: Prefix
121. Liquid measures: Abbr.

77 Partners by Eugene T. Maleska

People who naturally complement each other.

ACROSS

1. The core of rapport
5. Proceeded with difficulty
10. Bryan vs. Darrow event
15. River in Maine
19. Tub plant
20. Harden
21. One of the Beatles
22. The Oder, to Czechs
23. Author joins Miss Sheridan
25. Comic-strip team
27. Soldier on the watch
28. Aquarium units
30. Actresses Keaton and Varsi
31. Hot-day quaffs
32. One of a memorable trio
33. Comedian Sahl
34. World's most popular sport
37. Ron of baseball
38. Smallest Great Lake
42. Russian range
43. Martha co-stars with Joel
46. Do sums
47. Whittle
48. Worshipful trio
49. "Cielo ____," Ponchielli aria
50. Marshal at Waterloo
51. English cathedral city
52. Italian actress co-stars with Vereen
56. Kind of bore
58. TV newscaster
60. "Mack the Knife" was his big hit
61. Esprit de corps
62. Modern crusader
63. ____-arms (soldier)
64. Frankish king
65. Becky Sharp's victim
67. Tuesday, in Tours
68. Ripped up
71. Harmonium
72. Rote teams up with a journalist
74. ____ Marshall, U.S. historian
75. Golfers' org.
76. Spring period
77. Ancient Mariner's offering
78. First killer
79. Where Aaron died
80. Louise co-stars with Rowlands
84. Italian poet
85. Couturier
87. Clear, as a tape
88. Worlds, to Parisians
89. Meal for Spectacular Bid
90. Dyers' devices
91. Kind of brain
92. Reach for the gold ring
95. "____ horse to . . ."
96. Procrasti-nators
100. Starr teams up with Carney
102. Lombardo forms a combo with Birch
104. Pierre's girlfriend
105. Unworldly
106. Relative on the mother's side
107. Fit to ____
108. Guazuti or guemal
109. Did an autumnal chore
110. Fountain drinks
111. Harsh sound

DOWN

1. Glaswegians' caps
2. Seed wings
3. Loser to Joe Louis in 1946
4. Dangerous part of a sea anemone
5. Card that takes a trick
6. Backbone of S.A.
7. Like Jekyll's personality
8. Bald eagle's cousin
9. Tooth tissue
10. Where the Hessians got a surprise
11. Yugoslav port, formerly Fiume: Var.
12. Readies the presses
13. Moslem chieftain
14. One of more than 7,000,000 Britishers
15. Animal bodies
16. Capital of South Yemen
17. Hudson Bay Indian
18. Dumbarton ____
24. Support is their forte
26. Kind of pool or tricks
29. Show-biz group
32. Deposit
33. Mack's vaudeville partner
34. Part of S.S.T.
35. Papal cape
36. Grant co-stars with Cooper
37. More perspicacious
39. Sally joins George
40. Paragon
41. Force once linked to hypnosis
43. Not so easy to find
44. Figure in the red
45. Some of the Feds
48. Tightwad's wad
52. Thick woolen cloth
53. Take ____ (accept a challenge)
54. ____ Devi, Indian peak
55. Tub feature
56. Safari headgear
57. Crocus or gladiolus
59. Hacienda hall
61. Actress Oberon
63. Mediter-ranean island
64. External nodule
65. Last year's frosh
66. Grain disease
67. Winged talker
68. Part of a cactus
69. Typewriter type
70. Citizens of Aalborg
72. Clark and Rockwell
73. Mother Hubbard, e.g.
76. Member of the audience
78. Item named for Reggie Jackson
80. Regal headwear
81. Annulled
82. Book by Stowe
83. Sites for some sales
84. Catfish
86. What drugstore cowboys do
88. Writer A. A. and family
90. Height for a kite
91. ____ retreat (scram)
92. "Story of ____ Boy"
93. Identical
94. ____-dieu (kneeling bench)
95. Singer "at heaven's gate"
96. Pair
97. "Fine women ____ crazy salad": Yeats
98. These cross the bar
99. Fields of "Rippling Rhythm"
101. Venus or Minerva
103. Numero ____

78 Out of the Mothballs by George Madrid

And ready to be taken places.

ACROSS

1. Solzhenit-zyn's Archipelago
6. Beer containers: Abbr.
9. Tries
14. Kind of stress
18. For any reason
19. Old power agency
20. No ifs, ands ____
22. Asian mongoose
23. Prepares to go to the opera
26. Time of day
27. Type of can
28. North or South
29. Completely subdued
31. Boring
32. Prosperous one
34. Inter-school org.
35. Greek marketplace
38. Breather for a fish
39. As ____ can be (spiteful)
43. Changes a cribbage score
45. Fat movie part
46. Resident: Suffix
47. Waxed
49. School-reunion event
51. Number ending
53. ____ avion
54. King of Israel
55. Sounds in a library
56. Swedish measure
57. Avoids
59. Indian lutes
61. Placed on Elba
63. Sicilian resort
64. Musical ending
65. Jeeves or Ruggles
71. Jason's ship
72. King before 54 Across
73. Drench
74. Chat
76. Army release, in England
78. Explosive
79. High note
82. Jai ____
83. Gone by
85. Time period
86. Is diplomatic
89. Auto mishap
90. Drag
91. Wall St. shares, à la "Variety"
93. Scarlet letter, for one
94. ____ water (crash-land a plane)
96. Old World herb
97. Goose genus
98. Row
99. Defeated
101. Assn.
102. Item of formal dress
107. Not coy, old style
109. Bear, in Madrid
112. Et ____
113. Outfit for a fancy occasion
116. Army rank: Abbr.
117. Makes joyful
118. ____ Tse-tung
119. Opera by Bellini
120. Skating move
121. Meeting place
122. After dees
123. A.k.a. Clemens

DOWN

1. Infatuated
2. Western Indians
3. Wooden strip
4. Hirt and Unser
5. Dressy clothes
6. Pitching mistake
7. ____-mutton
8. Medieval impost
9. Distress signal
10. Of a clannish group
11. Red as ____
12. Half a Danube city
13. Stammer, old style
14. Kind of special clothes
15. Intensive suffix
16. Declare
17. Writer Thomas
21. "Faerie Queene" poet and family
24. Prepare, as plans
25. Literary caricatures
30. Trapezist's insurance
31. Primping
33. Ones parading their wardrobes
35. Curve
36. Colloids
37. Colorful fish
39. Items for a man drinking at a ball
40. One ____ time
41. Wartime fleet
42. Deep-water fish
44. Play for time
45. Garment for a younger child
48. Neighbor of Ill.
50. Robt. ____
52. Over or jury
58. Nautical dir.
60. Sherbets' relatives
62. Greek portico
65. Locked up, in Leeds
66. Opera by Verdi
67. Pub order
68. Appoint
69. Scads
70. Stringed instruments
74. Bounder
75. Item removed on entry into 77 Down
77. Household fixture
80. Falls behind
81. Summit
84. Baby's syllable
87. Hollywood quest
88. Sailor
92. Trademark of Charo or Liberace
95. Hack
96. Explorer William and family
99. Partner of itty
100. Mother of Perseus
101. Fall mo.
102. Long account
103. Holly
104. Wrinkle
105. Whip mark
106. Big cheese in old Moscow
108. Transistors: Abbr.
109. Gumbo vegetable
110. Truck, for short
111. Port in Algeria
114. Maker: Suffix
115. Nonpurple creature

79 Queries by H. Hastings Reddall

Tourists often have to ask for help.

ACROSS

1. Vanishing bag carriers
8. Closely knit group
15. Make a proposal
22. Vast
23. Beach damage
24. Hell and hair
25. Heavy grayish-white metal
26. Easing, as thirst
27. West Indian half-breeds
28. Rabbit ____
29. Alcohol problem: Abbr.
31. Singer Ed
32. Mr. Arden
34. Educ. group
35. Thorough-fares: Abbr.
36. Overfill
37. Road covering
38. Anoint, old style
39. Metric measures: Abbr.
40. German's query abroad
44. Moroccan city
47. Bellow
48. River to the Baltic
49. Climbing plant
52. Irritated
53. Kind of sized
54. Languishing one
56. Locker-room V.I.P.
58. Ozone
59. Put into order
60. Truck rigs
61. Nominal military rank: Abbr.
62. Prefix for nitrotoluene
63. Crowded
65. Stalin-era name
66. Delete
67. Friend of Uncle Tom
68. In the rear
69. Knight's enterprise
70. Snake of India
71. Beverages
72. American's query abroad
76. ____-turner (absorbing book)
79. Legal documents
80. Endeavors
81. Dreaded
85. Spring month: Abbr.
86. Lucky ____ of flying fame
87. Desolate places

88. Realty sign
89. New Deal agency
90. Egyptian goddess
91. Fishing reels
92. Goes amiss
93. Gun for a hit man
94. Contributes
96. Rent
97. ____-bang
98. Duchin, to friends
99. British spy of the Revolution
100. Flying prefix
101. Kind of sprout or curd
102. Long-legged bird
103. Frenchman's query abroad
109. Taxi
110. At full speed
111. In addition
112. Like under one's feet
113. Strike
116. Boat propeller
117. Spikelike flower cluster
118. Home for some owls
119. Discontinued draft: Abbr.
120. He fiddled
121. Small pitcher
123. Film ingredient
126. Fatima was one
128. Presiding at the bar
129. Scarlet
130. Windflower
131. Phoenician goddess
132. Infinite
133. Acts of retribution

DOWN

1. On the ____ (helpless)
2. Notoriety
3. Darlings
4. Felines
5. Black bird
6. Prolific ode writer
7. Dispersing
8. These, in France
9. Sooner ____
10. Unanimously
11. Gravel ridges
12. Reformer Jacob
13. Subatomic unit
14. Produce
15. Mosaic gold
16. It runs hot and cold
17. "____ or cut bait"
18. Superlative suffix

19. Charmed once more
20. Oak, linden et al.
21. Pile-on mount
30. Kind of hand or rate
33. ____-do-well
36. Harbor city: Abbr.
38. Mosquito genus
39. Roman 202
40. Downcast
41. Outdoor wear
42. Old district of Asia Minor
43. Drudge
44. Lariat
45. Ram constellation
46. Visorless cap
50. Effrontery
51. Melodies
53. Predecessor of pound foolish
54. In itself
55. Mimes
56. Way to the lonesome pine
57. ____ body (band of nerve fibers)

59. Spanish painter
60. Oozes
61. Boasts
64. Ancient Persian
65. Like divas of yore
66. Sea eagles
69. Tobacco chews
70. Actor Dullea et al.
71. Cries of surprise
73. Birdlife of a region
74. Money unit of Norway
75. Weights of India
76. Bearlike animal
77. Its strings are proverbial
78. Forebear
82. Stormed
83. Flush with success
84. Prevent from action
86. Unit of capacity
87. Cat call
88. Monk of the Assisi order

91. Argentine dictator
92. African antelopes
95. OPEC nation resident
96. Perform a séance feat
97. Red or Black
98. Dance step
100. Moslem call to prayer
101. Charlotte, Emily and family
102. Soundness of mind
104. Moan and groan
105. Come into view
106. Of a governing unit
107. Animal provisions
108. Poisonous gas
109. Troubles
113. Leander's friend et al.
114. Miss Bordoni
115. Carries
116. Eight: Prefix
117. Moslem ruler
118. Knee or South

120. "A rose by any other ____ . . ."
122. Oklahoma city
124. "Yes I ____"
125. Speech pauses
127. Precious stone

80 Going Downhill by Tap Osborn

It isn't too easy a trip.

ACROSS

1. Law-and-order band
6. Hiatus
11. Extract metal
16. Ex-Yankee pitcher Eddie
21. Reader of "Variety"
22. Do a tailoring job
23. ____ Rica
24. Obliterate
25. Start of a verse
29. Item for a lachrymatory
30. Standish
31. Beneath, in Germany
32. Hoopsters
33. Provoke
34. Andretti's forte
35. Admire oneself in the mirror
36. Bequeath
37. Greek letters
38. Writer Leon
39. "Phalarope" author
40. Second line of verse
50. African or shrinking
51. Black birds
52. Excavating aid
53. Knockdown start
54. In reserve
55. Prepare nutmeg
56. Soho chap
58. Ship's pole
60. Seat for Goren
61. Wastelands
62. In need of sandblasting
63. Most devious
64. River of Sardinia
65. Lily plant
66. Tatar, for one
67. Third line of verse
75. Arose
76. Globule
77. Sections
78. Fourteenth President
79. Bracelet attachment
81. Potato
82. Sunnybrook, for one
86. Pyle
87. Illegal lobster
88. Rank
89. Chrysalises
90. Little Edward
91. Undressed hide
92. Danish measure
93. Verbal contraction
94. Fourth line of verse
102. Nostrils
103. Worldwide cartel
104. Port sight
105. Cartographer
107. Furze
108. Whack
110. Glasgow headgear
113. "Inside ____"
114. Mr. Chips
115. British P.M.
116. Stubborn one
117. Last line of verse
121. French military force
122. Oily hydrocarbon
123. Recede
124. Zodiac sign
125. Loved ones
126. Collar supports
127. Rental sign
128. Thoreau

DOWN

1. Singer Page
2. Earth pigment
3. Swiss ____
4. Imitate Icarus
5. Work unit
6. Most scrawny
7. Right or obtuse
8. Increased
9. Knighted ones
10. Wine: Prefix
11. Part of an act
12. "Hostess with the ____"
13. Ruhr city
14. Purse material: Abbr.
15. Peking pagoda
16. Mideast trouble spot
17. Herb for Italian cuisine
18. Actress Debra
19. "He's ____ card": Dryden
20. Hamilton bills
26. Give, as knowledge
27. Groom a horse
28. George C. of Hollywood
34. Precipitous
35. What a doctor feels
36. Italian poet
37. Brilliance
39. Little finger
40. Profess
41. Baseball team
42. Polka ____
43. Home-run champ and family
44. ". . . as a bug ____"
45. Insect eggs
46. Energy source
47. Precede
48. Harmony
49. Irritate
55. "The ____ Show"
56. Flock
57. In ____ of (replacing)
58. Slovenly ones
59. Like Cape Cod woods
61. Canine disease
62. Sparkle
63. Vilify
64. ____ pie
65. Prevent
67. Poplars
68. Flowering bush
69. Faddish
70. Mata ____
71. Steel beam
72. Take up rope slack
73. Rounding out
74. Requirement
79. IOU's
80. Southwestern Indian
81. Final stage: Prefix
82. Frenzy
83. Mime
84. Ayn or Sally
85. Shea players
87. Killy, for one
88. Frothy stage offering
89. Phoebe
93. Twist violently
95. Having full control
96. Shallow serving dishes
97. Inexperienced
98. Time between A.M. and P.M.
99. Common ankle injuries
100. Samples
101. Bit of name-calling
105. Razor-billed auk
106. Emanation
107. Mrs. Meir
108. Of an ecological period
109. Dull finish
110. City on the Po
111. Birch tree
112. Littered
113. "Holy smokes!"
114. Word to a child
115. Tramp
116. Slue
118. U.S. soldiers
119. Prosperous
120. Word of disgust

81 Limited Fare by Mary Russ

But more varied than meat and potatoes.

ACROSS

1. N.Y.C. transit line
4. Acting award
8. Big D
14. Kind of cade or home
19. Rowing need
20. Unhappy word
21. Diacritical mark
22. Writer St. Johns
23. Certain islands' number
25. Chancel seat
26. Jeans' material
27. Dracula et al.
28. Squeal
30. Redhead
32. They go with kisses
33. Target of Lenin
37. Long times
38. News for little boy blue
42. "Fe, fi, fo, ____"
45. Code word for A
46. Guthrie
47. Algerian author of "Nedjma"
49. Boxer's features, at times
56. W.W. II alliance
57. Actress Signe
58. Card game
59. Like a straw to a drowning man
62. ". . . ____ I saw Elba"
63. Yeast acids: Abbr.
64. Renounce
66. At the peak of a slow burn
71. Lanky person
75. P.I. timber tree
76. Whittle down
77. Actress Joanne
78. Greenbacks
81. What charity does at home
83. Chinese spirit
85. Sandy ridges
86. Indistinguishable
90. Crush
93. Wine: Prefix
94. Dog-headed ape
95. N.Y. time
96. Certain walrus's concern
103. Where to buy baloney
104. Art devotee
105. After juillet
107. Flimsy paper
112. After part or mart
113. Bees' harvest
115. Moonshine
116. Sarcastic
119. Eellike
121. ____ tube
122. Busy N.J. airport
123. Mrs. Chaplin
124. Soak flax
125. Very small
126. "____ Delight"
127. Near, to poets
128. Type of dye

DOWN

1. Bungle
2. Elephant driver
3. Place for fodder
4. Kiln
5. Rocket launching
6. Fleming
7. Apocrypha book
8. Actor Hoffman
9. Spirit, in France
10. Law degree
11. Secular
12. Assembly hall
13. Rec-room equipment
14. Raphael subject
15. "Golden Boy" author
16. Omar product
17. Hodgepodge
18. Highway access
24. Opens
29. Uris hero
31. Calhoun
34. Shady place
35. Partners of fits
36. Number of sheets to the wind
39. Muse of history
40. High note
41. Heart
42. Prix ____
43. États-____
44. Disorder
48. Biblical spy
49. Chastity's mother
50. Swiss river
51. ____ to (accustomed)
52. Plant sheath
53. The moon does it
54. One of a Latin trio
55. Indian wheat
60. Kind of shine or burn
61. Work unit
64. Roman rooms
65. Machine guns
67. Sinus cavities
68. Sow, in Bonn
69. Comet trail
70. California oil town
71. Dressing flavor
72. Singer Adams
73. Kind of code
74. Convent dwellers
76. Tea types
78. ____ face (be humiliated)
79. Abbrs. on formal letters
80. Tense
81. Spree
82. Town, to a German
83. "____ soit qui . . ."
84. Popeye's favorite
87. One kind of story
88. Meadow
89. Becoming active
91. Actor's chew
92. Dutch painter
97. Brief beachwear
98. Boondocks
99. Cry of surprise
100. Wrestling hold
101. Leakage, in Spain
102. Spanish philosopher
103. Gross component
106. "____ Remember"
107. News item
108. "____ but the brave . . ."
109. Bulwer-Lytton heroine
110. Angry
111. "____ lay me down to sleep"
114. Greenland base
117. Medieval sailing ship
118. Relative of 1 Across
120. French jurisprudence

82 Tennis Shots by William Lutwiniak

Most of them going out of bounds.

ACROSS

1. To-dos
6. Prohibition
10. Bard's instrument
14. Flood
19. Of a Cretan age
21. "I met ____ with . . ."
22. Spanish month
24. Soft-pedaled
25. Touch off
26. Caroled
27. In a vertical position
28. Mr. Heep
29. Deuce
33. Take a stab at
34. A crowd, in Bonn
35. Meat cuts
36. Be in tumult
37. River duck
38. Social units
39. Grass-hoppers
43. Wife of Saturn
46. Turncoat
47. River of Russia
48. Cone producer
49. Teachers' org.
50. Singles
57. Peculiarity
58. Liter or meter
59. Panache
60. Writer Nin
61. Colleen's land
62. One-time girl
64. British guns
65. In a ____ (hurting)
66. Bursa
67. Attire
68. Golden
69. Sere region of Asia
70. Service aces
78. Singer Nancy
79. Greets
80. Textile fiber
81. Yalie
82. Ardent
85. Expenses
86. Pixilated
88. Noggin
89. Outlander
90. Stettin's river
91. Of flight: Prefix
92. Former pact
93. Doubles
99. Pindar reading matter

100. Honor cards
101. Revered one
102. Ending for meth or but
103. Fruit drink
104. Downstairs people
107. Abalone product
109. Defrost
110. Thine, to Pierre
111. Flexible branch
112. Ovid's boy
113. Balaam's mount
116. Foot faults
122. Fad
123. Similar
124. Situation
125. Mourn
126. Bring together
127. Get on, timewise
128. German article
129. Rated
130. Harass
131. Orch. offerings
132. Achievement
133. Laborers

DOWN

1. Afflicted
2. Stingy
3. Kind of tube or circle
4. Turbid
5. Japanese statesman
6. Curtain dangler
7. Fine violin
8. Seat in a Paris park
9. Impolite
10. Antenna hookup
11. Removes a diaper
12. Youthful time
13. Part of Q.E.D.
14. Smeared
15. Used a blender
16. Adjective ending
17. Ship wood
18. Anglo-Saxon letter
20. F.D.R. program
23. Czar's secret police

30. Lady with a lyre
31. Amundsen
32. Lotus-____
37. Weight allowance
38. Actress Jeanne
39. Potters' needs
40. Relative
41. Girl's name
42. Impertinent
43. Beseech
44. Outcast
45. Hard to find
47. Annapolis inst.
48. German physicist
51. Hurry
52. Ballroom dance
53. Source of arrow poison
54. Of oil

55. Words to a black sheep
56. Of Hindi, Urdu, etc.
62. Sloshed through
63. Spheres
64. Singer Ives and others
65. Golfer Jones
67. Twins of the sky
68. "Peer Gynt" girl
69. Insect
71. "Boléro" man
72. ____ scholar
73. Desert stopovers
74. Thrusting sword
75. Indian state on the Arabian Sea
76. Gladdened
77. Full of chinks

82. Portuguese folk songs
83. Avoid adroitly
84. More mature
85. Sheepfolds
86. English novelist
87. Viva-voce
88. Mars and Jupiter, to Livy
91. Spoke to
92. Diving duck
94. Dugout
95. Oral, in zoology
96. Place for a bust
97. Region of Africa
98. Irate
105. Grip
106. Finally
107. Small change
108. European capital

109. Like some mattresses
111. Take pen in hand
112. Inclined
113. Blazing
114. "____ evil"
115. Against-Thebes number
116. Kudos
117. Literary oddments
118. Neighbor of Y.T.
119. English painter
120. Fairway hazard
121. Williams and Kennedy
122. Fairy queen

83 Field Trip by Ruth W. Smith

Some specimens that might be encountered.

ACROSS

1. Lament
7. Extol
11. Abetted
17. Stir up
18. Like April weather
19. On land
20. Fashion plate
22. Stand to _____ (be obvious)
23. Gentleman, in Baden
24. Fork part
25. Beat at contract bridge
27. Flagmaker
28. Aims
31. Pitch
33. Certain get-together
36. Unwelcome dice throw
41. Musical deficiency
42. Form of poetry
43. Astronaut's wear
44. Knead, old style
45. Soft mineral
48. Ripped
49. "Luck be _____ tonight"
50. _____ in the back
52. Syrup
54. Rock, to a Scotsman
55. Orbital point
57. Chief of a tribe
59. Herb
61. River to the Rhine
63. George Eliot's Adam
67. Clothes or hair
68. Fountain or cracker
69. Burn
71. "_____ them eat cake"
72. Singer often toasted
73. Biblical city
74. Tillie of the comics
76. Government emblem
78. Dream of a sort
81. Start the defense at bridge
82. "To sleep: perchance _____"
83. Biblical brother
86. Initials on a letter from abroad
88. Fencing sword
89. Verb-forming suffix
93. Chess maneuver
95. Mechanic
99. Construct again
100. Place for money
101. Kind of job or track
102. Declaims
103. Volts' relatives: Abbr.
104. Sounded a car horn

DOWN

1. One of the musical B's
2. First name in detective fiction
3. "Wuthering Heights" backdrop
4. Offense
5. Residue
6. Born
7. Daft
8. "_____ moi . . ."
9. Downs' partners
10. Coloring matters
11. Hungarian composer
12. Peer Gynt's mother
13. Expert on roast pig
14. Shoshonean people
15. God of love
16. Thieves' places
18. Hair or T
21. Bustle
26. Expunge
29. Falling-out
30. Accessory at Ascot
32. Emissary
33. Agnès and Jeanne: Abbr.
34. _____ at windmills
35. Pilaster
36. Husband or wife
37. Averages
38. Mongol dynasty
39. Idea, in Platonism
40. Farm unit
42. Ordinal ending
46. Cabin material
47. Fine violin
51. Game accessory
53. Like a hollow stone
54. Cover
56. John Silver, for one
58. Small: Suffix
59. Uncle Remus relative
60. Wing, in Lille
62. Snead or Levenson
64. Singer Fitzgerald
65. Antelope's playmate
66. Being, in Cannes
67. Harm: Abbr.
68. Plants
70. Church court
75. Huge
77. Fries
78. Prickly pears
79. That is: Lat.
80. Mastery, in Scotland
82. Get ready to drive
83. Soil: Prefix
84. Boxer Max
85. Jane Austen novel
87. Org. for entertainers
90. Ricochet
91. Yield
92. Scrutinized
94. Presidential nickname
96. Aries
97. Playing marble
98. "_____ for my master . . ."

84 Heavy Going by Hume R. Craft
Luckily, the puzzle itself doesn't have to be lifted.

ACROSS

1. Miners' stakeouts
7. Part of Q.E.D.
11. Jewish month
15. Inventor Nikola
20. Jewish holiday bread
21. Magnet
23. Doorway
24. Front: Prefix
25. Cave men's weapons
26. Activating substance
27. N.Y.C. building
28. Poker stake
30. "____ Rheingold"
31. British gun
33. Egg drink
34. Acts of compassion
36. Fratricide victim
38. Assyrian god
40. Western sight
41. Heritage sources
43. Building-ceremony V.I.P.
45. Mountain-descent maneuver
48. Darjeeling
49. Giant armadillo
51. Lip-____
52. Old English letters
53. Spanish gold
55. One who works with granite
58. Throw out
59. Wernher ____ Braun
60. Something unique
61. Actress Sandra
62. Dine
65. 1,000 meters, for short
66. French season
67. Alice ____ Miller
68. Desirable cards
70. Baseball statistic: Abbr.
71. Freshwater fish
74. Cupid
75. Kind of face
77. ____ up (cinches)
78. Charged atoms
79. Mother or ladder
80. Stylish
81. Selected

83. Card game
84. Symbolic rings found in Puerto Rico
88. Current unit, for short
89. Gave a hint to
90. Road sign
91. College degree
92. Airport closer
93. Holmesian clue
94. Stone Age hero of comics
95. Late N.Y. restaurateur
96. Trump ace, in gleek
97. Honshu town
98. U.S. architect and family
103. Olive yield
104. Pindaric pieces
105. Anonymous Richard's kin
106. Lyric poem
107. Author Fleming
109. Star in Taurus
111. Footing pieces for lower walls
114. Where Stones River is
117. Columbo
118. Stringed instruments
119. Blacksmith's medium
120. Hides away
124. Inner: Prefix
125. Fairy
126. Pub order
127. Words specifying a date
128. Silkworm
129. Makes amends
131. Plant found on rocks
136. Swimming
138. Tendons
139. Poison antidote of old
140. Female adviser
141. Pours
142. Movie stages
143. "____ -boom-bah!"
144. Radio operator

DOWN

1. Attractive quality
2. Certain corporal
3. Wedding site
4. ____ -de-France
5. Glacial deposit
6. Forage herbs
7. Other
8. Twaddle
9. Commotion
10. It's often legal
11. Greek letters
12. Smoked salmon
13. French article
14. Not quite as tart
15. Pulled apart
16. Work unit
17. Ontario battle site in 1813
18. Woolly
19. Fermentation product
22. Engraved prehistoric rocks
23. Noblewomen
29. Lao-____
32. Wine cask
35. Highest points
36. Used up
37. Scarves
38. Flower
39. Danish glottal stop
40. Leo's hair
42. Resembling a boulder
44. Undergo decline, as a disease
45. Exudes fumes
46. Ticket word
47. Alchemist's quest
50. Male ant
54. Printing process, for short
56. Travel agent's offerings
57. River in Germany
63. Metric unit
64. Roofing material
67. Hollow
68. Word of assent
69. Finishing stroke
72. Farm animal
73. Cargo
74. At the summit
75. Degree in logic
76. Whetting devices
79. Emporium
80. Early street pavings
81. Presidential monogram
82. British ship initials
83. Higher: Abbr.
84. Sections of fired rock
85. Roman 202
86. Man of words
87. Kind of buckler
89. Landlocked
90. Fitted with footwear
94. Is obligated
95. Facing a glacier
99. Bucks' consorts
100. Molar menders
101. Graf ____
102. Of the Chinese: Prefix
108. Actress Rutherford
110. Foliage
111. Kind of swimming stroke
112. Mame, for one
113. Possessive
115. Builds
116. Old draft syst.
121. Audible
122. Correspondent Pyle
123. Shankar's instrument
125. Benches
126. Connectives
127. Animals
130. Thread: Prefix
132. Kind of dance
133. Kind of meal
134. Louis XIV, e.g.
135. Light-switch words
137. Hat gallonage

85 Supermarket by Herb Risteen

Some offerings of magnitude.

ACROSS

1. Miss West
4. _____-de-sac
7. Church section
11. Machine part
14. Embraces
17. Tower
18. Roman rooms
20. Wild area near Chesapeake Bay
23. Fishline dispensers
24. Wipe out
25. Adjusts
26. Between sum and fui
27. Boot-camp trainee
29. Separated
30. Allurer
31. Crepe de _____
32. Scenic U.S. range
41. Make unnecessary
42. Expels
43. Unknown John
44. Like some women's ears
45. Holds a meeting
46. Playing card
48. Vessel: Abbr.
49. Asian wild goats
51. Ry. stop
52. Bristles
55. Lahore garb
56. Sprinkle around
60. Siouan Indian
61. Rare violin
62. Adriatic port
63. Australia's coral breakwater
68. Carnival attractions
69. Buenos _____
70. Flowering plant
72. Swamp
74. Taciturn one
78. Companion of shorn
79. Actress Debra
80. Aussie animal
81. Russian V.I.P. and a Fitzgerald novel
85. Words of approval
86. Water bird
87. Pour at a party
88. Iniquity's place
89. Sweet _____
90. _____ Juana
91. Kobe coin

DOWN

1. Linear unit
2. Yule-log leavings
3. Fencing weapons
4. Stray dogs
5. Treat
6. Pasture
7. Tatar or Mongol
8. Group of good guys
9. Identical
10. Period
11. Stick one's neck out
12. Took sight
13. Treasure hunters' needs
15. Flirt
16. Sound system
18. Oblique
19. _____ day (pill-taking routine)
21. Consummate a toast
22. Rabbit furs
27. "_____ Roberts"
28. Equipped
29. _____ off (isolates)
30. Ancient spice
31. Expenses
32. Pol. party
33. Baseball abbr.
34. Time of day
35. _____ complaint (protests publicly)
36. Japanese admiral of W.W. II
37. U.S. naturalist
38. Cretan peak
39. Be off guard
40. Bishopric
46. Story connectors
47. Kind of noster
49. Pastries
50. Person from Jiddah
51. Frolics
52. Fixed, in the backwoods
53. Biblical verb ending
54. Part of Italy's anatomy
55. Madame de _____
56. Prepares a martini
57. Part of an African fly
58. Summer, in Soissons
59. Sports official
61. Sitting
64. Kind of image
65. Rebellious ones
66. Peep show
67. Lariats
70. Topic
71. Corroded
72. _____ Carta
73. Monsters
74. France has an azure one
75. Endures
76. American playwright
77. Yucatán Indian
78. Mining nail
79. Goriot or Marquette
80. Pepper shrub
82. Wise to
83. Hanoi holiday
84. Gypsy horse

86 Belabored Bard by Henry Hook

Some titles Shakespeare never thought of.

ACROSS

1. Mrs. Martin Johnson
4. "How ____ the little busy bee . . ."
8. Creator of Mickey
12. "____ Fox," Broadway play
15. Season for a Seine outing
18. Tennessee athlete
19. Part of U.S.A.
20. Diva's offering
21. College period
23. It's grounded Down Under
24. "Guys and Dolls"
27. Orders back
29. Cargoes: Abbr.
30. Receptacles
31. Clatter
32. Emulates Mark Spitz
33. Porter et al.
35. As strong ____ ox
37. Desserts
38. Singer Tennille
39. Welk's starting words
40. Arsenic's old partner
42. Silverman's old network
44. "The Barber of Seville"
50. Pungent, old style
51. Sci. course
52. Prefix for gram or cure
53. Czarist cavalryman
56. Invigorate
58. Give a new ____ (vary)
61. Painter Joan
62. "I ____ war": F.D.R.
63. Nickel or dime
64. Wyatt and family
67. "____ Sylphides"
68. Mr. Brummell
71. Not mine alone
72. Shindigs
73. Wisecrack
74. "Moby Dick"
80. King, to the French
81. Red hue
82. Club jack, in a way
83. Matchless type
84. Kipling hero
85. Gulliver's creator
86. Without, to Pierre
87. Dressmaker's dummy
90. Words of understanding
92. Old salts
94. Bird in a French song
98. Delivered
101. Naval branch: Abbr.
102. Has tea
103. Word of endearment
104. "The Sting"
110. F.D.R.'s Blue Eagle
111. Eight: Prefix
112. German song
113. Noble, to Nietzsche
114. 1970 Newman-Woodward film
117. Arizona Indian
119. Pond creatures
121. Blackbird
122. Dome athlete
124. Mink or nutria
126. Western state: Abbr.
127. They overcharge
129. "Through the Looking Glass"
133. Milne and others
134. Almost half a day
135. Western lake
136. Battle vehicle
137. Roman 1150
138. No seats
139. Harem room
140. Miss Ferber
141. Goddess of hope
142. Kind of jacker or line

DOWN

1. Exaggerate
2. "There must be ____ who are not liars": Maugham
3. Coat with a light metal
4. Condemns
5. "Bloomin' idol made ____"
6. Gumshoes
7. Initials for Elizabeth
8. Duck, sometimes
9. Came up
10. ____ Fail
11. A no-no
12. ____ precedent
13. Between K and O
14. Bear young
15. Principle
16. Annoy
17. Ocean birds
21. Well-known boulevard
22. Imperturbability
25. Solitary
26. Garden plant
28. In the center of
33. French nobleman
34. Enter quietly
36. Western org.
39. Flabbergast
41. Spartan king
43. Family members: Abbr.
45. Forsyte, e.g.
46. ____ pricing
47. Rather recent
48. Got a TD or HR
49. Snow-rain-heat ignorer
54. New Orleans cooking style
55. Dutch playwright
57. Sumac genus
58. Rich pastry
59. Homes on the reservation
60. Mountain lakes
63. Hill with one steep side
65. Footlike part
66. Compass point
68. Clara Peggotty's husband
69. Abélard's friend, in Soho
70. Food
71. "Welcome, ____!": James Joyce
72. Bewilders
75. Handy and Fields
76. Cut down
77. Beard of grain
78. Slowly, in music
79. Where the heart is
86. "____ Solomon"
87. Hit a pop-up
88. "____, sorry!"
89. Commuter's kind of hour
91. Governor of a people
93. Cautioner's word
94. Sackcloth's partner
95. ". . . like ____ of those who wake"
96. Bathroom fixture
97. On and on
99. Ended, to a poet
100. Mormon's last stop
105. Modern bikes
106. With unfriendliness
107. Home of the Grapefruit League
108. A Stockton alternative
109. Stink
114. Light-bulb units
115. Name in a Poe title
116. User of a pad
118. Kind of glasses or hat
120. Brutus was the noblest one
121. Conceals
123. Washout football score
125. "Sock it ____"
127. Suds maker
128. French river
130. Child's pie filling
131. G-man
132. Just claims: Abbr.

87 Title Tampering by A. J. Santora
Some variations on well-known works.

ACROSS

1. Confusion
6. Islands off Ireland
10. Far down, in poems
15. Heart, lungs, etc.
21. An agent for Murder, Inc.?
24. Surround closely
25. Basset's hereafter
26. Prefer
27. "Two Cities of a ___"
28. Slim, as a chance
29. Unit of bitters
31. Irish patriot
32. Startle
34. ___ Haute
36. Overdue balance
38. Cupid
41. Ending for huck
42. King, in Madrid
43. Kind of football pass
45. How Rome wasn't built
47. Transaction
49. Part of a harness
50. Pelion's partner
54. Pester
55. Tribulation's partner
57. ___ David
59. Adversaries
60. Georgia senator
61. Nonprofessionals
62. Literary form
63. Waste allowance
64. Padded shoulders?
69. Subway for Pierre
70. Break or cake
71. Roll or pie
72. More optimistic
73. Casual
75. Boston puckster
76. Gave the heave-ho
77. Like a faulty crystal ball
78. Bil of puppetry
79. Chinese nut
81. Hunter of English lore

82. Embellishment on an old factory?
88. Riga citizen
89. Refuse
90. Strain, as food
91. Galleries for concerts
92. Oil cartel
93. Merchant fleet
95. Riddle
96. Contemptuous laugh
97. Wildcat
98. Swami
99. Ham it up
101. Waco university
102. Iron Age period
104. Fleur-de-___
105. Get off ___ -free
107. Pen
108. Quick bread
111. ___ the good
113. Contends with
115. Not ___ in the world
116. Pacific sea
119. Liberate
121. ___ up (add zing to)
125. Fence
127. Love affair?
130. Charge
131. Cheating John Q?
132. Cascade peak
133. U.S. playwright
134. North Sea feeder
135. Sammy of football note

DOWN

1. Thai money
2. On the bounding main
3. False god
4. Glass eel
5. Golfer Elder
6. ". . . stirring, not even ___"
7. Roof beam
8. Social insects
9. Kind of game for a pitcher
10. Stuck
11. ___ volente
12. ___ Cologne
13. Alcohol burner
14. College degrees
15. London's Old ___
16. Belong
17. Jeremiah and Ezekiel
18. Flavor
19. Strong beam
20. Small barracudas
22. Like tapirs or anteaters
23. Part of F.B.I.
30. Rapport
33. "___ can you see . . ."
35. Whiskies
37. Like atoll waters
38. Miss Ross
39. Per ___
40. Billy's Mrs.
43. Rose of ___
44. Rebound
46. "Bon appétit!"
47. Church levy
48. Comedienne Martha
51. Combat mission
52. Become infuriated
53. John Jacob
55. Chewy candy
56. Latin or Eastern
58. Powerful one
61. Pompous
65. Swarm
66. Its first day is tricky
67. Kind of surgeon
68. Amino and boric
69. Israel's Dayan
72. Lace trimming
73. Drowsy
74. Redcap
75. Golf strokes
76. Water animal
77. Daphnis's love
78. Sooner than
79. Stinker
80. Concerning
82. Grade-school subjects
83. Walter of golf fame
84. Catch sight of
85. Objects of worship
86. Dormouse
87. Worship of: Suffix
89. Unit in India's pecking order
94. Cheer
95. Castle back gate
96. Surfeit
100. Old Lisbon money
101. Sheep hunter
103. Square matters
105. Rebuke severely
106. Pamper
108. Of John Paul II
109. Florida city
110. Becomes tiresome
111. Different, in Paris
112. Science, for short
114. Land of a famous queen
117. Boss of a shield
118. Eulogize
120. Newts
122. Korean War river
123. Puritan
124. Delineate
126. Commanding off.
128. Dynamite
129. Focal point

88 On the Offense by Dorothea E. Shipp

Concentrating on the operations of activists.

ACROSS

1. Cheek
5. Bumpkins
10. Edward the pirate
15. Engine component
18. Material finish
19. Monotonous recital
20. Russian range
21. Potentates
23. Habituate
24. Warehouses
25. Smiling
26. Zhivago's beloved
27. Attack
29. Came in first
30. Quake forerunner
32. Disappeared from view
33. Land of the rainy plain
34. Encouragement
37. Corrode
39. Augustus or Julius
41. Composer Ned
42. Morning occurrence
46. Maple product
47. John Jacob's family
48. Not wide: Abbr.
51. Acid salts
52. Skelton and Buttons
54. ____ Canals
55. Put on cargo
56. Bath adjunct
57. Otto's domain: Abbr.
60. Faucet dolings
62. Hats
64. Larva product
65. Leanings
67. Insect eggs
69. Insurance adjuster's concern
70. Daisy
71. Long John Silver's pet
73. Of an eye part: Prefix
74. Take advantage of
80. Brazilian state
81. Did some smooching
82. Peep shows
83. County in Northern Ireland
85. Genuine
86. Belgian port
87. Sheet-music sign
91. Ushers
93. Mock, in England
95. High note
96. Mystery
97. Feminine suffix
98. High crag
100. River of France
101. Starts a paragraph
104. Bishopric
105. Bear witness
107. Traffic situation
109. Cinder-sitting Polly
110. Deal's partner
111. Acid compound
113. Asian
114. Appeal to
119. Spanish mister
121. Ankles
125. Way out
126. ____ culpa
127. Take a wishful precaution
129. Et ____
130. Certain rib
133. "Take me to your ____"
134. Wispy clouds
135. Occasion for pistols
136. Leaked slowly
137. Fruit of the elm
138. Bone: Prefix
139. Univ. students
140. Ones adjusting cravats
141. Addicts
142. Red, White and Sulu

DOWN

1. Seasonal visitor
2. Take ____ for the worse
3. Retaliate
4. Search
5. Take revenge
6. Roma's country
7. Al's family
8. Recognized
9. Method: Abbr.
10. Fortunetelling card
11. Writers Glyn and Wylie
12. ____ premium
13. Half a dance
14. Start a trip
15. Biblical spy
16. Lizard
17. Morocco, to the French
18. ____ America
19. Occasional year
22. Cutty ____
28. Lauder of cosmetics
29. Conflict
31. Radiation dosages
34. Material for a prop moon
35. Have-____ (the poor)
36. Scout unit
38. Carney or Linkletter
40. Chalcedonies
42. Stipples
43. Jai ____
44. Cheerleader's offering
45. Home for Monroe
47. Persons with ambition
48. Famous Joe
49. Musical direction
50. Take umbrage
53. Miss Shore
55. Gold fabrics
58. Breakfast slice
59. Lures
61. Marked with lines
63. Nostril
65. Haggard book
66. Hog the conversation
68. Horse color
70. Parts of ships' keels
71. Like pencil ends: Abbr.
72. Cuttable part of the foot
74. Climbs
75. Cylindrical
76. Having branches
77. Moslem decree
78. Fisherman
79. Comedian Sparks
84. Satisfy
86. Mountain nymph
87. Regarding one's financial status
88. Night sight, in France
89. ____' acte
90. Actor Parker
92. Missives
94. Take pleasure in
99. Sail knot
102. Word before glycerine
103. Genetic initials
105. Barley spikes
106. Hoosegow
108. Identify wrongly
109. Brandishers of foils
111. Colombian native
112. Tree of the Far East
114. ____ of steam
115. Northern dwellings
116. One who never says die
117. ____ de chat (cat's eyes)
118. Wants
120. Soup ingredient
122. Blood carrier
123. Folk traditions
124. Personal: Prefix
127. New Zealand parrots
128. Cpls.
131. Louis, for one
132. Become like: Suffix
133. Baton Rouge campus

89 Pastoral Pastiche by Bob Lubbers

Celebrities lend their names to rural settings.

ACROSS

1. Gemstones
6. Mist or fog
11. Wapitis
15. Attends
21. Film director Hal
22. Hanging open
23. Chicago turnaround
24. Decimal fractions
25. Eats at
26. Baseball teams
27. P.I. native
28. Comeback
29. Property
30. Hired thug
31. Andes flier
33. "Yes ___!"
34. For the reason that: Abbr.
36. San ___
38. "Land ___!"
40. "___ for All Seasons"
41. Rural ditty sung by Jamie, Miss Loy and Gabriel
47. American realist painter
49. Criterion: Abbr.
50. Mine, in France
51. Oxhide thong
52. Tooth: Prefix
54. Revolutionary diplomat Silas
56. Kind of speaker or mouth
57. Perilous
59. Earth science: Abbr.
61. Theater district
64. Iron ___
65. Noncom
66. Sci-fi milieu
68. Mine entrance
70. Miss Albright et al.
71. Shake-spearean forest
73. Table spread
75. Lend an ___
77. Follower of upsilon
79. Dole out
80. Ireland's is old
82. Sign up
84. One showing esteem
86. Crosscut or rip
89. Little alma mater of Foxx, Cuddles and Sally Ann
94. Madrid Mrs.
95. Whiner
97. Soak up
98. Roman bronze
100. Japanese aborigine
101. Down, in bridge
103. Two: Prefix
104. Employs
106. Sky traveler
110. Mrs. Yokum
112. Pitcher Schoolboy
114. Literary initials
116. Mil. officers
118. Captain's aide
119. Win over
121. White or Blue
123. TV stem
125. Italian millet
126. Purviance and Ferber
128. Abate
130. This, to a Spaniard
131. Actor Blore
132. ___ and haw
134. Stripper's move
136. Vehicle for Bean, Dullea and Little
139. Galatea's beloved
141. Arab bigwig
143. Boxer Tunney
144. Profit
145. Italian historian
147. Clay-based rock
149. Actor Richard
152. Celebrity's writing aid
156. Parcels out
158. Hindu goddess
159. Shaping tool
160. Musical mishmash
161. Wanted
162. Debtor's nemesis
163. Hot spot
164. Dropsy
165. Levy a tax
166. Newts
167. Oglers
168. Pacific staples

DOWN

1. Miss Korbut
2. Writes
3. Turkish border river
4. Hazards for Edmund and Lloyd
5. Method
6. Guy rope
7. Currency changer's fee
8. Vista
9. Uncovered
10. ___ adjudicata
11. Fiery saint
12. Winged divers
13. Fuel supply for Alexander and Natalie
14. Eerie
15. Ocean liner: Abbr.
16. Shoe widths
17. Abstract beings
18. Refuges for Gale and Peter
19. Triple ___
20. Belgian port
31. Nat King ___
32. Marsh growth
35. Mr. Vance
37. Jason's helpmate
39. Br. pound base
41. Composer Manuel de
42. Parisian love
43. Circular
44. Starr
45. Got cozy
46. Coat's inside: Abbr.
48. Literally hard rain
53. Kind of sheet or drop
55. Ruth's mother-in-law
58. Fauna's partner
60. Kind of service
62. Spud
63. Bear's den, in Spain
67. Scold continuously
69. Alaskan spring event
72. Miss Bayes
74. Annapolis grad.
76. "___ Well That . . ."
78. Thought
81. U.S. labor leader
83. "Right on!"
85. Very brief time unit: Abbr.
86. Land or sea art
87. Suffix for libr or centen
88. Power sources for Ed, Cecil B. and Agnes
90. Colorist
91. Parasitic insect
92. Time units: Abbr.
93. Karnak monolith
96. Took pupils to school
99. Barn appearances for Elke and Miss Bara
102. Word after bon
103. Printing mark
105. U.S.A. unit
107. N.Z. native
108. Character of a people
109. What you can't do to an old dog
111. Yin's partner
113. Game stalked by Oscar and Ericsson
115. Memory fault
117. Done in
120. Thin
122. Ike's theater
124. Deserter
127. Jerk
129. Goad
132. Cigar capital
133. French schools
135. Cleopatra's ___
137. Street sign
138. Rue
140. English ware
142. Rosie's gear
146. French summers
148. Cans
150. Teen-___
151. Eliot
153. Finished
154. Japanese wrestling form
155. Oolong et al.
157. Former campus org.
159. Name for a ship

Wherewithal by Hugh McElroy

Some of the means for a bargain.

ACROSS

1. Use a swizzle stick
5. Tastes
9. Take a flier
12. Bayou native, often
17. Marie Wilson radio role
18. ____ skin paper
20. Gin flavor
21. Seed-to-be
22. Ready cash in a song
25. German river
26. Common verb
27. Null's partner
28. Harold of the funnies
29. Small change
30. Skateboard features
32. Was partisan
33. Slow musical movement
34. Dies ____
35. Amphibian
36. Heeled
39. Pays up
42. "A ____" (part of a thrift adage)
44. Inventor Whitney
45. Morse-code sounds
46. Goddess of healing
47. Military group
48. Town in Normandy
49. Elath's country: Abbr.
50. Early movie
55. Hebrew measures
56. Keep ____ (do guard duty)
58. Tête-____
59. "____ oui!"
60. Rub out
61. Blocker or Rather
62. Opposite of stem
64. Work out in the ring
65. Max and Buddy
67. Activated
70. Keats and Yeats
71. "Is a ____" (end of adage)
73. Ending with ox or chlor

74. A princess
75. Month segment
76. Dress up
77. Neighbor of the N.Y.S.E.
78. Word with horn or ear
79. English spending unit
83. Athlete's shoe feature
84. Places for rural hanky-panky
86. Biblical king
87. "Ballad of Reading ____"
89. Kiln
90. Tab settler
91. Home of the Braves
95. Rotisserie rods
96. Boo-boo
97. Preminger
98. Kind of bob or trumpet
99. Garbo is one
100. Dollars, pounds, francs, etc.
103. Baseball's Roger
104. Yankee Doodle's mount
105. Nostrils
106. Nile queen
107. Musial and Kenton
108. Carney
109. Junior arrow
110. Where to spend kopecks

DOWN

1. Instrument for Shankar
2. Cape Cod town
3. Urge forward
4. Criticize
5. Mexican state
6. Cut into
7. Kind of piper
8. Tippling one
9. Mixture
10. Long time
11. Early sportscaster Husing
12. Crouched in fear
13. Exact satisfaction
14. Old carnival pitchman's bargain
15. Endings with mod and glob
16. Saul's grandfather
19. Whim
20. Like a greyhound
23. Between Tinker and Chance
24. Kind of chair or auto
29. Editor's mark
31. Little white things
32. Cubic meter
33. Linda of TV's "Alice"
36. Craft for a Huron
37. Grasso and Logan
38. God, in Spain
39. Entrance
40. Reo's contemporary
41. Brecht-Weill musical
42. Walleyed or turn
43. Frying fat
46. ____ Homo
48. Kind of ribs or parts
50. Comes closer
51. Derivative suffixes
52. Bearing a burden
53. Eared seal
54. Like most forests
55. Correct
57. Talk on and on
62. Warbled
63. Three, in Napoli
64. Russian girl's name
65. Complaints
66. Singer Paul
67. Suffix for cyclo
68. Concert halls
69. Status of the first in line
70. Garden or primrose
71. Furrier's purchase
72. In conflict
75. Drifts on the breeze
77. Nazimova
79. Job for Mesta
80. Nook's partner
81. Colombian statesman
82. Titania's love
83. "____ me gray"
85. Stored for the winter
87. Assemble
88. Bear witness
90. To the ____ (pertinent)
92. Actress Patricia and namesakes
93. "Canterbury ____"
94. Chain mail
95. Ruth's sultanate
96. Oafish fellow
97. Other, in Málaga
99. Dress sizes: Abbr.
100. Audit man
101. Passing style
102. Old French coin

91 And So Forth by Arnold Moss

A bit of symbolism often provides a shortcut.

ACROSS

1. Sufficient
6. Moroccan capital
11. Idi ____
15. Tidies up, in Scotland
20. Actress Lee and others
21. Architect Jones
22. In Abraham's ____
24. Miss Fields
25. Shackles
26. Soak
27. Word on a Turin faucet
28. Sailor's call
29. Actor Dick's disguises
31. Jabber-wocky's frumious ____
33. ____ Street
34. Hesitating sounds
35. Shell member
38. Catchall abbr.
39. Western alliance
40. Worker in an Akron plant
44. Tales, in Toulouse
49. Line cutting a curve
53. Arithmetic word
55. "____ pronounce you . . ."
56. Palate part
57. Untruthful one
59. Roman helmet
60. Muscat native
61. Irving-Julie combo
65. Chilling
66. Drury and Memory
67. Sturm ____ Drang
68. Take a bus
69. Caesar of comedy
70. Actress Murray
71. Plants firmly
72. "The ____ is silence"
74. Bog fuel
76. ____ rum
78. Tire, in France
79. "Godfather" stars
82. Luminous glow
87. Be idle
88. Rhinal
90. Conductor Rapee
91. Kind
92. Swiss city, à la French

95. Flashlight unit: Abbr.
96. Legal degree
98. Sicilian city
100. Teutonic sky god
101. Conscious
102. Cote sound
103. Hold firm
106. Cheroot
107. Patois
109. Impose taxes
110. Uprush
111. Comic's fall
112. Zoo favorite from Asia
115. Singer Lena et al.
116. Ancient Jewish sect
118. Creatures without color
119. Actor Keith
120. Trojans' campus
122. Radiation measure
123. Puget, for one: Abbr.
124. H. H. Munro
128. Cave men
135. Hermitage resident
139. What Polonius hid behind
140. Self-evident truth
142. Scary
143. Horace's language
144. It's often purple
145. Electron tube
146. Checks
147. Make up for
148. Donkeys
149. Catch
150. Frozen raindrops
151. More undiluted

DOWN

1. Existing
2. Prospero's daughter
3. Stratagems
4. Gaunt
5. To be: Lat.
6. Step parts
7. Pilasters
8. Funeral frame
9. Mellowed
10. Garden need
11. Principles
12. O.T. land
13. Coney ____
14. Joint in a stem
15. Position
16. Variable star
17. "L' ____ c'est moi'
18. Platter
19. Son of Adam
23. Sir Thomas ____
30. Fix egg whites

32. London street
36. Carney
37. Sovereignty
39. Walking ____
40. Music-hall performances
41. Advanced accountant's degree
42. ____ for Progress
43. Female relative
45. Paintings of a Florentine artist
46. Silly
47. ____ down (subdued)
48. Guard or steak
49. Bedroom community
50. Smoothing device
51. ". . . eating her ____ whey"
52. "____ My Sons"
53. Famed chairman
54. Sand reef

57. Realty operation
58. Of the intestine
60. Ancient Mexican
62. Part of a baby's bottle
63. Pranks
64. Horace work
70. Weekday: Abbr.
71. Raise one's voice ____
73. Endure
75. King Arthur's birthplace
77. "Lost Weekend" star
78. Old Eastern R.R., for short
80. New England prep school
81. Vote against
83. "He Who Gets Slapped" author
84. Downtown street sign
85. Cower
86. Musical works

89. Height: Abbr.
92. Canadian peninsula
93. Pitchers
94. Hindu water spirits
95. Bolognese beard
97. Actress Mary et al.
99. Hot crime
102. After avril
103. Step
104. Teachers' org.
105. "____ Gang"
108. N.Y.'s horse-race org.
112. Exam
113. Compass pt.
114. Aromatic mixtures
115. "If I ____ Million"
117. Cavell and Nightingale
119. As a joke
121. African lake
123. Porkers
124. Roller or ice
125. Lady or Mary
126. Dialect of a region

127. Tube or city
128. Wine valley of Calif.
129. Deviates
130. "The Woman of ____": Wilder
131. Facilitate
132. Main line
133. Symbol of Venice's St. Mark's
134. Kind of cracker
136. Spool
137. N.Y. canal
138. Kind of bake
141. One of the "Little Women"

92 Dovetails by Raymond F. Eisner

Some ways to save space on people's names.

ACROSS

1. Name for a chubby one
6. George and life
11. Like some canaries
16. Ring arbiter
19. Actor Flynn and others
20. Of a geologic period
21. Climbing vine
22. Merit
24. Patriot, novelist and President
28. Get a move on
29. "___ ask?" (Is it discussable?)
30. City south of Moscow
31. Market for goods
32. Counterpart of Stockholm
34. Iranian coins
35. Was sorry about
36. Kind of boss
37. "The defense ___"
39. Depot: Abbr.
40. Revolver inventor
41. Gibraltar denizens
42. Rudiments
45. G.I. address
47. Light used at rock concerts
49. Certain iron
50. Fay of "King Kong"
51. Pays attention to
55. Downspout connection
56. Last
57. Competes at logrolling
58. Precede
60. Great warmth
62. Important part of a Wilde title
64. Dundee denials
65. Hawaiian lavas
67. Mix a martini
68. Religious-art subjects
69. Roman 155
70. Others, in Spain
72. Forearm bones
74. Bermuda grass
75. Star and novelist
82. Guido's high note: Var.
83. Old Azores air stopover
84. John La ___, U.S. painter
85. Suffer
86. Areas between mountains
89. "___ We Got Fun?"
91. Negative prefix
92. W.W. II battle site
93. Treat a metal: Var.
94. ___ health (ailing)
96. In an exclusive way
99. Indian princes
100. ___ over matter
102. Certain U.N. veto
104. Took a wrong turn
105. Certain voters: Abbr.
106. One of 52
107. What babies do
109. Hurok
110. Transform gray hair
111. Subside
112. "Get a ___ of this!"
113. Government rep.
115. Hebrew ceremony
119. Amundsen
121. Hard or soft
122. More mature
124. Singer Martin
125. Like a parquet floor
127. Church recess
128. South American liberator
130. Airboard initials
131. Pulitzer novel and musical star
135. Source of horsehair
136. Wine region in France
137. Miss Keaton
138. Cheapskates
139. Tack on
140. More sensitive
141. Posts
142. Night noise

DOWN

1. Topping for a French shortcake
2. Russian co-ops
3. Craggy hill
4. Took an icy spill
5. Levant of music
6. Warms up again
7. Having small interstices
8. Natives of Helsinki
9. Biblical weed
10. Curve of a plank
11. Bordeaux wine
12. Pointed at
13. Celt
14. Print measures
15. Bumped in a job shuffle
16. Designer Oscar de la
17. U.S. Chief Justice and film star
18. Wedge-shaped tool
19. Spartan magistrate
23. Court divider
25. Kristofferson
26. Unit of energy
27. Possessive
33. Mexican grasses
35. Two movie stars
36. Flowering shrub
38. Stepped on the gas
40. Havens
41. Southern constellation
43. Light wood
44. Body sacs
46. ___ toot (carousing)
48. W.W. II fliers
49. Divided country: Abbr.
50. Scatter, as chaff
51. Certain corporal
52. Wholly
53. Singing star and Alice's milieu
54. Declare
56. ___ honor
57. Barnyard family
59. Ground soils
61. Small bottle
63. Confuse
66. Big Apple's Bohemia
68. Tiny moths
70. Old Japanese coins
71. Leave in the lurch
73. Location of the Peacock Throne
76. F. Scott's wife et al.
77. Turkish regiments
78. Expectant
79. Actress Moorehead
80. City in northern France
81. Bridges or Nolan
86. Bird of the gull family
87. ___ occasion (always)
88. Supply's partner
90. Trifled with
92. Clambered over a wall
94. Neighbor of Ill.
95. Soak
97. Mil. officers
98. Greek god
101. Choler
103. Asian country
106. Certain museum mobiles
107. Vacancy sign
108. Realms
111. Lament
112. One of two evils
114. Group of beauties
116. Weight watcher
117. Unimpaired
118. White-flecked horses
120. Like a rowboat
121. Cactus leaf
122. Kind of type
123. Indoor-garage features
125. Doctrine
126. Campus sports org.
127. Hebrew lyre
128. French cheese
129. Picnic forecast
132. Even if, for short
133. Asner and Murrow
134. Movie initials

Finishing Touches by Alfio Micci

Some starts, with endings to be provided.

ACROSS

1. Out of fashion
6. Swahili master
1. Western sights
6. Essence
1. Mountain nymph
2. Tapestry
3. Mounted
4. Genus of flies
5. Two under par
6. Peter or Paul
7. Playwright Garson
8. Important inning
9. Des followers
3. Italiano's quaff
4. River to the North Sea
5. Possesses
6. Actually
9. Heavy-duty envelope
3. Neckpiece
5. Despot
9. In question
0. Atlantic City feature
1. Flowering shrub
4. Coin of old
5. Van followers
0. Compass reading
1. Ear-shaped shell
2. Zoo attractions
3. Engrossed
4. Versifier
5. Harem room
8. Monk
9. Native of Valencia
2. Zoroastrians
5. Madame Bovary
7. Sesame
9. Wallach
0. De followers
6. Rainbow
7. "___ transit . . ."
8. Swindles
9. Cupid
0. Nobility
4. Lao-tse's principle
6. Roman or Christian
8. Military prison
9. Pry
0. "___ Solemnis"
2. Abe of N.Y.C.
4. Gone by

107. Von followers
113. Feel remorse
114. Coal-gas hydrocarbon
115. Make a bridge faux pas
116. The transept crosses it
117. Ye ___ Tea Shoppe
119. Foreign or first
120. Double
121. Loathing
123. Deserter
125. Charity
127. French river
128. Del followers
138. Fall beverage
139. In a tumult
140. Ready for action
141. Disturbs
143. Twenty: Prefix
144. Permission to depart
145. Utopian
146. Water wheel
147. Magna ___
148. Attacked, in a way
149. Peter of horror flicks
150. Bedaub

DOWN

1. Author of "The Bells"
2. Ancient Syria
3. Utah state flower
4. Emulate Pavlov's dogs
5. Paradisiacal
6. ___ profundo
7. Prepare a gift
8. Seed covering
9. Pram pusher
10. Italian wine city
11. ___ pass at
12. Expunge
13. Sub's nemesis
14. "It's ___ to tell . . ."
15. "___ no money"
16. Loss of breath
17. Craving
18. Instrumentalist's concern
19. Liberal or fine
20. Stadium shout
30. Doorway: Abbr.
31. Hose
32. Wife of Theseus
36. Cordage fiber plant
37. Subject of a sentence
38. Golfer's cry
39. Stable occupant
40. Texas athlete
41. Zero
42. Miss Claire
43. Storage places
44. Calif. fort
46. Make oneself at home
47. One of a top four
48. Baseball statistic
50. French noblewoman
51. Have the lead
52. Sense of taste
53. Smell
56. Loop
57. Unsavory chap
58. Dickens's noted knitter
59. ___ tree (cornered)
64. Twosomes: Abbr.
66. Eastern state: Abbr.
67. Journalist Bierce
69. Seashore shindig
70. Chorister
71. Word with wit or pick
72. French breadwinner
73. Rose
74. Take to the slopes
76. Twice DIII
78. "Rose ___ rose . . ."
80. Place for baby
81. Lights and camera follower
82. Mideast nation: Abbr.
83. Bellini opera
84. Less humid
85. Barrister's wear
91. Down Under denizen, for short
92. "___ go marching . . ."
93. Gradually develop
95. Tennis star
97. Doubleday
100. Celebrated TV horse
101. More buoyant
103. Nervous
104. Open
105. Rendered
106. Joined
107. Hit sign
108. Brynner
109. Summer weather initials
110. Crew
111. Santa ___
112. Foyer
118. Borgnine
120. Sounded brassy
121. Attila was one
122. Bedecks
124. Roman courtyards
125. "Lorna ___"
126. Indian or orange
127. Confuse
128. Isinglass
129. Reputation
130. Old instrument of torture
131. One of the ages
132. Follow
133. Church calendar
134. U.S. citizen
135. At hand
136. Weary
137. Lamb
138. A Carter title: Abbr.
142. Men's org.

94   In Tune   by Anthony B. Canning

Dredging up some Tin Pan Alley oldies.

ACROSS

1. Spassky's game
6. Hopes
10. Over
14. Steeply cut, as palisades
21. Divine one of stage
22. Virginia willow
23. Coleridge's sacred river
24. Anybody
25. Occasion for hails in 1917
28. Iago's wife and namesakes
29. Comedian Jimmy
30. Snake
32. Miss Claire
33. Un-Victorian
36. Motor part
39. Great
42. Mortimer Snerd, for one
43. Stopover on the way home
44. Egg drink: Var.
46. Cinnabar, for one
47. Golf-course unit
48. What I'd never do in 1955
53. Bull and home
55. Fatima's husband
56. Yields one's place
57. Harp, in Italy
59. Shaping tool
60. Gas measure, in Europe
62. Roman money
63. Petrify
66. European's neighbor
67. Swing about
68. Disguise
70. Did spellbinding
71. ____ attention (be formal)
73. ____ Lane Theatre
75. Loch of note
77. Items in a purse
78. Tore
80. Gypsy husband
81. Varnish resin
83. Soprano Lucrezia
86. Indian "bird" tribesman
88. Called
91. Not voiced
95. Small cavity
97. Like a good cake
99. Clothe with authority

101. Musical show
102. Act of expanding
104. Doorway: Abbr.
105. Rugged crest
106. U.S. political org.
107. Egyptian object of worship
108. Removes
114. Slum pest
115. Greek region
117. Dancing accompaniment of 1930
119. Plaster holder
120. Greek letter
121. An enemy of Carthage
122. Village branch unit: Abbr.
123. Creator of "Gil Blas"
125. Psalms word
127. Rembrandt or Whistler, e.g.
129. Rescued
131. Old French coin
132. ____ Paulo
133. Sterilized condition
135. Rugged
139. Shade provider of 1905
146. Imply
147. ____ Carroll of old "Vanities"
148. Wings
149. Dandies
150. Did a teaching job
151. Stew
152. Fountain, in England
153. Yellow pigment

DOWN

1. Texas time: Abbr.
2. Exclamation
3. Prior to
4. Settle
5. Unit of a doubt
6. Spray of feathers
7. "____ broad as it is long"
8. Had in mind
9. Cure
10. Cry of dislike
11. Bar order
12. European herring
13. It was ended in 1927
14. Compass point
15. Everything's activity of 1959
16. Prefix for an acid
17. One who narrates
18. Food for Kamehameha
19. Spanish queen
20. From, in France
26. One outdoing a bikini wearer
27. Greek island
31. Like Bronx stadium fans
33. Worshiper of images
34. Emergency troops
35. Title for a French lady
37. Rikki-tikki-____
38. Like the Negev
40. Bookish
41. Habitué
45. Dress insert
47. George of Chicago Bears fame
49. Ring stone
50. Sham: Prefix
51. Light beam
52. Mariner of fiction
54. Progeny
56. "Don't ____ boy on a man's . . ."
58. Rhine feeder
61. Got out of hand
64. Gaelic John
65. Dead-language scholar
67. Doer: Suffix
68. Tito, for one
69. Urban district of England
72. Positive stresser of 1944
74. Tea-heating vessels
76. Blind component
79. Leads commandingly
82. Eel
83. Policeman's ID
84. Baseball team
85. Break
87. Solicit
89. Complete
90. Solid
92. No great shakes
93. Nodded
94. Canines
96. Meadow
98. Abbrs. on business names
100. Arrest
103. "____ pin, pick it up"
109. Stone: Suffix
110. First word of Mass. motto
111. Lacking a behavior code
112. Bidden good traveling
113. ". . . cast out your name ____ . . .": Luke
116. Allied landing site in Italy
118. Takes turns
119. Fall behind
124. Port of Japan
126. One taking a part
128. "Over There" creator
129. Bobby ____, black activist
130. Dismay
134. Neighbor of Wyo.
135. Merit-badge seeker: Abbr.
136. ____ sto (standing place)
137. Insect
138. Little Edward
140. Silkworm
141. Danube feeder
142. Whodunit figure
143. Cheer
144. Hotel plan: Abbr.
145. River to the Channel

95 Enneads by Sidney L. Robbins

That's a fancy way of saying this is about nines.

ACROSS

1. Kind of aleck
6. Prissy
10. Ball of yarn
14. Terms of sale
18. Hamelin employee
19. Italian philosopher
20. Sworn statement
21. Camper's pad
22. Staring
23. Wretched hut
24. "Do ___ others . . ."
25. Blade's feature
26. Nine
29. Trap
30. Miss Kett
31. ___ patriae
32. Curve
33. Sway
34. Silent, in music
36. Dover fish
38. Loaves' partner
39. Flight group: Abbr.
42. Mine deposit
43. Smoked ___
44. Furrow
45. W.W. II hush-hush org.
46. Czech capital, to Czechs
48. Beef ___
51. Biblical mount and peninsula
53. Ship channel
54. ___ into (scolded)
55. Collection of writings: Abbr.
58. Chess-match country: Abbr.
59. Pacific stopovers
62. Type of verse
63. Beginner: Var.
64. Ego
65. Nine
68. Hottentot
70. Trudge
72. Up: Prefix
73. Old
74. Genesis home
75. Strongbox
76. Car starter: Abbr.
77. Garment
78. Chemical compounds
80. Mad dogs' pals at midday
84. Numerous: Prefix
85. Roman 102
87. Author Deighton
88. Prevent
89. Type of confession
92. Electrical abbr.
93. Fisherman
95. East German kind of dam
96. More scarce
98. Mr. Bunker
99. Actress Rita
100. Verdi opera
101. Chalet backdrops
105. Sheds
106. Nine
110. Stub ___
111. Orchestra unit
112. Prognosticate
113. Day's march
114. Get up
115. Singer Seeger
116. Restrains
117. Post-___ drip
118. Arabian gulf
119. French seasons
120. Gaelic
121. Fishhook link

DOWN

1. Outpouring
2. Strength
3. Not together
4. Echo
5. Ash or catalpa
6. Upgrade
7. Funloving Tom ___
8. Summer refreshers
9. Dissolve
10. Part of a dinner
11. Shaded paths
12. Diminutive suffix
13. Pronoun
14. Nine
15. Gives drugs to
16. Entry
17. ___ clear of (avoid)
19. Pealed
27. Tortilla with filling
28. Phone greeting
29. Desperate letters
33. Marshal
35. Soviet range
36. Pay up
37. Poetic word
38. Vacation days
39. Point in an orbit
40. Muscle of the upper arm
41. Cinnamon bark
44. ___ cats and dogs
47. Nine
48. Chinooks, sockeyes, etc.
49. Henry VIII, for one
50. Type of chance
52. Dope
53. Entering
56. Merchants
57. Of epic proportions
60. Mobile home
61. R.R. depot
66. Electorate
67. Sheep
69. Handlelike parts
71. Place for Daniel
79. River duck
81. Type of club
82. Bikini-test weapon
83. Wrestler's pad
85. Neck artery
86. ___ formation (tightly arrayed)
89. One of Chicago's papers
90. Speed traps
91. River to the Caspian
94. Fleur-de-___
95. Check receivers
97. Porch-chair material
98. Singer Lucine
99. $1,000 bill
100. Protection
102. Lend-___
103. Of a religious leader
104. Sniff
106. Give backing to
107. Swiss river
108. Litigant
109. Camera part
111. Start, poetically

96 Acute Angles by Louis Baron
Some different ways to look at phrases.

Way Down by Martha J. DeWitt
Some observations on how it is below.

ACROSS

1. Attendant of a sort
6. Catch
11. Name for an elephant
16. Great ____ Lake
21. Century plant
22. Early ____
23. Make happy
24. Got a bead on
25. What the road to hell is
29. "Three Men ____ Horse"
30. Cult
31. Special committee
32. French brainstorm
33. Regret
34. Allergic reaction
36. Supplement, with "out"
37. Miss Rainer
38. Decimal base
39. Virginia ____
40. Snakes
43. College in Cedar Rapids
44. Guarantee
46. Diving bird
49. Uptight
51. ____ of time
53. Of an assessment
57. Tolerates
59. Seesawing Margery
60. Payable's associate
61. Having limits
62. Withdraws
64. Delaware Water ____
66. Work unit
67. Give, à la Burns
68. Teachers' org.
69. Cut across
71. Kind of geometry
73. Native of Ajaccio
75. Diana of films
77. Put in a box
79. Torment
80. What hell has
87. In accord
88. Venus, for one
89. Roman road
90. Infantryman's anathema
92. Goddess of crops
94. Even match
100. Skirt border
101. Counterpart of lv.
102. Beastly person
103. U-boat
105. Laggard
106. Muse of astronomy
108. ____ of hair
109. Beat it
111. Small anchors
112. Old-time fur man
113. Kind of tiger
115. Kind of code
117. English novelist
118. Off the sea
120. Jug handle
122. Repugnant ones
124. One of the three B's
127. Table scrap
128. Choler
130. Gypsy man
131. Liquefy
135. Labor org.
136. Con
137. Simple ones
138. Load
140. Cuckoo's cousin
141. What hell is full of
146. Ruling the roost
147. Reception
148. Greek physician
149. Mix up
150. Readings, for an actor
151. Ragouts
152. Slur over
153. Burgomaster

DOWN

1. Contrail content
2. Guam's capital
3. Etna's leavings
4. One of the first two
5. Kennedy and Sorensen
6. Great English game
7. Messed up the highway
8. Kind of can
9. Actor George
10. Kind of market
11. Gives medicine again
12. Follower of a rabbit
13. Early mo.
14. Mien
15. Those who pay attention
16. Surfeit
17. Roman weeks per year
18. Dean Martin hit
19. Jury trial locale
20. Ford's flop
26. Dandelion, for one
27. Sister Eileen's home
28. Hawaiian goose
35. Set
39. Pat pre-Nixon
41. Mr. who went to town
42. Riverboat hazard
44. ____ harbor (old sailors' home)
45. Makes an effort
46. Spar
47. ". . . ____ Alles"
48. Wealthy, in Spain
50. Exchange
52. "Life is but ____"
54. Destroyer
55. Comfortable
56. Had an inclination
58. Out at the elbows
61. Evergreen
63. Shrew
65. Kind of skirt
66. Recital comebacks
67. Blessing
70. Affliction
72. Sadat
73. Literary patchwork
74. Comparative suffix
76. ____ pilot
78. Small monkey
80. Belmont winner in 1955
81. The al. of et al.
82. General arrangement
83. Spanish article
84. Garage-bill items
85. Fire or narrow
86. What rusty hinges do
91. Depression org.
93. ____ thing
95. Creep
96. Most peculiar
97. Russian girl's name
98. "____ I say more?"
99. Gaelic
102. Contend
104. Judicial seat
107. Boat-builder of note
108. Disciplinarian
110. Cut down in scope
113. Gates
114. Backs out
115. Foretell
116. Like Elsa
119. Whet
121. Young, middle and old
123. Nonflying birds
124. Archie Bunker for one
125. Solo
126. Ducklike birds
128. Spiro
129. Of the kidneys
132. "St. Louis Blues" writer
133. Kind of Saxon
134. More hep
136. Elec. units
139. Factitious
142. Complete an "i"
143. "____ got sixpence"
144. Roman 551
145. "Sweet as apple cider"

98 Redefining by Bert Kruse

Some new approaches to old combos.

ACROSS

1. Carried on
6. Discernment
11. Disney flier
16. Preferred kind of tongue
21. Leave out
22. Heavenly
23. African stream
24. Cat-_____-tails
25. Oil drillers, e.g.
27. Visit a kennel
29. Feature of Orion
30. Patios
31. Brooklyn institute
32. Debases, in the past
33. Grow an identical twin
34. Former Asian pact
35. Perjurer
36. Home: Abbr.
39. Brew
40. Fed up
42. Henry, George or Lew
45. Deliver from evil
48. Does beauty-shop work
51. Opp. of longitude
53. O.T. book
54. English carbine
56. Fired pistols at dawn
57. French novelist
58. Straighten
59. Exhausts
61. Founded: Abbr.
62. Held fast
63. Fuel
64. Take a stand in court
65. Genus of mosquito
67. Moselle sight
68. Rider's seat: Abbr.
69. Fast buck
71. In good spirits
72. Place for traps
74. Arctic adventurer
75. Actor Brian
76. Like some skies
77. Late sextons
81. Took charge
84. "Valse _____"
85. British political author
86. U.S. hunter's quarry
87. Play tricks
88. Intend
89. Force

90. Comedian-singer Jim
92. Theme
93. Refluxes
94. Hashes
96. Moon goddess
97. Restaurant name
98. Grant's opposite
99. Electrocardiogram
101. Part of G. & S.
104. Goes off
106. Like an oboe or clarinet
108. Human projectile's need
109. Days of yore
110. Eggs of parasites
111. Gets wind of
113. Minneapolis suburb
115. Early ascetic
118. Words of confidence
119. Port-au-Prince's locale
120. Drama by Sophocles
124. Bud
126. Jogging spouse
128. Absalom's sister
129. Aesopian conclusion
130. Peace goddess
131. Torn
132. Hangs on
133. Girl's name, for short
134. Parents of babies
135. Hersey setting

DOWN

1. Actor Clifton
2. Lily plant
3. Lass
4. Use a blue pencil
5. Domestic retreat
6. Proceeds with care
7. Gives _____ (cares)
8. Fall sports event
9. "See you later"
10. Culbertson
11. Put down
12. Sneaky sea attacker
13. "THINK," e.g.
14. Take up ink
15. Cereal seed

16. Contemporaries
17. Mrs. Gandhi
18. Stringed instrument
19. American dramatist
20. Minus
26. _____-Curci
28. Rained ice
31. Hasty look
33. Hiding place
34. Roadside market
35. Washed
36. Plans again
37. Like Napoleon at the end
38. Mountaineer who likes company
41. Corrects
42. Whitman and Disney
43. Niggardly kin
44. Grill
46. Rave's companion
47. Breed or kind: Fr.

49. Soft leather
50. River to the North Sea
52. Neat
55. Shipbuilding wood
57. Kind of closet
59. Cut, to Shakespeare
60. Crusaders' enemy
62. Contestants
64. "Who steals my _____ . . ."
66. Always
67. Kind of withal
69. South American capital
70. Basra's land: Var.
71. Karpov's game
73. Kicks out
75. Marts of old
76. Influenced with gifts
77. One of the arts

78. Glyceride, for one
79. Permeated
80. Twelve
82. Word for "Beowulf"
83. Protect
84. Chinese weight
85. Joins
87. Nice, in Nice
89. Makes into cubes
91. Mt. Blanc, etc., to French
92. Island near Sicily
94. "_____ Roberts"
95. Be noncommittal
99. Climbing plants
100. Prefix for plane or gram
102. Accords
103. Red Square sight
105. Kind of street

107. Lambed
111. Stubble
112. See 118 Down
114. Do not, in Dundee
115. Newts
116. Bed part
117. Body
118. Chinese leader, with 112 Down
119. Tropical-tree genus
120. Surrounded by
121. Breakfast drink
122. Solar disk
123. Foreign: Prefix
125. Metric units: Abbr.
126. Free
127. Irish sweetheart

99 Roundup by Anne Fox

Long entries that need to be corralled.

ACROSS

1. Easter item
7. Film director Frank
12. Tennessee aluminum town
17. Ruth's husband
21. Adequate
22. In store
23. New Zealand native
24. Up to
25. He had a Doctrine
26. Physics Nobelist in 1938
27. Bulldog's relative
28. "____ Rose" (1957 song)
29. Mars, in old Greece
30. Former bandleader Ted
32. Whirled
34. Gyp
36. Cheese center
38. Victory site for Alexander
40. One-horse town of old
42. For
43. Words by Beaumont and Fletcher
50. Van Gogh's loss
51. Caravansary
52. April initials
53. Fixed up
54. Skulks
56. Restrict
58. Pirandello
59. New England river
63. Plus quality
64. Kind of metabolism
66. Prefix for puncture or men
68. Fixed course
70. Give the quick finish to
71. Kiwi
73. Sign on a busy street
76. Wound
78. Latin poet
80. Zodiac sign
82. Prayer
83. Novel by Gerald Durrell
90. Julius or Sid
91. Clergyman Henry ____ Coffin
92. Woollcott, to friends
93. ____ Kai-shek
94. Ratlike kangaroo
97. Shelley's elegy to Keats
102. Belonging to oneself
103. Math function
106. Cowboy actor Maynard
107. Brightness
109. Popular hero
110. Abominable one of Tibet
112. Things to count
114. Actress Ada
116. Big Ten team
118. Jury's decision
120. ____-disant
121. Makeup item
123. German article
124. Poem by Ernest V. Wright
130. Jinx
131. Farm animals
132. O.T. book
133. Even if: Lat.
134. Jockey Eddie
136. Baseball need
137. Crevasse
140. "Tell it not in ____"
144. Come together
145. N.Y. city
148. Nonsense!
150. Actor Don
152. Spar
153. Key ____
154. Its capital is Grenoble
155. Bacon unit
156. Honshu city
157. Conclusion
158. Very cold
159. Lengthen

DOWN

1. Early church chancel
2. ____ about
3. All's counterpart
4. Cared for
5. Capital "I"
6. Novel of 1931
7. Curtain or society
8. Listen!
9. Iran, once
10. L.A. player
11. Elian essay
12. Waylay
13. Capital of Aisne
14. Loser to Harding in 1920
15. Mispickel, for one
16. Critique by Henry Miller
17. "____ H'ai"
18. San Luis ____
19. Trees
20. Fanatic
31. Eastern title
33. Sets
35. Famous alter ego
37. Secretary
39. Companion of bones
40. Possessive pronoun
41. Starr
43. Seed coating
44. Medieval goblet
45. Not decumbent
46. Miss
47. U.S. missile
48. Ratite bird
49. G.P.'s
55. Devoured
57. Labor org.
58. Stagger
60. City near L.A.
61. Yule song
62. Golf tournaments
65. Plant part
67. General with a last stand
69. First name of 26 Across
72. Frequenters of the Forum
74. Make modern
75. Formerly named
77. Conrad character
79. Bad: Prefix
81. Relative of Mme.
83. "It's the real ____"
84. God, in Hebrew: Var.
85. Ring maneuver
86. Botanist Gray
87. Mountain
88. Cozy places
89. Wings
95. Kirghiz city
96. Busiest airport
98. Zilch
99. Ta-ta, formal style
100. Column type
101. Move furtively
104. Actor Nick
105. Tallinn natives
108. Space monkey
111. Car part: Abbr.
113. Ball or lid
115. Land of the Dail
117. F.F.V.
119. Fir pole
120. Kind of free
122. Salt Lake City team
124. Relative of "socko!"
125. Because of this
126. Kind of baggage
127. Big animals, for short
128. Poet Lindsay
129. Compendium
135. One of the Near Islands
136. Christmas trio
138. Espionage name
139. Struck with wonder
141. Hurt
142. Now and ____
143. Cowboy's charge
146. Lyric poem of old
147. Sea eagle
149. Compass point
151. Beerbohm

100 All's Well by Frances Hansen

Overcoming a minor crisis in a limerick.

ACROSS

1. Polynesian no-nos
6. Vinegary
11. Trotter's relative
16. He finds mischief for 60 Down
21. Writer St. Johns
22. Lumberjack contest
23. Grassy plain of S.A.
24. Place to remember
25. Of the feet
26. ____-Saxon
27. Artery
28. Sailor Shaftoe
29. Start of a limerick
33. Word in a Lost ad
34. Still
35. Notes between sol and do
36. Purple Sage people
37. Sgt., e.g.
39. Wood measure
41. Consumed
44. Spanish poppy
48. Pirates' gold
49. Do a grammar job
51. Syrian leader
56. Identical
57. "____ Been a Long, Long Time"
59. Wire measures
61. Income org.
63. Calcutta's was black
64. More of limerick
70. To the point: Lat.
71. German region
72. Kind of tamer or hunter
73. Made comparable
74. Feature of the tone-deaf
76. ____ Jima
77. Miss Kett
78. Indian ravines
79. Under, poetically
81. Inquiring sounds
82. Girder material
84. ____ interest in (got bored)
88. Miss Fitzgerald
90. Murray or West
91. Supple
96. "Bon ____!"
97. Midday
98. Moslem garment
100. Devon or Worcester
101. More of limerick
105. Actor Robert De ____
106. Time period
107. He, in Italy
108. Latin possessive
109. "Toyland" resident
110. Bloodhound's guide
112. Urn-shaped
114. Tease
117. Lagos is its capital
119. "Broken Nose" sculptor
121. Girl in "La Bohème"
122. Guido's high note
123. Poughkeepsie college
127. Lady of Spain
130. Harper Valley org.
132. Senior citizens
137. End of limerick
142. Thai or Burmese
143. "From ____ shining . . ."
144. Perfectly suited
145. Frequently
146. Stick in one's throat
147. Did a rattan job
148. Nemo's creator
149. Casper's wife in comics
150. Kind of trap or demon
151. In high dudgeon
152. Miss Millay and others
153. Nose partitions

DOWN

1. Long-snouted animal
2. Dote on
3. Sprinkle with moisture
4. Group of Koran scholars
5. Italian beachhead in 1943
6. Sheeted sheik
7. Island noted for rides
8. "Espolio" painter
9. One who narrates
10. Knucklehead
11. Western salt pan
12. Up in the air
13. Homing pigeon
14. Inner: Prefix
15. Wander
16. "____ Fair"
17. "Get ____ of this!"
18. Set aside
19. "Forever" girl
20. "The Highwayman" poet
30. 1654, Roman style
31. Like the gray mare
32. Three, in Turin
38. Horse opera
40. City on the Mohawk
42. ____ were (so to speak)
43. Earthly
44. Take ____ at (attack a fly)
45. Messianic Moslem leader
46. ". . . like ____ in spring"
47. Carolina river
49. Braids
50. ____ in the dark
52. Nautical hazard
53. Mosque student
54. Egyptian dancing girl
55. Scout's good things
58. African gulch
60. See 16 Across
62. Follow-up book
65. Spring from
66. "____ was in love with you"
67. In favor of
68. Western Pueblo
69. Somewhat tedious
75. Experience anew
80. Changed
81. Fictional Plaza pest
83. Uses a perforated line
84. Suburbanites' pride or despair
85. Of snakes
86. Kind of time or tire
87. Range of the Rockies
89. Mining finds
90. "O Sole ____"
92. "What care I how fair ____?"
93. Town near Jaipur
94. African antelope
95. Judith Anderson role
99. Attend an alumni affair
102. Shankar of the sitar
103. Convex moldings
104. Shadowed
111. Like a circus seal
113. Yin ____ (Chinese principles)
115. Hindered
116. Small heron
118. Awkward oafs
120. Hockey star
121. Spoil
123. Perfume containers
124. Fabulous man
125. Meanly nasty
126. It has wings and an apron
128. Out to get
129. Temperamental
131. Yoga posture
133. Crusoe's creator
134. Prevent, in law
135. Scarlett's Butler
136. Perceptions
138. Black measles
139. Adjective for Cassius
140. Take's partner
141. Cheers

101 Newton's Law by Mel Rosen

In this case it's word combos that react equally.

ACROSS

1. Research rooms
5. Carry on
9. Soaks
13. Boob
17. Matching: Prefix
18. Paul Bunyan's Babe and friends
19. Kind of culture
20. Cartoon light bulb
21. Fruit-filled pastries
23. Makes a better bargain
25. In a web
26. Sophia
28. Oil and wishing
29. German article
30. Enjoy shallow water
31. "____ company"
33. Of large proportions
36. Swan and jackknife
37. God in Nero's house
38. N.J. neighbor
41. Word of dismay
42. Cordage fibers
43. Convenient quantities
45. Feel under par
46. Ness and Lomond
47. Postal, for one
48. Etcher's need
49. Egad or drat, e.g.
51. Penicillin base
52. Miss Chase and others
53. It precedes sunrise
54. Flattered
56. Anjou's relative
57. Borders on
59. Law degrees
60. When tools first appeared
64. Discourse: Abbr.
65. Some are tight
66. Holey cheese
67. Took charge
68. Residents of Pierre and Bismarck
70. Short rides
71. Noisy dance
72. Endorses
73. Went underground
74. Sudden outpouring
75. Western movie riders
76. Beer-keg stopper
77. "Into ____ life . . ."
78. Execute a flimflam
79. Shillong's state
82. Laundry cycle
84. Its child has grace
88. Conductor's signals
90. Capsizes
92. Kind of bunt
93. Snicker-____
94. Ubangi River feeder
95. Violin silencer
96. Enervates
97. African village
98. Got ready to drive
99. Arabian chieftain

DOWN

1. Riga dweller
2. Color for a marine
3. Prove to be flammable
4. Lawrence and Gorme, e.g.
5. Like twill
6. Sacked from a job
7. Teutonic: Abbr.
8. Reduces to bondage
9. Hussar's weapons
10. Curved molding
11. Writer Rice
12. ____ still for (tolerate)
13. Shows partiality
14. Matinee ____
15. Whimper
16. Reviews harshly
22. Hodgepodge
24. Excalibur, for instance
27. Lyric writings
30. Keeps back, as evidence
32. Subside
33. Polite word
34. Et ____
35. Make noises in a blind
36. Water or air pipe
38. Dodge the phone
39. Kazan
40. Hallucinogens
42. Crawford
43. Agrees
44. Quiz choice
46. Stock-table listings
47. Actress Caldwell
50. Moro chief
51. Small metric units: Abbr.
52. Charged particles
55. Subjects for sofa-talk
56. Take charge
57. Ray of the movies
58. Bird's weapon
59. Kind of college
61. Fork feature
62. Washington and Sand, for short
63. Advantage
65. Cart
66. Justify a line of type
69. Barnum's General Tom ____
70. Bath and Banff
71. Use
74. Became aware of
75. Peasant's partner in an overture
76. Forehead cover
78. Healthy again
79. Supplies a postscript
80. Wading bird
81. Exchange
83. Willow
84. Mutual affinity
85. ____ up business
86. Opposed one
87. Belgian river
89. Curve
91. Churchill's gesture

102 Call of the Wild by Alice H. Kaufman

Some subjects for a nature-study course.

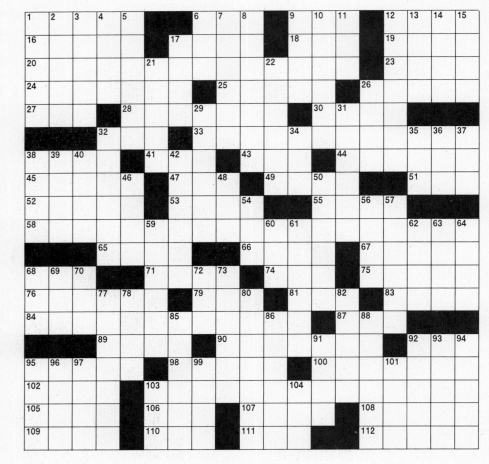

ACROSS

1. Assembly of witches
6. Container: Abbr.
9. Greek letter
12. Deserters
16. Cocktail greenery
17. Indonesian boat
18. Swoboda or Ziegler
19. Pennsylvania city
20. Cable terminals with jaws
23. Dandy's partner
24. Cultivated land
25. Horse's call
26. Shake-spearean forest
27. Red or Black
28. Lusitania's downfall
30. Shake-spearean villain
32. Through
33. Social parasite
38. Musical closing
41. "Exodus" hero
43. Liveliness
44. Irregular
45. Separately
47. Represent-ative: Abbr.
49. Soil
51. Nabokov novel
52. Blacksnake
53. Former Chinese leader
55. Something strained at
58. Tennessee Williams play
65. Sped
66. Cake's place
67. Glowing fragment
68. Botanist Gray
71. Maxwell or Lanchester
74. Abet's partner
75. Town near Salerno
76. Enlarge
79. Brattish child
81. One-liner
83. Soothe
84. 1943 Pulitzer novel
87. French season
89. Formerly, of old
90. Natives of a French region
92. Spanish pronoun
95. Starts a call
98. Put into order
100. One exercising power
102. Pre-bout wear
103. Not-so-good grief
105. Western Indians
106. California fort
107. Team-standing entry
108. Broadside
109. Cricket equipment
110. Stain
111. Insect
112. Actress Terry

DOWN

1. Layers
2. Kukla's friend
3. Country estate
4. Wicked
5. Nullify
6. Partnership abbr.
7. Home for Barnum's wild man
8. Fastened one's sneakers
9. Self-inflated one
10. Miss Tucker
11. Office holders
12. Chilled again
13. Barren
14. Prong
15. Observed
17. Feather: Prefix
21. Marketplace
22. Brother of John and Ethel
26. Opposed, in Dogpatch
29. Predicament
31. Class-reunion visitors
32. Graduation visitor
34. Mail center: Abbr.
35. Miss Gardner
36. Alert color
37. Factor in heredity: Abbr.
38. Small vehicle
39. Brilliant fish
40. Fish of the carp family
42. Playwright Crothers
46. The Fates or Graces
48. In addition
50. Things to be done
54. Mysterious aircraft
56. 1958 Pulitzer novelist
57. Kind of Western weed
59. Putting places
60. Power agency
61. Stature
62. ____ Ben Adhem
63. Dickens girl
64. Seed cover
68. Write a postscript
69. Title
70. Wing
72. ____ on one's hands
73. Of a simple form of life
77. Eternal
78. Craggy hills
80. Arbor or trellis
82. Lamp dweller
85. Like a clear night
86. Sinew
88. Fly
91. Birds of prey
92. Kennedy's Interior Secretary
93. Effrontery
94. Bean or Welles
95. Thump
96. Tiny amount
97. Incite
99. Ore deposit
101. Faithful, in Scotland
103. Fish-cake base
104. Adherent

103 Leisure Activity   by Evelyn Benshoof

The kind that's dealt out around a table.

ACROSS

1. "Cómo ____ usted?"
5. Killer whale
9. Gone by
12. Utah city
13. Unwilling
15. Kind of cheese
16. Personally suitable
19. Accompanying
20. Put on
21. Dances from Africa
22. Pep up
24. Author of "The Devil and Daniel Webster"
25. Yale people
26. Adm. bodies
27. Soviet agency
31. Fissile rock
33. Prefix for angle or pod
34. Plague
36. Step: Fr.
37. Scads
39. Chant
40. Curve
41. Ladies' afternoon diversions
43. Lacking color
44. Slipshod one
46. City in China
47. Mel
48. Esprit de corps
49. Include in
50. Skin problems
52. Place for a wish
53. Like fancy curtains
55. Yorkshire river
56. White poplar
58. Signs up
61. Garden blossom
64. ____ Jima
65. Took a photo
66. Speaks out
69. Choir recess
70. Silk hat
71. Alaskan native
72. Sewing or spelling
73. Fame
74. Warhol

DOWN

1. Puckish
2. Retaliate
3. Congress
4. Ozone
5. Baker
6. Legal point
7. Boasted
8. Nile city and dam
9. Soviet mountains
10. River to the Garonne
11. Umpire's call
13. Soon
14. ____ en point
15. Egyptian god
16. Wonder
17. Pindar offerings
18. Barbara and Lauren
23. Compete
24. Goren or Culbertson
26. Civil War photographer
28. ____ Gen.
29. Reveal all
30. Part of 3 Down
31. Spurt of energy
32. Platinum blonde of note
33. Rocky pinnacle
34. ____ entendu
35. Clefts
37. Drury, for one
38. Like a desert
41. Places for wine
42. Rabid
45. French lace
50. Suffer
51. Make firm and fresh
53. Instructive example
54. Syrian city
55. Celebes ox
57. Gravy server
58. Pitcher
59. Now
60. Fr. holy woman
61. Record
62. Otherwise
63. Drink
64. ____ fixe
66. Vehicle
67. Bright
68. RR ____

104 Gray Thumb by Tap Osborn

Lament of a never-to-be Burbank.

ACROSS

1. Sword
6. Shallow spot
11. Gullet
14. Dizzy
15. Of a time unit
16. ____ committee
19. Start of a horticultural verse
22. Bagnold
23. Ridiculous
24. Mrs. Simpson, wife of Edward
25. Grammar case: Abbr.
26. Deliberately-spread rumor
27. Most cunning
28. "I've ____ to the fair"
29. Danish measure
30. Second line of verse
39. Andretti, Unser et al.
40. That, in old Rome
41. Harness part
42. Light song
43. Eye troubles
44. Struck
46. ____ out (make do)
47. Rend
48. J.F.K.'s prep school
49. Third line of verse
54. Famed English town
55. Bismarck
56. Betray
59. Card markings
61. W.W. II sector in Asia
64. Cycle-race mishaps
65. Climb
66. Highlander group
67. Last line of verse
70. "A votre ____!"
71. Kind of soup
72. Maxim
73. Hershey's old org.
74. Repairs
75. French author Jean

DOWN

1. Did carpentry work
2. Coliseum
3. Prove appropriate
4. Donna or Walter
5. Building add-on
6. TV rock group
7. Golf champ of the 1950's
8. Prayer figure
9. Swiss river
10. Law degree
11. Supervises
12. Sweet girl of song
13. Early source of fuel oil
17. Medical suffix
18. Wen
20. Bathroom-floor workers
21. Danish national poet of the 1700's
26. Arctic explorer
27. Ski-pole substitutes, for some
28. Symbol of redness
30. About five bushels in Cairo
31. Japanese poem
32. Singing group
33. Soared sharply
34. Of Charles Lamb's works
35. Warning signal
36. German craft of W.W. II
37. The same
38. Painter Jan
43. Cut corners
44. Closes
45. Kissing disease, for short
48. Actor Joseph
50. Places for fives and tens
51. Develops
52. Extinguish
53. Rickshaw pullers
56. Speedy jets
57. Hebrew measure
58. Mortgages
59. Derision
60. Like a city street
61. Unsullied
62. Stephen Crane's was red
63. Garment addition
65. Pivot
66. Give in
68. Speed: Abbr.
69. Joker

105 Nature Tour by Ruth W. Smith

A good bit of it exploring the lowlands.

ACROSS

1. Lhasa ____
5. Hazard at sea
9. Haw's partner
12. Part of a play, in Paris
16. Astronaut Armstrong
17. Chemical compound
18. Cowboy Gibson
19. Verve
20. Mystery writer
23. Repudiate
24. Wallach or Whitney
25. Letter
26. Fleming and Smith
27. Intend
28. Alabama city
30. Crooner with a megaphone
33. Catbird's place
34. Gift for Adano
36. Michael or Harold
37. Greek island
39. Girl's name
41. ". . . he is mad, ____ true . . ."
44. Japanese mountain
47. Griffin et al.
50. Wriggling
51. Bon ____
52. Island in the Firth of Clyde
53. Threatened
55. Sculptor's medium
57. Danny or Sammy
58. Robin Hood's friend
61. Annoy
62. Ear or tube
64. Scolds
65. Dies ____
66. Regret
67. Singer Fitzgerald
70. King of Troy
71. Poetic twilights
72. Kind of rocket: Abbr.
73. Palm off
75. Kilns
77. Choose, in Arles
79. German poet
82. "____ crying shame!"
85. Portrayer of Norma Rae
87. Four: Prefix
89. Award
90. F.D.R.'s was new
91. Lend an ____ (listen)
93. Atmosphere
94. Bomb material
95. Actress-dancer
99. N.Z. evergreen
100. Handle, in Cannes
101. Hayworth or Moreno
102. Knee breeches
103. Hardy heroine
104. "____ thee behind me . . ."
105. Part of a ticket
106. Mine yields

DOWN

1. Backbone of S.A.
2. Rembrandt and Charles Wilson
3. Figure of speech
4. "Bravo!"
5. Entreats
6. Queen of Spain and others
7. King: Fr.
8. Honor, in Sèvres
9. Abounding in furze
10. Goddess of the dawn
11. Ordinal ending
12. Roman official
13. Christmas Eve chronicler
14. "La plume de ma ____"
15. Greek war goddess
18. Fly off the ____
21. Below, in poems
22. Hammer
27. Bowling and blind
29. Kind of idol
31. Place for flowers
32. Seed covering
34. Staggering
35. Missionary saint
38. Jane Austen novel
40. Pain-relieving dosage
42. Sea off Greece
43. Engraved pillars
44. Dervishes
45. Planet
46. Steve Allen's wife
48. Wind indicator
49. Steep slope
54. Biblical tower
56. Italian port
59. "____ them laughing"
60. Salinger girl
63. Pour another cup
68. Parrot
69. Gladly, old style
74. Give ____ (ogle)
76. Fertilizer base
78. S.A. animals
80. King of Israel
81. Sluggards
83. Dynamo part
84. Songlike
85. Bristles
86. Footnote abbr.
88. British composer and family
89. Marshal Dillon
91. "____, Brute!"
92. Pequod's captain
95. Spree
96. Kind of horse town
97. Small island
98. Greek letter

106 Quarters by Marion Moeser
But not the kind that can be spent.

ACROSS

1. ____ a customer
6. Soft drink
13. Singer Page
18. Cliffhanger White
19. Acted the hog
20. Scented root
21. ____ on (prodded)
22. Trappings
23. Form of trapshooting
24. One's faith: Abbr.
25. Popular diet item
28. Certain prayers
30. Hesitant sounds
31. Bearish show of affection
34. Exeunt ____ (everybody out)
35. Ross or Dors
38. Jog
39. South-of-the-border apparel
42. Presage
43. Creature in Alice's pool of tears
44. "It's ____ way to . . ."
45. Places for bookings
49. U.M.W. man
50. Triumphant sounds
51. Place
52. Marseille season
53. Desert Fox
55. Like Cal or an early movie
57. Decide on
60. Boss of a shield
61. Winglike parts
62. Dumb gals
66. W. H. Hudson's novel about Rima
69. Burma Road town
70. Ruled, as paper
71. Take on cargo
72. Contract-bridge move
73. Superlative suffixes
74. Elegance
76. ____ House, V.I.P. residence
78. Kind of lion or horse
79. Cry of contempt
80. Chooses in advance
84. Expensive steak
89. Writer Wallace
90. City linked to Columbus
92. Studies again
93. Not sensible
95. Practiced
96. Plant beards
97. Oslo people
98. Roman features
99. Zero and family
100. Say hello

DOWN

1. Sutherland's milieu
2. Beersheba's desert
3. Uncle Sam's feathered friend
4. Three, in Italy
5. Where the soldiers were "tenting tonight"
6. Military mission
7. Mrs. Hobby and namesakes
8. Painter of dancers
9. "To ____ and a bone . . ."
10. Feeble
11. Of the ear
12. Proud bird's mate
13. Artificialities
14. Unwieldy seagoers
15. One-time gift to Amy Carter
16. Collar's associate
17. Doer: Suffix
26. Novelist Sarah ____ Jewett
27. Historic time
29. Complaining one
32. Highly annoyed
33. Formation fliers
35. Morse-code units
36. Amin
37. Of a Greek region
38. Gehrig
39. Levenson
40. Whitney
41. Reagan
42. Semitic god
43. Activity of early American Indians
45. Brazilian dance
46. "If you were ____ girl in . . ."
47. Egypt's Blue and White
48. It precedes haw
54. Three thousand
55. Liquor-making plum
56. "I've had it up ____"
57. Pays unwelcome attention
58. Use a lever, in Britain
59. Octopus features
61. Helper
63. Mortar beater
64. "____ Blue?"
65. Old Irish material
67. Letters
68. Mineo
72. City in Normandy
74. Drinker
75. Aries
76. Happy couple's path
77. Hires
79. What some women have
80. Gabble
81. Irish county
82. Anxious
83. Like the uses of adversity
85. "Prisoner of Zenda" author
86. Relating to flying craft
87. "Exodus" author
88. First-grade
90. Maneuver a camera
91. Hubbub
94. Connective

107 Apt Authors by Mel Taub

Some writers' names lend themselves to irreverence.

ACROSS

1. Dick Tracy trademark
4. New Deal agcy. #300?
7. "____ my turn?"
11. Become a crew member
17. Half of snake eyes
18. Shout of surprise
19. Teamster's rig
20. Immature
21. Characteristic signs
23. Author who predicted a 1948 Dewey landslide
25. Polygamous households
26. Deal in secondhand goods
27. Soviet agency
28. Exceed in rushing yardage
31. Son of Jacob
33. Humorist in need of repentance
40. Between medium and jumbo
41. Footed vase
42. In need of Dr. Atkins
43. Iron or teen
44. Dies ____
45. Barbary pasha
46. Wear well
47. Consequently
48. Church payment
50. Garden festivity
51. Letters on an electric appliance
53. Area
54. Yiddish connoisseur
55. "____ are you now?" (birthday query)
58. Uptight
59. Not windward
60. Lincoln or Douglas in 1858
61. Fortune's partner
63. Rock's companion
64. Close-mouthed
65. Sunder
66. Accommodation in 25 Across
67. River to the Rhone
69. Put Fido to the chase
70. Used a trimming tool
71. Riotous poet
75. Cambodian's neighbor
76. Time on one's hands
77. Sea dog
80. Lark's milieu
83. Sonora snooze
87. Author, one of the angry young men
89. Color for Letter A
90. Current unit
91. Moslem official
92. Under the weather
93. Take measures
94. Plant anew
95. U.N. veto vote
96. Deletes
97. Questioning word

DOWN

1. Rib
2. Theater-group initials
3. Milldam
4. People's collective
5. Pure in behavior
6. Business orgs.
7. Native of northern Italy
8. Tranquil, in Italy
9. Hawaiian baking pits
10. Part of E.S.T.
11. Like Lapland winters
12. Cuttlefish secretion
13. Culinary word with au
14. Palm liquor
15. Musical work
16. Clears
22. Author who was a Lloyd assistant
24. Ready
29. Makes stick
30. Insubstantial
32. Compete
33. ____ de vaca (Spanish beef)
34. Ulster factionalist
35. Precisely
36. He wrote "The Wild Duck"
37. Stupefy
38. Guy, usually good
39. Old auto
40. Perjurer
45. Say it isn't so
46. Raze
47. Writer of salacious nonsense
49. Put on wearables
50. Overthrown
51. Attention getter
52. Kernel bearer
54. North Island native
56. Reception
57. Scott who lost a decision
60. Conduits
61. The other side
62. Tot up
63. Critical piece
64. Short, for short
67. Ending with fiend or devil
68. Marked indelibly
69. "____ the boys in the back room will have"
70. Quarterback specialties
72. Churchill's successor in 1945
73. Invest
74. Raw power
77. Prepare for a bout
78. "Alas!"
79. Utters softly
81. Island of Ireland
82. Roundup stray
84. Deli salad
85. Georgia ____
86. Bar man, for short
88. Dudgeon
89. Hockey team

108 Buttonhooks by Herb Risteen

They have gone out of fashion except in puzzle gimmicks.

ACROSS

1. Easy runner
6. Word after Bath or Beer
11. Track-meet event
16. Place for a stoa
17. Bulgarian weight
18. Dropsy
19. Novelist; President
22. Square in Moscow
23. Swift's specialty
24. Hinder
25. Throw pebbles at
26. Literary forms
27. Western Indian
30. Extremely
31. Fill-in piece
32. Lowlife
35. Moderating agents
37. Sweet flowers
38. Chemical suffix
39. French painter
40. Of aircraft
41. Earthen jar
42. President; painter
47. Beginning
48. Manufacture
49. Turkish inn
50. Massachu-setts cape
51. Variegated
52. Vacation spot
54. Plural ending
55. Bundle
56. Mast
57. Curve
58. Large containers
59. Knife for a hood
60. Harbor boat
62. Wall St. purchases
64. Cry of disgust
67. Commenta-tor; novelist
70. Isolated
71. Hourly

72. Mountain nymph
73. Pro football team
74. Starts the bidding
75. Musical Mel

DOWN

1. Bert of comedy
2. Curved molding
3. Backdrop for Thoreau
4. Blunder
5. Beta and X
6. Old Greek coins
7. Sermon
8. Turn outward
9. Despicable
10. Long part of the law
11. Save
12. Blue-pencils
13. _____ majesty
14. Cupid
15. Penn _____, N.Y.
20. Player of jokes
21. Steele's colleague
26. Actress Maureen

27. Feudal Japanese warrior
28. Clam's big brother
29. Grand and Bryce
30. Ex-fighters
31. Farsighted one
32. One of 25 or so in a pat of butter
33. Gets rid of
34. Prepares
36. Acid _____
37. Summoned
41. Is indebted
43. Put on a jury list
44. _____ into (scolds)
45. Winter-sports item: Var.
46. Monarch
52. Inflation shapes
53. Building parts
55. Instruments for reveilles
56. Medicine man
58. He had a last case
59. Songstress Dinah
60. Heavy knife
61. G.I. offense
62. Kind of lifter
63. Photo

64. _____ Rabbit
65. Furniture style
66. _____ Park, N.Y.
67. Varnish base
68. Nevertheless, for short
69. Nigerian native

109 Prom Time by William H. Ford

And all the youthful zest that goes with it.

ACROSS

1. Junior Class dinner dance, e.g.
6. Govt. unit
10. Texas univ.
13. ". . . the students shall be bravely ____"
17. Tropical Asian tree
18. Only
19. Graduate degrees
20. Sacred: Prefix
21. Enjoys the big event
23. Where some dancers feel they are
25. Bill-sending time: Abbr.
26. Duck genus
27. Highway sign
28. "By me," in bridge
29. Attired for the big event
34. Cupid
35. Prefix for dynamics
36. Chinese date
37. The urge to cut loose
40. When the last celebrant flakes out
42. Univ. of Hawaii locale
46. Go like blithe spirits
49. Indelible or India
50. Word for the ball
53. Dancer, to escort: "Don't tread ____"
54. Fraternity letter
55. Least liable to injury
56. Her word for her chic dress
57. Nimble
59. Big shot, in a way
61. Cambridge campus
62. Reduce
64. Bit of truth stretching
65. Wave ____ wand
68. American humorist
70. Arabian port
71. All aflutter
73. Aurora
74. "____-ce pas?"
75. Golfer, at times
76. Recent: Prefix
77. Shows radiance
80. Christian monogram
82. Former soccer star
83. "____ go Mets!"
86. Dazzles the eyes at the ball
92. Morning-after drink
94. French goose
95. Have ____ of fun
96. Army rating
97. Teeth
99. Under full steam
102. Dab, as of bitters
103. Wall décor
104. Maple genus
105. French storm
106. Fencing sword
107. Cobb and others
108. River of Italy
109. Bridge expert

DOWN

1. Handled rudely
2. Off the ship
3. Customer for Mrs. Hoople
4. Bout's end, often
5. Jabber
6. Have ____ to (intend)
7. Be rebuked
8. Robinson and family
9. Uh-huh
10. Happy expression
11. Result of a base hit
12. Escort, for short
13. Traditional party pooper
14. Eruptive outpourings
15. Several weeks, to teeners
16. Uproars
22. So, to Burns
24. German article
27. "____ 'nuf!"
30. Fête nocturne
31. Certain missile: Abbr.
32. Scottish breeches
33. Footnote abbrs.
38. Lulu
39. Deprive of official rank
40. Ready and able
41. "Roger!"
43. High mark on an exam
44. Throws with effort
45. Pressing
46. Underside, in architecture
47. Handy, as to a rail link
48. One-celled creatures
51. ". . . the King of Siam, ____"
52. "Because ____ June!"
58. Game marble
60. Black-____ affair
63. Gretel's sib
66. Capital of Belorussia
67. Brook's relative
69. Feminine suffix
72. Paris's Arc de ____
78. Banquo's son
79. Pipe bend
81. Barrel part
82. Sweetie ____
84. Tone deafness
85. Land tenure
86. Partner of fast
87. Word after oops
88. Heels over
89. Miss Shearer
90. Participial ending
91. Onetime Yankee Irv
92. Between A and F
93. Musical work: Abbr.
98. What to do at 1 Across
99. Fleming
100. Kind of wash or tie
101. Dozen dozen: Abbr.

110 Who? by Mary Virginia Orna

Some roses that are indeed called by another name.

ACROSS

1. Aristocrat's trademark
6. Ladies
11. "Come Back, Little ___"
16. Of one's heritage
17. Court decision
18. Stately dance
20. Who's Herbert Khaury?
21. "Cloister and Hearth" author
22. So-so
24. Personate
25. Eland's relative
27. Meeting record
29. Wee one
30. Kind of rug
32. Like some apricots
34. Viennese psychiatrist
35. Enter
36. Blood fluids
37. Caper
39. "The Eagle ___ Landed"
40. Model-airplane wood
41. Papal vestments
44. Bridge-bidding convention
46. Bach products
47. Swan genus
49. Chemical substance
50. ___ the future (electric auto, maybe)
51. Kicked up one's heels
55. Scenario: Abbr.
56. Common colds
59. ___ Culp Hobby
60. Shunner of grapes
62. "Pale ___ offerings...": Macbeth
64. River island
65. Concave or convex item
66. Who's Frances Gumm?
68. Singer Paul
69. Sea bird
70. Loading-platform worker
71. Miss Merkel
72. Kitchen utensil
73. Certain incomes
75. Pen point
77. People using olive forks
79. Drums' companions
80. Money in Sonora
82. Who's Hector Hugh Munro?
83. Go-betweens
85. Examples
87. Pee Wee and Della
91. What one is often out of
92. Toot
93. Italian town of W.W. II
95. Cult
96. Japanese premier during W.W. II
97. Novelist Cornelia
99. Faint
101. Fib
102. Ancient name for Tokyo
103. Rant and rave
105. Who's Vladimir Ilich Ulyanov?
107. Sal of song
108. Rifle
110. Kind of ends
112. Repeat
114. Boil
115. Diminutive suffixes
116. Medieval helmets
117. Endured
118. Oglers
119. Snare

DOWN

1. Blare of trumpets
2. Aloof
3. Who's Josip Broz?
4. Thane's countryman
5. City on the Chemung
6. Who was naughty?
7. Land measure
8. Thomas Hood's "The Dream of Eugene ___"
9. Press, etc.
10. Who's Marie Henri Beyle?
11. Gushes
12. Actress June
13. Vigil times
14. Tavern feature
15. Who's Jacques Thibault?
16. More opulent
19. Vain one
20. Italian poet
23. Liquid heaters
26. Storage places
28. ___ Bator
31. Bumpkins
33. Phones
35. One of the Bowls
38. Who's Tula Finklea?
40. Adriatic winds
42. Who's Charles Lamb?
43. Relative of an org.
45. One who broods
46. Ended a chess game
48. Pays back
50. Dozes
51. Parts
52. Chris ___ Lloyd of tennis
53. Who's Phyllis Isley?
54. Princeton president: 1933–57
56. Actor James and family
57. Trail habitué
58. Deneb and Rigel
61. Wood: Prefix
63. Rights org.
66. Fonda and Withers
67. Hackman and Lockhart
68. Most sprightly
70. Weighs by lifting
72. Hogarth subject
74. Spotted pony
76. Dummies
78. It houses the stapes
80. Who's Norma Engstrom?
81. Like frustrated skiers' slopes
83. Fall flower
84. As ___ gold
85. Den
86. Blackthorn
88. Rolling ocean swell
89. Dazzling effects
90. Arrow shaft
92. Yanked
94. Sea off Greece
97. Virile
98. Black
100. Part of TNT
103. Supporter of Cicero
104. Memo
106. Verne's captain
109. Gel
111. Offering of a rev.
113. Thing, in law

111 Forget-Me-Nots by Henry Hook

Of a variety that flower in the mind.

ACROSS

1. Ishmael called him crazy
5. Early Dickens
8. Balder's killer
12. Nonpicket
16. Inept one
17. Bean
18. "What are you? Some kind of ____?"
19. ____ order (tough job)
20. Kind of prize
21. Actor Richard
22. "Curiosity Shop" girl
23. Home for about 2.5 billion
24. Way to keep track of time changes
28. Diminutive suffix
29. Poet Lazarus
30. Half the title of a 1970's best seller
31. Old vaudeville-circuit name
32. Jersey's Garden State is one
34. Shebat's follower
35. Pi-R squared, etc.
36. Author Rand
37. Magis' beacon
38. Arab garment
39. Composer of "Symphonie Espagnole"
41. Tabby's remark
42. Salad ingredient
44. Urban rainy-day scarcities
48. How to dispose of old ties
49. "____, though I walk through . . ."
50. Aunt, in Sonora
51. Melville book
52. Appreciative song, with 54 Across
54. See 52 Across
56. Goshen or Nod
57. Clod
58. Poetic word
59. Ohio city
60. Doggy-bag contents
61. "What's the ____?"
63. Em halves
64. Habiliment
65. Makeshift piggy bank
66. Work
68. "____ a mo'!"
69. Lhasa ____ (dogs)
72. Bit of repartee
73. It starts on a Roman-numeral page
77. Sore
78. "The ____ rim dips . . .": Coleridge
79. Kilmer offering
80. French wall
81. Fact about the ninth month
85. Nonpick of the litter
86. Output from St. Helens
87. Hebrew letter
88. Soprano Frances
89. Two-toed sloth
90. "The ____ Love"
91. Arrow poison
92. Not masc. nor fem.
93. Advantage
94. City on the Aar
95. Fire: Prefix
96. Angelic strings: It.

DOWN

1. Makes sense
2. Press-agentry
3. Stage-door Johnny
4. Singer Lucrezia
5. Saying "I do, I do," maybe
6. Boys Town's nearest city
7. Author Grey
8. Gateway Arch, e.g.
9. "____ the money . . ."
10. Russian farmer
11. 'Twill, updated
12. Steadfast
13. Winter melon
14. Mrs. Longworth et al.
15. "Tiger! Tiger!" poet
17. Certain girl watcher
25. Big Apple
26. Verdi's dedication to the Suez Canal
27. Theme-song girl
33. First of each month, in old Rome
34. Like the U.S. in 1941–1945
35. Nautical position
37. Attend a bon voyage party
38. Boat people, often
39. "Merry Widow" composer
40. ____-garde
41. "____ Lady"
43. Where stoas abounded
44. Prove satisfactory
45. Surrounded by
46. Karloff
47. Sauce source
48. Town in France
53. Sal and vanilla
54. Prepare to drive
55. Tending to overdo
62. Clarinetist Pete
65. Clown, in circus jargon
67. Partner of tush
68. "But where ____ snows of . . .?"
69. Preposition for Phileas Fogg
70. Slow-moving horse
71. Pygmalion's Galatea, e.g.
72. Tremble
73. Corn or eye
74. Novelist Eric
75. Got in line: Var.
76. Typos
77. "____ Madeleine": Cagney film
78. Ladd role
79. Showy flower
82. Boor
83. Between hop and jump
84. "A ____ plan, a canal: Panama"

112 Getting in Shape by Dorothea E. Shipp

Doing exercises from Euclid's how-to book.

ACROSS

1. Give the glad eye to
5. Ionian Sea gulf
9. Freshwater fish
13. Lively dance
18. Secular
19. Novelist Uris
20. Palm leaves: Var.
21. Convex molding
22. Area of watery riddles
25. Lotus or pumpkin fan
26. Marshal of the old West
27. Anent
28. Certain feast
29. "____ a lovely day?"
30. Ranch denizens
32. Apollo's path
34. Unvaried recital
36. "____ Brute!"
37. Cherish
38. Show disdain
39. Call-up letters
40. Seize
42. Live it up
45. Carpentry disk
49. Bridle bit
53. Pirogue
54. Reply: Abbr.
55. Barbara ____ Geddes
57. "____ in the mind!"
58. Estonian city
59. Miss Gardner
60. Miss Swit
62. Meadow sound
63. Utter monotonously
65. Toper
66. Eleven-year-olds, e.g.
68. Year, in Spain
69. Disparage
71. ____ -Anne-de-Beaupré
72. Move at ____ (run easily)
73. French Impressionist
75. Ocean farer: Abbr.
76. ____-Magnon
77. Hose disasters
78. Popular whodunit poison
80. Be ready with a scheme
83. Having a fancy edge
85. So, in Perth
86. Instance: Fr.
89. Nastase's namesakes
90. ____ on to (grab)
93. Fertile valley of Calif.
97. "On ____ night"
99. Month before mai
100. Stage of progress
102. Risky
103. Kind of arts or print
105. French resort
107. Not bright
108. Paying-guest house
109. As you were
112. Uneven
113. Olive genus
114. Fear: Fr.
115. Word before body or freeze
116. Mural artist and family
117. Auto pioneer
118. Luge
119. Certain eating place

DOWN

1. Ester of an acid
2. Attic
3. Clinging mollusk
4. Old French coin
5. King of Mowbray
6. Retraced one's steps
7. Bullfighter
8. Black bird
9. Diner's dunker
10. Seaweed
11. Slander
12. Vane letters
13. Digresses sharply
14. ____-garde
15. Gambling games
16. Fat ingredients
17. French gateways
22. Egyptian god of pleasure
23. Underworld god
24. Outsiders
29. Endless
31. Behave in a disorganized way
33. Fox and Rabbit
35. Some paintings
37. ____ Simbel, Nile sight
38. Farmer in the spring
41. Powerful card
43. Blouse decoration
44. Letters
45. Market containers
46. Division word
47. Tennis's Rod and family
48. Of each, in prescriptions
50. Famous Easter-egg maker
51. Plains of South America
52. Stretchable quality: Prefix
53. Soup-factory worker
56. Old coin of Greece
58. Royal wedding wear
59. Lawyer: Abbr.
60. Auctioneer's offering
61. Prefix for foil
64. How Berlin was supplied in 1948
65. Abandon
67. Common Latin abbr.
70. Friend of Porthos
71. Spanish wife: Abbr.
74. Faroe winds
76. Lebanon growth
77. Precipitation in Scotland
79. Roman 152
81. Sheathing for some claws
82. Certain Wednesday
84. Drop
86. Hidden stores
87. Beached
88. Part of a turbine
91. Christmas decoration
92. Coterie
94. Mr. Lupin
95. Some lights
96. Aphrodite's love
98. "____ of robins . . ."
99. Paul and relatives
100. Okhotsk, for one
101. Lamb
104. Like summer tea
106. Cheese component
109. Sound of derision
110. Goddess of the harvest
111. Ruminant

113 Unstill Life by Phil Spiegel

A bit of nature here and there.

ACROSS

1. Portliest President
5. Electric or reclining
10. Graduated
16. S.F. time
19. Prefix for syncrasy
20. Lena
21. Potluck
23. "_____ we forget"
24. Irregular
25. "_____ wouldn't work!"
26. Hebrew measure
28. Scottish denial
29. Furtive
30. Indians
31. Indulged in thievery
32. Straying
34. "_____ and I want to go to . . ."
38. "_____ up, wear it out"
40. Before la
41. Modest poker opener
42. Founded: Abbr.
44. Fastener
46. Scrooge was one
48. Poet's word
49. Former Vice President
51. Result from
52. Nile killer
55. Comic-strip sound
56. "_____ that is alone when he falleth"
58. Half: Prefix
61. What F.D.R. hated
62. Things often passed
64. Woo with song
66. Shoe part
68. Progenitor
71. Type of finish
72. Windsor, for one
73. Chant
74. Newbiggin _____, England
76. Distant
78. Meet a poker bet
79. Prescribed amount
81. Secretary's put-off
84. Camel-hair fabric
85. Bank employee: Abbr.
86. Abbr. on a white-sale tag
88. Aromatic plant
89. Letters of endearment
90. Pie fruit
94. Hitch
95. Oolong, for one
96. Vaunted
97. Swiss river
99. Rubble
101. One who does a gate job
102. Not _____ (less)
104. Layers
107. Horse color
108. Prohibition org.
109. Seminary degree
110. German port
111. "If _____" (Ink Spots song)
116. Western brick
118. Apple: Prefix
119. Relative of Pandora's box
120. Of the kidneys
121. Get a camera ready
122. W.W. II org.
123. Nethermost
124. Trillion: Prefix
125. Sea flier

DOWN

1. Mah-jongg pieces
2. Proficient
3. Misfit
4. Wholes
5. Cuban revolutionary
6. Trouble
7. Noisy
8. Put into
9. Ruff's partner
10. Milk not be cried over
11. _____ slicker
12. Past
13. Abner
14. Too
15. Flat fish
16. Sulky one
17. Hit a high fly ball
18. Eastern holidays
22. _____ down the drain
27. Mulish sound
29. Villain
33. "_____ longa . . ."
34. Pervade
35. Skirmish
36. Carpentry abbr.
37. Fleming
39. Othello's adviser
41. Offs' partners
42. Common Latin notation
43. British officer and shell inventor
45. Smith or Seeger
47. Prisoners
50. Like some apples
52. Unwelcome visitor
53. Suitable for marketing
54. Canada's Grand _____
57. British moor growth
59. Casualty designation: Abbr.
60. Elected ones
63. Rialto letters
65. Russian river
67. Depot: Abbr.
69. It's often bitter
70. Recent: Prefix
72. It's often let out
73. Follower: Suffix
74. North African Moslem
75. Eternities
77. Worthless, biblical style
80. Leningrad ordeal of 1941–43
82. River to the Danube
83. Void
87. Stalin or Lenin
90. "The Godfather"
91. Cruces or Palmas
92. Sound of disgust
93. Edible root
96. Intellects
98. Tiller's linkup
100. Like Simon
101. Musical passages
102. Weapon trial
103. Hag
105. Replace a crew
106. Nasty
107. Puerto _____
108. Munitions
112. Pete Roselle's org.
113. "_____ for the show"
114. Chicago culprit
115. 100 square meters
116. _____ Deco
117. High note

114 Double Takes by Mary Russ

Presenting second ways of looking at familiar things.

ACROSS

1. Encircle
6. Nursery word
10. ____ loss
13. Sloping
19. Beppo's wife
20. Geraint's beloved
21. Pester
22. Nova ____
23. What football linemen do
26. Actor Al
27. French president's palace
28. Substituted
30. Things to be known
31. Italian port
33. Wander
35. Remain at home
38. Dessert for Enrico Fermi
45. Move stealthily
48. Home for Two Gentlemen
49. Old school items
50. After a fashion
51. Olive stuffing
53. Golden king
54. Camera from Rochester
55. Rich rum cake
56. Tempt Satan
59. Property claim
60. State without proof
62. Partner of shine
63. Partners of subways
64. Activity for James Wong Howe
68. ____-relief
71. Arrivederci city
72. Melodic
73. "____ We Be Friends?"
74. Midriff problem, for some
79. Feed the kitty
80. Kind of drum
81. Radium pioneer
82. Hodgepodge
84. Clergyman
85. Rainbow
86. Ball-park offering
88. Short lecture
90. Have matching pupils
92. "____ Butterfly"
93. Starter for monde or john
94. Ape
98. Venice's Polo
101. In a calm manner
105. Bunny or Island
110. "I ____ that I dwelt . . ."
112. Actor Walter's language
114. Cugat
115. Chill
116. Ivan or Nicholas
117. Soprano Lehmann
118. City of woodsy tales
119. ____ brio
120. Swiss herdsman
121. Verse form

DOWN

1. River to the North Sea
2. Shopping center
3. Channel marker
4. Circle segments
5. Talkative beast
6. Ex-boys
7. Composer Previn
8. Widows' offerings
9. Acclimatize
10. Singer Paul
11. Soft mineral
12. Author James
13. Cleo's killer
14. Egyptian talisman
15. Lunatic cause
16. "Take ____ from me"
17. Supreme Court number
18. New Mexican pueblo people
24. Vaporize
25. Cling closely
29. Albanian river
32. Cadmus's daughter
34. Wood sorrel
35. Relative of Exxon and Mobil
36. Hebrew letters
37. Nile sight
39. Care for
40. Northern Italian lake
41. Anchor
42. Skirt length
43. American painter
44. Double curve
45. Small field, in England
46. October stone, in Spain
47. Land of the lamas
52. Wise men
53. Unit of pottage
55. Puff up
57. Rub out
58. Terrible
60. Sighing words
61. Spanish queen
64. Miffed
65. ____ Chaco, S.A.
66. Gives a certain recital
67. Symbolic pole
68. Small fowl
69. Luanda is its capital
70. Baby bringer
71. What Eve did
73. Rib
74. Kind of thing
75. ____-dieu
76. "For ____ be Queen o' the May"
77. Counsel, old style
78. Arizona town
80. Bird needing a toupee
81. On this side: Prefix
83. Growing old: Var.
84. Typewriter roller
86. Finish a skirt
87. A Skinner
89. "I ____ Camera"
91. Royal guardsmen
95. Satisfies
96. Defeatist's words
97. Critic-author Kenneth
98. Roman 1515
99. Central Honshu town
100. Dream, to Napoleon
102. "Iliad," for one
103. Puerto ____
104. Paradise
106. Slush
107. Yugoslav name
108. Part of a co. sign
109. Korea's Syngman
111. Start of a refrain
113. Sea bird

115 Option by Louise Earnest

Presenting a query on personal choice.

ACROSS

1. Thick-shelled clam
7. Spring event
11. Barber's offering
16. College in East Orange, N.J.
17. Sewing-machine inventor
18. ". . . where angels fear to ____"
19. Start of a question, with 35, 55, 61 and 71 Across
21. Castor-bean product
22. Pentateuch
23. Diversify
24. Coin in Málaga
25. Sign of success
26. Bar order
28. Monday morning feeling
29. Shaw's "____ House"
32. ____ Paulo
35. Second part of question
38. Rundown
39. Neighbor of Wis.
40. Some are instant
42. Rue ____ Paix
43. End in ____ (come out even)
44. Moral nature
45. Miss Hopper
47. Theater offering
48. Merchandise
49. Con (animated, in music)
50. Kind of bliss
52. Arrow-poison tree
53. "This ____ Eden . . ."
55. Third part of question
56. Architect I.M.
57. Christmas plant
59. "A time to ____, and a time to dance"
61. Fourth part of question
62. ____ the wrong way
65. Victor of films
67. Cordon ____
69. Sub ____ (secretly)
70. Keen
71. End of question
74. British measure
75. Occupy
76. Like sailors on leave
77. Billy Sol ____
78. Creation
79. Saint Joan, for one

DOWN

1. Call it ____
2. ____ grabs
3. National League player
4. Happy sound
5. Hooray for Pele
6. Civil War vets' org.
7. Throws a monkey wrench into
8. Field worker
9. Out of kilter
10. Like Willie Winkie
11. Do an X-rated act
12. Kind of stew or potato
13. Call for
14. Pace or trot
15. Best or Ferber
20. "Be it ____ so humble . . ."
24. Desert basin
26. Early pulpits
27. "____ does it!"
28. Confusion
29. Celestial wear
30. Author who asked the question
31. Yellow-fever conqueror
33. Orwell's farm
34. Score for a 43 Across situation
35. Drafted
36. Erase and start over
37. Arthur Train's lawyer
39. Actress-model Berenson
41. A ____ the dark (wild guess)
46. People: Prefix
47. Legal right
49. Marianne or Victor
51. Leaf-cutting ant
54. Repairs by fusing
57. Thick soups
58. Dull sound
60. Far-out
62. Character in "R.U.R."
63. Shylock's offense
64. German astronomer
65. Rosalind Russell role
66. Four-pointers in bridge
67. Flapper Betty
68. Comic-strip girl
69. Essen's river
71. Word before dunit
72. Southern food
73. Explorer Johnson

116 Tourist Traps by Louis Baron

Places partly hidden from public view.

ACROSS

1. Shaker sprinklings
5. Bacchante
11. Pride of Hannibal, Mo.
16. Heart
19. Eastern nurse
20. Court session
21. Tidal rush
22. Arrah's cousin
23. Advice to a Rumanian bibliophile
26. Marvin or Grant
27. Parking-meter limit, often
28. Ta-ta, in Turin
29. Blurt out
30. Checkpoint Charlie complaint
37. Kind of goat or grace
40. Old French measure
41. Mutual haters
42. Hope's on-the-road crack to Crosby
47. Ended, to poets
48. Hokkaido native
49. Aged beer
50. Kennel arrival
53. "_____ Joey"
54. Miss Langtry and namesakes
55. Piece of mag. art work
56. Madeira wines
58. Germ-free
60. Make _____ of it (jot down)
61. Fringed two-seater
62. Tass review of a striptease
66. Different: Prefix
68. Delicacies
69. Davis and Lansbury
72. Think-tank output
73. Conduits
74. Deck out
76. Crocked
77. Crag

78. Italian novelist Matilde
79. Borscht base
80. Fire stair: Abbr.
81. Quote from a bored London tourist
87. Russia's noman's land
89. Vincent Lopez theme
90. Commune in Algeria
91. Greeting to Tarzan from a King
96. Not in town
97. "_____ Majesty"
98. More like men's pockets
102. Needlefish
103. Rebuke to Mrs. Truman on her African tour
109. Mouth: Prefix
110. Poet W. H.
111. Vicar's aide
112. Condition: Suffix
113. Zenana quarters
114. Antler tip
115. Eaglestones
116. Fork part

DOWN

1. Palm starch
2. Entebbe name
3. Cleanse
4. Prime targets for reducers
5. East Indian tree
6. "Pure joy of knowledge rides as high _____": Conquest
7. Boston time
8. Point
9. Gypsy in "Il Trovatore"
10. Noise unit
11. "_____ coffee?"
12. Range or price
13. Mature
14. Tax initials
15. Hair or drag
16. Sheepdog
17. Expanses

18. He didn't give a damn
24. Heavy literature
25. Have, to Burns
29. Gusty, in Ulm
31. Lion-colored
32. Garden asset
33. Associations
34. Author Hammond
35. Kind of do-well
36. P.O. boss
37. Pickup points
38. Two-timer
39. Winged missive
43. "_____ thee, blithe Spirit!"
44. Did a lube job
45. Gives license
46. Conference site of 1945

50. Analogies
51. Caucho tree
52. Freud's field: Abbr.
54. Forked-tongue artists
55. Curares' cousins
56. Like some midriffs
57. Hankering
59. Large bird
60. Hard-sell phrase
61. Beethoven's Kreutzer, e.g.
63. Mite or tick
64. Fountain nymph
65. Seaweed
66. S.R.O. play
67. Tokyo's old name
70. Usher's domain

71. France's West Point
73. Radio, press, etc.
74. Mount opposite Gibraltar
75. Resuscitated tire
78. Hypodermic device: Abbr.
81. Mess sergeant: Abbr.
82. Wine: Prefix
83. Proclaim
84. Gush
85. Barrymore or Dors
86. "This _____" (complaint about coffee)
87. Alaska's purchaser
88. Aegean island

91. Nearsighted cartoon Mr.
92. Almost extinct
93. Hebrew letter
94. Make joyous
95. Part of m.p.h.
99. City of Rumania
100. Galway's land
101. Go up
103. Chatter
104. "_____ Town"
105. Japanese salad herb
106. Hangout
107. Part of TNT
108. Krazy _____

117 Brevity by Stephanie Spadaccini

A bit of space-saving to get ideas across.

ACROSS

1. Sticky
6. Coop occupants
10. Alas, in Augsburg
13. Friend, in France
16. Spanish lady
17. Criminal
18. Kind of monk
21. City due west of Butte, MT
23. Romantic pl.
24. Believer: Suffix
25. Abner's creator
26. Carpenter, sometimes
28. Tree juice
29. Calif. time
30. Dusky
33. Confused
34. "A Farewell to ____"
35. Army supplies, for short
36. Instructs
38. Sphere
39. Run in
41. Discredits
42. Significant
45. Gives off
47. Impressario Hurok
49. Ticonderoga et al.: Abbr.
50. ____ easy (informal)
51. Street urchins
53. Lanterns
55. TV horse
56. Half a fly
57. Morsels
58. Help prepare for publication
60. Imbiber
61. Home of the C.I.D.
63. X-lge. wrestler
68. Buttery spreads
69. Predicament
70. Kind of review
71. Angry
74. Stout's Wolfe
75. Trojan king
76. Vassals
78. Composer Gustav and family
80. Mountain
81. Offices for gens.

83. Coffins
84. Metallic blue colors
85. Fauna's sister
87. Conductors' needs
89. Actress Myrna
90. Certain night bird
92. Youth orgs.
93. Ladd or King
95. German composer
96. Without visible ____ support
98. Roman 605
101. Family member
102. Preacher McPherson et al.
104. Tchaikovsky's lake
105. "Vive ____!"
107. N. Coward play
109. Where you are after you've burned your brs.
112. Florida tribe
113. "The Stranger" author
114. Actor John and family
115. Adam's ____
116. Nautical rope
117. Biblical victim
118. Like tree-lined lanes

DOWN

1. Things to shift
2. Dark
3. Genus of sunfish
4. R. and F. Lockridge sleuths
5. Swing off course
6. "I can't ____" (no choice)
7. Runs out
8. Immediately
9. Photo
10. Reference books
11. hags
12. ____ heart (be kind)
13. Spring mo.
14. Old-time gambler's trans.
15. Eastern religion
16. Make a trade
17. Antiaircraft fire
19. ____ diem
20. Soldier's good night
22. Not up and down
27. Comic Bert and family
31. Soul, in Saint-Lô
32. Sml. person
34. "Rule, Britannia" composer
35. Painter
37. Slices
38. Steinbeck's "East ____"
39. "We ____ please"
40. City on L. Erie
42. Electra's brother
43. Heavy wts.
44. Dutch commune
45. Relatives of ids
46. Playwright Connelly
48. ____ maid
50. Dowdy one
52. Mountain climbers
54. Word before night or summer
55. N.F.L. fan, the day after
59. Individuals of distinction
60. Divine actress
62. "The Heart Is a ____ Hunter"
63. Ovid's 1101
64. Water pipes
65. Roof parts
66. Declare
67. Loch of note
69. H.S. dance
71. ____ Pinafore
72. Trotter fodder
73. Final walk on Alcatraz Is.
75. Scheme
77. Poetic pmt. due
79. Jaworski or Errol
80. Solitary
82. Refuses
85. Envision
86. Impressive
88. Chinese truth
90. Plain-looking
91. Legal
93. Snakes
94. Calves' ____
95. Gold digging
97. Drew and Hanks, for short
98. Ancient priest
99. Old-fashioned
100. French drinks
102. Own, in Glasgow
103. Animal lover's org.
106. Miss Kett
108. Women's
110. Mr. Hunter
111. Ethiopian prince

118 Carte du Jour by Elaine D. Schorr

Possible selections for a balanced intake.

ACROSS

1. East Indian tree
5. Kind of Prophet
10. In ____ (chaotic)
15. News item
19. Accommodation
20. City of Turkey
21. Riveter of W.W. II
22. Pain in the neck
23. Topic on the Walrus's agenda
26. Son of Seth
27. Old French currency
28. Shine's sidekick
29. Artistic quality
31. Weight deductions
32. Bloodhound's forte
34. Actress Damita and others
35. Stephen or William Rose
36. Cold Adriatic wind
37. Ballroom dance
40. Might and main
41. "____ in My Soup"
45. Easy gait
46. Adds poundage
48. Miss Lee of silents
49. Long yarn
50. Wife of Athamas
51. Harvard club
54. Native of Bengal
55. Restraining ropes
57. Light gas
58. Honor, Dean Martin style
61. Gives out
63. Writer Yutang
64. Rainbow or brook
66. Pentagon oversupply
68. Gunther's "Inside ____"
70. Ski-lift trips
74. Recent: Prefix
75. Secretary of State under Grant
80. Alley of comics
81. Fitzgerald
83. Dumb one
84. Marilyn of the Met
85. Word with à la
86. Fruitless labor
90. Summer refreshers
91. Quasi
92. Got the dander up
93. In chivalrous style
94. Ladies of the opera
95. Lab heaters
97. Prize money at the track
98. Northern constellation
100. In the thick of
101. Title for Foch or Pétain
104. "Woe is me!"
105. Edwardian dress style
109. Ballplayer's gear
110. Take to the podium
111. Like sheep
112. Fastener of a sort
113. Comme ci, comme ça
114. What the pieman had
115. Prince Charles's domain
116. Peter Duchin's father

DOWN

1. Old money box
2. N.Z. birds of yore
3. Crustacean trap
4. Environment
5. Strong picker-upper
6. Mental products
7. Political cartoonist
8. "____ clear day . . ."
9. Got on the ticket
10. Alan of the screen
11. Like a good layer cake
12. Anglo-Saxon laborer
13. One's John Henry: Abbr.
14. Provençal verse form
15. Cleopatra's Needle, etc.
16. T-____ (gourmet food)
17. Word with bound or clad
18. Midterm event
24. Correspond
25. Alice's journey, for one
30. Author Waugh
32. Jolson's boy
33. Like fresh celery
34. Navigation aid
35. Richard or Daniel
36. Hector
38. Plant fungus
39. School sports org.
40. Go hither and yon
42. Bashful lover's proxy
43. Resort near Venice
44. Eastwood
46. Like carnival lighting
47. Girl Fri.
51. Partners of haws
52. Eastern Church member
53. Pointe near Detroit
56. Babylonian god
59. Cry of displeasure
60. Corroded
62. Aegean island
63. Spring shrub
65. Kind of check
66. Contradict
67. Breakfast offering
69. Beget
71. Simple Simon was one
72. "Here ____, gone . . ."
73. Roman goddess of hope
74. Daily TV fare
76. In ____ age (long time)
77. "Appointment in Samarra" author
78. Pries
79. One of the Allens
82. Accepts responsibility
85. Highlight of a De Mille movie
87. Take's tag-along
88. "____ Boat to China"
89. Certain Indian
90. Stendhal character
93. Ministers to
95. Be conspicuous onstage
96. N.Y.C. or London paper
97. Lustrous fabric finish
98. Hoodwinks
99. Assortment
100. Culture medium
101. Drudge
102. Enthusiastic
103. Dutch painter
106. Historical period
107. Kind of head
108. Power org.

119 Compendium by Marie West

A listing of various compatibilities.

ACROSS

1. Greek letters
6. Mall tenant
10. Running track
14. Oafs
19. "Thy word is _____ unto my feet"
20. Young salmon
21. Pitcher Blue
22. Peking's province
23. Barbers
27. Endless, to Pedro
28. Propriety
29. Breakfast fare
30. German article
31. Cochineal, for one
33. Takes ten
34. Chief exec.
35. Miss Verdugo
37. Slithery fish
38. Old French coin
39. W.W. II agency
42. Finns
49. Embrace
50. They, in Paris
51. In medias _____
52. Mutiny ship
53. Gallic exclamation
54. Author of "Fables in Slang"
55. Carry
57. Souvenirs
58. Tennis replays
59. Vindicated
61. English composer
62. Opposite of WSW
63. Parks; Park
66. Sat. performance
69. Ann and Thérèse
71. Sows a new crop
72. Portuguese dance
73. Surpassed
76. Fuss
78. Duct
79. Starch palms
80. Detective Pinkerton
81. Father's Day gift
82. Sun. talk
83. Seat for the mighty
84. Heros

89. Author Deighton
90. Carved totem pole
91. Diff. version
92. Bergen's Mortimer
93. Catch sight of
95. Jason's wife
97. High, in music
98. Certain sister
101. Penalize by fining
104. Miss Griffith of early films
106. Kind of block
108. Beards
111. Hanoverian general
112. Hawaiian food fish
113. Antic
114. Surrealist paintings
115. Brants and solans
116. Essence

117. Meredith's Harrington
118. Trapshooting

DOWN

1. Founded
2. Buoy up
3. Lion trainer
4. Siberian border river
5. Become frugal
6. Dax or Evian
7. Hired worker
8. Moose or Odd Fellows
9. Total returns
10. Openly
11. Flu bug
12. "Madam, I'm _____"
13. _____ Vegas
14. Belfry sound
15. Theater boxes
16. Ring gem
17. Streeter's "_____ Mable"

18. Massé or carom
24. Paint coats
25. Propounded
26. Tribunal
32. U.S.N.A. grad
34. Pea jackets
35. People who stare
36. Tolerant one
38. Old dirk
39. Dust Bowl victim
40. Noted Quaker
41. Senate votes
42. Gamut
43. City in West Germany
44. Penned
45. Suffix for fraud or corp
46. Op or pop
47. Niche object
48. Soap unit
54. Wide sts.
55. Doctrine
56. Bookie's quote
57. _____ bien

59. Not yet up
60. Depot, in Paris
61. Does arithmetic
64. S.A. rubber tree
65. Longs for
66. Gog and _____
67. Town in India
68. "We're off _____ the Wizard"
69. Bridge
70. Look after
72. Electrical unit
73. Equal a poker bet
74. Wind-sheltered
75. Floor or Five-Year
76. Printing pointer
77. Kin: Abbr.
79. Remnants
81. Cafeteria burden
82. Swain's song

83. Actress Ritter
85. Force out
86. Gormandize
87. "Quo _____"
88. Genetic abbr.
93. Iroquoians
94. Public spat
95. Faultfinder
96. Reunion time: Abbr.
98. Fashion
99. Jack of films
100. Consecrated
101. Slowly, in music: Abbr.
102. Drake or cob
103. Grafted, in heraldry
104. City of Colombia
105. Icelandic poetry
107. Neighbor of Minn.
109. "A _____ of wine . . ."
110. Paul Hindenburg

120 October Lament by Tap Osborn

Halloween can often lead to a lot of trouble.

ACROSS

1. Police-jacket décor
6. Like gas-station air
10. Assessment amount
15. Iroquoians
16. "What's ____?"
17. Actress Verdugo
18. First line of verse
21. Roman highway
22. Grassy marsh plant
23. Indolent
24. Sailor
25. Spread out
26. Nigerian people
27. Conjunction
28. Engage in logrolling
29. Baum martens and lapins
31. Second line of verse
40. "____ at a Time"
41. Nostrils
42. Elegance, usually with de
43. Blood relatives
44. Feature of a sun hat
45. Ace of trumps, in gleek
46. Served a winner
48. Schisms
49. Go too far
52. Third line of verse
55. Proclivity
56. Biggie on the Beaufort scale
57. Diamond or ruby
60. Greek letter
61. ____ de León
63. Kind of sack
66. ____ play
68. Of a time period
69. Miss Gluck

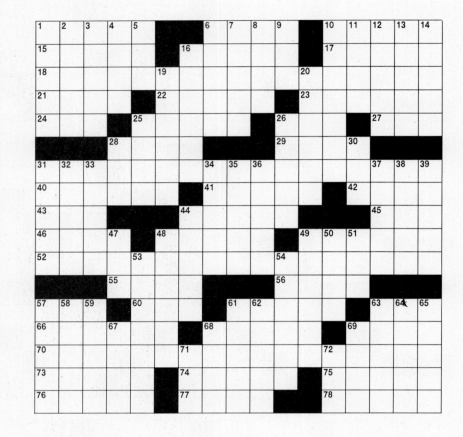

70. Last line of verse
73. Strike out
74. Dull finish
75. Jagged
76. Merits
77. Self, to Caesar
78. Barfly

DOWN

1. Suit
2. Japanese porcelain
3. Scuba ____
4. Late actor Will
5. Sixth sense
6. Peter or Henry
7. Like sharp mountaintops
8. Otherwise, in Scotland
9. Self-importance
10. Pastor's home
11. Jai ____
12. Mortise's partner
13. "____ to bed"
14. Cake part
16. Rules of dawn combat
19. Fish hawk
20. Halls of debate
25. Hindu deity
26. Before's partner
28. Offer
30. Open shoe: Abbr.
31. Sweet wine
32. In reserve
33. French novelist Jean
34. Bring together
35. Delicious
36. Stood
37. Bizarre
38. Zinc ____
39. Jazz
44. Objets d'art
47. Cotillion honoree
48. Adler or Tebaldi
49. Prophet
50. Despicable
51. Candidate for shearing
53. Fodder plants
54. On the father's side
57. Name for an office errand boy
58. ____ Gay
59. Deserve
61. Burns, Frost and others
62. Take the stump
63. Sailboat
64. Tickle
65. One with courage
67. Staff worker
68. Overfill a plate
69. Hair style
71. Southern campus: Abbr.
72. Take-home pay

121 Wintry Advice by Frances Hansen

Hints for what to do on a cold day.

ACROSS

1. "Steam____," Haney hit
5. Fashionable
9. Biblical giant
13. Pushes rudely
19. Preminger
20. "Ten thousand saw ____ glance"
21. Lasso
22. Place to be in winter
23. Act I for a winter day
27. Donuts
28. Noted penologist
29. Most unusual
30. Tax agent: Abbr.
31. "An eye ____ eye . . ."
32. Arias
33. Act II
37. At a ____ (bewildered)
38. Loki's daughter
41. "It is ____ wind that blows . . ."
42. Stashed away
43. Place to be in winter
44. Corrida entrant
45. Pencil stub
46. Jazz style
47. Set-to
50. Containing a metallic element
52. "On thy cold gray stones, ____!"
54. Número ____
55. Raccoon's relative
56. Pitch woo
57. Forbidden, in Frankfurt
59. Ancient country east of Jordan
60. Fiddle amateurishly
61. Intimidate
62. Eden resident
64. African antelope
67. RR employee
68. Shrimp: Suffix
69. Western hemisphere
72. Kind of collision
75. Fred's sister
76. American editor
77. Millay or Best
78. "Winnie ____" (Milne bear, Latin style)
79. Coney Island attractions
80. Mystical mantras
81. Attention
82. Dash
83. Do a road job
85. Short haircut
86. Ipso follower
88. "____ Kapital"
89. "Don't throw bouquets ____"
90. Act VII
94. Superman's friend
95. Aromas
96. Ripen
97. Hair-raising locales
100. Where Greeks met
101. Gambols
105. Acts VIII and IX
108. Stritch or May
109. Nagy of Hungary
110. Robt. ____
111. Actress Thompson
112. Curtain-stretching frame
113. Misplace
114. Bambi, for one
115. Arduous journey

DOWN

1. Beer ingredient
2. Needle case
3. Abbr. on an office memo
4. Became under the weather
5. Fruitcake rind
6. Exultant cries
7. Resident: Suffix
8. Large shipment
9. S.A. Indian
10. ____ volens (willy-nilly)
11. Bird of Paradise constellation
12. "D'ye ____ John Peel . . . ?"
13. Act III
14. Phil or Julie
15. "____ ain't got a barrel of money"
16. Competes
17. State: Fr.
18. Echo's title
24. Perfumery base
25. Antony
26. Water at the mouth
31. Act IV
32. Act V
33. Dancer Valery
34. Brand-new
35. Religious responsory
36. Glistened
38. King of the road
39. "Red" explorer
40. Ness, notably
43. O'Hara's "The ____ the Bed"
44. Like the Channel, for most swimmers
46. Act VI
47. Like Capone's face
48. Gather together
49. Name of 12 kings of Egypt
51. Japanese porcelain
53. Be ____ on (rely too heavily)
58. In control of
63. She was a lady in song
65. Adorn
66. Inherent
70. Small jazz band
71. Fortunetelling card
72. Made tracks
73. Miss Fitzgerald
74. "Woe is me!"
84. Mennonite sect
85. Scolded roundly
86. Bundle of twigs
87. "'We ____!' the captain shouted"
89. United
90. Will or Ginger
91. Renée of the silents
92. Heart of the matter
93. Miser Silas
97. Store event
98. Family group
99. Came down
100. G.I. supply
101. Liberated
102. Cousin of a T-beam
103. Yield
104. Neighbor of Neb.
105. Progeny
106. Olive or midnight
107. Rubber tree

122 Hookups by David A. Scully

Wherein some letters are called on to do double duty.

ACROSS

1. Barrelhead deposit
5. Reprove
10. Long or big follower
14. Kind of bank
18. Norwegian hub
19. Wading bird
20. Lorelei's home
21. Areas in the Seine
22. Particle, in Scotland
23. Irish isles, fish, guide
25. Time or Twain
26. Book, defrost, heavy weight
28. Jacob's ___
29. Can of ___ (mess)
30. Meter experts
31. Sucker
32. Heavy liquid
34. Kind of bath
36. Money in England
37. Phase out a debt
40. Hirt and Smith
41. Palmer, trite, barter
44. ___ humble pie (retract)
45. Honey badger
47. Things found in lodes
48. Muses or Mets
49. "He loved his country ___ other man . . ."
50. Solar disk
51. Self: Prefix
52. Like ___ of bricks
53. Imitate a peacock
54. Climatic foursome
56. Riviera resort
59. Dipsomaniac
60. Medical pioneer, land tracts, contest, ripped
64. Mil. officers
65. Hooker, old style
66. Does a brake job
69. ___ Mile Island

72. Observance
73. Field animal
74. Venetian traveler
75. Robin or Red Riding
76. Finished
77. Close
79. Teutonic gods
80. Terminus
81. Protected, fender woe, powder
85. Author of "Fables in Slang"
86. Almost, caustics
88. Money transactions
89. More weird
91. Perch
92. Approximately, as a date
93. Like a trireme
94. Dull finish
96. ___ princeps (first printing)
98. Out of the audience's sight
101. Skip
102. Swap, winter mo., California city
104. Med. subject
105. Heap
106. "___ your hat, what's . . ."
107. Caniff's Canyon
108. Run disengaged
109. All-knowing one
110. Neisse joiner
111. Principle
112. Humorist Bill and family

DOWN

1. Kind of accountant
2. Regarding
3. Lean, tax, purloin
4. "___ the Range"
5. Idle talk
6. Leander's love and others
7. Pahlavi's old domain
8. Budge of tennis
9. "Walk upon ___ mountains green?": Blake
10. Of questionable merit
11. Pelt
12. Unit, Roman tyrant, certain numeral, educator Horace
13. Thrice: Prefix
14. Air-raid precaution
15. Disturb, multitudes, compass pt.
16. School-year unit
17. Inquires
20. Suez Canal terminal
24. Fastener
27. Authorized
29. "___ in the Money"
31. Soccer great
33. Deposit
34. Teasdale et al.
35. Blue or home
36. Wine from the Douro valley
37. Melodic
38. Author Grey
39. English school
42. "It's ___" (can't be done)
43. Explosive, trial
46. Stored fodder
49. Skill, trash
51. Picnic intruders
52. ___ mundi
53. Devil's tool, in "Music Man" song
55. Bone: Prefix
56. Deep U.S. lake
57. Rhine feeder
58. Naught
59. ___ the tide
61. Zoo animals
62. ". . . that bloom in the spring, ___"
63. Adam's grandson, spoke, fop
67. Suppress
68. More painful
69. And ___ some
70. Whet
71. Pole, move rapidly, floor covering
72. Gypsy man, measured
73. Informers
76. W.C.T.U. members
77. What Florida has a lot of
78. City in Sicily
79. Hard tennis servers
81. Drug plant
82. Type sizes
83. Kind of Greek column
84. Handbill
87. Cad
90. Remember
92. Fall drink
93. "The Three Faces ___"
94. Swabs
95. Parisian friend
97. Have the nerve
98. Augury
99. Strong blast
100. Summers, in Savoie
102. Even if, for short
103. Way: Abbr.

123 Meanings by George Madrid
Presenting some definitions that usually are answers.

ACROSS

1. Kind of rich
5. Expert
8. Rude homes
12. Postal initials
15. Dialect
16. Yutang
17. Lop, old style
18. Black: Prefix
19. "____ not amused"
20. Iron or coon's
21. Catarrh
22. Ref. books
24. Lib people
25. Ais
28. TV store trade-in
30. Old lace's partner
31. Well-known whaler
32. Nautical direction
33. Certain previews
35. Make possible
37. Cruel one
39. Attracted
40. Gets ready, for short
41. Ball or bid
44. Through train: Abbr.
45. W.W. II spy org.
47. Erie, for one
49. Destroyer, often
51. Be of advantage
53. Ike's military field
55. Seed of a vetch
57. Top-notch
58. Saki
63. Parl. members
64. Kind of type or plasm
65. Inferior fleece
66. Penthouse
68. Org. for Snead
70. Another name for 82 Down
76. John Dickson of mysteries
77. Social reformer Jacob
78. Famous Giant
79. Spanish head shawl
80. Having credit
83. Prepared for knighthood
85. Garb for a priest
87. Triumphant cry
88. Ginza currency
89. Wiliness
92. Wither
94. "Do ____, not as I do"
96. "How ____ my heart . . ."
98. Time for old TV movies
100. Between K and O
101. Part of A.M.A.: Abbr.
103. House mover of a sort
106. Hit tune for Arnaz
108. Western sample of 2 Down
111. Dress trimming
114. Places for asides
115. Catch a fish
116. Good card
117. Blanched
118. Right away, for short
119. Kind of diluvian
120. System: Suffix
121. Adapts to
122. Campus org.
123. Gardener's bane
124. Work on edging
125. Bones

DOWN

1. Thought: Prefix
2. 78 Across was one
3. Miss Lee of blonde note
4. Correct
5. Typewriter part
6. Avenged
7. Singular person
8. Hitters' dream feats
9. Pocket shapes
10. Pang of pain
11. More composed
12. Get a fresh fuel supply
13. Decamp
14. Russian villa
15. Labor org. of early 1900's
18. Manila airport designation
22. Fire or narrow
23. U.S. org. for senior citizens
26. Gen. Ira of W.W. II
27. Patronize a cafe
29. Speedy planes
32. Ingenuous
34. "The ____ the Fugue"
36. Humanities degree
37. Word with dash or happy
38. Kind of heat or eclipse
40. Member of the O.A.S.
42. Samovars
43. French season
46. Take care of
48. Cartoon deer
50. Badge of a tourist
52. Not totally
54. "Here's ____ absent friends"
56. Represent
59. Apple-pie baker
60. ____ hand (abjectly)
61. Lariat
62. Cornet, to a cockney
67. Metrical feet
68. Part of a sheet of stamps
69. Other words for 8 Down
71. ____ of Samothrace
72. ____ home (out)
73. Since
74. Allen
75. Breed of sheep
76. Like a shrinking violet
81. Ottoman title
82. Pack animals
84. Hear
86. Gentle person
90. Roman road
91. Borrower's safeguard
93. Sunnybrook Farm resident
95. Maltreats
97. One of Churchill's words for Russia
99. Least colorful
101. Med. group
102. Gown material
104. Climbing vine
105. Owner of la plume
107. Small lunar crater
109. Touched
110. Trot, for one
112. Juno, to the Greeks
113. U.S.N.A. grad

124 Mr. Malaprop Speaks by Bert Kruse
And, like his wife, he has his own way with words.

ACROSS

1. Lean eater
6. Roof border
10. Part of A.F.L.
15. Evergreen
16. Writer Horatio
17. Florentine painter
19. Crucifixion site, to Mr. M.
21. Not to be believed, according to Mr. M.
23. Vast ages
24. Evolution-trial name
25. On the deep
26. Curve
27. Dill plant
28. Delirious, to Mr. M.
30. Kind of skirt
31. Steal from again
33. Dutch commune
34. Organic compound
35. Beer brewings
36. Fathers of jrs.
37. Ameliorate
39. Treaty
41. French novelist
42. "___ We Trust"
43. Adventuress Johnson
44. Genie's home
45. Whitman home
47. Very favorable, to Mr. M.
50. Shade of blue
54. Seriously injured
55. Old instrument
56. Dictionary name
57. Kind of pike or stile
58. Knightly attire
59. Kind of sum
60. Image seekers' problems
61. Tobaccos
62. Look like a wolf
63. Truck, for short
64. Crib

65. Party
66. Old Icelandic work
67. Former enemy, to Mr. M.
69. Parisian caps
70. Guardsman portrayer
72. Silkworm
73. Heads
74. Campus plodder
76. Dice thrower's plea
77. Cleo's attendant
78. Investment bonds: Abbr.
81. Muse
82. In a jiffy
84. To's follower
85. Dolly Varden
87. Flycatcher
88. It was the Spanish ___, to Mr. M.
91. Sicilian city
92. Panay islander
93. Slay
94. Leave-takings
96. Artless
97. Russian dictator, to Mr. M.
100. "___ the Breakfast Table," à la Mr. M.
102. "One man, ___"
103. Thin dress material
104. Props for Ozawa
105. What some laws lack
106. British composer
107. First U.S. tennis champ

DOWN

1. "Kinquering cong" man
2. Tree surgeons
3. Totals
4. Have a role
5. Gumshoes
6. Pass
7. Lace part
8. Recto's opposite
9. Ending for rook or fish
10. Kind of descendant
11. Have ___ (dine)
12. Spoiled
13. Oriental sash
14. German measles
15. Daubs
16. Skirted
17. Kid of Western fame
18. Cow and Dinsmore
20. Former Secretary of State
22. Superlative endings
25. "___ Misbehavin'"
29. Résumé
30. Mr. M. loves those of Haydn and Brahms
32. Toot
35. Art or chewing
38. Like a good brandy
39. In a childish snit
40. Caama
41. Verve
42. Living forever, to Mr. M.
44. Grazing grounds
45. Got involved
46. Used sights
47. TV part
48. Metal unit
49. Water bird
51. Container size
52. Prods
53. Handle: Fr.
54. Sire
55. Like Dali's watches
59. Book to study
60. Singer Tennessee
61. Most miffed
63. Exhilarate
64. Sentence
65. Bristle
68. Ad signs
69. Rank above a knight
71. Numero ___
73. Dugout canoe
74. Cave
75. Like an angel's face
76. Its age is often mentioned
78. One who gives
79. Foot problems
80. Groups of reporters, etc.
81. Greek letters
82. Unctuous
83. Give one's views
84. Conclusion
86. Singer Tebaldi
88. Goofy one
89. Gods' blood
90. Car-wheel inclination
95. Weeps
98. Grant's counterpart
99. Opposite of arr.
100. Energy initials
101. Half of a life vest

125 Take Two by Alfio Micci

And pair them up by watching them repeat themselves.

ACROSS

1. On ___ with
5. Prefix for ton or phone
9. Composer of "The Bohemian Girl"
14. Trouble
17. Place for a hero
18. Mideast trouble spot
19. Met offering
20. Spew out
22. Loose change; fragment
25. Sassy
26. Material for boxer shorts
27. Smart or jet
28. Perfect place
29. Nobility
32. Statesman Dean
35. Have ___ for (desire)
36. Gasoline rating
37. Haydn or Hemingway
39. Hammer part
41. Palm leaf: Var.
42. Fitting; fitting
46. Did a lawn job
50. Deerlike animal
52. Kind of goose
53. Bombeck and namesakes
54. Brisk, in music
55. Downing St. number
56. Observance
57. Musical piece
58. Capitol feature
59. Kind of ager
61. Indistinct
62. What piu lento means
64. Inhaled; unlike
70. Smooth
71. Parliament people
72. Branch of math
73. ___ avis
74. Arthurian lady
75. On the briny
77. Emulate Thespis
80. Bakery installations
82. "___ plan, a canal: Panama"
83. Ilk
84. Okinawan port
86. Deaf, in Milan
87. Parasite; stannum
89. As the occasion arises: Abbr.
90. Secondhand
92. Overlay
93. Card games
96. His, in Germany
99. Crusader's foe
103. Brazilian tree
104. Bicuspid's neighbor
106. Afflict
107. What hams chew
110. Egg-shaped
111. Rank indicator; goblin
116. Doctrine
117. Pours
118. Versifier
119. River to the Baltic
120. Half a fly
121. Black-ink item
122. He, in Italy
123. Hack

DOWN

1. Madison Ave. products
2. Architect I.M.
3. What some winners take
4. Noted muralist
5. Desert phenomenon
6. Clear the blackboard
7. Wolfe character
8. "The King ___"
9. S.A. country
10. Silly
11. Wharf
12. Worries
13. Musical instinct
14. Sobbing
15. Actor Davis
16. Allen or Frome
20. Salamander
21. Complain; musical instrument
23. Dash
24. ___ Flow
28. French article
29. Mastwood
30. Brilliance
31. Storehouse
33. Beat; cotillion
34. Chooses
37. Lose one's breath
38. To ___ (exactly)
40. Roman or Christian
42. It's of no return
43. Priests of old
44. Improve
45. Soprano Adelina
47. Plains Indian
48. Irish patriot
49. Steel-plow pioneer
51. Disjoin; join
52. Like Gatsby
60. Sea bird
61. "Our Gang" comedy member
62. Small herring
63. Medieval ballad
64. Certain hairdos
65. Prefix for a Balkan
66. Less polluted
67. Gum resin
68. Mr. Chips portrayer
69. Violinist Isaac
75. Italian wine center
76. Taint
78. Blue Grotto site
79. Pulsate
81. Desperate letters
82. Time ___ half
85. Anatomical loop
88. Like some forests
91. Ending for Siam or Senegal
93. Magician's cry
94. Famed marshal
95. Timber disease
96. Sir Walter
97. House features
98. Pointless
100. Earns V.I.P. treatment
101. Buenos ___
102. Region, to poets
103. Aconcagua's range
105. After taxes
108. Superman garment
109. Slaughter of baseball
111. RR stop
112. Western time zone
113. Lupino
114. Nickname for an oilman
115. "___ tu" (Verdi aria)

126 Good Sports by Jack Luzzatto

Some things all in a day's play.

ACROSS

1. Diffracting glass
6. Enriched soil
11. Tough bounce for a shortstop
17. Other-worldly session
18. Residents
20. Athletic bird
21. One reaping a net profit
23. Flinches
24. Sly designs
25. Multitudes
26. Cried like a kitten
28. Do-it-yourself item
29. Pooh's partner
30. Comedian Sahl
31. Asset on the bases
32. The B in N.B.
33. Check
35. Pitcher Newsom
36. Litigants
37. Word after sooth
38. Office note
40. Pele and Chinaglia
43. "What are little boys ____?"
45. Castle ditch
46. Contract stipulations
50. Tenement, often
52. Festive affair: Abbr.
53. In addition
54. Ancient Toltec capital
55. Blank out
56. Gold-quality standard
58. Algerian port
59. Arab country
60. Tit for ____
61. Grand National and other races
65. Cambridge campus
66. Andes thatch grass
68. Man without competition
69. Send back
70. Boxing rendezvous
72. Spill over
73. Prohibit
74. Height measure: Abbr.
75. Stern talks
77. Where to lay an egg
79. Throat-clearing sound
81. African big game
82. Conduct ____ (have all play each other)
86. Slanted type: Abbr.
87. Nip and tuck
90. ____ the job (just starting)
91. Tough-luck player
93. Printing error, for short
96. Aid for guessing
97. Farm fields
98. Legendary ship
99. Unruly bunch
100. Soul: Fr.
101. Merman
102. "Beat it, Polonius!"
104. Eject suddenly: Var.
105. Kind of football pass
107. Shady profits
110. Gorgon with snaky hair
111. Darlings
112. Ace-queen, for one
113. Sets up a show
114. Pairs
115. Base-stealing maneuver

DOWN

1. Look closely
2. Completed 26 miles plus
3. Taverns
4. ____-fi, fiction of the future
5. Netty fabric
6. Clearance
7. Not fulfilled, as obligations
8. Plans
9. One: Prefix
10. One who dances heavily
11. Executed a salaam
12. Waterless
13. Racket
14. Islanders' game
15. Liquid part of fat
16. Annoy
17. Pierces
18. Beats steadily
19. Taunting expressions
22. Italian resort lake
27. Ram, Dodger or Angel
31. Fatty, as certain meat
32. South African Bantu
34. Old Persians' partners
35. Surly one
36. Random, as gun pellets
37. Spanish Mrs.
39. Measures out
41. Tropical tree resin
42. On one's own
43. Unbelievable happening
44. Feinted
47. Quadrennial sports event
48. Arthurian maid and others
49. Anita and Clara
50. Prepos-session
51. Song of triumph
53. Way of the hiker
57. Concern of a racing driver
58. Electrical unit
62. Forbidden
63. Famous person, for short
64. ____ out (rode the bench)
67. Tossed skyward
71. Charge an opponent
74. Ex-Giants boss Wellington and family
76. Note of debt
78. Metal source
80. Leaves to live elsewhere
83. Sea nymph
84. Lived at
85. Lacking intestinal fortitude
87. Abysses
88. Mollusk hard to detach
89. Upstate N.Y. lake
92. First-class
94. Leap upon
95. Portly
97. Reference book
98. Shun
101. Make comfortable
102. Taj Mahal city
103. Blasting explosives
104. Word element for healthy
106. Axminster, for one
108. Put down
109. Solidify

127 Last Stop by Sidney L. Robbins

And nevermore to roam.

ACROSS

1. Plate
5. Cutting remark
9. Snakes
13. Ark builder
17. Type of meat
18. Evergreen shrub
19. Word before dash
20. Thessaly mount
21. Perfume
22. Without equal
23. ____-kiri
24. Spots on cards
25. What Boston is the home of
28. Manorial court
29. Buddhist sects
30. Gentle moisture
31. Spat's coverage
32. Italian river
33. Fort ____
34. Hurok
35. Takes a flier on
38. Schooling: Abbr.
40. Auto
41. Roman foot soldiers
44. Author Sinclair
48. Nonfatal disease
50. Choose
51. Muscle woe
53. Oklahoma city
54. Egyptian deity
56. Pastoral poem
57. French philosopher
58. Violins' cousins
62. Swan feature
64. Church levy
65. Forty acres and a mule
68. Parapet structure
72. Italian host
74. Various
75. Busy airport
76. Leaf part
79. Jug-of-wine poet
82. Anger
83. Hotsy's partner
84. Most unusual
86. What charity does
91. Violin
92. Exultation
93. Chemical suffix
94. Bits
97. "Where have you ____?"
98. Graduate degrees
99. Naval missile
102. German Mr.
105. Shock
108. Kind of luck
109. Ancient Mariner's sighting
110. Mélange
111. Homely words
116. Hatred: Prefix
117. Mother of Apollo
118. Long account
119. Seductive singer
120. Vous ____
121. Old Dead Sea land
122. Bad-tempered
123. Antelope
124. Hire
125. Generators: Abbr.
126. Kind of school: Abbr.
127. Take it easy

DOWN

1. Excitement
2. Mean
3. Strike-breakers
4. ____ and now
5. Local ordinance
6. Neuron appendage
7. Melon leaving
8. Borscht basis
9. Pale
10. Negligent
11. Convict's break
12. Did garden work
13. Part of Payne's sentiment
14. Willow
15. Quivery tree
16. Must
17. Seder item
18. Type of discussion
26. Dote on
27. Speed
34. Tastes
35. Show one's poise
36. Antlered animal
37. Type of horn
39. Rubber tree
40. What chickens do
41. TV part
42. Mental-process initials
43. Fast plane
45. Married
46. Like winter streets
47. Cardinals' city: Abbr.
48. Moss or Larry
49. Indian chief
50. Pronoun
51. Time zone
52. French king
55. "So near ____ so far"
59. Bandleader Brown
60. Big Ten campus
61. Stopping place: Abbr.
63. Medicinal plants
66. Light man
67. Island off Scotland
69. Appointment
70. ____ poetica
71. French marshal
73. Little one
76. Spanish Mrs.
77. Highland wear
78. Age
80. Honest ____
81. Bro. or sis., e.g.
85. Dear one
87. Clark
88. Follower: Suffix
89. Never, in Germany
90. Moor
95. Postponed
96. Fleet
98. Sullen
99. Israelis
100. Like early movies
101. Merge
102. Certain pigeon
103. Top-notchers
104. Up
106. Climber's need
107. Molecule parts
108. Twenty-third, for one
109. Umbrella substitute
112. Gripper
113. Jewish month
114. Laugh, in Paris
115. Consumer

128 Visiting Hours by Gene Gellis

People who might make bedside calls.

ACROSS

1. Importer's outlay
7. Cheese
11. Fraternity letter
15. One who degrades
16. Shows the way
17. Feudal estate
18. He'll have to stomach you
20. He's a smooth operator
22. Miss Teasdale
23. Sherbet's relatives
24. Word before assured or in peace
25. Miss Farrow
27. Like the Titanic
30. Plato and Pericles, e.g.
33. Samoan port
36. Lawyers: Abbr.
37. Tote-board listing
39. Gets the soap out
40. Vase
41. Suit to _____
42. Pacific fish
43. Regular: Abbr.
44. Emeritus
46. Twelve inches
50. U.S. publisher
54. Tack on to a bill
55. More obese
57. Spread
58. Jargon
60. Oceangoers: Abbr.
61. Spanish pot
62. Iranian coin
63. Shipping box: Abbr.
64. Proportion
66. Cold
68. Digits: Abbr.
69. San _____ Rey of bridge note
71. Comedian Crosby
72. To-do
74. Permitted
76. Gaelic
77. Towers
79. Understood
81. Gala event
82. Contestant
83. Less important
85. Brief pool visit
88. Erode
89. Further
90. Enzyme suffix
91. Show up
94. Rickey ingredient
95. Imp
96. Stake
97. Newspaper come-ons
99. Crusaders' foes
102. Very old: Abbr.
103. Coin
104. Beef order
105. Husband of Jezebel
108. He fills his spot well
111. His concerns are small
115. Downpours
116. Happening
117. Elusive one
118. Air pollution
119. Reviews unfavorably
120. Classes

DOWN

1. Reunion lapel wear
2. Arab garments
3. Tabula _____
4. Adriatic peninsula
5. Wild
6. Back
7. Procreates
8. Poker move
9. Psyche motivators
10. N.Y. time
11. Negotiates
12. Chang's twin
13. Kind of hold
14. Perfumes
16. Find
17. Command to an Eskimo dog
19. Swiped
20. Foils a bridge contract
21. Diamond number
24. He'll see through you
26. Fool
28. Of _____ (recently)
29. Affectionate people
31. Insect egg
32. Kind of rainy-day activity
33. Distinctive trait
34. Not ready yet
35. He gets to the nitty-gritty of things
38. Eccentric
41. Passion
45. Participial ending
46. He'll look you straight in the eye
47. Connective
48. Lubricating can
49. Archer of legend
51. His bedside manner is impersonal
52. Most cordial
53. Suns
56. Kind of road or splitter
59. Light colors
60. One with allure
63. Treble or bass
65. Carry
67. Likewise
70. Sowed
72. Schedules
73. Bowling-pin number
75. Kind of fish or walk
78. June dance
80. Oak, for one
83. Vote of assent
84. This, in Spain
86. Adjective suffix
87. Doing comparison shopping
89. Biblical mountain
91. Cry of triumph
92. Hang fire
93. Race horses
94. Sacrificial period
95. Intellectuality
96. Backyard receptacle
98. Eliot _____
100. Eve of TV
101. Simple
106. _____-de-camp
107. 1930's boxing champ
109. Viet _____
110. Spanish relative
111. Vigor
112. Uncle Tom's friend
113. Not spec.
114. F.D.R. agency

129 Family Tree by David A. Scully

Blood is always thicker than water.

ACROSS

1. North Pole worker
4. Childish writing
7. Bangkok native
11. Words from Major Hoople
16. Mars: Prefix
17. Hodgepodge
18. Steps to the Ganges
19. Go, in France
20. Kind of cabin
22. Sophie Tucker was the last of these
24. Superstitious hang-up
25. Headband
27. He reigned in Asgard
28. Corroded
29. Garden flower
30. Sack or port
31. Novel by Theodore Dreiser
35. Err
36. Family members
39. Dogwood
40. "____ a great life if . . ."
41. Convenes
42. Abnormal sac
43. Perverse person
44. Kind of bet or swipe
46. Asian sheep
48. Air base near Kansas City
50. Call's opposite
51. Mal de ____
52. Barely enough
53. Family member
54. Word in tennis ranking
56. Artist Jean ____
57. Mail, in Médoc
58. Word before sucker
59. Kind of coffee
61. "I arose ____ in Israel"
63. ____ up (intensify)
65. Injury
67. French relative
68. Kind of curve
71. Indian weights
73. "Sufficient unto ____ is the evil . . ."
75. Inflexible
76. Japanese statesman
77. Neptune's home
78. Hoosier poet's family
79. Arrow poison
80. Camera eye
82. Bone: Prefix
83. The same, in a footnote
84. Dies ____
86. Letter
87. Western range
89. Chess pieces
90. Haggard novel
91. Kind of banquet
95. Marquand sleuth
97. Strange
98. Part-time work: Abbr.
99. Leaky vessel
101. Thyroid, for one
102. Aptitude
106. "____ me Will"
109. Area of Killingly, Conn.
112. Writer-director Woody
113. Bitter drug
114. With, in Dijon
115. Suffix for tonsil
116. Like Williams's menagerie
117. Time for pistols
118. Green
119. Heart

DOWN

1. Sea flier
2. Formal talk: Abbr.
3. Having leaves
4. Mideast org.
5. Intention
6. News media in China
7. "The Catcher in ____"
8. ____ bite (supped)
9. Part of N.C.A.A.
10. Prefix for gram or bar
11. De Valera
12. Open place in the woods
13. Egyptian dancing girl
14. Inge was a gloomy one
15. Upperclassmen: Abbr.
16. ____ wiedersehen
17. Different
18. Brünnhilde's horse
21. Chemical compounds
23. Romulus and Remus, e.g.
26. Comparative suffix
29. Words for George Washington
30. Humor
31. TV serials, for short
32. Emerged
33. Ballad by Dante Rossetti
34. Fall drink
35. Ruth McKenney's relative
36. TV series for Fred MacMurray
37. Arthur of tennis
38. Ragout
41. Health, in Le Havre
42. French kings after Louis V
45. Miss Hogg
46. Certain terrier
47. Bollixed up
49. Pinky and Peggy
52. Kind of cake or rubber
55. Crown
60. Entreat
62. Its coast is rock-ribbed
64. Quick musical movement
66. "Thou art my mother, and ____"
69. Direct
70. Dombey's relative
72. Lucifer
73. Neat
74. Seek's partner
81. Banana split, for one
85. Greek letter
86. English cheese
88. Pastoral
91. Like some arches
92. A lad and ____
93. Kind of type or horn
94. Place for toys
95. ____ and bounds
96. Drying chambers
99. Threshold
100. Cuba's ____ de Pinos
101. Type of worm
103. This, in Spain
104. Monte Carlo color
105. Small cities: Abbr.
106. Economic decline
107. Uncouth one
108. In the manner of
110. Miss Gardner
111. Deal or Testament

130 Quiet, Please by A. J. Santora

Readers must have a place to concentrate.

ACROSS

1. Kinsmen
5. Relative of an H-hinge
10. Neighbor of Ky.
13. Washed-out
17. Coagulate
18. Useful kind of book
20. City in Oklahoma
21. Swan genus
22. Reading matter with medieval locales
24. Alarm clock, for one
26. "____ each life . . ."
27. Former outfielder Del
28. Well-known London street
29. Exchange premium
30. Inquisitive Paul
31. Yale man
33. Supplement, with "out"
34. Old English letter
35. Moo goo ____ pan
36. Cabell of baseball
37. Roman writer
39. Literary collection
40. Early part of a book
43. "____ Were King"
44. "The ____ Story"
45. Brooder
46. Transmitter: Abbr.
47. Gratuitous
50. Retired: Abbr.
52. Emerson name
56. Library cataloguing system
59. Miss Venner
60. Emulate W. A. White
61. Like goods that can be set aside
62. June grads
64. Eisenhower

65. "Hansel ____ Gretel"
66. Reagan, to friends
67. Hot item on the book rack
71. Sturdy tree
72. Enrich
73. Part of Latin "to love"
74. Drabowsky of baseball
75. Wire measure
76. "____ Whom the Bell Tolls"
77. The sun
78. Ignited
79. Idol
81. Hungarian
84. Not spoken
86. Salvation or Coxey's
87. Earlike part
88. Bookish people
91. The ____ pajamas (hot stuff)
92. Acting part
93. Long short story
94. Smell ____
95. Freshly
96. Writer LeShan
97. Arab prince
98. Fishhook attachments: Abbr.

DOWN

1. Barges' relatives
2. ____ ease (uncomfortable)
3. Certain critiques
4. Variable
5. Coaxed
6. "To ____ not . . ."
7. Frequently, to poets
8. Bethlehem, Pa., campus
9. ____ Lopez (recording artist)
10. Japanese box
11. Sgt., for one

12. Faults
13. Author Robert ____ Warren
14. Like Coleridge's mariner
15. Hides
16. Asner and Ames
19. Outside: Prefix
23. "Knock on ____ Door"
25. Compass pt.
29. Nabokov title
30. Dime novels, e.g.
32. Kind of metrics
34. Maroon
35. Yiddish thieves

36. Printing lapses
37. Otto zur ____, German writer
38. "____ Pretty"
39. Flute (recorder)
40. Presidential Arthur
41. Kind of sphere
42. Writer Lear
44. Philadelphia skaters
48. Believers
49. Seat for Gene Autry
51. Formal observance
53. Certain borrower's need
54. Sorrow

55. Upright
57. Word with winder or dish
58. ____ out (stall)
63. Half step
67. College degrees
68. Love or hatred
69. Having commercial value
70. Fate
71. Upton Sinclair book
72. Like some of Lewis Carroll's nonsense
75. Wanton harm
76. So ____ (up to now)

78. Roman 52
79. Burnsian hillside
80. Abundant
81. One who meditates
82. Constellation Ara
83. What F. Lee Bailey's defense never does
85. Ball of thread
86. Irish town
87. Comic Johnson
88. Bikini part
89. "____ Is My Co-Pilot"
90. Summer, in Paris

131 Formalities by William Lutwiniak

Some fancy ways to express simple things.

ACROSS

1. Volcano of Japan
4. Diamond features
9. Sedan
12. Clad
17. Plant of the Southwest
19. Pointed arch
20. "Quién____?"
21. Mountain crest
22. "Take it easy!"
25. River mouth
26. Recluse
27. In the dark
28. Comedienne Phyllis
29. Zebra's pride
30. True up again
31. Charter
32. Ohio athlete
33. Classical medic
34. Snafu
37. Handles successfully
40. What this puzzle does, with 77 Across
42. Ring decision
43. Part of m.p.h.
44. Fictional whaler
45. Famed publisher
46. Irwin or Artie
47. Banking abbr.
48. Ranch hand
52. "Some of ____ Days"
53. Man of many affairs
56. Niche objects
57. Lazy one
58. Salad garnish
59. Recipe meas.
60. Château unit
61. Paderewski
63. Make slow progress
65. Dismayed
68. Mini-mesa
69. Helicopters
71. Call ____ day
72. North Carolina hero
73. Hairdo
74. Not aspirated
75. Put-down
76. 1 or 66, e.g.
77. See 40 Across
81. Miss Verdon et al.
82. Folksy
84. Concerns
85. In favor
86. Reeking
87. Others, in Sonora
88. Maryland athletes
92. Allied groupings
94. Win them all
95. Small tube
96. Ghostley or Faye
97. Costly flops
100. French historian
101. Many millennia
102. Accrue: Var.
103. Molds for metals
104. Horn sounds
105. Implore
106. Passé
107. Dehumidify

DOWN

1. Rheumatic woes
2. In arrears
3. Garage man, at times
4. Shod
5. Malarial symptoms
6. Gentleman's title
7. "All About ____"
8. Literary follow-ups
9. "____ be true?"
10. Give backing to
11. Musical notes
12. Tires
13. Threatening words
14. Did a risky thing
15. Ending for kitchen
16. Cherished
18. Beau
20. Woodland deities
23. Kennel sounds
24. Like certain gems
28. Strikes out
30. Shul V.I.P.
31. Workshop adjunct
33. Tropical jelly fruit
34. Simoleons
35. Fiat
36. Kind of house or play
37. Modish
38. Mrs. Chaplin
39. Behaves fancily
40. Jostle
41. Pawn
44. Superior
46. "____ We Dance?"
49. Saltpeter
50. Car that flopped
51. Flower in Flanders fields
52. Indian weight
54. Winged
55. Pleasing
57. Oversight
60. Disburse
61. Construction beams
62. Relish
63. Reproach
64. Raff's partner
65. Declares
66. Vingt-____
67. Smidgens
69. A stage, to Shakespeare
70. Purgative drug
73. Game fish
75. Passed out
77. Crowded places
78. Musical groups
79. Street show
80. Prepared Xmas gifts
81. Routine
83. Polar feature
85. Entreated
87. Due
88. Earth pigment
89. Sensational
90. Davis or Rice
91. Impertinent
92. Apparel
93. Robt. ____
94. Drop the other ____
97. Trap of a sort
98. Group of sayings
99. Prune

132 One-Upmanship by Sidney Frank

Giving above and beyond one's duty.

ACROSS

1. It's often au lait
5. As easy ___
10. Impressions
15. Petty evasion
18. Neat as ___
19. Regatta boat
20. Eugene of "Strange Interlude"
21. "___ dreamer, aren't we all?"
22. Yield
23. Signal to Paul Revere
25. Road mover
26. Suffix for Siam
27. Fleet animal
28. Ballots
29. Checks
31. What Old MacDonald had
33. Regaled
34. Repair places
35. Authentic
37. ___ even keel
38. Jacket for Ravel
40. Mountains
41. Pairs
42. Hesitant
43. Shinto temple
46. Game score
47. Child, in Clydesdale
49. Expect
50. School orgs.
51. Sprite
52. Famed Grandma
53. Kind of patch or bow
54. Chinese weights
55. Body of water
57. Boadicea's tribe
59. Noted existentialist
61. Librarian's word
62. Stroke on a letter
63. "___ up to his neck"
64. Miss Muffet's visitor
66. Add one for a musical instrument
67. Upstate N.Y. silver community
70. Mournful sounds
71. Fencing swords
73. Extinct Western Indians
75. Spanish queen
77. Horse play
78. Dams
79. Perfect joy
80. Peter or Nicholas
81. Jeanne d'Arc, for one
82. Heads
83. Study hard
84. Face the ___
85. Having wings
87. Eschew
88. City in Kenya
90. Showed reverence
91. Article of food
92. Lofty aim
93. To 638,000.000 or so, it's home
94. Miss Thompson
95. Ampersands
96. Equal: Prefix
99. Army unit: Abbr.
100. Neil Simon play
104. Tie the ___
105. Order's partner
106. Less troublesome
107. Certain droplets
108. Before naut or plane
109. Nigerian native
110. Office copies
111. Artist Max
112. Certain aircraft

DOWN

1. Batting-practice backstop
2. Sacred bull
3. Stem to stern
4. Compass reading
5. Nautical position
6. Intrigue
7. Contented sound
8. Seine area
9. Companion of a mortise
10. Not up
11. Old Algerian rulers
12. German drink cooler
13. Beverage
14. Cut
15. Kind of bed
16. Moslem priests
17. Forbids
20. Frequently
24. Insignificant amounts
27. Place for a mike
30. Rocky hill
32. Coal or peat
33. Chekhov girls
34. Narrow cut
35. Pledge
36. Organic compounds
38. Slant
39. What carets usually indicate
41. Small cube
42. Another signal for Revere
44. Patriot Nathan
45. Silly one
47. City in Idaho
48. Shrewd
49. Ludwig von ___, German poet
50. Singer Page
52. Tennyson's lady and others
53. Game fish
54. Stabs
56. Large animal, for short
58. Harvest goddess
60. Christie and namesakes
64. Chimney grime
65. "Why so ___, fond love?" asked Suckling
68. Jacques I of Haiti
69. Diarist Nin
70. Army lawmen: Abbr.
72. Jumbled, as type
74. Use a gunsight
76. Ancient box
78. Light-bulb unit
79. She has fun, too
80. Yuba's instrument
82. Blenheim and Crystal
83. Preside
84. Marseille ladies: Abbr.
86. Waikiki wear
87. East or West
88. Forty-niners
89. Queerest
90. Work on dough
91. Ancient Gallic seers
93. Like the rich
94. Shoal
95. Islands off Galway
97. Classify
98. Siouan Indians
101. It's in the ring
102. King of Judah
103. Part of H.M.S.
104. Neighbor of Colo.

133 Color Scheme by Stephanie Spadaccini

Some subtle nuances of shading.

ACROSS

1. "____ My Heart in . . ."
6. Not care ____
10. Weeps
14. C.P.A.'s
18. Large trucks
19. Singer Vikki and family
21. Baseball's Felipe
22. Prefix with stat or scope
23. Black
25. Supposedly like the rich
26. Congers
27. Rocky and Blue Ridge: Abbr.
28. "Close Encounters" vehicle
29. Heeds
31. Lend a hand
34. Seashore souvenir
36. Little one
37. Seer Edgar
38. Yellow
41. Relative of a glad
42. Blemish
44. N.Y. time
45. Compete
46. Johnny ____
48. North Sea feeder
50. Musical work
52. Circuit
55. To-do
56. Put on cargo
57. Spring harbingers
60. Bother
61. Like poorly knotted laces
62. His tomb is famous
64. Courage
66. Favorite places
67. Pigeon sound
69. Green
72. Fastest way to Eur.
73. In the ____ (about to happen)
75. Town near Buffalo
76. Get ____ (throw away)
78. Blazing
79. Saloon
80. Shoe machine
82. Grate
85. Counting units
86. Heraldic band
88. New York river
89. Preminger
90. Hotel's forerunner
91. Author Levin
92. Hammar-skjöld
95. Bus
97. Underworld goddess
98. Blue
103. Take ____ (look)
105. Westchester and Dade: Abbr.
106. Family members
107. Western conserva-tionist club
108. Candy
111. News-service initials
112. Musical passage
113. Puff
114. In ____ (going nowhere)
115. Orange
120. Foot part
121. Same, in France
122. Creepy
123. Film actress Nancy
124. Tints
125. Jewish month
126. Dispatch
127. Peggy and Robert

DOWN

1. Begin's land: Abbr.
2. Tolstoy
3. Large bird
4. Of motion pictures
5. African flies
6. Vaudeville turns
7. Actress Charlotte
8. Strawberry trees: Lat.
9. Book part
10. Move vigorously
11. Somewhat elderly
12. Red
13. Fat
14. "We ____ amused"
15. Brown
16. Hibernian
17. O.K., barely
20. Herons' relatives
24. Blasting material
30. Raison d'____
31. High points
32. ____ Ste. Marie
33. White
34. Hedge material
35. Greek cheese
38. Famed gangster
39. Islet
40. Believers
43. Step in cooking fruit
47. Treaty of ____-Litovsk
49. Sheep
51. Smirks
53. Auto buyer's concern
54. British gun
55. Old Cannes coin
58. "All You ____ Is Love"
59. Sunset or Gaza
61. Actor Alan
63. "____, ten, a big fat hen"
65. Prong
66. ____ the throne (successor)
67. Tropical animal
68. Hurt
70. Winter hol.
71. Cockscombs, e.g.
74. Fed. collection agency
77. Gold, in Granada
79. Turn purple
81. Catches one's breath
83. Ranch animal
84. Kind of dot
86. Day of the wk.
87. England's Anthony
91. Smithsonian, for one: Abbr.
93. Mention
94. Fishbowl inhabitants
96. Bought and ____
99. Artists Andrew and Newell
100. Shock
101. Alice's mad friend
102. ____ d'
104. Like heaven's gates
107. Mayday's relative
108. W.W. I plane
109. Guarded
110. "I Remember ____"
112. Fed lines to
116. ____ Tin Tin
117. Dos Passos trilogy
118. Atom
119. Ship wts.

134 Happy Hour by Hume R. Craft

Time to say prosit, skoal and all that.

ACROSS

1. "____ du lieber!"
4. Two-faced god
9. A-one
13. Bandleader Count
18. Minstrel's offering
19. Actress MacMahon
20. Occupied
21. Calculator for Fu Manchu
23. Drink for a patriarch
26. Cowboys
27. Misses
28. Anatomical network
29. Drink for the fox-hunt set
31. Footless creature
32. Shillong teas
34. Old blade
35. Fiscal initials
36. Radiation dosage
37. Baseball gear
38. Questioning sounds
40. Recipient
42. Move back
44. Bumbling
46. Like a saw
49. Went into second base
50. Doer: Suffix
52. Emitters of fumes
54. Kettle and Barker
55. San Francisco team
57. Paintings by Guido
58. English name of the Thames
59. Spree
62. Confused
63. U.S.-England golf cup
64. Landis or Lombard
66. Owners of contiguous lots
68. Rib beneficiary
69. Made a point
71. Ford and Pyle
72. Toward the ventral side
74. Himalayan goat
75. Part of to be
76. Stare
77. Angled edge
78. Librettist Alan Jay
80. Nigerian
81. Mrs. ____, Pickwick admirer
83. Murder, ____ (assassination squad)
84. Vassal
87. Made a new try at a script
89. Barnyard dwellings
91. Pollen container
93. Greek letters
95. Relig. school
96. Le Gallienne et al.
97. "Fe fi fo ____!"
99. Whale: Prefix
100. Courtroom people: Abbr.
102. What a blabber spills
104. Wool: Prefix
105. Sweet cordial for writer Sholem
108. Kind of music or food
109. Cremona creation
110. Conrail's counterpart
111. Drink for a bomb squad
114. Cleopatra's Central Park landmark
115. Arcadia
116. Epidermal opening
117. Hazel, for one
118. Strong beam
119. Dried up
120. Robert Devereux's earldom
121. Sneaky Northern apple

DOWN

1. Sour brew
2. Measurers of thickness
3. Honey and water drink
4. Containers
5. Mass robe
6. Rhine wine for writer Gertrude
7. Discontent
8. Syriac script
9. Marble
10. American inventor
11. Bottle sizes
12. Glasses for a rathskeller
13. More sterile
14. Ben Adhem
15. More inane
16. Drink from a certain jerk
17. God of the east wind
22. Lower division: Abbr.
24. Old times
25. Its capital is San'a
30. Poet Lizette and family
32. Support
33. Winy name of riders' leggings
37. Act as a go-between
39. Accelerated
41. Hosp. affiliates
43. Smoke, for short
44. "____ about time!"
45. Chromosome suffix
47. One of Dorothy Sayers's nine
48. Dead Sea Scrolls writer
51. Hid away
53. Opera star Dorothy
56. Grieg's "____ Death"
58. Anger
59. German rifleman
60. Rub off
61. Brew for Guy Fawkes
63. Liquefies anew
64. German botanist
65. Blotter entries
67. Jazzbow
70. Portuguese wine for nurse Edith
73. Nights before
77. In the same ____ (simultaneously)
78. Fleur-de-____
79. Deer, in Dresden
81. La Paz's country: Abbr.
82. One on the initiative
85. Holds back
86. Dieter's dessert
88. Checks
90. Ancient Syrian city
92. Cole or Turner
94. Plant stems
96. Does a Mount St. Helen's routine
98. Half
99. Humpbacked animal
101. Underhanded
103. Thicket
104. Zoo attraction
105. Word before grove or handle
106. It's white in January
107. Hotshot
109. Trojan War hero
112. Opposite of WSW
113. Scottish uncle

135 Working Letters by Mel Rosen
Sometimes one can do the job of two or three.

ACROSS

1. "A plague on ____ your . . ."
5. Bassoon's relative
9. Mince
13. Stare at
17. Yearns
19. It'll get you ten
20. Japanese native
21. Anglo-____
22. Playground gear
24. Louvre treasure
26. Move like Mopsy
27. Arab chief
28. Follows relentlessly
29. He obtained more than 1,000 patents
30. Commandeered
32. Bolivian capital
34. Fed
35. He's even
37. French playwright Jean
38. Fancy dive
40. Flagging
41. Dresden denial
42. Baltimore team
43. Simpleton
46. Napoleon and Nero: Abbr.
47. Heavyweight champ of the 1930's
49. Hebrew letters
51. Highland group
52. Saul's grandfather
53. Ladies of Spain
54. Mellow
55. Dandelion tufts
56. Kind of sin
58. Disconcerts
59. Drive-in attendant
60. Western Indian
61. ____ de France
62. ". . . maids all ____"
64. Of the pelvis
66. Frozen

68. Priest, for one
71. Foreign
72. Don Juan's mother
73. Matinee V.I.P.'s
74. "____ Misérables"
75. Van Winkle and Torn
76. Forum platforms
78. Part of S.A.R.
79. Pierre's state: Abbr.
80. Ocean: Abbr.
81. Musically slow
82. Empty, in Edinburgh
84. Selected
85. Belabors a role
87. Shrink
88. Paying guest
89. Rara ____
90. Lurking sea danger
91. Martinique peak
92. Cast gloom on
95. Distress
96. Homer masterpiece
98. Hitting stat
101. Iowa rail center
103. Tacit
105. Molding edge
106. Furniture wood
107. Facilitate, as the way
108. River of Europe
109. Used a hair rinse
110. Dilettantish
111. Dived for third base
112. Spanish weight

DOWN

1. Take a ____ (lose one's shirt)
2. Eight: Prefix
3. Theory of promotion through ineptitude
4. Possessive
5. Recurrently
6. Go for the hook
7. Superintendents
8. Poetic contraction
9. Bound about
10. Gate holder
11. Burden
12. Kind of elec. charge
13. Tomboy
14. Line of symmetry
15. Mallet sport
16. Town near Springfield, Ohio
18. Provided grub money
21. Automobiles
23. Straw in the wind
25. Resigns
28. Confederacy premise
31. Rtes. of approach
33. One: Prefix
34. Strong wind
35. Amanuensis, nowadays
36. Racing official
37. They bark up family trees
38. Buckminister Fuller creation
39. Well-known essayist
42. Hatteras or May
44. Sodium-based soap
45. Impertinent one
47. Insipid
48. Eastern nurse
50. ____ up (estimated)
51. Mediterranean tree
53. Parlor piece
55. Priam's son
57. French depots
58. Office worker
59. Wall Street moves
63. Gas for signs
64. Teasdale
65. Landed
67. Within: Prefix
69. Annoy
70. Glacial deposit
73. Of the same magnetic dip
76. Eye part
77. Persons
79. Old woman's home
81. What Frankie and Johnny were
83. ____ tear
84. More aloof
86. City of the Prado
87. Scotch or redeye
88. Kind of admiral
90. Begin's counterpart
91. Aped Pan
92. Pompano-like fish
93. ". . . out of these wet clothes and into a ____ Martini"
94. Defy
95. Atlantic City's is steel
97. Roman 66
99. First commercial gas auto
100. Notion
102. School org.
103. Good times
104. "____ 'nuff!"

136 Toujours l'Amour by Raymond F. Eisner

Cashing in on that universal sentiment.

ACROSS

1. Act often read
5. Rum cakes
10. This can be reserved
14. Tristan's beloved
16. Site of the Alcazar
18. Peter Pan, for one
20. A ___ (fashionable)
21. Barbara Cartland romance
23. City on the Dnieper
24. Despotic ruler
26. Portion
27. Bird's beak
28. Yucca's cousin
29. Scandinavian name
31. Land measure
32. Poet Pound
33. Barbershop-quartet gal
34. Singer of "Darling, Je Vous Aime Beaucoup"
38. ". . . unto us ___ is given"
39. Turndown words
41. Miss Street
42. Guitarist Paul
43. Native of an Italian city
45. Roman date
46. Fancy
50. Some South Pacific natives
51. Skin layers
52. Rulership: Sp.
54. Shank
55. Work by Anaïs Nin
58. Comparative ending
59. Everglades locale: Abbr.
60. ___ about
61. Arab ruler
62. Where Solomon was king: Abbr.
63. Pacific porgy
64. Song hit of 1931
68. Sandwich for Luis
70. Johann Strauss was one
72. Electronic device
73. Ed of TV
74. More pretentious
75. Norwegians' neighbors
76. Composer Nelson
77. Prior to
78. Frutti's partner
79. Eggnog garnish
81. Concordat
83. Silent-screen star
85. Lake, in Lille
87. Other shoe
88. Sp. lady
89. ___ it (amen)
90. Norwegian king
92. Baseball Hall of Famer
93. Sweet potato
97. Woeful word
99. Diverse: Prefix
100. Barbara Cartland romance
103. Kind of board
105. Dealer in legwear
106. More ill-natured
107. Metal tips of laces
108. RR depots
109. Cousins of T-Beams
110. Painter of two Majas

DOWN

1. Star-cross'd lovers
2. Song from "The Band Wagon"
3. Like Neil Simon's couple
4. Harold of the comics
5. Partner of lo
6. "___ atque vale!"
7. Partners of pieces
8. Helm direction
9. Smelting waste
10. Tender
11. Building addition
12. Amos ___ Stagg of football
13. Neighbor-hood oasis
14. Miss Chase
15. Lateen and mizzen
16. Go down lovers' lane
17. Spain's pride in 1588
18. Etna's shape
19. Hebrew weight
22. Dried up
25. Silkworm
30. Hat
32. Eat, in Dresden
34. ". . . a big fat ___"
35. Disposition, in Durango
36. Shake like ___
37. Literary monogram
38. Mosquito genus
40. "___ Rheingold"
42. Biblical precious stone
43. G.I.
44. Where pylons are seen
45. ___ Dame
47. Star-cross'd lovers
48. Male hawk
49. Sound receiver
51. Garlic unit
52. Staff again
53. Playwright Bagnold
55. Ache, in Genoa
56. Seth's son
57. Miles and Zorina
62. Cole Porter perennial
63. Pride of Sen. Norris
64. Sluggish
65. Entrances to collieries
66. Producer Carlo
67. Golfer Palmer et al.
69. Coin of Norway
71. Nephew's sister
73. Intent
75. Body of a plane: Abbr.
76. 1 or 66, for short
78. Like weepy eyes
79. Having more dignity
80. Eye part
81. Sympathetic pity
82. Verify
83. "Dracula" author Stoker
84. Fishes' Biblical partners
86. Insert mark
87. It's nonresistant to flame
88. Jutting rock
91. These have needles
93. Bull and Olsen
94. Forty-nine minutes to twelve
95. Conservation agency: Abbr.
96. Can. province
98. It's often at bay
101. ___ de siecle
102. Hear: Sp.
104. Vanity

137 Missing by A. J. Santora

Some things prove hard to find.

ACROSS

1. A bit of this is walcum, said Nash
7. ____ out (make do)
10. Rainbow shapes
14. Of the eye
19. Melodious
20. "____ any drop to drink"
21. Marco's game
22. Lost, in the Argonne
23. Reputed roots of the American Indians
27. Within: Prefix
28. Singer Brewer
29. Russian ruler
30. Sac
31. Bright performers
33. Meadow
34. Time past
36. Writer Wolfert
38. Kind of jack or pie
40. "Utopia's team got beat!"
45. Tree surgeon, at times
48. Savage
49. Proper behavior
50. "Days of Wine and Boozes"
53. Place for an in-basket
54. Neighbor of Pa.
55. City in Iowa
56. Advice to Kelly
57. Indian butter
59. Singer Frankie
61. Sportsman Turner
62. Like Telly or Yul
63. Bunk tellers
65. Cloth-stretching frame
66. John Wayne movie
69. Hair slickum
72. As easy ____
73. Decays
74. Globe
77. Heiden and Ambler
78. Fraternal org.
79. "____ cold, starve . . ."
81. On ____ (equal)
82. Large quantity
83. Greek letters
85. Out of this world
87. Food-flavoring base
89. Oarlock
91. Minnesota player
92. Oft-rewarding newspaper column
94. What squad cars do
96. Cool drink
97. Bancroft
98. Parseghian
99. Weeping figure
103. Old World apple
106. Haughty pose
108. Most despicable
111. Sailing
112. Tourist sight in the Andes
116. Assisted
117. Kind of vision
118. Place
119. Put in a box
120. Simpleton
121. Pelion's underpinning
122. Deceitful
123. Detects

DOWN

1. Poet Allen and family
2. Common contraction
3. Actress Lavin
4. Dyes
5. Org. for a Bob Hope visit
6. Largest part
7. Menu listing
8. Neighbor of Japan
9. Greek goddess
10. Copy
11. Of a pulpit
12. Shop sign
13. Lounge lizard's place
14. Harvest goddess
15. Sheet fabric
16. Canapé carrier
17. European fish
18. Devilism or fetishism
24. Blab
25. Magic medieval horse
26. Eye parts
32. Pour forth
35. Mouths
37. Irresponsible
39. Forebode
40. She waited for Ulysses
41. ____ fixe
42. Bit of gossip
43. Setting
44. Texas city
45. Piece of ground
46. City in which one must conform
47. Took advantage of
48. Sustained
51. She, in Paris
52. Commits a major crime
53. Proposed Mormon state
57. Accordionlike magazine page
58. Royalty initials
60. Army insect
62. Four-poster frame
64. "____ Were King"
65. "It takes two ____"
66. Resinous substance
67. British award
68. California wine city
69. Rose feature
70. "Stein Song" town
71. Certain skirts
74. Oceanic food fish
75. Lineage
76. Storied Mr. Fox
78. Writer Schulberg
80. Suffix of origin
81. Toaster or electric fan
84. Virgilian hero
85. Friendless
86. Dispersed
88. Hostlers' digs
89. Adenoids' kin
90. Vandal
93. Mockeries
94. Attractive
95. Impetuous
98. Very bad
100. Native of Campania
101. Animal
102. Calms
103. Party
104. "Beautiful" river
105. Change, as a room
107. "Tell ____ Sweeney!"
109. Butterfinger's word
110. Ball holders
113. Horatian work
114. Party
115. Part of a corp. name

138 Making Good by Cornelia Warriner

A few ways of beating the system.

139 Hard Going by Anthony B. Canning

Not necessarily referring to the difficulty of the puzzle.

ACROSS

1. Not yet up
5. Mile-high town of Eritrea
11. Army woman
14. L.A. time zone
17. Biblical spy
19. Argentine lariats
20. Biblical high priest
21. Skyline: Abbr.
22. Missilelike dancing group
24. Pilot's distance units
27. Luanda's land
28. Wanton
30. Omar I, e.g.
31. Seaweed
32. Avalon visitor
34. "The ___ is cast"
35. Water buffalo
37. Old porch piece
43. Tack on
44. Pronouncements
46. Nickname for actor Colman
47. Way up
49. Writer James and family
50. Straight
51. Partner of drink and be merry
53. Kind of tone
55. Like Nero, in a way
59. Fussily exact
61. Zoroastrian
65. Advance
66. Fight
68. Quantity
69. Metric unit
72. "___ in White"
73. Solomon, in a way
74. Do a school assignment
75. Focusing device
77. Took a chance
78. Signs
79. Old coronation seat
85. Bit
87. Moscow square
88. Amazon port
89. Scenic view
94. Bingo's relative
96. Signoret
97. Baked goods of a queen
98. Shy
100. Eluder of moss
104. Farrow et al.
105. Cargo for Gary
106. Minnesota village
107. Louis XIV et al.
109. Spoils
111. Censure
116. Kind of job
119. Without a lap
121. Talking aids for Demosthenes
123. Brit. award
124. Durocher
125. Revenue man's target
126. Miss Korbut and others
127. Bar order
128. O.K.
129. Tenant
130. Old laborer

DOWN

1. Official proceedings
2. German road
3. Tasteful style
4. Disparage
5. Ararat caller
6. Bishops' units
7. Anatoly Karpov's aim
8. Business-letter abbr.
9. Scottish explorer and family
10. Mitigate
11. King Midas's obsession
12. Famed boaster
13. When it's short, there's trouble
14. Bandleader Harris
15. Very firm
16. Timorous
18. Cattle entangler
23. John Dickson of mysteries
25. Flawed
26. Constructor's shelter
29. Bend
33. Dispatch
35. Nabokov girl
36. Equip
38. Mountain: Prefix
39. Preserve
40. On bended
41. Creep
42. Chilean export
45. Agree to
48. Browning's passer and namesakes
51. Gaelic
52. Solar disk
54. Cotton thread
56. Heads, in Dijon
57. Plan
58. Kaiser's place of self-exile
60. Fitting return
61. Equal: Prefix
62. Modify a bill
63. Advice before a bough bends
64. French neighbor, to French
67. Clergyman
69. African plant
70. Tear
71. Compass point
76. Edna Ferber's prize book
80. Fish while moving
81. Women, familiarly
82. Cash taker
83. Recent: Prefix
84. Black cat, to some
86. Damaged
90. Corset's cover-up
91. Rebellions
92. School org.
93. Curve
95. How children play, usually
96. Irritable red fish
98. Cornfield leavings
99. Cicero, for one
101. Slow musical movements
102. Mutated water
103. Creator of discord
108. Preposition
110. Arrow poison
112. Dream, to a Frenchman
113. Old Japanese coin
114. "Yr. ___ servant"
115. Escape
117. Acheson or Inge
118. Latin being
120. Identity word
122. Misdo

140 Fulfillments by Norton Rhoades

Acquisitions dear to varied collectors.

ACROSS

1. Dieter's fare
6. Archeologist's accessory
11. Theda of silents
15. Tax acct.
18. Miss Massey
19. Yalta participant
20. It's rara
21. Place for some castles
22. Antique-car collector's dream find
24. Night letter, for one
26. Collection
27. "____ the Greek"
28. ____ culpa
30. Praises
31. Time spans: Abbr.
32. Rests at anchor
33. Things often cut
36. Broz
38. Old hands
39. Genus of butterflies
40. Cherished ones
41. Area of influence
44. Wrapper's need
45. Settles comfortably
47. Boscs
48. Gets ready to dream
50. Market that's the Amex now
51. Meter's counterpart
52. Scarf
53. Like peas
56. Saragossa's river
60. Art collector's dream find
63. Of a knot
64. Missile lost in the air
65. Use a pulpit
67. Time units: Abbr.
69. Post-banquet woe
70. Fire or steam
71. Beiges
72. Summarize
74. Egyptologists' finds
76. Historian's time
77. Calms
79. Airport abbr.
80. Reporter's paragraph
83. Cassini
85. Sniff
87. ____ all others
88. Tequila cocktail
93. Palm
94. Best ____ (hot book)
95. Use energy
96. Special-interest promoter
98. Marquette
99. Certain monster
100. Condenses on a surface
101. "I carry," to Cicero
102. "The Naked ____"
105. Flavor
107. Follower of fa
108. Upstate N.Y. city
109. Uno, ____, tres
110. Ancient Greek jars
113. Musicologist's dream finds: Abbr.
116. "____ Kapital"
117. Boss Tweed's enemy
118. Piles of rocky debris
119. Join
120. Cockney's aspiration
121. Tennis star
122. English cresses
123. Parisian pates

DOWN

1. Mama's boy
2. Change
3. Yokels
4. Hill dweller
5. Eye strikers
6. Quick tries
7. Kind of rubber
8. Rubbing fluid: Abbr.
9. Trash collector's dream find
10. Intestine: Prefix
11. Go to the plate
12. ____ Maria
13. Small brooks
14. Confused
15. Of the heart
16. Mideast currency
17. ____ of the sea
19. Ecological stages
23. Bistro's relative
25. Bibliophile's dream find
29. British queen
33. Heals
34. German article
35. He ran around the rugged rock
37. Secret service, once
38. Signature collector's dream find
39. Miller or Doakes
40. Beetle
41. Le Carré figure
42. Princess's mattress problem
43. Certain Ferry
44. Fought
46. Hound-dog signal
48. Desperate signal
49. L.A. specialty
52. Scrooge's word
54. Mrs. Cantor et al.
55. Met's counterpart in Italy
57. English port
58. Ziegler
59. Have a debt
61. Metric measures: Abbr.
62. Whale
64. Literary collection
65. Kind of pills
66. Entertainment giant
68. Nile queen of the gods
70. Go wrong
72. Add a new coat of gold
73. Philatelist's dream find
75. Exist
77. Indian weight
78. Skitters
81. Adam's find
82. Mal de ____
84. ____ and long.
86. After Mar.
87. Balloonist
88. Little Woman
89. W.W. II cartographer's dream find
90. Fall back
91. Places to send wires: Abbr.
92. Australian natives
94. Eastern inn
97. Visit a bookstore
98. Lords
100. Tapestry
101. Escapes
102. Concede
103. French mail
104. Letters
106. Mrs. Chaplin
108. Outstanding person
110. Fuss
111. Residue
112. Calais summer
114. Jacques' pleasure
115. Direction: Abbr.

141 State Secrets by Diana Sessions

Some of them are revealed in one way or another.

ACROSS

1. Discarded
8. Chair piece
13. Frog, at times
20. San ____
21. Teeming
22. Waterloo native
23. Sometime
25. Put to rest
26. Young rascal
27. Speak excitedly
28. Crafty
29. Theater abbr.
30. Downy surfaces
32. Stableman
33. Bouquet
34. Portico
35. Narrow valleys
37. Biddy
38. Strong wind
39. ____ up (agitated)
40. Where Damascus is
41. Letter
42. Coated with zinc: Abbr.
43. Sidetracks
44. Proposed undertaking
46. Where the natives are skeptical
49. Answer
52. Deer
53. Range over
54. New Mexico people
57. Get one's bearings
58. Draw a ____ on (aim)
60. Lear or Midas
61. Actor Conried
62. Spirited tunes
63. Suburban activity
65. Moorings
66. Collect a tax
67. Kind of cracker or fountain
68. One-time gold-rush city
69. Bell sound
70. Full of: Suffix
71. Buy ____ in a poke
72. Clay's name today
73. Stubborn

74. Edward Gibbon subject
78. Large nonflying bird
79. Cigarette, in Britain
81. Grate
82. Dorothy or Fort
84. Infants' disease
88. Take place
89. Wax fabric finish
90. Home of the Reds: Abbr.
91. Brownish gray
92. Trireme equipment
93. Sugar source
94. Wheezy whodunit suspect
97. Castor or Pollux
98. Presidential monogram
99. Tweed's outfit
100. Invalidates
102. Actor Whitman, for short
103. Busy place for Utah
105. Birds for Alabama
107. "Random Harvest" plot element
108. Steve or Woody
109. Summer menu item
110. Consideration
111. Stations
112. Cheese vat

DOWN

1. Sausage covers
2. Inconsistent quality
3. Cork, for one
4. Large amount
5. Do ____ thing
6. Dempsey opponent
7. Certain paradise dwellers
8. Lacking flavor
9. Part of a typewriter
10. Metric unit
11. Declare
12. Part of N.W.T.: Abbr.
13. It's often longue
14. Mass meeting
15. Having a quizzical look
16. Woody vine of N.Z.
17. Second bases
18. Goldenseal
19. North American trees
24. Babe and kin
28. Ann Arbor athlete
31. Unduly curt
33. Tree in the Sunshine State
34. Fasten
36. Art exhibition halls

38. Stare
39. Counterfeit
41. Cessation
42. Large pearl oyster
43. Adult deer
45. Red or army
47. Kind of count
48. Dance's partner
49. First duke of Normandy
50. Great Lake Indians
51. Movies
55. Colored linen tape
56. Resource
58. Harassing
59. Pitching abbr.
60. Miss Novak
61. Country on the Pacific
63. Enter
64. Café ____
65. Guide

67. Do ring training
69. Article of headwear
71. North, Central or South: Abbr.
72. Projecting building part
73. Put the whammy on
75. First part of op. cit.
76. Dark area on the moon
77. Newspaper runs
79. Mr. ____, who was waited for
80. Where Plato taught
83. Relative of sorts
85. Beginnings
86. In trouble

87. Attentive study
89. "All you ____ for 85 cents" (old diner sign)
90. Schnitzel
93. Municipal
94. Invoices
95. System of moral values
96. Attain
99. Upward slope
100. Tricycle, for short
101. Pintail duck
104. ____ cat
105. Shrill bark
106. Physicians: Abbr.

142 Gifts from the Sea by Olga Kowals
Our waters yield strange and varied things.

ACROSS

1. Inventor Howe
6. Chafe
10. Not big, to Burns
13. Miss Murray
16. Move furtively
17. Make over
18. Stanford's home
21. Suspect a bit of finagling
24. Once more
25. Dash
26. Spanish year
27. Embroiderers' needs
30. Up and about
32. Supervise
34. Mexican uncle
35. Exclamation
39. Line member
40. Gull's cousin
41. Genus of shad
42. Carte or mode
43. One's digs
44. Apiece
45. One-liner
46. Make a second basketball shot
50. Some transport lines
51. Endures
54. Wall or Main
55. Toddy or plate
57. Victim at Little Big Horn
58. Sky saucer
60. Resort near Trieste
62. Textile machine
64. Ivy Leaguer
65. Lack privacy
69. Deplorable
70. Insects
71. Contrition
72. Curve
73. Infancy's opposite
75. Discontinued car
76. Ready for action
78. ____ à manger
79. ". . . sing thee to ____ rest!"
81. Material for a gray suit
83. Moslem title
86. Bartender's frequent loan
87. Cry's partner
88. Scottish river
89. Plume
91. Chocolate and gold
93. Capp's Abner
94. Irate nontalkers
98. Nursery-tending letters
99. Peanut genus
101. Belt out a soliloquy
102. Extirpates
105. Take it on the ____
106. Belligerent god
107. Time segments
111. Awkward situation
115. Union Civil War general
116. Cookbook instruction
117. "____ lunch"
118. Miss Muffet did it
119. Plaines or Moines
120. Frying and bed
121. Entreat

DOWN

1. She, in Italy
2. Delineate
3. ____ fixe
4. In ____ (inclusively)
5. Piquancy: Fr.
6. Romp
7. Theatrical aside
8. Author Phillpotts
9. Youngster
10. Gem mineral
11. Baronial residence
12. School subj.
13. Kind of fist
14. ____-ran
15. Ordinal endings
19. Creates displeasure
20. Dishes for R-months
22. "____ thief to catch a . . ."
23. Enjoy oneself
28. Goddess of healing
29. Family-business member
31. Kind of aleck
32. Escutcheon border
33. Pribilof denizen
35. Kind of fish or ridden
36. Wave, in Spain
37. Object easy to roll off
38. Veterinarian's marker
40. Parties
43. Sulky mood
44. Lead sounding weight
47. Royal robe material
48. French dye
49. Zeus's sister and others
52. Archer William and son
53. Hindu title
54. Part of U.S.S.R.: Abbr.
56. Military weapons: Abbr.
57. Stick together
58. Russian city
59. Musical crustacean
61. Be down in the dumps
62. Napkins, sheets, etc.
63. Campania inhabitant of old
66. Kind of beaver
67. Genus of shrubs
68. British ref. book
69. Sea call
74. Woeful word
75. Grain
77. Make a choice
79. Cravings
80. Kind of hoop
82. Alkaline solutions
83. Altar constellation
84. Pearl or ruby
85. Siamese coins
90. Merry
91. Heating initials
92. Jungfrau or Blanc
93. Inactive
94. No great ____ (just average)
95. Legendary magician
96. Arab chiefs
97. "I can ____ much and no more"
100. Firth of Scotland
103. Work
104. Odd, in Scotland
106. Indian flour
108. Ceremony
109. Malaccan measure
110. Having footwear
112. Rx directive
113. Cook's meas.
114. Dandy

143 Outdoor Life by Manny Miller

A few specimens from the world of fauna.

ACROSS

1. What a buffalo does
6. "____ the mornin' to you"
10. Hair arrangement
14. First president of Germany
19. Dismay
20. Mosque leader
21. Going before: Abbr.
22. Buddhist monks
23. Spanish market fete
24. Festivity
25. Vivacious
26. Intense
27. Whence the best info
31. Singer Janis
32. Relative of RBI
33. Miss Lupino
34. Chinchilla-ranch worker
38. Declare
41. Some H.S. students
43. Actress Verdon
45. Turkish money
46. Love story
49. Mountain climber of ditty
50. Greek architecture style
51. Avocados
55. Broadway flop
56. Me, in Montmartre
57. Pleads
58. Legendary bird
59. Plug
61. Entangle
62. Candor
68. Feudal slave
69. Southern spreads
72. Writer Wiesel
73. Curbs
75. Mistress Quickly
76. Rental agreement
77. Pique
78. Determine
81. Downy surface
82. Koala's relative
86. In earnest
89. Hodge-podges
90. What snakes do
91. Land region
92. Siberian river
93. Sharp pain
94. Balaam's ____
95. Foliated rock
99. Dance
101. ____ party
103. Equal: Prefix
105. Picture
106. Relative of "coming down in buckets"
112. Resin for varnishes
115. Celebes ox
116. ____ session
117. Israel's southern port
118. Champagne bottle's place
119. Poke
120. Source of sugar
121. Confound
122. Subject of labor disputes
123. Wash. legislators
124. Landed props.
125. Biblical verb

DOWN

1. Basket fiber
2. "Louise" and "Martha"
3. Protective clothing
4. Injure
5. Louver
6. Animal not to be dismounted
7. Triple Crown winner
8. Alto's start
9. Egypt's Sharif
10. Raised the bet
11. Prophet
12. Skin: Suffix
13. Ale time
14. Excite
15. President Buchanan, for one
16. Ostrich's relative
17. ____ on (betray)
18. Between Mao and tung
28. Cossack leader
29. One of the family
30. Coffee dispenser
35. Actor Bogarde
36. Empire State canal
37. Risqué
39. Son of Gad
40. Author of a word book
41. Room dividers
42. Meal
44. Common verb
47. Old coin of Siam
48. Conquest of 1066
49. Low, in Bordeaux
50. Donald or Daffy
51. Like waves of grain
52. Relaxed
53. ____ share
54. Grain alcohol
55. A lot
58. Norse sea goddess
60. Adjust
62. Steals
63. High ____ (heavy gambler)
64. Born
65. African antelope
66. Strong rope fiber
67. Inclined to ooze
69. Role
70. Recline
71. Principles
74. Inlets
76. Admit
78. Mountain pass
79. Org. for Nassar
80. St. George's foe
82. ____ in sheep's clothing
83. Margarine
84. Pert one
85. Regatta
86. Gained
87. Gary Cooper film
88. Chemical ending
90. Short siestas
93. Food on Maui
94. Of early times: Abbr.
96. Tristan's beloved
97. Eric and George
98. Six-line piece
100. Breathing sounds
102. Mild oaths
103. Key
104. Flavors
107. Pertaining to
108. French cleric
109. One of seven: Abbr.
110. Kind of wood or aim
111. Prank
112. Moon orbiter
113. Actress Munson
114. ____ Latin

144 Bartender's Guide by Jordan S. Lasher

Some mixtures designed for esoteric hangovers.

ACROSS

1. Of a resistance unit
6. City on the Irtysh
10. Cotton applicator
14. Piano in the raw
18. South Pacific atoll
19. Comedienne Martha
20. Attention-getter
21. Where the Owl and the Pussycat were
22. Chamber of an Egyptian tomb
23. Brandy drink
26. Actress Ullmann et al.
27. Get ____ of confidence
29. Half a Chattanooga sound
30. Minnesota resort town
31. Hearty drink
32. Full assemblies
33. Marie and Anne: Abbr.
34. In the open
35. Persevere at
36. Suffer
37. Biblical prophet
39. Relative of a hockey stick
43. Bird's song
46. Progress laboriously
47. More meager
48. Vodka drink
51. Sweet wine
52. Bit of deception
53. Overact
54. Miscalculate
55. Lounged
56. "Come ____ Faithful"
58. Guinness
61. The Censor
63. Get the brass ring
65. Collar
66. Gin drink
71. Portrayer of Maude
72. Here, in Spain
73. Captain of the Nautilus
74. Gateway
75. Bloodhound's quest
77. Suffix with differ or defer
79. Essex or Hudson
80. Willow
84. Sacred chest
85. Former German area in Africa
87. Creamy drink
90. ____ Paix
91. Faction
92. Without pretentiousness
93. "Life ____! Life is earnest!"
94. Real people
96. Jackie's one-time mate
97. Bikini part
100. Radical campus org.
101. Atmosphere
102. Preminger and Klemperer
104. Time delay
105. Yawning
108. Not pro
109. Like a paperhanger's hands
110. Gerrymandered product
111. Gin drink
114. Settle a score
116. Is sorry
117. Viva voce
118. Medieval weapon
119. Cum ____
120. Monster
121. Newsman Ernie
122. Prune, in Scotland
123. "... in someone ____ arms"

DOWN

1. "Anna Christie" playwright
2. Fruity drink
3. Beauty applications
4. Author Levin
5. Rum drink
6. Welles
7. Rum drink
8. New Year's word
9. Container
10. Fool
11. Wind-tunnel sound
12. Of aviation
13. "Ta-ta!"
14. Certain photoengravings
15. Words of assumption
16. Italian painter
17. Leaf
22. Stick or dash
24. Goings-on
25. French Pointillist
28. Parchment-like paper
32. Central or Hyde
33. Casa room
34. Cross one's mind
38. Did a sideshow promo
40. Rhine-wine drink
41. Perceptiveness
42. Prior to
44. ____-deucy
45. Inner: Prefix
47. Teasdale and Roosevelt
48. Safari title
49. Purplish
50. Line member
51. Jiffies
57. Lone, long time
59. Nigerian tribesman
60. Singer Rosemary
62. Hindu mantras
64. Brazilian port
67. Notices to car owners
68. Iowa church society
69. Lille's department
70. City on the Ural
76. One of the Reiners
78. "... who shall pretend ____ Art and Science!": Blake
81. Mr. Kabibble
82. Liken
83. Drink containing 51 Across
85. Part of TNT
86. Gloomy
87. Acid for dyes
88. "____ good deed daily" (Scout's boast)
89. Bird on the Nile
91. Put the kibosh on
94. "How-to" book
95. Cheer up
98. Alps, Andes, etc.
99. U.S. author
103. Worked on a piano
105. Hairdo
106. Bottle-pouring sound
107. Massachusetts town
108. Thirsty, old style
109. Fed
110. Chief on Olympus
112. Elephant, in politics
113. "____ Pinafore"
115. Actress Harper, for short

145 Snippets by H. Hastings Reddall

Presenting key parts of a few familiar declarations.

ACROSS

1. Lists
6. Stone pillars
12. Merganser
16. Like a Treasury service
17. Brazilian river
18. Profanities
20. Fighting figure of 1844
22. Intelligence
24. Operatic piece
25. Land maps
26. Enjoys Rotten Row
28. Start a beer keg
29. Orange remnant
30. Lady Macbeth's bane
31. More rational
32. One often apparent
33. Pool-ball mover
34. Game requiring 22 Across
35. ____ of remorse
36. Strong thread
37. Feminine suffix
38. Loser to the tortoise
39. Desires
40. Gloomy
41. Quagmires
42. "Wish you were here" medium
43. Yiddish thief
44. Romantic coals
47. ____ majority (small margin)
49. In a slow way
52. Parisian room
53. Centers
54. More mature
56. Wise to
57. Sea-speed unit
58. Scotland's bonnie ____
59. Amateurs: Var.
60. Teddy or brown
61. Kind of trip
62. Kind of towel
63. Instruct
64. Bridge bid
65. Squirrels and beavers
67. Destroys documents
69. Bishops' headdresses
70. Connects for a homer
71. See 15 Down
72. Refer to
73. Carpenters, at times
75. Accumulate
77. Store-ad word
78. Actor O'Brien
81. Pastry workers
82. Chic
83. Security deposits
84. Dixie state: Abbr.
85. Chinese teas
86. Part of 46 Down
87. Box-score entries: Abbr.
88. Trim a photo
89. ____ one's heart out
90. Carpentry machine
91. Necktie woe
93. County of N.C.
94. New York or Tokyo
96. Part of F.D.R.'s reassurance
100. "Tennis, ____?"
101. Nathanael or Lorne
102. Mimickers
103. Stupid
104. Haunt
105. Foul-up

DOWN

1. Changes oil to gasoline
2. Group of eight
3. Take a stab at
4. W.W. I force
5. No-trump bidder's needs
6. Jack and wife
7. U.S. President
8. Love god
9. Gibbon
10. Joiner
11. Maxims
12. Sedate
13. Earth's neighbor
14. Greek letter
15. Bunker Hill sighting, with 71 Across
16. Bright star
19. ____ pace (slow gait)
20. Low comedy
21. Marked by: Suffix
23. Frolic
27. From, in France
30. Chases flies
31. Finishes floors
32. One taking on help
34. Task
35. Reduces
36. Unsocial one
39. Merchandise
40. Horse features
41. Suspenders' successor
42. Galley marks
43. Medieval jacket
44. Sandy drift
45. Tropical fruit
46. Three of Churchill's famous four, with 86 Across
47. Snakes
48. Musical chords
50. Renter's paper
51. Flanders town of W.W. I note
53. Garnish plant
55. Rainbow goddess
58. Ashtray leavings
59. Some toads' homes
60. Moderate
62. Growls
63. Rendezvous
64. Ceremonies
66. Wide-mouthed jugs
68. Gets wind of
69. Mr. Standish
72. Confining
73. Indian grooms
74. Patras is its capital
75. Oriental nurse
76. Town of northern Italy
77. Ancient Italians
78. Grammar pupils, at times
79. Hilo greetings
80. Come to a point
82. Parlor piece
83. Oats, wheat, etc.
86. High lakes
88. Left Bank spots
90. Crazy as a ____
91. Holy women: Abbr.
92. Quaker word
95. English poet laureate
97. Spherical body
98. O'Shanter
99. Start, poetically

146 Reaching Out by Louis Baron

Dictionaries don't always have all the definitions.

ACROSS

1. The "d" in LSD
6. Speaker's word
10. Classical walk
14. Tire city
19. Style of expression
20. Recital offerings
21. Central Italian city
22. Rough's mate
23. Chief of police
25. Pet-food star
27. Cornered
28. Locater device
30. Kind of role
31. Word from Sandy
34. O.T. book
35. Spike Jones favorite
36. Snowmobile's ancestor
39. Honked
41. Major
42. Item in an auto trunk
44. Story baddies
45. Presidential yacht
48. "____ little teapot"
49. Serenade instrument
50. In a while
51. Tops
52. Over again
53. Bucharest money
54. Prestidigitation
58. Symptom for Freud
59. Hidden dissuaders
61. Womanizer
62. "Give him the old ____"
63. V.I.P.'s of some lamps
64. Shankar's instrument
65. Gout's target, usually
66. Like a deadpan stare
67. Immature hooter
68. Place for some jewelry
69. Miss Massey
70. Hive genius
72. Between U.S. and Eur.
74. Kind of eyed
75. Follow orders
76. Pianist Petri
77. Roman emperor
78. Comic-strip scream
79. Crooked casino, in a way
83. He introduced Friday
84. Slave and pile
86. Magyar hero
87. Rebounds
88. Pines
89. Overindulge
90. Trouble call
91. ____ judicata
92. Direction: Abbr.
93. O. Henry touch
94. Ekberg
96. Van Gogh exhibit
100. Like Gertie's garter
105. ". . . who lived in ____"
106. Madame Bovary
107. Big name in Rochester, Minn.
108. Dashboard set
109. Very small
110. Temporary release
111. First, in Frankfurt
112. Boutique purchase

DOWN

1. Photog's product
2. Tokyo, formerly
3. Frosty feeling
4. Egyptian Christian
5. Becomes visible
6. Bloodless
7. Worked the bean patch
8. Old note
9. Between bow and stern
10. Advice to an earbender
11. Connective tissues
12. Glacial ridges
13. Use sights
14. Backward, to Pierre
15. ____ cool (stayed calm)
16. Writer Santha Rama ____
17. Word with bodikins
18. Initials in Albany
24. Marsh grass
26. Flattened at the poles
29. Butter-knife target
31. Eniwetok, e.g.
32. Alcatraz art show
33. Rich dame
35. Pants cloth
36. Studies poetry
37. Defending Dracula
38. Sugar daddy's pad
40. Word before total
41. Furry dogs
43. Lay down the ____ (be strict)
45. Fungus diseases
46. All there, plus
47. Brouhaha
50. Newspaper, familiarly
52. Pico de ____, Pyrenees peak
54. Anatomical column
55. Bit of fanciness
56. Stopover
57. Stradivari's teacher
58. Consecrate, old style
60. Meaningless
62. Ears, in Essen
64. Garbo or Bergman
65. Small drum
66. Gripped tightly
67. Cockney aspirations
68. Incited, with "on"
70. Creator of the Grinch
71. Katmandu's land
73. Wind-deposited loam
75. Stinger
77. Poet's word
79. Chocolate center, Pa.
80. Famous "Das"
81. He goes for the heart
82. Summary
83. Cur
85. Basque
87. Invent
89. Ashram V.I.P.
90. High-hat
93. ____ con variazoni
94. Phrygian god
95. Winglike
96. One Margery
97. Put to work
98. Article
99. Graycoat
101. Former Mideast initials
102. Chemical suffix
103. Wrong: Prefix
104. Cattle genus

147 Age-old Subject by Henry Hook

Another barb at those who try to stay young.

ACROSS

1. Starts a pump
7. Telly on the telly
12. Horror-struck
18. Does a cobbling job
20. Salamis event
21. Barry Fitzgerald's trademark
22. Middle-ager's remark
25. Flap
26. Sets out
27. Piece of writing
28. Chess pieces: Abbr.
29. City of North Dakota
32. My, in France
33. Asp's victim and others
35. Brogan
36. Prehistoric creature
39. Dijon darling
40. Former Green Bay QB
41. Degree seekers' hurdles
42. NATO ex-general and kin
43. Fritz's comic-strip brother
44. Nom de crime: Abbr.
47. Sanctions
48. Westmore of Hollywood
49. Feather: Prefix
51. Sofas
53. Wings
54. 1978 scandal
59. "I'm ____ forgiving man"
60. Rescue signal
61. Put ____ writing
62. To ____ (unanimously)
63. Start of a catty reply to 22 Across
67. Foot part
68. Cheat at hide-and-seek
69. Reacts to reveille
70. Words before never or declare
71. Pitchers' dreams
73. Shelley output
74. More lurid, as a whodunit
75. Whistle blast
76. OPEC exec, maybe
77. ____ Mahal
78. Drink
79. Mr., in Utrecht
81. Allen Ludden or Bill Cullen
83. Tennis champ after Tracy
85. Track event
86. Paul Bunyan and others
87. Three-time Derby winner
91. One-time spouses
92. What Billie Holiday sang
93. Chinese tea
94. 1956 Dior creation
95. Joke
96. Ship's spine
97. Quest
100. McTavish's topper
101. Remainder of catty reply
107. Wolf Larsen's creator
108. Make possible
109. Chanted
110. Definite thing
111. V.P. under Coolidge
112. Matted

DOWN

1. Belonging to Hector's father
2. Do this, then weep
3. "When day ____ . . ."
4. May honoree
5. Wallach
6. Stage manager's concerns
7. Philosopher Immanuel et al.
8. Mel and family
9. Elbows and knees: Abbr.
10. Andy Capp's quencher
11. Finders, traditionally
12. Start of a Nichols title
13. Metric unit
14. Greedy one
15. V.I.P. in Moslem history
16. Swains
17. Not as calm
19. Occupy a howdah
20. Injurious insect
23. Warm work jacket
24. Kubrick's "Space Odyssey" year
30. U.S. science satellite
31. City on Lake Ontario
33. Fashionable
34. Grauman's souvenir print of Grable
35. One in reverie
37. Broadway producer Gene
38. Jolson and Capone
39. No housewives, these
40. N.L. stadium
42. Miss McCullers's lonely hunter
44. ". . . as ____ June?"
45. Garb for Cio Cio San
46. Guarantee
48. Campaigners' footings
49. Stuffy people
50. Oak Ridge's state: Abbr.
52. ____ a sheet
53. Birch's cousin
54. Punch line
55. Indians of Nebraska
56. Earhart
57. Pursued
58. Complete
60. Flag officer's charge
64. Capable of
65. Lady of song
66. Key Pacific isle of W.W. II
72. No liberal, he
74. Rail stop, in France
76. Part of a deadman's hand
77. Nevertheless, for short
79. Six-sider
80. Refined
81. Went on an ego trip
82. Tussaud or Defarge
83. Hospital footboard hanging
84. Gal of song
85. Play the lavish host
86. Hebrew letter
87. Clayey rock
88. Tampering with checks
89. Ceramist's coat
90. Panacea
92. Campus headwear: Var.
93. Honeycomb units
96. Granny or slip
97. "Quién ____?"
98. Comiskey Park site, for short
99. Trace
102. Ugandan name
103. Alfonso's queen
104. Inexperienced
105. Grand Cent. or Penn
106. One sixteenth of a song load

148 Erudition by Alfio Micci

It always helps to improve one's mind.

ACROSS

1. Milan's La ___
6. Members of the force
10. Vague or Miles
14. Golf shout
18. Midwest Indians
19. Race track
20. Musicologist Downes
21. Of an age
22. Fits like ___
23. Money for Mario
24. Diplomacy
25. Heron's kin
26. Sophocles's advice, with 70 and 112 Across
30. Ringworm
31. TV's talking horse
32. Spleen
33. Loosen
35. Remnant
36. Blue Eagle measure
38. Sullivan et al.
40. Weir
42. Chang's twin
43. Certain linemen: Abbr.
44. Andrea ___
47. Commemorate in verse
50. British honor
51. What Alexander Pope belittled
54. Stubborn one
56. For men only
57. Empty, in Edinburgh
58. Lex. and Mad.
62. Group of five
64. Oregon Indian
67. Word with Thule
69. Bis!
70. See 26 Across
72. Vacillate
73. Eagle's weapons
74. Come to ___ (conclude)
75. Stemmed
76. British gun
77. Preserves
79. Milieu for an R.N.
83. King of guard
84. What Pope said 51 Across is
89. Fitting
92. Resilient
93. New Zealand native
94. Miss Hagen
97. S.A. country
98. After taxes
99. Medieval tale
101. Proscribe
102. Part of R.S.V.P.
103. Physicist Enrico
105. Beast of burden
107. Asian tongue
110. Salute
112. See 26 Across
117. City on the Orne
118. Put to flight
119. Aura
120. Gardener's tool
121. Part of a French play
122. Regarding
123. Champagne bucket
124. Miss Sedley of "Vanity Fair"
125. Kind of seller or man
126. Nobleman
127. Mountain lake
128. Tropical ant

DOWN

1. Showing one's relief
2. First day of each Roman month
3. Love, in Rome
4. Apt words for getting along
5. Confused
6. Kind of blind
7. Sheeplike
8. Easter event
9. Thick slice
10. One with a secret trust
11. Gladden
12. Impersonator Little
13. Con
14. Pretend
15. Traveled in space
16. Former grapes
17. City lines
18. Importance
27. Stings
28. Fine cotton thread
29. Divine spirit
34. Kind of centric
37. French monarch
39. Dolores ___ Rio
40. De Laurentiis
41. Astronomical arc
45. Corporation initials
46. Neighbor of Ga.
48. Trencherman
49. Sound of distress
51. Pa. city
52. Equal, in France
53. Type of table
54. "___ work" (repair-site sign)
55. Remus or Sam
59. Botanical streak
60. Eastern potentate
61. Chalcedony
62. Teachers' (favorites)
63. Clean fish
65. Actor Cariou or QB Dawson
66. Hindu holy man
68. Classroom hours
70. Penetrating flavors
71. Start
78. Med. study
80. Odor: Prefix
81. Train stop: Abbr.
82. Fear
85. Durable fabric
86. Austrian poet Rainer Maria
87. Wood sorrel
88. Author Levin
89. Strauss's "Ariadne ___ Naxos"
90. Book opener
91. Castle features
94. Utilitarian: Var.
95. Cravat adjunct
96. Ex-tennis champ Gibson
100. Cornell locale
104. French Impressionist
105. "___ the Top"
106. Fall bloom
108. Nine-___ (golf course)
109. Oak in the making
111. Insurgent
113. Stumble
114. Whetstone
115. Speck
116. Neighbor of Minn.
117. Rush-hour rarity

149 Getting in Focus by Maura B. Jacobson

And coming up with reasonable facsimiles.

ACROSS

1. Genre
4. Harm grievously
8. Greek group of W.W. II
11. Kiddie cart
15. Santha Rama ____
16. Darius's domain
18. Bangkok citizen
20. Swings along
22. Words to an old beauty expert
26. Fervency
27. Bartholdi creation
28. "Wishing will make ____"
30. Word to a dogie
31. Sir, in Singapore
32. Mao ____ -tung
33. Plus
36. W.W. II aces
37. U.S. satellite
39. Neighbor of Jaffa
42. Human
44. Between Q and U
45. Colloids
47. Word after inter or sub
51. Ancient Jewish believer
53. Word before smoke or cow
54. Not dense
55. Perfect replica
58. They're often doux
59. Part of the psyche
60. Warbucks
61. Embellished, on French menus
63. Humorist's forte
64. Post and box
66. Foot the bill in a major way
68. Partner of order
71. Cabal
72. Total again
73. Wolfed down
75. North Atlantic nemesis
77. Macles
81. Composer Harold and family
82. Gardener's bane
83. Actresses Parsons and Winwood
85. Kind of rampart
86. Ancient reliquary
87. Where, to Caesar
89. Preoccupy
90. Did blood sampling
92. Secant's kin
94. Like some verbs: Abbr.
95. Trapezist's insurance
96. Sky sighting
99. Martian prefix
101. Roman 250
102. Revue segment
104. Like Dorian Gray, at first
109. Nods
113. Film star's handout
115. Petite
116. Lupine look
117. Comfort
118. Maiden-named
119. Miniature maelstrom
120. Depression org.
121. Saucy
122. Pro vote

DOWN

1. La Douce
2. Hideaway
3. Caucasian nomad
4. Matelot's milieu
5. In the ____ Morpheus (asleep)
6. "____ true what they say . . . ?"
7. Optical illusions
8. Raison d'
9. Not give ____
10. In a virile way
11. West Point novice
12. Schoolboy of baseball
13. Separated
14. Becomes runny
16. Jennifer Jones film
17. Creator of likenesses
19. Joan Didion's "Play It as ____"
21. Roy Rogers's real name
23. Reine's mate
24. Scoreboard info
25. Female deer
29. Latin dance rhythm
33. Electrician's word
34. Japanese dramas
35. Hang in folds
38. Popeyed
40. Game for Goren
41. Soviet sea
43. Spanish wheat
44. Edit
46. Composed of verse couplets
48. Caldron contents
49. Italian wine city
50. Hatching place
52. Suffix, e.g.
53. Manger input
54. ____ Fein
56. Forms notions
57. A.M.A. members
58. Mathew and Diamond Jim
62. Gromyko
65. Trappers' sales
66. Bog
67. Meat marts, in Marseilles
68. False witness
69. Real-estate unit
70. Fuse metal
72. Disencumber
74. Author Glasgow
76. Tempo
78. Immerses
79. Leggy bird
80. Mobutu ____ Seko (Zaire leader)
82. Like Western spaces
84. High-speed plane
86. Farina, for one
87. Removes a lid
88. Hotel worker
91. Henry VIII's sixth
93. Like summer tea
94. Babylonian goddess
96. Tree of Java
97. Adriatic port
98. Eightsome
100. "Having a mind ____ own"
103. "High ____"
105. Tattled
106. Unsightly
107. Wife of Zeus
108. Enameled metalware
110. Wacky
111. Fencer's weapon
112. Mets' home grounds
114. Fall mo.

150 Rebus by Frances Hansen

You'll need to draw on your knowledge of the heavens.

ACROSS

1. Intimidated
6. Ann or May
10. Humpy beast
15. Neighbor of Nor.
19. Slacken
20. Sch. of higher learning
21. Egg-shaped
22. "____ a little nut tree . . ."
23. Church designation: Abbr.
24. Scott's setting for "fair Melrose"
26. Tower city
27. She was a lady in song
28. Relatives of T-beams
29. ____ for news (reporter's asset)
31. Writer Josephine
32. Japan
36. Coty and Descartes
37. Arias
38. Polaris
41. Clay's new name
43. Cavalry weapon
46. The Feds
48. Wing, in Wassy
49. "____ dong bell . . ."
51. Name for the twenty-eighth state
53. Overcharge
56. River of Mongolia
57. Philistine god
59. "I ____ Girl . . ."
61. People who don't drink till five P.M. or so
63. Adequately fed
65. Pell-____
66. "And the skies ____ not cloudy . . ."
67. Meat pies
69. "Tono-Bungay" author
72. Race advantages
77. African antelope
78. Hutch's TV partner
80. On high
81. Football lineman, often
86. Cook, as clams
88. Prefix for sanct or iliac
89. "____ and shine"
90. Celtic sun god
92. Head cavity
94. Miss Pitts
95. After Aug.
96. Foolhardy
99. Twangy
101. Asian holiday
102. Drink ____ to (honor)
105. Kind of miss or beer
107. Stretch of land
109. Everything, poetically
116. Cousin, to kinfolk
118. Actor Fernando
119. Star, in France
120. English writer of the 1600's
121. Melville book
123. Disobey the revenooers
125. ____ a tie (be stalemated)
126. "Take away that ____ garter"
127. Dunne or Castle
128. "____ it with my little hatchet"
129. Bright lights
130. Snick's partner
131. Tea container
132. Computer components: Abbr.
133. Irish dramatist

DOWN

1. West Point student
2. West Indian sorcery
3. The planets, to early astronomers
4. Prima ballerina
5. Robs of dignity
6. Upper-lip shape
7. Philippine fiber shrub
8. Rice dish
9. Turns inside out
10. Neighbor of Okla.
11. Abodes for birds
12. Great: Prefix
13. Community character
14. Permits entry
15. Taste
16. Pentecost season
17. Facility
18. June 6, 1944
25. NASA venture
30. Wine: Prefix
33. Actress Patricia
34. Desire-inspiring tree
35. Birdseed
39. Another name for Aegir
40. Ones who gaze intently
41. Arrive at a total
42. Climbing vine
44. Hindu land grant
45. Magazine plea
47. Beach visitor's frustration
50. Ruling body: Abbr.
52. Surprise
54. Wife of Esau
55. "M*A*S*H" locale
58. Horse's vote
60. Mays, Musial, DiMaggio, etc.
62. Has on
64. Star in Cygnus
68. "You bet!"
70. W.W. II craft
71. Length of yarn
73. One of The Cid's names
74. "Among the Guests ____ the Grass"
75. Concise
76. Facial feature of a tapir
79. Early Calif. Indian
81. Bear in the sky
82. Russian refusal: Var.
83. Solar-equator area
84. Javanese wax
85. Scull
87. Has to, redundantly
91. Southwest tip of England
93. Chalcedony
97. Tennis unit
98. Laughing sounds
100. Triangular sails
103. Recital piece: Abbr.
104. Of a tidal wave
106. Forward a consignment
108. Actor Lon
110. Soprano Lucine
111. Wearing less than a fig leaf
112. Lunar-sea phenomenon
113. German poet Ludwig
114. Common U.S. bird
115. Common, horse or sixth
116. Shares the billing
117. Arabian Sea gulf
122. Pindar product
124. Tom ____, labor leader in 1916 bombing

151 Visiting the Sphinx by Evelyn Benshoof

And learning to keep one's mouth relatively shut.

ACROSS

1. Work on a balloon
5. Mop
9. Biblical wise man
14. Word with space or dynamics
15. Languished
17. Ballet movement
19. Shiny mineral
20. Bury
21. Rush a football passer
22. Keep silent
25. Work unit
26. Told a story
27. Like some humor
28. Breeze, in Madrid
29. Kind of feeder road
32. Off Broadway award
34. Enhance
35. It's often felt
36. Related
37. _____ marché (French bargain words)
38. Western Indians
39. Droop
40. Stuff
43. Legal point
44. Two steps above Confidential
46. Wanting
47. Quivers
49. Guinness
50. Mince
51. Island in S.F. Bay
52. Put the last item in the suitcase
53. Beat soundly
54. Look down on
56. Prying
57. Vehement
58. _____ monde
59. Miss Ullmann
60. They're usually high
61. Disposed
62. Behind-the-scenes figure
68. Upholstery fabric
70. Kind of highness
71. Hebrides island
72. Actress Stevens
73. Pomme de _____
74. Bus rider's place
75. Checks texts
76. Sly look
77. Informality

DOWN

1. Lively party
2. Scale: Prefix
3. Kind of surgeon
4. Not speaking
5. Porcupine quills
6. Regaled, in a way
7. Insects
8. Horn sound
9. Lenity
10. Away from the wind
11. Circulate
12. Secret
13. Sports official
16. Enticed
18. Incite
23. River to the Seine
24. "Some _____ born great"
28. Effluvium
29. Leftward
30. More like your own baby
31. Reticent
32. Trappist cheeses
33. What little pitchers have
34. "Not on _____!" (no way!)
36. Mont Blanc's range
37. _____ plaisir
39. Word that makes golfers duck
40. Utah city
41. Make _____ -in-one
42. Relegated to repeated roles
44. Split
45. Pottery material
48. Trade center
50. Discipline
52. Secret
53. Gradual impairment
54. Frauds
55. Writer Truman
56. Zero
57. Time, as regards wounds
59. Turkish coins
60. Reserve
62. Fine sand
63. Yule singer's offering
64. Old Phoenician port
65. _____ bene
66. Son of Seth
67. Plunder
69. Miss MacGraw

152 Wet Goods by Bert Kruse

A look at an era when things dried up.

ACROSS

1. Nondrinkers' org.
5. Underworld group
10. Brother
13. Urchin
17. Inter
18. Become used to
19. Laughter: Fr.
20. Originate
21. Importers of a sort
23. Chicago king of crime
25. Actress Sandra
26. Arrest
27. Business light
28. Rocky peak
29. Kind of squad
30. Out of control
33. Bill
35. "In Cold Blood" author
38. Milkmaids' props
40. Adjective for 1 Across
44. Nimble
45. Crates on wheels
47. Mrs. Chaplin
48. Kind of shop
49. Indication
50. Wedding-story term
51. S.A. monkey
52. Hangers-on
54. "Down the hatch," e.g.
56. Quieted
58. Tom and Jerry ingredient
60. Chief Assyrian god
62. Drink sometimes spiked
63. Knocking sound
67. All in
69. Plug-uglies of myth
73. Footless creature
74. Joe College's word
76. Diamond figure

77. _____ Friday
78. Greek letter
79. Antinuke events
81. New Hampshire city
82. Construct
84. Street _____ (worldly wisdom)
85. Broke down a sentence
86. Doll, for one
88. Miss Maxwell
89. Opponents of 91 Down
90. Lamb's mother
93. Cradle
95. Soprano's offering
96. Neckpiece
99. Bugbear of 31 Down
101. Causes of gang wars
104. Ending for mob or gang
105. Uno, due, _____
106. Caesar's "veni"
107. Dr. Jonas
108. Serf
109. Cut
110. Speakeasy hostess Guinan
111. Railroad supports

DOWN

1. Watch and _____ Society
2. Hint
3. Magazine born in the Roaring 20's
4. Nasser's org.
5. Threat
6. Gun girl of song
7. Feed
8. Verb variety: Abbr.
9. Roman bronze
10. First name of Repeal proponent
11. Upset
12. Bit of neckwear
13. Reptile
14. Kind of act
15. Cartoonist Peter
16. Near _____ (mix of the 20's)
22. Come together
24. Duck genus
29. Dry enforcement law
30. Anyway
31. Hooch producers
32. Alley of comics
34. Spirited people of the 20's
35. Live outside
36. Author James
37. Bowlers' targets
38. Pacific island group
39. Spots
41. Bubble
42. Heraldic term
43. Law-enforcement action
45. Iota
46. Bristle
53. NCO
55. Sightseer: Sp.
57. Nuptial declaration
59. "The World According to _____"
61. Landlords' income
63. Level
64. Mimic
65. Carry
66. Tobacco byproducts
68. _____ Moines
70. Meadow barleys
71. Ocean flier
72. Winter transport
75. Spirit of the 20's
80. Cymbals of India
81. Eskimo canoe
83. Municipality
85. Vincent and Leontyne
87. One nearing adulthood
89. O'Neill product
90. Gaelic
91. Backers of the 21st Amendment
92. All knotted up
94. Word with bagatelle
95. "Iliad" hero
96. _____ B'rith
97. Come-hither look
98. Inquires
100. Before
101. S.R.O. show
102. Diamonds
103. Ending for moral or reform

153 Songs in Retrospect by Frances Hansen

Presenting appropriate titles in appropriate order.

ACROSS

1. Get started
7. Island near Antigua
14. Mysterious
20. Saver on wedding costs
21. Parker or Powell
22. Wreath material
23. Song in retrospect
26. Frying pan
27. Actress Charlotte
28. Splendid dress
29. Clement
30. Lace town of France
32. Give it a whirl
33. Mehta's namesakes
36. "Up" times
37. Toward the stern
38. Sounds of laughter
42. Slaughter of baseball
43. Teed off
44. Same: Prefix
45. Chemical compound
46. Song in retrospect
51. K-Q connection
52. Morse-code unit
53. Tatum or Ryan
54. "____ most unusual day"
55. Flint instrument of early man
56. Region of Ghana
58. Actor Max of "Barney Miller"
59. Bill's partner
60. Song in retrospect
67. Adam's clock
68. Allies' enemy in W.W. II
69. Absorbs
71. Member of Loyola's order
74. Clublike Maori weapon
75. Cobra's cousin
77. Org. for senior citizens
78. Make an all-out effort
79. Song in retrospect
82. Heavy book
83. Courage above and beyond
84. "M'appari," for one
85. Start of a cockney toast
86. Bagnold
87. Author Yutang
88. Where van Gogh played it by ear
90. Ever so
92. Musical notes
93. Prepare to be knighted
94. Will-o'-the-____
95. Dead set on
99. Doctrine
100. Fare at the yacht club?
103. Song in retrospect
108. ____ Olde England
109. Soprano Patti
110. Out of this world
111. Takes an oath
112. "You Know Me, Al" author
113. Come to one's ____

DOWN

1. Call, in poker
2. Desirable trees
3. Had effect
4. Owner of rose-colored glasses
5. "I got a beautiful ____ . . ."
6. Airline extras
7. Submitted
8. Crested parrot, in Acapulco
9. Johnny of the C.S.A.
10. Barbershop lotion
11. Robs of virility
12. Okey-____
13. Rainbow
14. Belgian king: 1909–34
15. Like jazz tunes
16. Panamanian people
17. Seed covering
18. Saint Philip
19. ____ Exile isle
24. Rorem or Sparks
25. Word for a certain Dodger
30. Atoll or necklace material
31. Leopold's partner in crime
33. Fictional prisoner's castle
34. Foolish
35. One of Clare Luce's names
36. ____ Raton
37. Not have ____ about (have no scruples)
38. Last drink for Socrates
39. Years, to Cicero
40. Gibson of westerns
41. River of Xanadu
43. Length of yarn
44. Miss Dinsmore
47. Judgment against a plaintiff
48. Purpose
49. Enlists
50. Japanese noh singing
51. "A cat may ____ king"
55. Like yodeling
57. Confident
61. Tablecloth's companion
62. Raise on high
63. Broz
64. "Venice of Japan"
65. State firmly
66. Traditional light-hider
70. Fall guy
71. Baryshnikov's leap
72. Governor of Nebraska: 1971–78
73. Trailer type
75. Capek
76. Baseball stats
79. Barley beard
80. Cole Porter's alma mater
81. Custom-made, in England
83. ____ off (ricochets)
88. Solution
89. Shape anew
90. Gourmet's victuals
91. "O that man's heart were ____"
92. Moslem ascetic
93. "My ____ Love," Crosby's first hit
94. Old British weight
95. Navy V.I.P.'s
96. Sketched
97. Swiss river
98. Pianist Hess
100. Fly high
101. Peruvian plants
102. Title for 98 Down
104. Gala event for Marie Antoinette
105. Part of a sen
106. One, in Wassy
107. Bridge passes

ACROSS

1. Mast timbers
6. "____ Most Unusual Day"
10. Not of the cloth
14. Buddhist narrative
19. Village near Harrisburg, Pa.
20. Throat-clearer
21. Lucasta or Sten
22. Like a wild shooter's target
23. Zagreb native
24. Champagne Tony of golf
25. Steel city
27. Hack writer's output
29. Err
31. City near Phoenix
32. Amour-propre
33. Steel-making method
38. ____ now (pronto)
41. French cloak
42. Author of "These are the times . . ."
43. Place, to a lawyer
45. War of 1899–1902
46. Clumsy ship
48. Pipe fitting
52. Petty despot
54. French possessive
55. ____ Tech
56. Lustrous woolen fabric
57. Perfume ingredient
59. Part of F.B.I.
60. Men's org.
61. Capuchin monkey
62. Composer Copland
63. Sights around 25 Across
66. Long-necked pear
69. Kin of Mrs. and Sra.
70. Memorable period
71. Arikara
72. Take ten
73. Passageway for 65 Down
76. U. of Maine site
78. Police-blotter initials
79. Old English letter
80. Hindu mantras
81. Hoosier
85. Spin yarns
87. One of a litter
88. Rio de ____
89. Despise
90. Pass legislation
91. The Censor
92. Traditional knowledge
94. Look down one's nose at
95. Jimmy Valentine, for one
97. Melancholia
100. Supporters of the 18th Amendment
101. About 1,400,000 Americans
106. Derek and Diddley
107. Coll. subject
108. Shoe size
109. Baker Street visitor
113. Alternative to 33 Across
117. Like campus walls
119. Neutral color
120. Town near Zurich
121. Famous Virginia
122. Advantage
123. Ms. Abzug
124. Robert ____ Jones, golfcourse designer
125. Culbertson et al.
126. Leak slowly
127. River to the Danube

DOWN

1. Call's partner
2. Cross inscription
3. Shape of Italy
4. Smeltery item
5. Paige of baseball, for short
6. Suffix with editor or janitor
7. Another example of 64 Down
8. Low-carbon cast iron
9. Ones who collect
10. Once around the track
11. Varnish resin
12. Worldwide crime-fighting agency
13. Dupe
14. Bench warmer
15. Burmese statesman
16. A crowd
17. Bobby of tennis
18. Cohort of Aramis
26. Garment for a rani
28. Do some stitching
30. Kara or Sulu
34. Girl of Gilbert's ballads
35. Like Mr. America
36. Feature of a Las Vegas bandit
37. Early Briton
38. As well
39. Go hang gliding
40. After hepta
44. "The Forsyte ____"
47. Sagan or Reiner
49. City on the Rhine
50. Doctoral exams
51. Gibson girl's shortage
53. Alter
56. Relative of 57 Across
58. Sex appeal
59. Golfer Julius
60. Dummy Mortimer
63. Bring back, as a tax
64. The Mesabi or the Gogebic
65. Major U.S. industry
66. Cacophony
67. Kind of old bucket
68. Actress Lilia
74. Pay up
75. Win convincingly
77. Ancient Greek shrine
81. What stainless steel resists
82. "Take ____ leave it"
83. Nautical greeting
84. N.B.A. team
86. Room to swing
87. Arcadian
88. Certain tale-tellers
91. Mt. Rainier is one
93. Alaskan native: Abbr.
96. French thought
98. Martino and Pacino
99. How to save nine
101. German sub
102. Wall Street term
103. Grenoble's river
104. Race contestant
105. Harry Kemelman hero
110. Ledge
111. Certain look
112. Adjacent
114. Nickname for Fabray
115. Rude house
116. Men
118. Gary Cooper affirmation

155 Category by Sara Helleny

Getting into a rut with a letter combo.

ACROSS

1. Sensible thought
6. Glacial pinnacle
11. Invitation letters
15. Smith or Bede
19. Dispatch boat
20. Turkish city
21. Gemstone
22. Golden in color
23. Children's story, with "The"
25. Region of Spain
27. Friend of Toklas
28. Infatuated
30. Crocus bulb
31. Kind of belly
34. Vestment
35. ____-depressive
36. Dozes
39. Muse of astronomy
41. Product of a destructive metabolism
43. Gypsy
44. Range animal
45. French composer Erik
46. Sweetsop
47. Between sine and non
48. "The ____ Hurrah"
49. Baby distress
50. Bright burner of poem
52. Contented sound
53. Feminine suffix
54. French chicken
55. Bundles
56. Bee product
57. California island
59. Kind of pneumonia
60. Rumples
61. Fairy godmother's prop
62. Unwanted prize
63. Small whales
64. "____ eat bats?" (Wonderland query)
67. Having painful joints
68. Night prowler
72. Inclined, as a mast
73. Author of 23 Across
74. Act haughtily
75. King or Newburg
76. Flying object
77. Nuisance, in Paris
78. "____ a Hot Tin Roof"
79. Sandpiper
80. Explorer Johnson
81. Wood strip
82. Moro priest
83. Discussion group
84. Of a TNT acid: Prefix
85. Of oral instruction
88. Stealthy
89. With ____ (looking ahead)
91. Final passages
92. Title for Churchill or Raleigh
93. Letter addenda
94. Recent: Prefix
95. Happen
96. Rustler's nemesis
98. Type of schizophrenia
101. On a diagonal line
106. Panay people
107. Political cartoonist
108. School for Jacques
109. Saltpeter
110. Finesse
111. Opposite of dele
112. Rustler's prey
113. Grate leavings

DOWN

1. Resin
2. Eggs
3. Command to a dogie
4. Wife of Osiris
5. Hold
6. Master, in old India
7. Famed couple's home
8. Hooray!
9. Rising upward
10. Chains of related things
11. Over-elaborate
12. Shoe cover of yore
13. Cistern
14. One who mediates
15. Enhance
16. Creator of archy and mehitabel
17. Jackie's second
18. ____ culpa
24. Tissue
26. Lurks, old style
29. Kinsman
31. Word after notary
32. Name for Elizabeth I
33. Armor plate: Var.
35. Young herring
36. Mentions
37. ____ merite (Prussian order)
38. Stings
40. ____ in the least
41. Lily type
42. Brew
45. Barrier or box
49. Rupees and pesos
50. Brindled female
51. "Now ____ me down . . ."
52. Kind of willow
54. Blue or home
55. Footwear for a posse
56. Library sign
58. Ready to get up
59. Lowdown heel
60. Fruit for stockholders
62. Contest
63. Single-masted boat
64. Siouan group
65. Prayer
66. Lacking a syllable, in verse
67. Beau ____
68. Dido
69. Treat for 50 Down
70. Foreigners
71. Often-turned items
73. Former pact acronym
74. Wear for ranis
77. Football team divisions
78. River rapids
79. "My Gal ____"
81. Hunting hound's forte
82. Leads astray
83. One often non grata
86. U.S. suffragist's signature
87. Ad ____ committee
88. Treasury
90. It's on the up and up
92. More peeved
95. Seine tributary
96. Hawaiian volcano goddess
97. Greek troublemaker
98. Cool one
99. ____ loss
100. King Cole
102. Drive slantingly
103. Type of degree
104. Prior to
105. Thing, in law

156 Straightedges by Mel Rosen

Everything going directly from here to there.

ACROSS

1. Yin's partner
5. "Here's ____"
10. Gem
14. Discards
19. Indeed, in Ireland
20. ____ liar
21. San ____
22. Gables near Miami
23. Gags
25. Fishes
27. Open
28. Lists at sea
30. Fixed a charge
31. Comic Louis and family
32. Nucleus
33. Not on tape
34. Pitcher's opponent
37. Trivial objection
38. Gas-company employee
42. Biographer Leon and family
43. "Buckle up" and "Watch your step," e.g.
45. Stir
46. Kimberley sight
47. St. Paul's architect
48. Wild sowings
49. Protection
50. Sauce for chow mein
51. Relatives of sems.
53. ". . . to make a house ____"
55. Soot
56. Weasels' relatives
58. Pajama strings
60. Egg masses
61. Fool
62. Texas city
63. "Please," to Henny Youngman
67. Do a bit of check juggling
70. Lectures
71. For ____ (cheaply)
72. O'Kelly and O'Casey
73. W.W. II craft
75. Rara ____
76. Feathers' partner
77. Winglike
78. Mention
79. Review harshly
80. Crackleware features
83. Poisons
84. Gold and silver
86. Relative of keen
87. Least
88. Western Indians
89. Charles's principality
90. Western alliance
91. Gold and ivory
94. Like some wands
95. Indifferent
99. Fencing
101. Walk a tightrope
103. Pink flower
104. Bakery worker
105. Confidentially, with 3 Down
106. Aplenty, poetically
107. Stock-exchange assets
108. Cool apartments
109. Give one pause
110. Belles of the ball

DOWN

1. Manchurian border river
2. Galway Bay islands
3. See 105 Across
4. "Do not ____ into that good night"
5. Harder to believe
6. Tonys' relatives
7. "____ Cassius has a lean . . ."
8. Danish coin
9. Bearded
10. Hospital worker
11. Hostess Mesta
12. Book before Obadiah
13. Cut off
14. Mufflers
15. ____ than thou
16. Leif's father
17. Victor Borge, e.g.
18. Dogboat
24. Helen or Rutherford
26. Shows malice
29. Do a job on copy
32. Sidewalk sights in Paris
33. Somber
34. Makes speech pauses
35. Local language
36. Critical gridiron spot
37. Wise guys
38. River to the Ohio
39. French flop
40. Stop on ____
41. What to count
43. Kind of dive
44. Amoral
49. Writer Jong
51. Crowns worn by Osiris
52. "L'état ____ moi"
53. Accompanying
54. Hydrant attachment
55. Showy flowers, for short
57. Swindles
58. Specie
59. Verdon
61. Veneer
63. Public warehouse
64. Part of U.S.N.A.
65. Visits frequently
66. Twists
67. Arctic explorer
68. Unusual
69. ____ Park, Colo.
72. Narrow openings
74. Try
76. New York's ____ (police)
77. Unnatural
78. Sang
80. Correspondence
81. Wild asses of Asia
82. Thread: Prefix
83. Miss Davis
85. Relative of a blunderbuss
87. Flirt
89. Abated
90. Gunpowder ingredient
91. Tax-time V.I.P.'s
92. Seine tributary
93. Recorded proceedings
94. Isinglass
95. Riga dweller
96. German one
97. Hoity-toity one
98. ____ up (concludes a deal)
100. Back talk
102. United

157 Hoedown by Olga Kowals

Contrary Mary would have no trouble with this.

ACROSS

1. Presided at a party
7. Addams of cartoons
11. Put on
16. Punctual
17. ____ the rag (gabs)
18. What Macduff did
19. Tempt a weakling
22. Person to cherchez
23. Textile worker
24. Bread or whisky
25. Reaction to a touchdown
27. Windy City center
28. Play the romantic field
30. Snow, in Scotland
31. "____ Town"
32. Scottish alders
33. U.N. veto
34. Splinter group
35. Kind of jack or chase
38. Medieval fabric
41. Halloween wear
42. Boone or O'Brien
43. Frustrater of thieves
46. Filthy
47. Disparage
50. Hobgoblin
52. Cuts to shape
53. Quarry product
54. Sheepish opinion
57. High-toned lady
59. Forbear
62. Classified items
63. Use a sled
67. Van Gogh's brother
70. One of the Three Stooges
71. Suffer for one's sins
75. Ivanhoe's beloved
78. Lingers
79. Cuckoo
80. Sheeplike
81. Say Hey Kid
82. Magnitude
86. Prefix for phone or gram
87. Harbor of Guam
90. Getting louder, in music: Abbr.
92. Health spot
93. Suffix for tank or dull
94. Promote misgivings
98. School orgs.
99. Noncoms
101. Doll stuffing
102. Narcotic
103. Rabbit and Fox
104. Give a person a dressing-down
108. ____ Hound (Canis Major)
109. Arctic menaces
110. Molten-metal crust
111. Takes off a habit
112. Basic Latin verb
113. One who destroys

DOWN

1. Sink a putt
2. Increment for a baker's dozen
3. Rubber or postage
4. Bay of Fundy feature
5. Flightless bird
6. Lament
7. Of a science: Prefix
8. German philosopher
9. Tony or Oscar
10. Eur. unit
11. Most reasonable
12. Burden for a diner-out
13. Jewish month
14. Peter out
15. Made nicer
17. Black-tongued dogs
18. Gulf south of Samar
20. Hall or house
21. Cart
22. Ziegfeld and others
26. Rundown
28. City of Uruguay
29. Carousing
34. Steer clear of
36. Spartan magistrate
37. Windy-weather wear
38. Feels peaked
39. No-credit initials
40. Corn predators' calls
41. Angel's delight
43. Hole-in-one
44. Kind of blow
45. From ____ Z
46. Algonquian
47. Excels
48. War ____
49. Sign up
50. Org. for retirees
51. Cradle of the pea
54. Minstrel, as of Avon
55. Pocket, brake or duct
56. Prefix for body or thing
58. Collegiate sports org.
60. Highland ____
61. Arrested
64. Lawyer: Abbr.
65. Medicine man
66. Buddhist temple
67. "____ way, please"
68. Betake one's self
69. Hesitant sounds
71. Coty of France
72. Chemical suffix
73. Ironic
74. Pride of the Gibson girl
75. Rosters
76. Become weedy
77. Variety of vetch
82. Tropical evergreen
83. Parsons or Winwood
84. More meager
85. Back talk
87. Bakers' wear
88. Blueprints
89. Latest thing
90. Red wear for the British in '76
91. Dancer St. Denis
95. Smokes, in Scotland
96. Imitative ones
97. Mournful song
98. Madrid sight
100. Shadow: Prefix
103. Bottled in ____
105. Long time
106. Brit. decoration
107. Against

158 Groupies by Hume R. Craft

Common denominators on various fronts.

ACROSS

1. Kinsman
4. Oodles
9. Studio wear
14. Chess problems with two answers
19. Creator of Artie
20. Passion
21. Kind of lily
22. Marble
23. White ties
27. "Pilgrim's Progress," for one
28. Dentist, at times
29. S.R.O. show
30. Friend of Pierre
31. Dutch painter
32. Dress fabrics
35. Wax products
38. Andy's radio friend
39. Loom
41. Gives off a stench
42. Great northern diver
43. Bullfighter's cloak
45. Cow's mouthful
46. Md. landmark
47. Fourth-down move
48. Greetings for the newborn
49. Regions
52. State on Can. border
53. Pulitzer writer: 1958
54. Fodder plants
55. Flagler's rail terminus
56. Come before
58. Munchausen
59. Frank's kin
60. Brownies
64. John and Maureen
66. Vanquishes
67. Important word to Oscar Wilde
70. Like Ivy League buildings
71. Western chaser
72. Word between "well" and "ends well"
74. Prom partner
75. Confuse

76. Jack Sprat or Peter
77. Portnoy's creator
78. Molding
79. Eccentric piece
80. Savoyard seasons
81. They're rouge and blanc
82. Cotton-field hand
83. Vichyssoise ingredients
85. Loudness unit
86. Natives of eastern coal-mine areas
87. As ___ ice
89. Do some hamming
91. Mr. Pry
92. Kind of important
93. Troika accessory
96. Distinguished one, usually a poet
100. Holy of holies
104. Zoo-bred hybrid
105. Noisy
106. Infirm
107. Keats output
108. Excited display
109. Cheer-leaders' repertory
110. Length units
111. ___ troppo (without excess)

DOWN

1. Hero's life story
2. Matinee V.I.P.
3. Brontës' pseudonym
4. Ceramic furnaces
5. Emulates Der Bingle
6. Worship
7. Actress Goodman
8. Acad. higher-ups
9. Five o'clock fare
10. Canada's leaf
11. Upstate N.Y. city
12. Component of weak feet
13. Orson Welles role
14. German article
15. Word of disgust
16. Golden weddings
17. ___ ambush (lurk)
18. Clans
24. Mr. Doe's movie namesakes
25. Succeed accidentally
26. Bucket contents
31. Struck hard
33. Mme. ___, French beauty
34. Miss Rooney's storied namesakes
35. ___ up (concoct)
36. Odin, Thor et al.
37. G.I.'s radio and campus namesakes
38. Lloyd's Register designation
39. Tack on
40. Goren declaration
42. Olympic coasters
43. Bow and Barton
44. Composer Copland
47. Some hors d'oeuvres
48. Track official
50. Soul, in France
51. Chaplin or Raleigh
57. Scholastic world
58. Chaliapin and others
59. Word in a Steinbeck title
61. Lord Jellicoe's tormentors
62. "Beau ___"
63. Policemen's tours
64. Reproductive elements
65. Obscured
68. Mosshorn
69. Starting golfers
71. Hammer part
72. Threefold
73. Sharpen
81. Citizen, in November
82. Security exchanges
84. Skagerrak port
85. Becomes serious
86. Warm ale drink
87. Broadway groups
88. Fatty
89. Flynn
90. Kind of auxiliary verb
91. Certain button
94. Call it ___
95. Small opening
96. Miss Turner
97. In a while
98. Commotion
99. Elysium
101. Presidential nickname
102. Partner of all
103. Vermont harvest

159 Here and There by Emory H. Cain

Refresher course on some old familiar places.

ACROSS

1. European blackbird
5. Corpsman
10. French friends
14. Moslem call to prayer
18. Met fare
19. "Do as I say, not ____"
20. ____ majesty
21. Insipid
23. Site of a Civil War battle
26. Unit of capacity
27. Actress Parsons and namesakes
28. Broadway flashers
29. City on the Rio Grande
30. McMahon and Ames
31. Nuclear experiment
32. Fog's relative
33. Culture mediums
36. Barren
37. Marquis of note
38. Wall Street word
41. Site of a Bonaparte victory
42. Gay ____
44. Word with crow
46. Foot: Prefix
47. Suffix with whole or win
48. Ladd and Lerner
49. Actor Richard
50. French seasons
51. King of Judah
52. Bandleader Louis
53. Nautical position
54. Fence straddler
55. Holy city in India
57. Wander
58. New York island
59. Site of a noted Benedictine abbey
64. 100-yard dash, for one
67. Italian town
68. Mideast, politically
72. Kind of wind
73. Mockery
74. Agitates
76. Cadmus's daughter
77. Demolish
78. Valletta's island
79. Where Orono is
80. Moslem judge
81. Troubles
82. Think-tank results
83. Spreads
84. Celebes ox
85. ____ qué? (Why, in Spanish)
86. Ran away
87. Insects
88. Black wood
89. Woe!
90. Fountain drinks
92. Labor initials
93. Site of the Coast Guard Academy
96. Meadowlands entry
97. Harassed
102. Ulan ____
103. Where Tarzan had an adventure
105. Word with deaf
106. Appointment
107. Adjust
108. Neat as ____
109. Bishoprics
110. Get rid of
111. Shangri-la people
112. Lease

DOWN

1. A gender
2. Love god
3. Uprising
4. Separator of Ohio and Ontario
5. Handles roughly
6. Italian family
7. Low-beam lights
8. Wedding words
9. Sligo, Clare, etc.
10. Chorus voices
11. Had significance
12. Egyptian goddess
13. Sun Yat-____
14. Burning
15. Site of an Ali fight
16. Feed the kitty
17. Ointment
22. Sky animal
24. Auto pioneer
25. Exigency
29. Burdened
31. Atlanta's Omni, for one
32. Seraglio
33. 1942 Preakness winner
34. Word with step or flesh
35. Madison Avenue worker
36. Ancient Syria
37. Deli purchase
38. Kind of jury
39. An Astaire
40. Ascended
42. Family member
43. Leaning
44. Wooden shoe
45. Best part
46. Flower parts
52. Recumbent
53. Golfer with an army
54. Proofreaders' marks
56. Chemical compounds
58. Props up
60. Conquered Everest
61. Blood carrier
62. Early Peruvians
63. Uniform material
64. Word with hanger
65. Where to see a Goya
66. Keen-edged instrument
69. Kind of bar or forte
70. Hamburger topper
71. NBC morning show
73. Sinks away
74. ____ away (saves)
75. Old-school items
78. Site of Teatro alla Scala
79. Seat of McGill University
80. San Francisco transit
86. Island of the Azores
87. What Robert E. was
88. Newts
89. Make up for
90. Rough finish
91. Yearned
92. Ruins
93. Literary monogram
94. Cry of frustration
95. Oklahoma Indian
96. Egyptian god of creation
97. Decorous
98. Sicily's perennial threat
99. Cheap cigar
100. "____ go bragh"
101. Parking-lot souvenir
103. TV commercials
104. Menu words

The who, what and who else of whodunits.

ACROSS

1. Indy-500 circuits
5. Like a bartender mixing 50 martinis
14. Raiment
20. Relaxing color
21. Fortified, as a castle
22. Melodic sound-makers
23. He said 61 Across
25. Emulates Eve's serpent
26. Sonnet feature
27. Prized possession
28. Palindro-mist's word
29. Certain atom
30. English lawmakers: Abbr.
33. Theseus's aid in the labyrinth
37. Roman 409
38. Language of Pakistan
40. Mrs. Claus's laundry woe
41. Comes (from)
42. Cheater's aid
43. U.N. denial
44. "____ the Dozen"
46. Garment for a wahine
48. Bo Derek
49. Is skeptical
50. Shapers in olden days
51. Bone: Prefix
53. Between bi- and quadri-
54. Corsage flower
55. Parlor piece
58. Not spec.
59. One of Henry's Catherines
60. Anderson's "High ____"
61. The quotation
67. Army mini-brass: Abbr.
68. Screwball
69. Long-time Bruin star
70. Early Kremlin resident
71. Drawing a metaphor
74. Lippo or Angelico
75. What asterisks do
79. Men on base
80. High-school area
85. Scottish explorer
86. Antics
87. Keynes's adjective for Marxism
88. Micro-organism
89. Upright beam
90. Ta-ta!
91. City on Norton Sound
92. Wine: Prefix
93. Actor Douglas
94. Evening star
95. U.S. output initials
96. ____ Plaines
97. One ____ time
98. Possessive
99. Penna. city
102. Light lace scarves
104. He wrote 61 Across
112. Seat of Howard County, Ind.
113. Saturday, in Stuttgart
114. Dog's bane
115. Honor an R.S.V.P.
116. Ordeals for role seekers
117. Ending for song or gab

DOWN

1. Smaller
2. Result of over-exercising
3. Leader
4. Frock coat
5. Name for a Dalmatian
6. Middle of three in a row
7. Be a thorn in the side
8. Cheer-leader's remark
9. Navy rank: Abbr.
10. Electrical unit
11. Air: Abbr.
12. Zuyder or Tappan
13. Gridiron units: Abbr.
14. Played Hamlet
15. The bad guys
16. Tiny Cratchit
17. Baggage
18. Tit for tat
19. English earldom
24. Actor Cariou
27. All talk
30. ____ scale of hardness
31. Keats or Shelley
32. TV outer-space series
33. Quotation source
34. Paint's rider in old westerns
35. Keel attachments
36. Bert Parks's successor
37. Small container
38. "Do others . . ."
39. Bar drinks
40. ____-fi
42. Element of Miss Muffet's diet
45. Boil and strain
46. Chair man
47. Employ, in Spain
49. Entry
50. 3.086 grains
52. "C____ la vie"
54. Moll's leg
56. Hindu ascetics
57. Uninformative sigs.
59. Movie designation, at times
61. Thing gained
62. Parts of talking film
63. Magog's partner
64. Baker Street scout: Abbr.
65. Teasdale
66. Relig. degree
67. Social zilch
72. Actress ____ Aimée
73. ____ off (irritated)
76. Olympic swimming event
77. Make
78. San ____
80. Curtail
81. Protected, on board
82. Adam Smith's field: Abbr.
83. Highway access
84. ____ aux Noix, Canada
87. Name cards: Abbr.
88. Explodes
90. Noted Illinois monogram
93. "The Trial" author
94. Windshield attachment
96. Breadwinner, sometimes
98. Actor Cronyn
99. Linemen
100. Corrida cheers
101. Undiluted
103. Hello, to Tonto
104. Retiree's org.
105. Creditor's reminder
106. Three mins. in the ring
107. Black bird
108. Type of tractor, for short
109. Accessory for Madame Butterfly
110. Not of the old guard: Prefix
111. Raggedy girl

161 Activation by Alice H. Kaufman

Various ways to get things from here to there.

ACROSS

1. Mexican sandwiches
6. Finish third
10. Cleric
15. The one specified
19. Kind of setter
20. Elf
21. Garnish
22. German title
23. Prepare a dinner course
25. Isaac's mother
26. Ceremonial act
27. Somewhat tardy
28. Entreaty
30. Evergreen droppings
32. Gaelic
33. Landon et al.
35. Bankbook abbr.
37. Garden tools
38. Chinese symbol of longevity
39. Yorkshire river
40. Defeats at bridge
41. Record of a year's events
45. Lops, as twigs
49. Asserts
53. Lands held by rental agreements
55. Coward or Harrison
57. Prior to, in the boondocks
58. Ageless film dog
59. Relative of yep
61. Network
63. Author of "Picnic"
64. Decorate gaudily
66. Wings
68. Lindbergh's field
70. Kiltie's dance
73. Pigment
77. Like the fox's grapes
78. Bring to life
83. Margarine
84. Allen and Ott
86. Becomes chilled
88. Floors, in France
89. Respond
91. New Zealand tree
93. Devices for producing suction
95. Obtain by force
97. As one
99. Orange, in heraldry
100. Ingenuous
102. Caviar
103. Lake in Lombardy
105. H. M. Pulham, for one
108. Contents of a certain bag
109. Burner
110. Biblical king
114. Mel Tillis or Roscoe Ates
116. Wheezy piano piece
118. Color pic
120. Calendar abbr.
121. Of a membrane
123. Gets romantic
125. "Right on!"
126. Peruvian beast
127. Over
128. Ruhr city
129. Actor Grant
130. Squeals
131. Idol
132. Channel

DOWN

1. ID of a sort
2. Noisy
3. Neolithic graves
4. Actor Davis
5. Wild Asian sheep
6. Health resort
7. In a constructive way
8. Tests
9. Off target
10. Ethiopian prince
11. Accommodate
12. Soprano Lucrezia
13. Wild geese
14. Belongs
15. Becomes furious
16. German poet
17. Russian collective
18. Braid
24. Eastern ruler
29. Broadcasts
31. Word after terra
34. Off one's rocker
36. Kind of sign
38. Trickery
39. Towns in Minnesota and Ontario
41. "____ right with the world"
42. Minimum range tide
43. Astronauts' agency
44. Society: Abbr.
46. Perfect
47. One-time London trademark
48. Brutal
50. Singer Tennille
51. Thus
52. Perceived
54. Airship filler
56. First Roman empress
60. Asian capital
62. One of a daily trio
65. Heron
67. Train
69. Restless, in music
71. Spartan serf
72. Impertinent
73. Sped
74. Holly
75. Shipshape
76. Target game at English fairs
79. Defeat at chess
80. Dramatic struggle
81. Sea bird
82. Existence
85. Theater sign
87. One in the stands
90. Feature
92. Monster
94. Do housework
96. In a weary manner
98. Of the dawn
101. Old switch for punishing pupils
104. Sound-barrier word
105. Old sword
106. W.W. II German bomber
107. Odd
108. Kind of steamer
109. Superior group
110. Charge facing a firebug
111. Julia Ward and Elias
112. Romance, in Rome
113. Plug
115. Of an epoch
117. Large marine fish
119. Prefix for sphere
122. ____ Palmas
124. Naval noncom

162 Liquid Centers by Alfio Micci

They slosh around at the drop of a definition.

ACROSS

1. Former Austrian coins
7. Stood the gaff
13. Choir lofts
18. Hand-thrown weapon
19. Off the boat
20. Sweetheart
21. Visitor; place for same
23. Beer
24. Kind of transit
25. 402, in Roman times
26. Raptorial
28. Jargon
29. Accompanying
31. Bowling item
32. Corroded
34. Sprout; talk freely
42. Showed clemency
46. Washed out
47. Gazelle
48. Memorizes
49. Medicinal units
51. Hank of baseball
53. "God is light, and in Him ___ darkness"
54. Final totalities
57. Cars that were flops
58. Car type
60. Dud car
61. Kind of machine
62. Neatness; decide on a dessert
70. Hibernia
71. Singer Obraztsova
72. False face
73. Circle or ocean
76. Shows kindness to
80. Data, for short
81. Partner of chapter
82. Ran
83. Pay attention
85. Alfonso's queen
86. Middle: Prefix
87. Sour notes from the choir
89. Make a debut; result
92. Tricks
93. G.I. mail center: Abbr.
94. Straw bundle
96. Circus employee
101. Pay
108. Prefix for culture
109. Finnish lake
110. With force
111. Musical instrument; musical direction
114. Mother-of-pearl
115. Sign up
116. Prima ballerinas
117. King Midas's downfall
118. Certain leathers
119. Holed up

DOWN

1. Drummer Gene
2. Plastics base
3. Nervous; abut
4. Shrew
5. Instruct
6. Teased
7. High-school subject
8. Bat wood
9. Emporium
10. Kind of de force
11. Scottish language
12. Legal document
13. Labor-union conglomerate
14. Lamentation
15. Starch source
16. Cassowary's kin
17. Sunday talks: Abbr.
18. End
21. Time periods: Abbr.
22. Jewish homeland: Var.
27. Footless
30. Fails; endures
33. Handlelike part
35. Out of tune
36. Beethoven's "Grosse ___"
37. Fr. holy women
38. "For ___ a jolly good . . ."
39. Fairy-tale heavy
40. Ass
41. Aficionados
42. Skin fold
43. Noted fabler
44. Made hastily
45. Little spits of rain
49. Major-___
50. Swan genus
51. Hitler
52. Referrer to a footnote
55. Yeasty pancake
56. Understand
57. Cockney's SOS
59. Uncanny
61. Nail for a miner
63. Movie, for short
64. Author Wiesel
65. Rex or Donna
66. Mass. cape
67. Bridge, in Bologna
68. Deduce
69. Jackets and collars
73. ___ plaisir
74. Splitsville
75. Prepare for finals
76. Judge's seat
77. Within: Prefix
78. Old MacDonald's property
79. Meager
82. Shea player
84. Shoe part; shoe
86. Asian wild dog
87. Like overdone toast
88. French privateer
90. ___ State (New York)
91. Started the bidding
92. Utah's flower
95. Sword handles
97. Old-womanish
98. Bleated
99. Marine fliers
100. Vintage car
101. Wooden punishment collar
102. Sharif
103. Self-defense item, at times
104. Goddess of hope
105. Japanese aboriginal
106. Chaucer specialty
107. Author Bagnold
112. Simple sugar
113. Long time

163 Keeping Company by Elaine D. Schorr

The Elks and the Moose aren't the only ones to organize.

ACROSS

1. Conductor Caldwell
6. Dreiser's Carrie
12. Tarzan portrayer
18. Hersey's town
19. Menu offering
20. Creator of Uncle Remus
21. Game birds assembled
23. Creator of the Marches
24. Corrida cry
25. Gounod opus
26. Bone: Prefix
28. Inhabitant: Suffix
29. See to
31. Society-page word
32. South African statesman
34. Aberdeen's river
35. Military acronym
37. They get pearls thrown at them
38. Kind of cellar or door
40. Sleeve style
43. ____ for (tolerate)
44. Unheeding
45. Ph.D. requirements
46. New Zealand native
47. Foxhole's relative
49. Long yarn
50. Learned Moslem
51. Jack of TV
52. All ____ up (miffed)
54. Work units
55. Formicary
57. Dam's mate
58. ____ ammoniac
59. Formosa Strait island
60. George, William or Apache
61. Utmost limit
62. German
64. Have ____ to pick
65. Alan of the films
66. Hematite and limonite
67. Become dependent on
68. Place for wallowers
69. Worse than bad
71. French site of Roman ruins
72. Give a reference
73. Doll stuffing
74. Make ____ at (be amorous)
75. Scale tone
76. Blind part
80. Malta or Elba, to the French
81. Element unit
82. Titan with a load
84. Spanish she-bear
85. Shows anger
87. Kenyan family
91. Seed coats
92. Pawnbroker, for one
93. Resource
94. Miss Franklin
95. Sand ridges
96. Wallace or Noah

DOWN

1. Low Countries footwear
2. Fred's sister
3. One-word bird
4. "Have you ____ wool?"
5. ____ it (walk)
6. Continuance
7. Busy
8. Bit of sports info
9. Kind of corn
10. Moray or conger
11. What echoes do
12. Fireside items
13. Respiratory sound
14. Clara Barton's org.
15. Fowl family
16. Hang on to the ____ end
17. Treasure
22. Papal garment
27. Holy one: Abbr.
30. J. R. Ewing's locale
32. Hive horde
33. Kind of bus
36. Part of to be
37. Zeno follower
38. Forecaster
39. Administer a beating
40. Attar sources
41. Turkish mount
42. Flying flock
43. Risqué
44. Rural conveyance
46. "____ Lescaut"
47. Oncle's partner
48. Asocial one
51. Adult bookshop offering
53. ____-bopper
55. O.T. book
56. Sacks
57. N.C.O.'s
59. Defective: Prefix
63. S.A. country
64. Isn't up to par
65. Little island
67. Ride roughshod over
68. Rice concoction
69. Insect bristle
70. Raleigh or Camp
71. Detached: Prefix
72. Flag
74. Bewildered
75. Range roamer
77. Partner of fast
78. Lou Grant player
79. Toothsome
81. Oriental nurse
82. Egyptian skink
83. Bacon unit
86. Court fig.
88. Legal matter
89. Kind of stand
90. Bay of Honshu

164 Parlay Voo? by Raymond F. Eisner

If so, this lesson in French lit shouldn't be difficult.

ACROSS

1. Leaf's lifeline
5. Spectral type
10. Elec. current initials
14. Roman 1150
17. Certain code
18. French or shore
19. Purchase, in Paris
20. Make ____ (get on base)
22. Saint-Exupéry work
25. Singer Abbe
26. Inventor Howe
27. Southern evergreen
28. Gloomy song
29. Finally!
31. Novelist Meyer and family
32. "L'____," Rostand play
33. In one's element
34. Sequence, in Soissons
35. Unique
36. Anna who portrayed Nana
37. Novel by 78 Across
40. Lush
43. Moccasins
44. "To ____ not . . .''
45. Quay
46. Patriarchal title
47. Sign of a crowd
48. Swann's creator
52. Vientiane's land
53. Expose
55. Undermine
56. Hebrew months
57. Columbus was one
59. Town in Norway
60. Balzac's "La ____ Humaine"
62. Choir voices
63. Pear-shaped music makers
65. Lourdes has a famed one
66. Slapstick props
67. Rimbaud prose poem, with "A"
70. New Guinea town
73. Common French verb
74. Old man, in Dresden
75. Sky animal
76. Partner of furious
77. Opp. of plaintiff
78. Friend of Jean-Paul Sartre
82. Catalogue
83. "Für ____," Beethoven piece
85. Biblical mount
86. Helots' home
88. Electron tube
90. Cocktail preparers
92. Actor Jack and family
93. Adjust one's shoelaces
94. Winter melon
95. Skewered meat: Var.
96. Further
97. Famous work of 15 Down
102. Simon ____
103. Every 60 minutes
104. Sea call
105. Paper or pudding
106. Red letters
107. Obligation
108. Acceptances
109. Seethe

DOWN

1. Cliché
2. Part of TNT
3. Poetic contraction
4. Molière snob and namesakes
5. ____ Pascal, French writer
6. French legislative branch
7. Urchins
8. Burma's old capital
9. Melts down, as fat
10. City near London
11. Disorder
12. Patch
13. Coins: Abbr.
14. Speak evil of
15. French symbolic poet
16. Vernacular
19. More pallid
21. Suffix for a young age
23. Bridge bid
24. Ship's crane
28. French couturier
29. Perfume oil
30. Novel by André Gide
31. Emptiness, in Ems
32. Bright
33. Small cobras
34. Kind of wave
35. Dark and Middle
37. Laconic
38. Having no feet
39. Isle near the Tongas
41. Old coins of Greece
42. Word after demi
44. Pasture plaints
46. Ethan or Mel
48. Sras., in St.-Lô
49. Musical direction
50. Show off
51. Italian pianist Bruno
54. Briefly-worn necktie
56. Actor Jannings
57. Stared
58. Typewriter type
60. Anatoly Karpov's game
61. Border, in Barcelona
63. Word on a E.T.A. board
64. Consumer
65. Hedge material
67. Mud volcano
68. Dresden's river
69. Presiding spirit
71. Staff members: Abbr.
72. Singer James
76. "Madame Bovary" author
78. ____-de-camp
79. Person in bondage
80. Small dance band
81. Sunken court outside a cellar
84. Hang around
86. Wooden shoes
87. Faculty member, for short
88. Springe
89. Picture puzzle
90. Max and Buddy
91. ____ as a pig
92. Tired, in Toulon
94. Late Chinese leader
95. Tomorrow, to Tacitus
97. Clerical degree
98. Second person
99. "La ____ en Rose"
100. Type of bag
101. Moon-landing vehicle

165 Getting Around by Sidney L. Robbins

And getting nowhere in the process.

ACROSS

1. V.I.P.'s of old Russia
6. Old madrigal
10. Clerical leader
15. Frolic
19. Boredom
20. Wading bird
21. Fairies
22. Sin
23. Consumed
24. Bridge seat
25. "___ of do or die"
26. Explorer Cabeza de ___
27. Twister for climbers
30. Heights of the Mideast
31. Avers
32. Electrical units
33. Squirmy fish
34. Beret's relative
37. Type of show or block
38. Pintail duck
39. Balkan native
43. Writer Jong
45. You, in Berlin
46. Director Federico and family
47. Type of skirt
48. Ironic development
53. Convent dwellers
54. Partridge's tree
55. Wars of the ___
56. Bits
57. Correspond
58. Tuesday event
60. Rival
61. Henry and Clare
62. Golf position
63. Used a baton
67. Certain verb: Abbr.
68. Lower-priced whisky
70. Type of loft
71. City near Paris
76. Miss Two-shoes
77. Swallow
79. Oakley
81. Blockhead
82. "Thanks ___"
83. Deserving maneuver
85. Chariot route
86. Troubled
88. Negative of sorts
89. In agreement
90. Attar
91. Son of Noah
93. Rivals of Reps.
96. Gangsters beat it
97. Type of constrictor
98. Word to a horse
99. Moonlight, for one
101. Type of vote
104. Asian twister
109. Socials
110. Puts on weight
111. Type of brush
112. Furious
113. Add liquor
114. Formal mall
115. Row
116. Money of Iraq
117. Mineral rocks
118. Pub drinks
119. G.M. car, for short
120. Antelope

DOWN

1. Mounds
2. Type of dragon
3. One opposed
4. Sorry ones
5. Old Blue Eyes
6. Celebration
7. Lessened
8. Little Elizabeths
9. Spumante city
10. Southwestern Indian
11. Resulted in
12. Army V.I.P.'s
13. Seine feeder
14. Half a fly
15. Money turnover
16. Well-known office
17. Transparent metal
18. Prepare
28. Thai language
29. Lover
30. Earth science: Abbr.
33. She, in Paris
34. Apollo's vale
35. Prospero's sprite
36. Old Hebrew weights
38. Holds court
39. Beats a bridge contract
40. Accustom
41. Dressed to the ___
42. Basic Latin verb
44. Homered
45. Opposite of NNW
46. Mrs. Sprat's fare
48. Partner of true
49. Coax
50. Negative contraction
51. Type of proof
52. Type of lance
57. Gold: Prefix
59. Undersized
60. Prepare eggs
61. Type of closet
64. Tory's rival
65. Stage villain
66. Celtic goddess
68. Hacking knives
69. Freeboots
72. Knightly title
73. Helicopter part
74. Princess ___ (Mme. Lupescu)
75. Kind of throat
76. Newscaster Pressman
77. Old dirk
78. Join
79. He ribbed Eve
80. Certain degree
83. Whale
84. Tatum or Patrick
87. Sufficient, poetically
89. On horseback
91. Black eye
92. Stallions
93. Trailed closely
94. Tail and bitter
95. Miss Murray
98. Word after mean or worth
99. Delicacy at Maxim's
100. Paris month
101. French town
102. Rip
103. Meet event
104. Ridge
105. Words of proportion
106. Collective suffix
107. Laurel of comedy
108. Cattle group
110. Blarney-stone gift

166 Cruise Stops by A. J. Santora

Spots of land we might or might not visit.

ACROSS

1. Danish astronomer
6. Oahu food
9. Iceberg-lane message
12. Eskimo settlement
16. Hockey champs of 1980
18. Asian nanny
19. Tear off
22. Plea of girl enjoying the sun
25. Barge canal
26. Knight's shoes
27. _____ poetica
28. Ordinary
31. More enthusiastic
32. Big bin
33. Piled up
34. "_____ from the Bridge"
37. Answer
40. Donne would say no to this fact
44. _____ man (mortal)
45. "Alive and Well" Jacques
46. Irritate
47. Am, to Madame
49. Elk
52. Swerve off course
53. Greek sorceress
54. Kind of type: Abbr.
55. Where Andretti goes a lap
56. Penalty
57. "Le Rouge _____ Noir"
58. "Oh, _____ a home . . ."
60. Barnum import
65. Ancient rival of Athens
67. Remove, in printing
68. Young salmon
69. Cod's kin
70. Two, to a Berliner
71. Mediterranean cruise stop
73. Cold-cut item
76. Urfa's old name
79. Greek letters
80. Hercules' captive
81. Elephant boy
82. As the _____ would have it
84. Chic shorts
87. Enzymes from molds
90. Most tiny
91. Spanish bayonet
92. Part
93. Small, hard bed
96. Filming units
97. Alder tree
98. British comedienne
101. One lamenting
102. Stop on a Canadian cruise
108. Stud with diamonds
109. Nurse in Hyde Park
110. Rum-coke in Havana
111. Shadow: Prefix
112. Opposite of exo
113. "_____ My Man"
114. Ref. book

DOWN

1. Proposal
2. Supply sgt.
3. River to the North Sea
4. Spiteful missives
5. Snares
6. Show dog, for short
7. Lode contents
8. Beliefs
9. Show satisfaction
10. Like an old bucket
11. Worcester and Talia
12. Tone down copy
13. Miss Trueheart
14. _____ loss
15. Cruise stop in TV Guide
17. _____ Eireann
18. Lament from a certain island
20. Sophia's mate
21. Green tea
23. Bumpkin
24. Wolfe and others
28. _____-pamby
29. Scarlett
30. Continue
32. One-night stand
34. Chaplet
35. Kind of durance
36. Mallorca is one
38. Kind of tide
39. Miss Merkel
41. Program
42. Tough _____ crack
43. "_____ for Murder"
48. Arabian nomad
50. Dundee cap
51. Martinique is one
53. May of baseball
56. Certain bargain event
58. Chef's utensil
59. Concerning
60. Drowsy one's need on a Pacific isle
61. Trimming tool
62. Tritons
63. Angle of a sawtooth
64. Sea anemone
65. Pronoun
66. Notebook
71. Give an example
72. Plunders
73. Wore
74. Lessen
75. Goddesses of inspiration
77. B.&O. stop
78. J.F.K.'s U.N. representative
81. Feudal lord
83. Plant leaf
85. Bind again
86. Structure of a synthetic fabric
87. Mideast native
88. Kind of game or nylons
89. Like ocean water
94. Minnelli and others
95. Southwestern plain
96. Elamite city
98. _____ B'rith
99. Saarinen
100. Engrave
101. Adam's spares?
103. Common abbr.
104. Cry's partner
105. Rival of CBS
106. Kind of wit
107. Moment, for short

167 Dual Entries by Judson G. Trent

Some roses are known by other names.

ACROSS

1. OTB participant
7. Habituated
13. Butter-coloring dye
19. In
20. Orange fragrance
21. Daub thickly
22. John C. Frémont
24. Cerium or helium
25. Loom bar
26. Korbut et al.
27. Millay and Best
29. Brouhaha
30. Cuckoos
31. Astronomer Tycho ___
32. Grafting shoot
33. Pro ___ publico
34. Fleet letters
35. Bed parts
36. "Ring of Bright Water" star
37. Greek letter
38. Rapidly
39. ". . . nor ___ of night . . ."
40. Places for cuisses
43. N.T. gospel writer
45. Closet lining
46. Pitt's earldom
47. Stick together
48. Jacques of song
49. Blessing
50. Carioca's city
51. Rarities
52. Hit the deck
53. Nantes's river
54. Pester
55. Batty
56. Shays led one
58. Unused
59. Japanese statesman
60. Tiresome ones
62. Feet for Frost
63. Dream: Prefix
64. Labor initials
65. In the center of
66. Moslem judges
67. Trail markers
68. Mine air shafts
70. Hebrew month
71. Bristly
72. More filmy
73. Rings
74. Midweek god
75. Part of E.T.A.
76. Scandinavian
77. Greek physician
78. Hay place
81. Dream, in Dijon
83. Boxer Archie
84. Essential parts
85. Sonoran Indian
86. Zeta's neighbor
87. Early Calif. missionary
88. Domain
89. Held and Moffo
90. Volcanic crater
92. Erie Canal
95. Fitting
96. Kind of bonnet
97. TV aerial
98. Cactus of the Southwest
99. Gazed
100. Cubic meters

DOWN

1. Canadian river craft
2. Allen and Frome
3. Ph.D. requirement
4. Hits the bottle
5. Caliph slain by a slave
6. On a pension: Abbr.
7. Distend
8. Welcomes from Whirlaway
9. Jars: Lat.
10. Items for Walton
11. Moray; old style
12. Capra or Hitchcock
13. Historian Nevins
14. Scottish denials
15. Air: Prefix
16. Roosevelt's regiment
17. Mortise's partner
18. One ___ (a few)
21. Title in Iberia
23. Ode specialist
28. Per ___
31. Actress Amanda
32. Piraeus porticoes
33. Lure
35. Rowel holders
36. Gen. George Thomas or Tommy Henrich
37. Cawdor title
38. DEW-line signal
39. Flyway users
40. Kon-Tiki's Heyerdahl
41. It recedes, regrettably
42. Meerschaum users
43. Musical brevity
44. Stonewall Jackson's men
45. Uses a pony
46. Mints
47. Will adjunct
48. Disengaged
49. Simpletons
52. Gallico's "Mrs. ___ Goes to Paris"
53. Curtail
57. Dips
58. Skull protuberance
60. Sherlock's street
61. Measure for Micah
63. Like Dobbin's diet
66. Kind of fire
67. Relinquishes
69. Yorkshire river
70. Series of slopes
71. ___ as a judge
73. Meager
74. Militaristic ruler
76. Bayes and Kaye
77. Chin growth
78. Adviser
79. Delphi's attraction
80. Hopes for
81. Kind of tire
82. Marching distance
83. Old Ethiopian capital
84. Middle: Prefix
85. Woodcock's kin
87. Clan
88. Laughter, in Lima
89. Comstock entrance
91. Cock-a-doodle-___
93. Livy's lang.
94. Former campus org.

168 Homely Gathering by William L. Canine

In which 75 Down runs away with 49 Across.

ACROSS

1. President from New Hampshire
7. Gather
12. One at the top
20. Went along with
21. Single diner
22. Adapt to Caesar's world
23. Observes thoughtfully
25. Northwestern's home
26. Sweet gum or cedar
27. Up and about
28. ____ one's whistle
29. Holiday time
30. Las Vegas strip feature
33. Incense
36. Helps for detectives
39. Fleet cat
42. Noted puppeteer
44. ____ jolie fille
45. Talk about
46. Muse
49. Locale of a Masters piece
53. Fragile lizard
56. Famous dining area
57. Unwritten
59. "Do it or ____"
60. Small portions
62. Medley
65. African wildcat
68. Breach of unity
70. Beginning
71. Service coups
73. Period of time
74. Old French coins
76. Carriage
80. Actor Brian
83. Churchill's successor
87. English landscapist
89. Region in Israel
91. Spain's Duke of ____
93. Neighbor of Mass.
94. It was promised in the Bible
96. Team in a Jan. 1 event
99. "1812 Overture" instrument
103. Mister, in Cádiz
104. Before
105. Marsh elder
106. Word form for an Asian land
107. Lecturers
109. Word with ink or grand
111. Medicinal plant
114. Moslem priest
115. ____ Diavolo
117. "Beer on ____"
119. African antelopes
121. Greek W.W. II group
125. Summer cooler
128. Weill protagonist
131. Amazon denizen
132. Walking ____
133. Life of the party
134. Depicts
135. John Marshall's successor
136. Speak up

DOWN

1. Covenant
2. Stravinsky
3. Sea bird
4. Resinous hydrocarbon
5. Letter
6. Teacher's deg.
7. "____ well . . ."
8. Castle guards
9. Caper
10. Cassandra
11. Fourth-yr. people
12. Gang
13. Mansion's opposite
14. Dabbler
15. Writer Fleming
16. M.D.'s associates
17. Small bits
18. Black Sea arm
19. Hawaiian goose
24. Beg
31. Summers in Nice
32. Rows
34. Postprandial breaks
35. Scout units
37. Tropical cuckoo
38. Heartfelt
39. Hockey goal
40. South Dakota has black ones
41. Clean off
43. "You Can't ____ Again"
47. Sailor
48. Turkish weights
50. "No, no ____ me!"
51. Bobbles the ball
52. Beef preference, for some
54. Sun. event
55. Dais leader
58. Like candles in use
61. Fleeced
63. Sulk
64. Depose
66. Cosmic
67. Zoological suffix
69. ____ sanctum
72. Side dishes
75. Plug of tobacco
76. Depression org.
77. Peter Pan's enemy
78. Mrs. Lindbergh
79. "It's a small world, ____?"
81. France's I through IV
82. Concerns of Freud
84. Salic or Murphy's
85. Actress Terry
86. First German president
88. French wheat
90. Direction: Abbr.
92. Warlord of Olympus
95. Beach sight
97. Flourish
98. Killer whale
100. Energy agcy.
101. Tropical plant
102. Treasure State
108. Corrects
109. Island north of Leyte
110. Annie's Warbucks
112. "____ do" (nix)
113. Okie's relative
115. To-do
116. Gaming city
118. Hash-house bullets
120. Give it ____ (make an effort)
122. Parasites
123. "____ and asunder"
124. Seven: Prefix
126. Birth month for D.D.E.
127. "____ any drop to drink"
128. Smart remark
129. Estonian river
130. Neighbor of Mo.

169 Showing the Way   by Ruth W. Smith

Some familiar routes for tourists and locals.

ACROSS

1. Away from the coast
7. Play parts, in Paris
12. Okra plants
18. Dreamy one
19. Hang loosely
20. Like some strong breaths
21. Familiar D.C. avenue
23. Lorraine's partner
24. Winter road hazard
25. "Othello" character
26. Whitney or Wallach
27. ____ gestae
28. Swiss herdsman
30. Revue offering
33. One of Lincoln's sons
35. ". . . and ____ well!"
39. Win by a ____
41. Concerning
43. Booty
46. Atlanta hub
48. Donkey, in Bonn
49. "The ____ of a Tub"
50. Principal dish
51. Son of Jacob
53. Steeplechase occurrences
55. Sister, in Bordeaux
56. Kiln
58. Evening, in Arles
60. Krazy ____
61. Jazz artery of the South
65. Cheer
68. Andes dweller
69. Besides
70. Indian thrush
74. ____ -the-clock (continually)
76. Unless, to Caesar
78. Moorish drum
79. Sharp bark
80. Taro root
82. New York winos' hangout
85. Shaker or mine
86. Gun or squad
87. Kind of cracker
88. Portico
89. ____ Kippur
91. Small pest
93. Bones
95. Labor org.
97. Exclamations
99. Wine pitcher
101. Homes for Araby sheiks
106. Swell!
108. San Francisco cable-car route
111. Like early skirts
112. Minneapolis suburb
113. Part of the mouth
114. To sit: Lat.
115. Garden accesses
116. Mountain ridges

DOWN

1. Annoying children
2. Playwright Coward
3. Single
4. Boleyn
5. Aeries
6. Prohibitionist
7. Move forward
8. Projecting rock
9. New Mexican Indians
10. Roof adornment
11. "Alone on a wide wide ____"
12. Objective
13. Dark
14. Wrong: Prefix
15. New Jersey's casino thoroughfare
16. Fairy-tale first word
17. Descends, old style
22. Steamship
26. Existence: Fr.
29. Grafted, in heraldry
31. City in the Ukraine
32. Maintains firmly
34. Italian wine city
35. Mimics
36. Fabric weave
37. "Miniver Cheevy, born too ____"
38. Prepare to operate
40. Famous race horse
42. Well-known cow
44. ____ breve
45. Exploit
47. Narcotic
52. Heating devices
54. Magician's word
56. Grampus
57. What to do to a sinking ship
59. Spanish gold
62. "Keep it ____ your hat"
63. Narrow openings
64. Melts
65. Goulding and Noble
66. Kind of code
67. Vine's crossroad in L.A.
71. Support
72. "Odyssey" priest
73. Star in the Serpent
75. ____ -date
77. Very small degree
78. Arab garments
81. One's pad
83. To-dos
84. One of the Fords
90. Inciter
92. Namely
94. Perfume
95. Expressions of disgust
96. Pacific island group
98. Jekyll's partner
100. Nonaspirate
102. Writer Gardner
103. Spruce
104. Head, in Lyon
105. Agnès and Marie
107. Poetic word
108. Cribbage piece
109. Harem room
110. Health resort

170 Finales by Mary Virginia Orna

Some things that dieters usually pass up.

ACROSS

1. Mr. Milquetoast
7. Czech premier in 1919
12. Lodge member
17. Charlotte ___
18. Pen filler, in Angers
19. Conference
21. Summer dessert
23. Muscle producing rotation
25. Horned antelope
26. Fanfare
27. Type of gasket
28. Nigerian tribesman
29. Solar disk
31. Fall dessert
33. "Metamorphoses" author
34. Vex
35. Date for Caesar
36. Wine: Prefix
37. Broadway musical
38. Town near Canberra
39. Give ___ of approval
40. Boodle
41. Orchestral section
42. Kind of slip or resistance
44. Name for a ship
45. Intend
46. Infused
49. Rowboat feature
52. Incision
56. ___ the saddle
57. Restaurateur Toots
58. Part of a three-piecer
59. Friend of Narcissus
60. Monarchs of the Mideast
61. Dessert, in general
63. Chinese or Indian
64. Rover's relative
65. Painter Mondrian
66. Jargon
67. Plan
68. Bolted
69. Islands in the Bay of Bengal
71. Music makers, to Pythagoras
72. Miss Adams
74. Approves
75. Kind of nonsense
76. Kind of transit
78. Ocean eagle
80. Encountered a banana peel
81. Stream feature
85. Dammar or elemi
86. First Chinese dynasty
87. Singe
88. N.C. college
89. Wings
90. Dessert for Seward
93. Ironwood
94. Prefix for givings or take
95. Sam of Watergate hearings
96. Annoys
98. Poke, in Paisley
99. Summer dessert
101. Topping for 99 Across
103. Town near Milan
104. House for Poe
105. Tragus
106. Hydrophobia
107. Necro-mancers
108. Downbeat

DOWN

1. Stampede site
2. Intellectual deficiency
3. Butler and Barber
4. Arafat's assn.
5. "___ She Sweet?"
6. Tire with a new life
7. Arched ceilings
8. Wild
9. Cliffs
10. Pianist Claudio
11. Buttons or Grange
12. Breed of sheep
13. Amidst
14. Join the choir
15. Miss Munson
16. Locals
19. Botticelli season
20. Birds in a Kilmer poem
22. Like light coats
24. Teased
27. Concert halls
30. Cream dessert
32. Wooden pin
33. Cooling dessert
37. Levin or Gershwin
39. Dutch measure
40. Dessert often served with fruit
41. Crooked
43. Bee, to Brutus
44. It may need a horn
45. Perfume spray
46. Crosier, e.g.
47. Dravidian language
48. Skip
49. Greek letter
50. Smooths
51. Fuel often bogged down
53. Quaker gray
54. Disgrace
55. Sharpens
57. Scand. country
61. Trig ratio
62. Le ___, race city
63. Smart
65. Reimbursed
67. Emulated A. J. Foyt
70. Simple organism
71. Loafer
73. Uproar
75. Jack the Ripper et al.
76. Vestiges
77. "Set me ___ upon thine heart"
78. Nose rubber
79. Nothing, in Nancy
80. Splinter
82. "You've got to give ___"
83. Takes heed
84. They were often errant
85. Branches
86. Prized cigar
87. Fit out
90. Stens' relatives
91. Dishonor
92. Upbeats
95. Son of Aphrodite
97. "Get out!"
100. Proclaim
101. Mass-transit unit
102. N.H.L. trophy winner

171 Combos by Dorothea E. Shipp

Sometimes things can get slightly repetitious.

ACROSS

1. Lurch
7. Don Ho's welcome
12. Gold coin
17. Isolate
18. Gawked
19. Structure on a tank
20. Gossip
22. Point in the right direction
23. Winged
24. Day or Duke
25. Weaken
27. Bristle
28. Broke the tape first
30. Minnesota politician
32. Symbol of U.S.-China détente
35. Sailor's words before "sir"
36. Sass
39. Certain chicken
40. ____-toothed tiger
42. Mexican food
44. "Cry I ____ more"
45. Drama of 1920
46. Lying deep in the earth
48. Bishopric
49. Sounds of disgust
52. Cad
54. Flickertail State: Abbr.
55. Streamlets
57. Word before ho
59. Hajes
63. Hang around
65. With: Prefix
66. Creek
69. Like Key's banner
71. Word before corn or gun
73. In the thick of
75. Tax-return listing
76. Taunted
78. Rector's home
79. Photo-grapher's abbr.
80. Flavorings in cordials
83. Tear roughly
85. Milliner, for one
87. It turns litmus paper blue
88. Seventh king of Israel
90. Zodiac animal
91. Singer Gluck et al.
92. "____ Lynne"
96. Counterpart of parental
98. Sound of tiny feet
101. Queen of mystery
102. Mideast weights
103. Uncut
104. Italian physicist
105. Oregon or Long, Long
106. Dinner meats

DOWN

1. Whale
2. Blue dye
3. Moreno
4. Hormone
5. Old cloth measure
6. Must
7. Culture medium
8. Paris's ____ Quarter
9. Chooses
10. Goddess of the underworld
11. ____ fideles
12. Ger. and Den. are part of it
13. Come up
14. Eric's discovery
15. Time for fasting
16. Miss Kett
19. Upside down
21. Rip's family
26. Motorists' org.
29. Din
30. Neighbor of Leb.
31. Rush-hour bus prize
32. Enlisted men: Abbr.
33. Dies ____
34. Dorothy Sayers's tailors
35. Flying prefix
37. Pelvic bones
38. Hunt and ____ (typing system)
41. Explode
43. ____ ami
46. G.I.
47. Meadows
50. Without choice
51. Type of gin
53. Pulse
56. Cover
58. Part of a tooth
59. African fox
60. Extend over
61. Old relatives of croquet
62. Scottish precipitation
64. Finials
66. Miss Barrett
67. Part of M.I.T.
68. Pulitzer writer
70. What a sr. hopes to be
72. Lickety-split
74. City near Atlanta
76. Relative of gosh
77. Capital of Senegal
81. Japanese bay
82. ____ nothing (go all out)
84. Wyoming city
86. Theater awards
87. Asian range
88. West wind
89. Hawaiian port
91. Indian flour
93. Panay natives
94. Mural artist
95. ____ bien
97. Greek name
99. Kind of verb: Abbr.
100. Upward: Prefix

172 Author by William Lutwiniak

Featuring a Britisher whose works are often revived.

ACROSS

1. Visored cap
5. Xanadu's river
9. Eastern European
13. Bakery unit
17. Niche object
18. Farm feature
19. Place
20. Winnie ___ Pu
21. Play by 51 Across
25. Aaron's forte
26. Run easily
27. Most peculiar
28. Play by Capek
29. Unadorned
30. Ballet position
31. Targets
34. Jalopy feature
35. Cover girl's pride
39. U.S. publisher
40. MacMurray
41. Part of NASA
42. Greek letter
43. Bar offering
44. Misinforming one
45. Vivacious
46. Ubangi feeder
47. Reflex movement
49. Out of plumb
50. Tapestry
51. His middle name is Brinsley
54. Goldbrick
56. Heavy reading
57. Set apart
60. Roomy bag
61. Nile bird
62. Bronze and teen
63. "___ Misérables"
64. Ring legend
65. Plus value
67. Hurt
68. Nontalker
69. Seeks talent
71. Grow together
72. Bit of poetry
73. Poetic works
74. Twosome
75. The ___ Canals
76. They're often drawn
79. Contort
80. Chorister
84. Where 51 Across put on plays
87. Indicator
88. Best
89. Unassisted
90. Luxurious fabric
91. "Bird thou never ___"
92. Tosspots
93. Meadowlands event
94. Baseball's Slaughter

DOWN

1. Friends and neighbors
2. Repeat
3. Sonnet
4. Extras in Sunday papers
5. Assyrian deity
6. V.I.P.
7. Arafat's org.
8. Kind of gin
9. Ski trail
10. Colleen's land
11. Musical notes
12. Rural
13. Basswood
14. Ye ___ Tea Shoppe
15. Neighbor of Can.
16. Sensed
22. Shank
23. Worth or Wayne
24. Stop on ___
29. Taproom offering
30. 51 Across, e.g.
31. Ketch, for one
32. The Bruins
33. Another play by 51 Across
34. 51 Across et al.
35. Bender
36. Forever
37. Hacienda room
38. Presses charges
40. Angle
41. Certain Indians
44. Indiana's is French
45. Dunderheads
46. Orsk's river
48. Bore
49. Own up
50. Fusses
52. Hospital wear
53. Words of ken
54. One in the limelight
55. Doughnut center
58. Side
59. Salinger girl
62. Tart
65. Wystan Hugh
66. Naps
67. Metrical foot
68. Bach composition
70. Mouse or squirrel
71. Certain Iraqi
72. Material for an old Indian trick
74. Has the nerve
75. Not ___ (just fair)
76. Harbor craft
77. Word to James
78. Declare
79. Desire
80. Manche's capital
81. ___ impasse
82. Verne's captain
83. Smelter input
85. Muck
86. Neighbor of Swed.

173 Color Coded by Hugh McElroy

Without any need for a whole palette.

ACROSS

1. Certain records, for short
4. Jungle home
7. Display paintings
11. Jacques of Paris
15. Escape suddenly
16. Cotton unit
17. Swan genus
18. Travel fancy-free
19. Garden flowers
21. Sapphire stolen by Beau Geste
23. "Laura" author Vera
24. Kind of party
26. Type of chair
27. Cat or goldfish
28. Wishy-washy
30. Customary: Abbr.
31. Not stoned
34. Taker of legal action
35. Part of N.Y. Harbor
40. Word of regret
41. Fall bloom, for short
42. Under-garment
43. Middle name in Menlo Park
44. Writing point
45. Alternative to the Devil
50. Nasser's alliance
51. "____ Green," Heston film
53. Rents
54. Addison's partner
56. Finish off a book
57. Football actions
58. Some turkeys
59. "Stein Song" singer
61. "To hell ____ Connacht" (old Irish cry)
62. Hotel maid's need
65. Large bird
66. Texas flowers
69. Anger
70. Song, in Munich

72. Wall and Wimpole: Abbr.
73. Galena, for one
74. Nashville,
75. Scenery expert
78. Villa d'____
80. Takes off weight
81. Ginger follower
82. Stopover for F.D.R.
84. Relig. school
85. Permits
88. "____ Yankee Doodle . . ."
89. Movable property
93. Wife-killer of note
95. Puritans
97. Potentate
98. Gin flavor
99. Indian flour

100. Brewer's need
101. Colleen
102. English river
103. "Waste Land" initials
104. Advanced students: Abbr.

DOWN

1. Miss Falana
2. In addition
3. Siberian plains
4. Augustin of theater note
5. Pipe curve
6. Snuggle
7. White House architect
8. "____ ashore!"
9. Highest intellect
10. Matured
11. Brilliant showing

12. Kyle of sports
13. Knievel
14. Sea god
15. London TV initials
16. Wheeler or Parks
20. Max or Bugs
22. On to
25. Corn unit
28. Like a ____ on a log
29. Coercion
31. Word with souci
32. Mixture
33. Light colors
34. Bird-feeder item
36. Dance step
37. Irving Berlin song
38. Grand-parental
39. Maneuver-able, as a ship
41. Pioneer in heredity laws

42. Olympic skater Dick
45. Star in Cygnus
46. Book-jacket teasers
47. Slow, in music
48. Landed property
49. At ____ of a coin
52. Diamond lady
55. Printers' measures
57. Ogden Nash output
59. African grassland
60. Parisian friend
62. Dumas ____
63. North Irish river
64. Desires
67. Get service from
68. ____ bene
71. Phone-booth occupants

74. Jungle drums
76. Sticky mass
77. Most novel
78. Name of many streets
79. Make a ____ (try)
80. Jack Sprat's choice
83. Helpers
84. Queens ball park
85. College in Michigan
86. San ____ Obispo, Calif.
87. White or fire
89. Winsome
90. Ivan or Peter
91. Lampreys
92. D-day landing craft
93. Barbara ____ Geddes
94. Shad dish
96. Future capts.

174 Figures of Speech by Louis Baron

Or how to tell when one's number is up.

ACROSS

1. Croat or Serb
5. "____ Dance," Kern song
10. Mischievous one
13. Dimensions: Abbr.
17. Gambling city
18. Direct
19. Greenhorn
20. Genus of monkeys
22. Dickens novel
25. "That's ____ idea!"
26. Like machine-gun bursts
27. John O'Hara novel
29. Old Dutch liters
30. African antelope
31. "____ kleine Nachtmusik"
32. Go from 1st ____ (advance a base)
35. Of a cranial gland
37. More sullen
41. "Life Begins ____"
42. Slow developer
45. Cpl., for one
46. Exclamations
47. Sea off Borneo
48. Vincent Van Gogh's brother
49. 5 P.M., in the service
50. In the past
51. Agent
55. Mideastern weights
56. Curmudgeon
58. "A Room with ____"
59. Common finch
60. Guard or admiral
61. Astaire and Allen
62. Large ocean fish
63. Size up
65. Action site
66. Lucidity
70. Natterjacks
71. They foiled a home wrecker
73. "Gotcha!"
74. Vallee
75. Partner of ready and willing
76. Charismatic leader
77. White House office
78. ____ loss
79. Unfriendly persuasion
83. Pom's cousin
84. Natural science, to Pliny
86. Spring gardener
87. Trait carriers
88. Sniff, in Seville
89. Word after ill or thorough
90. Kind of owl
92. Belles' letters
97. Bolshevik
101. Wide open
102. De Mille subject
104. Historic alarmist
105. Counterpart of the Pac.
106. Actress Dickinson
107. "Cut it out!"
108. SSE and NNW
109. One of the Stooges
110. High and after
111. Disseminated

DOWN

1. Mex. ladies
2. Resident of Riga
3. Tuamotu atoll
4. Krakatoa and Popocatepetl
5. ". . . sad and dreary ev'rywhere ____"
6. Warp-crossing threads
7. "Do you have change ____?"
8. ____ non (also): Lat.
9. Grandstand, in Spain
10. Sign briefly
11. Powwow
12. ____ a question
13. W.W. II line that failed
14. Diatribe
15. Asian weight
16. Pompano's relative
20. Member of a crime ring
21. "Dinner ____"
23. Adjusted organism
24. Spinet mechanic
28. Rouse, in Rouen
30. French form of mister
32. African weaverbirds
33. N.Z. province
34. Constantly
35. Howard and Ernie
36. Lenya and Lehmann
38. On cloud 9
39. ____ des Beaux-Arts
40. Boasting, old style
42. "Little we see in Nature that ____"
43. Certain soft drinks
44. Work on a quid
49. Hawkeye
51. Bridge player's words
52. Insert-a-word mark
53. It makes news
54. Of nests
55. Things to know
57. Thin
59. Language
61. Pullets, to cooks
63. Walk into ____
64. One of the Americas
65. Complete trio
66. Cook Inlet peak
67. Yorkshire river
68. Fair or milk
69. Store events
71. Ursid family
72. Pelted
75. "____ this kind persuasive strain"
77. Candor
79. Rudder handles
80. Disaster
81. Cuenca ____ (river basin): Sp.
82. Physiology Nobelist: 1972
85. Association football
87. Humorless
90. Nigerian river
91. Aconcagua's locale
92. Neighbor of Syr.
93. Didn't drag
94. Rikki-tikki-____
95. Anna's destination
96. Marquand's sleuth
97. Italy's Como, for one
98. Division word
99. Pack
100. Recipe meas.
103. L-P liaison

175 Here and There by Herb Risteen

Offering different things for different places.

ACROSS

1. Radar spot
5. Where Cedar Breaks is
9. Siamese and alley
13. Sea bird
17. Swiss river
18. High point in "Ben Hur"
19. Oriental nurse
20. Busy as ___
21. Unreliable one
22. Ancient warfare weapon
24. Scads
25. East German city
27. Legal paper
28. Small kite
30. Right, in law
31. Containers
32. Box
33. Water growths
36. Horsy event
37. Lewis's street
38. Boxing blow
41. Do patchwork
42. Distinctive flavor
43. Wrist holder's reading
44. Roof decoration
45. Shaping tool
46. Hollow
47. Sacred Jewish work
48. Reproach
49. Evangeline's home
51. Ancient Iran
52. Wouk's ship
53. Jellied candies
58. Flirtation Walk visitor
60. Food fish
61. Hurried
64. Exam
65. Wing-shaped
66. Leveling strip
68. ___ gratias
69. Danube feeder
70. Italian river
71. Oregon peak
72. Certain Sunday
73. Antagonist
74. Water bird
75. Welshman, for one
76. Authority
77. Kind of cash
78. African lake
79. Hamburger accessory
80. Adventure-some expedition
83. It's usually accompli
84. Transport for a doge
88. ___ Holden
89. Cook, in a way
92. Heroic poem
93. Swamp growth
94. Mining product
95. Where Sligo is
96. Allergy symptom
97. Confederate
98. Saarinen
99. Be worthy of
100. Do away with

DOWN

1. Unadorned
2. Hiding place
3. Dies ___
4. Kind of melon
5. Yens
6. Mountain pool
7. Fearless flier
8. Being responsive
9. Paris attractions
10. In the thick of
11. Seagoer
12. Awkwardly bashful
13. Asian tribesman
14. Black
15. Director Clair
16. Love ___
23. English county
26. Proper
29. Rustic way
31. Diamond maneuver
32. Deli meat
33. "___ pinch of salt"
34. Nonclerical
35. Dog of stature
36. Chinese river
37. Rivera work
38. Sunset to sunset
39. Neat as ___
40. Be caught
42. Wood for a ship's deck
43. Person from Poznan
46. Gossip
47. Kind of bear
48. Works with thread
50. Fight
52. Fast friend
54. Long or Coney
55. Cut
56. Hounds' quarry
57. Grating
58. Close-fitting cap
59. Pisa's river
62. Slippery fish
63. Major-___
65. Weapon for a child
66. Real-estate sign
67. Like a tamale
70. Orchard product
71. British moor growth
72. Caters to
75. Stylish
76. ___ Valley
77. Blues composer
78. Seabees' motto
79. River to the Irish Sea
80. Immunizing agents
81. Biblical brother
82. Be aware of
83. N.C. cape
84. "True ___"
85. Ring gem
86. Mona ___
87. Having hurts
90. Western Indian
91. Brother

176 Democracy by H. H. Reddall

Highlighting part of the American way.

ACROSS

1. Eastern Church altar
5. Reputed wart sources
10. Grape residue
14. Faced up to
15. Fiber plant
16. Numbskull
18. Rule book of a sort
20. Appeared out of nowhere
22. Feed the pot
23. Place to head 'em off
24. Gives up
26. ____ Tse-tung
27. Joseph Conrad milieu
28. Actress Diana
29. Denominations
30. As ____ as an owl
31. Shakespeare's blow
33. Rocky hills
34. Fixed courses
35. Chemical ending
36. Shadings
37. Wrongful act
38. Verb-forming suffixes
41. Century plants
42. Small sea extensions
45. Anglo-Saxon letters
46. North Dakota city
47. Court advocates
48. Mauna ____
49. Certain hill dwellers
51. Drinking cup
52. Find a new homeland
54. Arctic sights
55. Agreement
56. French painter and family
57. Nom de plume
58. Glass units
59. Rumple
60. Disturbances
61. Disfigure
62. Peculiar opinion
64. Warmwater fish
65. Sounds of little feet
69. Writer Leigh
70. Unsocial one
71. Navy sweeper's target
72. Kind of stick
73. Switch positions
74. Did needlework
75. Mother of F.D.R.
76. Tivoli Park visitor
77. Town near Newark, N.J.
79. Revolving door for V.I.P.'s
82. Laughing
83. Singer John
84. Makes comfortable
85. ____-dieu
86. Villa
87. Pair

DOWN

1. 113-pound boxer
2. Gaelic
3. N.L. player
4. Fatty
5. Rigid framework
6. Horse fodder
7. "____ my brother's . . ."
8. Church districts
9. Eastern Indians
10. Standish
11. Stirs
12. ____ de Janeiro
13. He often has a hearing problem
14. Gift recipient
17. Disentangle, as wool
18. Throw
19. Like some apples
21. Performs
25. Bowery problems: Abbr.
28. Thieves' places
29. Where legislators get to the bottom of things
30. Pulitzer's paper
32. Apple, mince et al.
33. ____ City (Detroit)
34. Kind of nose or candle
36. Slight coloring
37. Forest hiders, in saying
38. Went after morays
39. Mouth: Suffix
40. Gavel-wielding status
41. Liquid measures
42. Egyptian dancing girls
43. Prelude to peace
44. Top enlisted men: Abbr.
46. Laments
47. Loin muscle
49. Movie critic Judith
50. Cuts lengthwise
53. Haggard
55. Constituent
57. Large terrier
58. Balding area
60. Kept subscribing
61. Ran the business
62. Restaurateur Toots
63. Of the moon
64. Hurdler of the moon
65. Scottish fishing reel
66. Small kite
67. Peels
68. Chancy thing, for short
70. Philippine island
71. "As ____ goes . . ."
74. Healthy: Prefix
75. Whisky serving
76. Doctor's portion
78. "First in first . . ."
80. City ways: Abbr.
81. Greek letter

177 Partners by Reginald L. Johnson

To the extent that they share some letters.

ACROSS

1. Kind of hand
5. Mineral with a soapy feel
9. Shower time: Abbr.
12. He knows books
15. City west of Chicago
17. Peek-____
18. Choler
19. Spheres
21. Smitten by Thespis
23. Dimwits
26. Suffix for broad or along
27. Pies
29. Venture
30. Squid's calling card
31. Old cloth measures
32. ____ Palmas
33. Pear, to Pierre
35. Contrary current
36. ____ off (begin)
37. Franklin or Blue
38. Alias Santa
41. Deity of Thebes
43. Planet
44. Polynesian god
45. Correctly fine
48. Raised, in Paris
49. Not quite
51. Holiday or candle
52. Mah-jongg pieces
53. Plagiarize
54. English elopers' haven
57. Windjammer feature
61. Snicker ____
62. Concert or baby
63. Communion-cloth case
64. Electric light in cartoons
66. Certain poisons
68. Tige's cartoon master
70. Suit part
71. Heart queen's production
72. Coquettish glances
73. Stupidity
76. Exclusively
77. In a body
79. New Zealand island
80. Magna ____
82. Gists
83. Wild pansy
86. Lawyer: Abbr.
87. Barnyard sound
90. Itinerant farmhand
91. ____ Domingo
92. Gator locale
93. Charge per unit
94. Before amas
95. Nothing more
96. Use a hat check
100. Concerning
101. Modish young man
104. Fictional tec
106. Checks
107. Call ____ day
108. Mata ____
109. Directs
110. Dolt
111. Bill
112. Certain cartel
113. Moscow agency

DOWN

1. Treetop bed
2. Stalls
3. Part of to be
4. Kind of waist
5. Highlander's emblem
6. Borders
7. Places
8. Fuel
9. Pitch in
10. Like a prig
11. Mention
12. Body of law
13. Tom Watson, e.g.
14. Shortens
15. Word on a statement
16. Practical
20. Ballplayer's cradle
22. Ability
24. "Uncle Remus" relative
25. Scottish island
28. Skyline sights
34. East, in Bonn
35. Within: Prefix
37. Candy or style word
38. Turned over
39. Black
40. Poetic feet
41. Marbles
42. American educator
45. Work units
46. Blackmore heroine
47. Islamic prince
48. Property charges
49. Originate
50. QE2, e.g.
52. Region
53. Hauls
55. De Mille
56. Gray, to the French
57. Smelling of mold
58. Combustible vapor
59. Objects of worship
60. Yukon river
63. Potato-sack material
65. French handle
67. ____-les-Bains
68. South African language
69. Kind of shell or shelter
71. Suspended animation
73. Scholar
74. Selassie's land
75. Ribbon: Prefix
77. Involve of necessity
78. Queer one
80. Wedge-shaped
81. Sum: Abbr.
83. "Grapes of Wrath" family
84. River in W.W. I news
85. Garden, in Versailles
86. Conqueror of Rome
87. Prepares potatoes
88. Fragrance
89. Long periods
92. Sudden outburst
93. Preakness and Belmont
95. Hodgepodge
97. Nature's back talk
98. Crack, as a lip
99. Cloud
102. After-afterthought
103. Arrest
105. Greek letter

178 Science Test by Barbara Weakley

Some specialties one might or might not go in for.

ACROSS

1. Verve
5. Perch
10. Flat-bottomed boat
14. Spanish sword
16. Boredom
17. Make soda water
20. Trouser-length measure
21. Entertained
22. Wicker-chair material
23. Hillside for Burns
24. Tooth
26. Of sound
28. Football linemen
30. Tatter
31. Varnish ingredients
32. Cap
33. Relation of gosh
34. Horace's writings
36. Presage
37. _____ for (reserved)
40. Like unsuccessful soufflés
41. Science of body fluids
43. Put on
44. Willows
46. Marked with streaks
47. Carry across
48. Explorer Hedin
49. Table linen
52. Gem weight
53. Lab scientists
57. Secret for the audience
58. Long and slender
59. Leave port
60. Narrow opening
61. Turkish weight
62. Colorado's is Royal
63. Foot woes
64. Bravo!
65. Repairman: Abbr.
67. "One of _____"
68. Urbane
69. Pith helmet

71. Study of doctrines
73. Granite city
74. Ale house
75. State bird of Hawaii
76. City near Marseilles
77. Celsius freezing point
78. Agreement
81. Cooked in a pan
82. Science of heat
86. Like the Cratchits
87. Dormant
89. Condemn
90. Gem
91. Attention
92. Intelligence
93. Art _____
94. Seine area
95. Hospital photo
97. Synagogue platforms
99. Florida city
101. Product of Gilead
102. Twisted
104. Senseless
106. Showy
108. Property
109. Witches' group
110. _____ up (accelerated)
111. Asian country
112. Like Adeline
113. Ivy League member

DOWN

1. Otherwise
2. Shelter
3. Genesis man
4. Science of the laws of the mind
5. Repair a surface
6. Unique persons
7. Can. province
8. Bird food
9. Science of sea levels
10. Procession
11. Genuine
12. Painting or sculpture
13. Deck officer
14. Harangue
15. Wild ass
18. Snarl
19. Win over
23. Friars: Abbr.
25. Duke's daughter
27. Greek goddess of victory
29. Groupings
35. Did shoe repairs
36. Like unfilleted shad
37. Wander
38. Segment
39. Some reading matter
40. Finale
42. Corso money
43. Suiting
45. Relig. school
47. Snakes' weapons
48. Glisten
49. Ruth's mother-in-law
50. Inquired
51. Fragment
52. Partner of cash
53. Chisel
54. Skiing locale
55. Worker on floors
56. Relative of umpteen
58. Item of makeup
59. Flies high
62. Indian thug
63. Preserved
66. Renown
68. Starchy tubers
69. Poi ingredient
70. Convex molding
72. Celtic sea god
73. French cheese
74. Sea bird
76. Science of virtue
77. Science of fermentation
78. Highest point
79. Crude
80. Atoll ingredients
81. Word before flam
82. S.A. rodent
83. Narcotic
84. Irritated
85. Original substance of the elements
88. Nobel's country
89. Proper
93. Gift recipient
96. Tibetan monster
97. Alpha's follower
98. Plow's winter target
100. Region
101. Like the Hubbard cupboard
103. Word before paint or cry
105. _____ Maria
107. Indian reed

179 Sick Call by Tap Osborn

Some illnesses that seem to afflict certain people.

ACROSS

1. Warm dry wind
5. Spicy rice dish
10. Tackle a task
15. Recipe measures: Abbr.
19. Writer Seton
20. British pathologist: 1862–1926
21. Orinoco tributary
22. Mother of the gods
23. Economist's illness
25. Union organizer's agony
27. Prepare for the printer
28. "Hard Cash" author
30. United, T.W.A., etc.
31. Unit of stock: Abbr.
33. Haul
35. Untactful
37. ___ time (in the pen)
38. Banker's affliction
42. Land a fish
45. Thought: Prefix
46. Preener's problem
47. Preppie's polite response
49. Make sure of
50. Morton Downey, e.g.
52. Floating haven
54. Flew
56. J.F.K. users
57. Questioned
59. Watchmaker's malady
64. Joined Chubby in a dance
66. Lawn base
67. Vintage listing
68. "Bank Dick" star's monogram
71. Wattlebird
72. Eskimo knife
73. Pivotal
75. Hearst captors, for short
76. Louis XIV, for one
77. Writer Rand
78. Submerged
80. Lotto's cousin
81. ___ store or piece
83. Auto mechanic's trauma
86. Cheerful
87. U.S.T.A. 1968 singles champ
91. Gain
92. Parking ticket
94. Made a parabola
96. Accumulate
98. Overlooked
102. Half a bikini
104. "___ Nice," Gershwin song
105. Charges
107. Lawyer's distress
110. ". . . the ___ the ocean"
112. Dwarf: Prefix
113. Scott's Roderick
114. Prosecutors: Abbr.
115. Affected
118. Cooler items
120. Satie or Estrada
122. Comedian's injury
124. Critic's ailment
128. Bjorn's occasional opponent
129. Skiing maneuver
130. Sharp, to Luigi
131. Woodcarver's material
132. Tennessee gridders
133. Selected
134. Sweetheart, in olden days
135. Kite's lookout

DOWN

1. Mood ring or skate board
2. Back-from-lunch time
3. P.R. man's illness
4. Matgrass
5. Farm area
6. License, passport et al.
7. Resting place
8. Tiny parasite
9. In conclusion
10. Lead ores
11. Mileage rating agcy.
12. Marching-band instrument
13. Spiky plant
14. Dread
15. Military tyros
16. Roofer's virus
17. Bolt, to Henri
18. Lip
24. Bygone time, to Angus
26. Thicknesses
29. Trick
31. Loretta of "M*A*S*H"
32. Retreat
34. Foolish
36. Fabric, in Paris
39. Closet adjuncts
40. Eroded
41. Comic Russell
43. Big Board initials
44. Digits: Abbr.
48. Try again
51. Rounded, as a leaf
53. Edible seaweed
55. Phone user
58. Sumptuous
60. Mulcts
61. Godfrey or Jeeves, at times
62. Certain Arabian
63. Anthropological finds
64. Relative, in Málaga
65. Dancer Katherine
68. Plumber's injury
69. Duchessa's inferior
70. Wearability
74. Cheer for
79. ___ Kahn of Persia
82. Actress Leslie
84. Disavow an heir
85. Arrests
87. Rhine tributary
88. Mustangs' campus
89. Carpenter's sore
90. Perfumes
93. Kind of iron
95. Brighton bunk
97. Hebrew letter
99. Gave it to Caesar
100. Bonn article
101. Ulster county
103. Truman Secretary of State
106. Bull stalker
108. Belmont cancellation notice
109. Actor Kasznar
111. Disgusted
115. Roman 1104
116. Guthrie
117. Word from an annoyed one
119. Ghetto
121. Smidgen
123. European fish
125. Helium-style craft: Abbr.
126. Head part
127. Shoot high

180 Paging Ponce de León by Bert Kruse

Everyone wants to turn back the flight of time.

ACROSS

1. American painter
6. Snowmobile's relative
10. Hit by a police weapon
15. Times Square problem
16. Biscuit
17. Soft drink
19. Hemingway classic, with "The"
21. Frog-to-be
23. Spoken
24. Will Rogers was one
25. Noon, in Nantes
26. Highest note
27. Heraldic design
28. Michigan pro athlete
30. Stuffed shirt
31. Model-airplane wood
33. Sot's nightmare
34. _____ bien
35. Garbo
36. Upward curve at the bow
37. Java's neighbor
39. Cantor and Tarbell
41. Kind of remark
42. Free-for-all
43. Mountain pass
44. Satyr
45. The Pequod, for one
47. "Good heavens!"
50. Actor James
54. Secretes
55. Writer Grey
56. Anne Nichols character
57. C.P.A.-to-be's hurdle
58. Neapolitan bills
59. Scads
60. Candidate for a spanking
61. It went down in Cuba
62. Grocery-list unit
63. Diving bird
64. Sticks out
65. Classical odist
66. Marquette or Goriot
67. Actor Victor
69. Hereditary-law man
70. Smooth, as the way
72. Possesses
73. Shelley subject
74. Uncouth
76. Housing money
77. Be unfond of
78. Quid pro _____
81. Basement problems
82. Edible ball
84. Flew
85. Long Island or Puget
87. Lohengrin's wife
88. Siege of Troy prop
91. Copy Cauthen
92. Ht.
93. Not matched, in Scotland
94. Red dyes
96. Black: Prefix
97. Rimsky-Korsakov's last opera
100. Gingham dog's friend
102. Potential graduates
103. Miss Bordoni
104. Drug lilies
105. Wind-borne soil
106. Bones
107. AK and HI, formerly

DOWN

1. Highland purse
2. With fidelity
3. Papal capes
4. Miller or Harding
5. Becomes bored
6. Perfumes
7. Also-ran
8. Spanish month
9. Goddess, in old Rome
10. Connecticut community
11. Off the cuff
12. Clamlike Pres.
13. Finial
14. Like a rich bride
16. Footwear embellishment
17. Nutmeg or pepper
18. Courteous
19. Idiots
20. Methuselah
22. Doting
25. Engines: Abbr.
29. "Boot" of Europe
30. Rodgers-Hammerstein duo
32. Poplars
35. Antelope
38. Beers' cousins
39. Religious figures
40. Alms
41. Base call
42. Puccini's Cio-Cio-San
44. Move lightly
45. Like Moby Dick
46. Boss, at times
47. McKinley's friend Mark
48. Menu
49. Arabian garments
51. Zinc _____
52. Root or Suez
53. Hebrew measure
55. Camera distance lens
58. Sass
59. Dictionary or atlas, e.g.
60. Explode
61. Cuts up
63. Like some TV
64. San _____
65. Kind of house
68. Dissertation topic
69. _____ harm (acted innocently)
71. TV plugs
73. Church goblet
74. Strings
75. Find new courage
76. Indian ruler
78. Coward
79. Prepare for bed
80. Greek theater
81. Circus performer
82. Bobbles
83. _____ Rebellion of 1842.
84. "Barber of Seville" soprano
86. Spellbinder
88. Commotions
89. Approaches
90. Old King and Nat King
95. Card game
98. Número _____
99. Cry of shame
100. Labor org.
101. De France, for one

181 Observations by Sophie Fierman

Presenting some notable thoughts that have been expressed.

ACROSS

1. Fine meal
7. Slave
11. Feathered neckpiece
14. Imposing home
19. Pencil top
20. Betrayers
22. Hawaiian rope fiber
23. Where beauty is, to Margaret Hungerford
26. Donate to a Scot
27. Clever
28. Silk gelatin
29. Exist
30. Pack compactly
32. S-shaped arch
33. Joist supports
35. Capri, for one
37. ____ boo-boo (goofed)
42. Kind of do-well
43. What Lincoln wouldn't do
51. Cowboy's appurtenance
52. Roundworm
53. Courtroom response
54. Stringed instrument
55. Norse god
58. Pirate's gold
59. Facilitate
63. Criticize
64. Doing a double take
66. Knobbed: Prefix
67. Tightwads
69. Kind of sized
70. Preminger
71. Lovers
75. Salic or Murphy's
78. Infallible
82. Spigot
83. Thrive
84. Anglo-Saxon coin
85. Tableland
86. Nonprofessional
87. Renaissance, for one
88. Contributes, in poker
91. Antiseptic compound
93. What Lovelace said after "Stone"
100. Off balance
101. Defeat
102. French handle
103. Bewildered
106. Andes dweller
108. Rip-off
112. Honey
113. Shipworms
117. Foot troubles
119. Sash
120. Jefferson said it
124. More crafty
125. Measure a firearm
126. Words of threat
127. Tries out
128. ____ out (make do)
129. Took to court
130. Inattentive one

DOWN

1. Govern
2. Correspondent Pyle
3. Liver spreads
4. Cigar leaving
5. Observes
6. Musical flutter
7. Cubic measure
8. Question marks
9. English heroes of W.W. II
10. Suits
11. South African
12. Heavenly path
13. Get ____ opinion
14. Sky event
15. Entire
16. Of a knot
17. Standouts
18. Unusual
21. Article
24. Short rifle
25. Employs
31. Gratuities
34. Use poor judgment
36. "The ____ of Dan McGrew"
38. Broad tie
39. Pepys's trademark
40. Join in
41. "Where ____?"
43. Aspersion
44. Path
45. Confused
46. Played the stool pigeon
47. Assassination date
48. Land of the Dail
49. Jewish month
50. Floor cleaners
56. Hash house
57. Task for an emcee
60. Make amends
61. Localities
62. Starts a rail trip
65. Navy rating
68. High hill
71. Hearty dish
72. South American rubber
73. Iridescent jewel
74. Kind of song
75. Numbers game
76. Astern
77. Stingers
78. Group of Kaffir warriors
79. Former opera star Frances ____
80. Leader, in India
81. Newcastle's river
89. At present
90. Cause nettle rash
92. Cockney pads
94. Young one
95. Roof workers
96. Dirty ____
97. Superintend
98. "____ bleu!"
99. Unceasing
103. Popular damsel
104. ____ Island
105. Bo of "Tarzan" note
107. Eminent
109. Was able
110. Downgrade
111. Distance runner
112. Spar
114. "____ Mable"
115. Fall mo.
116. Indian titles
118. Body fluid: Prefix
121. Encountered
122. French drink
123. Abbr. after a math problem

182 Proper Names by Mel Taub

Or, to be more exact, appropriate names.

ACROSS

1. Enervates
5. Bohemian reformer
8. Sticky stuff
11. Latin he
15. Turkish capital
16. Doorway: Abbr.
17. Paleozoic, e.g.
18. Secluded spot
19. Port of Yemen
20. Gal featured in the Sunday papers
23. Pitcher Tom's cheerful kinswoman
25. Added gin, e.g.
26. Drowsy person
27. Violinmaker of Cremona
28. Superior of a capt.
31. Sotheby declarations
32. Propriety
35. Malayans of Luzon
37. 14 pounds of Man
39. Portuguese enclave annexed by India
40. Out of _____ (panting)
41. Gore Vidal subject
42. Generation _____
43. D.D.E. et al.
44. Greek physician
45. Wire measures
47. Hanticipation
48. Fleur-de-lis
49. Chew out
51. Spring month: Abbr.
52. Swag
54. Categorized
55. Joker
57. Minnesota Fats's game
58. Good sign for angels
59. Having horny projections
60. Daring and courageous
62. Warbles
64. Seeker of the Fountain of Ute
68. Ventral terpsichorean
70. Need an aspirin
71. "M*A*S*H" star
72. Fall back
73. Descendant: Suffix
74. Modish
75. Taproom orders
76. Caustic substance
77. Hallucinogenic initials
78. Screwball

DOWN

1. Steel-mill waste
2. Verdi work
3. Fly, to a spider
4. Dennis or Duncan
5. By this means
6. Lets go of
7. Kitchen units
8. Reverse, e.g.
9. Assn.
10. Shell team
11. Send out R.S.V.P.'s
12. Reflective fellow
13. Body of tradition
14. _____ out (barely made it)
21. _____ Führer
22. With speed
24. Footgear for Hans Brinker
27. Bedeck
28. Taw
29. Roman statesman
30. Oscar's cardplaying kinsman
33. Drink-glass underpinning
34. Fido's cry
36. Little Rachel
37. Tarnish
38. Deuce topper
41. Trout fly, e.g.
44. It's old and red, white and blue
45. African corn
46. The tax folk
47. Boob
49. Deep crimson
50. Tokyo of yore
52. Superstar of early TV
53. Excel as an insurance agent
54. Figure controllers of yore
56. Diva Maria
57. Lead or eyebrow
60. Destructive person
61. Chatter
62. Vail conveyance
63. Look to for aid
64. Summon in the lobby
65. Sympathetic response
66. Louisville's river
67. Narrow strip of land
69. Eight hours of work, e.g.

183 In Good Standing by Elaine D. Schorr

Presenting a liberal assortment of gerunds.

ACROSS

1. Actress Thompson
5. N.L. players
9. Main point
13. Nickname for H. H. Arnold
16. Supreme being of myth
17. Skater's jump
18. Inter ____
19. Lucille's first
20. Kinder gartner's product
23. They're sometimes wild
24. Duke in "The Tempest"
25. Yea or nay, e.g.
26. Miss Vanderbilt
28. Majors or Radziwill
29. Sandwich shop
30. Eastwood
31. God in the New Testament
34. Composer Weill
35. ____ to (curries favor)
38. Pass between peaks
39. Orthopedist's specialty
42. Author Levin
43. C
44. Eye part
45. Ladder component
46. Defacement
47. Tiny tear
49. Dutch cheese center
51. Athlete's weak spot
52. Nursery playmate
53. Garden bloom
54. Icy mass
55. Fatuous
57. Lord's lackey
58. Like a king's head
61. Orchestral instrument
62. Holding device
63. Thai people
64. G. & S. princess
65. Ring name
66. Presidential pastime
69. Spiciness
70. Means to an end
72. Not on the level
73. Noncoms
74. ____ vincit amor
75. Fine ____
76. In the manner of
78. "Moonlight ____"
80. Where the Owl and the Pussycat were
81. Fairway club
85. Consanguineous
86. Quid pro quo of a sort
89. Kind of cab or skirt
90. Novelist O'Flaherty
91. In fine fettle
92. Harp player in Le Havre
93. Put one's finger on
94. Feminine ending
95. Jannings
96. Kind of book

DOWN

1. Sleeping accommodation at times
2. Tennis point
3. Forcefulness
4. Its capital is Luanda
5. One of the Curies
6. Public exhibition, for short
7. Bag or ball
8. Small pieces
9. Miss Page
10. Nastase
11. Cheap horn material
12. Engaging in barter
13. Consuming with torment
14. Italian wine city
15. Arno River city
19. Blackmore heroine
21. Compass direction
22. Nick of films
27. Cod's relative
29. Club-joiner's obligation
30. Cabinet occupant
31. Kind of test
32. Vulgarian
33. Toxic malady
34. Use needles
35. Contemplate
36. U.S.S.R. mountains
37. Reduce
39. Policeman's club
40. City on the Oka
41. Income producer
46. Goose or leopard
48. Author of "An Essay on Man"
49. Laughter amounts
50. ____-way street
51. ____ with (side by side)
53. ____ deux (duet)
54. Tarkenton of football
55. Be up in the air
56. Having the know-how
57. Periwinkle
58. Kitty sweetener
59. Give a going over
60. Maneuvers a baited hook
62. Inconstant
63. Slopes gear
66. Abou Ben Adhem's creator
67. Hopping creatures
68. Case carried to court
71. Muscat native
73. Flounce off
75. "Don't ____!" (I don't know)
76. Soviet co-op
77. Resinous substance
78. Hominy porridge
79. "Grapes of Wrath" character
80. "____ can look at . . ."
81. Exotic isle
82. ____ qua non
83. Actress Swenson
84. "Rome of Hungary"
87. Little isle
88. L.A. player

184 Angels of Mercy by A. J. Santora

Some of the people who helped the lives of others.

ACROSS

1. Renaissance-period dress
6. One ____ (stickball)
10. Mister, in Madrid
15. Surgical group
19. Coeur d'____
20. Weathercock
21. Sierra ____
22. Together, in music
23. Hospital mainstays
26. First-aid ____
27. Critic Huxtable
28. Cast off
29. Friends, to De Gaulle
30. Tropical fish
31. Fishing gear
32. Waterproof
33. Agreed
34. Teases playfully
35. Medicinal plant
37. Frozen, as a pond
39. Abdominal disorder
40. Hospital volunteer
42. Secluded
45. Mag. publication
46. Mus. piece
47. Edict
48. Letter with Tee
49. Entr'____
51. Kind of Lizzie
53. Defense org.
54. Take a flat
55. Famed Crimean War nurse
61. False witness
62. Active one
63. For
64. Blue river
65. Go astray
66. Terns and ernes
67. Craft
69. Western alliance
70. Walrus
72. "General Hospital" nurse
78. Singer Pat
79. ____ the chance (took advantage)
80. ____-Coburg
81. Nebraska river
83. Actress Shirley
84. Historical times
86. Where to enjoy eaux
87. Vigorous
88. Murder by suffocation
89. Andrea ____
90. Conway
91. Concerned with
92. Nurse's prescription
95. In a stir
96. Coup ____
97. Part of a range
98. Raring to go
99. Zoom, for one
100. Musial and Kenton
101. Ice mass
102. Double runners

DOWN

1. Lake group of New York
2. ____ Cité
3. Unit of explosive force
4. Black bird
5. Takes a break
6. Emote
7. Noel singers
8. Over again
9. Knight of TV
10. Popular girls' party
11. More frightening
12. ____ out (just beaten)
13. Some cash items
14. Home: Abbr.
15. ____ easy (relaxes)
16. Famed W.W. I nurse
17. Other, in Paris
18. Flat-topped hills
24. River of Europe
25. Not wised up
30. ". . . ____ down in green pastures"
33. Scott of jazz fame
34. "Mammy" singer
36. News worker
38. Calorie counters
39. Raccoon's cousin
41. River of Belgium
42. Card game
43. Ms. Richards of tennis
44. Furthermore
47. Throw a rider
49. Burning
50. Red Cross pioneer
52. Partner of tuck
54. Uplifts
56. Mosque town of Turkey
57. Kind of mythology
58. Relinquish
59. Comprehends
60. Growl
61. Bandleader Brown
66. Swag
68. Sustain for a while
69. Procure
71. Ballpark purchases
72. Tours for freeloaders
73. Arab ruler
74. Pendant
75. Loss through carelessness
76. Ran out
77. Juice squeezers
79. Mideast country
81. Small bottle
82. Actress Hope
83. Faction
85. Wise persons
88. Garden vegetable
89. Billie or turtle
92. Six-pt. scores
93. Soft toss
94. One of the Techs

185 Riffraff by Alice H. Kaufman

Society always has its misfits.

ACROSS

1. Mongoose's target
6. Forms
12. Plaid textile
18. In profusion
19. Unattractive
20. Come into view
21. Kenneth Roberts novel
23. Livy and Brutus
24. Wholly
25. Ocean eagles
26. Boar's feature
28. Wrestlers' need
29. Prepared to golf, with "up"
31. Comedian Skelton
32. Present ones
34. Capable of
35. Cupid
37. Dishonor
38. Goose genus
39. Deliverer
42. ____ out (chides)
43. Memorandum
44. Independently
45. Sketched
46. Dickinson or Millay
49. Torpid
50. Decorative headdress
51. Uninviting
52. Quick-witted
53. Ex-Gov. Wallace's state
54. Purpose
56. Bleat
57. Ecclesiastic's vestment
58. Run off
59. School officials
60. Lively
61. More temperamental
63. Orange color in heraldry
64. Port in the Azores
65. Ointment
66. Dormouse
67. Feudal tenant
68. Move unobtrusively
70. Member of the electorate
71. Clarinetist Fountain
72. Threatening
73. Tennis star of the 60's
74. Author Fleming
75. Cracker sprinkling
79. Wine: Prefix
80. Mrs. Chaplin
81. Good will
83. Flying insect
84. Various
86. John Gay musical, with "The"
90. Timeless, to poets
91. Quantity of type in printing
92. Lawn shrub
93. Suit fabrics
94. Hardened
95. New Hampshire city

DOWN

1. Small weight
2. Religious cape
3. Southern Belt
4. Steal
5. Asian evergreen
6. Silvery minnow
7. Sharpened
8. Japanese women divers
9. For each
10. Hardwood tree
11. Networks
12. Concise
13. In a murderous frenzy
14. Radiation dosage
15. Ocean wanderers
16. Related paternally
17. Elder counselor
22. Fault
27. Put into service
30. Farm building
32. Old poem about a homeless warrior
33. Actress Goldie
34. Single thing
36. Witty saying
37. Portion
38. Throat-clearing sound
39. Eastern salutation
40. Handsome Greek god
41. 1929 Rudy Vallee role
42. Beat-up car
43. Invents
45. Dog wagon
46. Predisposed
47. City in Greek history
48. Of a government unit
50. Like many bathrooms
51. Jack's victim
55. Male voice
58. Discharge
60. Sits
62. Former "What's My Line" host
63. French head
64. Toque or pillbox
66. Cuddly
67. Outlets
68. Shoe leathers
69. Inflame
70. Heflin
71. Two by two
73. Gets no ribbon
74. Mirror's offering
76. Fred's dancing sister
77. Navigational system
78. Track down
80. River of France
81. Culture medium
82. Part of an egg
85. Work unit
87. German article
88. Wildebeest
89. Dessert

186 Sing-along by William H. Ford

Bits of lyrics that should be familiar.

ACROSS

1. How a certain bicycle is built
7. Word before cheap
11. Top diplomatic offs.
15. Hemingway
19. Hydrocarbon prefix
20. Invader of Spain
21. He composed "Le Roi d'Ys"
22. Basic coin of Cambodia
23. What I left
27. Atlanta university
28. To ___ (on the dot)
29. Innisfail
30. River into Solway Firth
31. Scottish winter fall
32. ___-de-lance
33. When it's blue, it moves fast
35. An actor may steal it
36. Sarcasm, in France
39. Mortar box
40. Latin wraths
42. Stableman
45. "To ___ with Love"
47. Cuckoo
48. Family or whiffle
52. "Over ___"
53. What love makes
58. ___-mill
60. Beside, at sea
61. Bermuda or pearl
62. Ballet's Pavlova
63. Chicago Bears' George ___
65. Ballyhoos
68. Student org.
69. He sailed on the Beagle
71. Jet or Gulf
73. Wooden pail of old
76. Strasberg and Glaspell
78. Intervening, in law
79. Deviates, at sea
83. Napoli isle of song
85. Give the ___ (prompt)
87. Certain Austrian
89. What happiness is
93. Auk's cousin
94. Which's partner
95. Who my gal is
96. Call, in poker
97. Duelist's man Friday
98. Employ, in Spain
100. Time zone east of N.Y.
102. Make a levee
105. French revolutionist
108. Ironhanded one
111. Trick or witch follower
112. Hebrew letter
115. As ___ (generally)
116. Roué
117. Place of shelter
119. Bonfire leavings
121. Where she'll be
125. Enzyme suffixes
126. Norwegian port
127. Whit
128. ___ grudge against
129. Vamoosed
130. "___ a man with . . ."
131. Snide
132. What the lady is

DOWN

1. Fortune's partner
2. Endings for pseud and hom
3. Title for an Eng. lord
4. What I've been workin' on
5. "King Kong" star
6. Put one's ___ in
7. Shostakovich
8. Pompeiian girl of fiction
9. How everything's coming up
10. Musical sound
11. Director Hitchcock
12. What they call the wind
13. Shutting out, in sports
14. Favorite ___, in politics
15. Tigers' home
16. Argonne Forest river
17. Kind of roll or pie
18. How you'll never walk
24. Ribbon: Prefix
25. Pianist Peter
26. House, in the Southwest
32. Favoring
34. Heart ___ (sweetie)
37. Skipper's hazard
38. Direction: Abbr.
41. Where to fly down to
42. Other, in Cádiz
43. Shy from
44. Between Ark. and N.C.
46. "When ___ a lad. . ."
47. Owns up
49. Do in
50. Slaughter of baseball
51. Miss Millay
53. Warms up
54. Of the sun
55. Legal matter
56. Memory problem
57. Ponselle
59. From end to end, for short
64. Invalidate
66. Comics-artist Bushmiller
67. Killing look
70. "It's ___ to tell a lie"
72. What you are
73. Git!
74. Take an ___ (swear)
75. Hebrew bushel
77. Salt, in Paris
78. A la ___
80. Of aircraft
81. Tip off
82. Lop, in Scotland
84. Exorcist, for one
86. Musical libretto
88. Harbinger
90. Youth org.
91. Certain rec area in a club
92. Relative of golly: Var.
97. "You don't ___!"
99. Relative of a Tommy gun
100. "___ what your country can . . ."
101. Gunned it
103. Star of "Gypsy"
104. Con (with spirit)
105. Aviary bird
106. What he's mighty lak'
107. Bossie's cud
109. ___ Cologne
110. Western lake
113. "Butterfield 8" author
114. Religious belief
118. Alpha's follower
119. Dill
120. Spell, especially a cold one
122. Hitting stat
123. Conway
124. City north of Rio

187 Up and Around by Sara Helleny

And off and away and out and whatever.

ACROSS

1. Executive head-rolling
8. Harbach and Preminger
13. Pass the cards
20. Swiss lake
21. Inlaid decorations
22. Unknown, to Pierre
23. Opening hymn
24. Boo-boo
25. So-so poker holding
26. Little, in Nice
27. Ships: Abbr.
29. Connective
30. Large antelope
31. Interdict
32. Turkish weights
34. Up and down
36. Go back on: Var.
38. Siouan
39. Like interlacing
41. Macaw
42. Opposite of WSW
43. Jeanne d'Arc's execution site
45. Memento
47. Big bash
49. Rope fibers
50. Colorful fish
52. Malayan sirs
53. Boggy places
54. Boone or Paulsen
57. ___ es Salaam
59. American humorist
60. Roman 152
61. Me, to Jacques
64. Loos or Bryant
67. Kind of duck
69. Tense event for NASA
71. Remove from a list
73. Mitch Miller forte
74. Connecting rail track
75. Famous puppeteer
76. Old Chinese coin
77. Owns
78. One with a habit
79. Linkletter
81. Quentin or Salvador
83. Coin-toss call: Abbr.
84. Moslem noble
85. Lizard: Prefix
87. Last call
90. Late singer Bobby
92. Join again
94. Packed cotton
97. Work on a clock
98. Person
99. Fit for ___
101. Fragrant bloom
103. Little green men's craft
104. First German president
106. Secondhand deal
108. Brazilian rubber
109. "Nic ___ paddy whack . . ."
110. Altar constellation
111. Animal farm
112. Hawaiian bird
114. Apiece
115. Yellowish green
118. Colorful decade
120. Blind alley
122. Displays brazenly
123. Boleyn and Bancroft
124. Well filled
125. Disagree
126. San ___, L.A. harbor
127. ___ a dime (jams the brakes)

DOWN

1. Kind of sweater or shoe
2. U.S. author and critic
3. Arouse
4. Prefix for plunk
5. Love god
6. Components
7. Woody vine genus
8. Brit. decoration
9. Reversal
10. Junk mail, usually
11. Swan genus
12. Soviet constituent
13. Quintuplet name
14. Boredom
15. Part of a blackjack
16. Trim the twigs
17. Go ___ (expatiate)
18. Eastern Church members
19. Activate
28. Balkan
30. Classy guy
33. W.W. II city
35. Weaponry pact
36. Defendant, in law
37. Coarse sherbets
40. Rover's cry
44. W.W. II spy org.
46. No gentleman
48. ___ and only
49. For the time ___
51. Invited a friend
53. Tossed toward
54. Passover festival
55. Bone cavities
56. Amateurs: Var.
58. Redirect
60. Coconut fibers
61. Cadge
62. Possessed
63. William and Dean
65. "___ the season to be . . ."
66. Ancient Abyssinian
68. Dark Cont.
69. Jeff Davis org.
70. Every 24 hours: Abbr.
72. Red dye
75. Sloppy typewriter correction
79. U.S. sports org.
80. Pillar-to-post treatment
82. Snatch
84. Before
85. Dispatched
86. Elevator man
88. Crony
89. Ferry berth
90. Composer Manuel
91. Word for a hermit
92. ___ avis
93. Hindu land grant
95. Slips by
96. Has the nerve
97. Tie breaker
98. Least
100. Egg-white liquids
102. Lurch
105. African tribesman
107. Irish patriot
111. Writer Grey
113. Sweetheart, in England
116. Bridge-game situation: Abbr.
117. Daughter of Cadmus
118. Glove-compartment item
119. Within: Prefix
121. Height

188 Consuming Thoughts by Sidney L. Robbins

It's always time for a feast of some sort.

ACROSS

1. Part
6. Macho party
10. Novak
13. Squeezably ___
17. Biblical mount
18. Franchot
19. Fifth of five
20. Accustomed
22. Bakery items
25. Ripe
26. Cupid
27. Cowboy Rogers
28. The Lip
29. Bread additives
30. Generator: Abbr.
31. Passing fancy
32. Eastern U.S. wine
35. Lease
36. Gaelic
37. Harem room
38. Shade tree
40. Nicholas was one
43. Western Indian
46. Nonfare for a fox
50. Begin, poetically
51. Gladden
52. Type of billy
53. "Get your ___ franks!"
54. G-man or T-man
55. Habit
56. Raced
57. Comparative word
59. Type of rocket
61. Type of hold
62. Future cow
63. This, in Madrid
65. "Get ___ it!"
66. What apple sellers undergo
72. Lion's growth
73. Prospector's find
74. Jutting rock
75. Oath
77. One of the five W's
79. French river
81. Breathing space
82. Taunt
83. Sicken
84. Follower of a Chinese leader
88. Caps
90. Murmuring trees
91. Hit sign
92. Baloney, to some
94. Gobi, for one
95. Be on the back burner
97. Even-steven situation
98. Poem for a skylark
99. For fear that
100. Edgar Allan
102. Terminates
105. Fore and ___
106. Swimsuit part
109. Juice bases
112. Access: Abbr.
113. Hasten
114. Ooze
115. Senility
116. Bakery items
120. Medic
121. Golfing area
122. Type of hat
123. High flier
124. Not now
125. Type of pit
126. Metallic rocks
127. Bit of hair

DOWN

1. ___ of evidence
2. White-haired
3. Hot crime
4. Agents, for short
5. Type of tide
6. Took long steps
7. Conservative
8. Kind of one for tennis
9. Obtain
10. Inchon's country
11. Being hauled
12. ___ amis
13. Escargot
14. Start
15. Grapes et al.
16. Sea bird
20. "___ little teapot"
21. ___ Moines
23. Eradicate
24. Where to say "I do"
29. Kramden or Edwards
31. Gratis
32. On ice
33. X-rated
34. Draw a ___ on
36. Heraldic term
39. Indian caste
41. Mimic
42. Fix over
43. Saucy
44. Above it all
45. Juicy site
46. Wicked
47. Grip
48. French income
49. ___ beans
52. 50 percent
56. Value
58. Spells
60. Common abbr.
62. Movie
64. Penny ___
65. Last
67. Former Mideast org.
68. Type of change
69. Makes corrections
70. Spring flower
71. Not drunk
76. Bridge seat
77. Hornet's relative
78. Take on
80. Evade
82. Core
85. Keen
86. English painter and family
87. Holly
89. Summer desserts
90. Picnic ant
93. Hearty vessel
94. Put off
96. Heed a charity plea
99. Scottish landlords
101. Urge
103. Simon, later
104. Against a thing, in law
106. Tan color
107. Movie spools
108. Church parts
109. Unusual
110. Type of beer
111. Suffix for mountain
113. On hand
114. Box
116. Depot: Abbr.
117. Another of the W's
118. Chocolate or sand
119. Still

189 Just Desserts by Anne Fox
Polishing off repasts with a flourish.

ACROSS

1. Easy
7. Legendary horse
13. Islamic spirit
18. Leon Uris opus
19. Greek marketplaces
20. "Robin ___"
21. "Victoria ___," Housman play
22. Platitude
23. Arkansas town
24. U.S. folk song
27. Retiree's gift
31. Drink flavor
32. Tenn. athlete
33. Andes grass
34. Cutting tool
35. School org.
38. Riddle
42. Story by Arnold Lobel
46. Carnival SOS
47. Trojan-horse builder
48. 100 cts.
49. Skill
50. For
51. Meadow sound
53. Adriatic wind
54. Story by Richard Connell
60. Certain French art works
61. Le ___ Soleil, Louis XIV
62. Poetic word
63. Bluff King ___
64. Escapee from a bag
65. Military survey, for short
67. Monikers
71. Dance of 1883
76. Withdraw formally
77. Clumsy boat
78. Deplore
79. Miss Chase
80. Presidential monogram
81. Virginia specialty
83. Upstage
84. Stupid dessert
91. Soprano Lucine
92. Cake covers
93. Straying
98. Badgerlike animal
99. Fountain offering
100. Composer Gustav
101. Kind of alcohol
102. Fauns
103. Flycatcher

DOWN

1. ___-de-lance
2. Fire
3. Slip a ___
4. Amin
5. Kind of counter
6. Son of Isaac
7. More wacky
8. Zagreb, to the Germans
9. Words by Cole Porter
10. Jejune
11. Type of berry
12. Word with monde or tasse
13. "With the ___ of an ass . . ."
14. Charmingly simple
15. "Greatest athlete" of Disney film
16. Kind of pin
17. Angers
25. Pizza order
26. Steven's partner
27. In agreement
28. Hurt
29. People in general
30. Piece of armor
34. Mortgagee, e.g.
36. Scottish uncle
37. Sagacity
39. "Waiting for ___"
40. Marianne or Thomas
41. Reference book
43. Remedy
44. Saarinen
45. Glacial ridges
50. Druid, for one
52. Quivering
53. Winter apple
54. Ceremonial staffs
55. Clerical cape
56. Of the eye
57. Scandinavian goddess
58. Camera part
59. Citizen of a 1941 movie
66. Neck, in France
67. Does teamster work
68. Composer Edouard
69. Nevada city
70. Card game
72. Baron ___ Amherst
73. Kook
74. Wife of Zeus
75. Wrinkles
82. English composer
83. Conductor Caldwell
84. Also-ran of fable
85. One of a Latin trio
86. Slat
87. Partner of tell
88. Quito's land: Abbr.
89. Force
90. Bandleader Hal
94. Greek letter
95. Companion of cakes
96. Bill
97. After due

190 Social Register by Hugh Holland

Some names that might or might not have made it.

ACROSS

1. Word to get attention
5. Mrs., in Quebec
8. Original person
12. Terra ___
17. Musical finale
18. Bern's river
19. Bantu-speaking tribe
20. Biblical treasure source
21. Plymouth couple
24. "If a body ___ body"
25. Mexican state
26. Fallow animal
27. Prefix for dermis
29. Smart remark
30. Bro. or sis.
31. Charged particles
32. Play part, in Spain
34. Highway users
37. Fleming and Smith
38. Having a brownish color
42. Gums: Prefix
43. Beatrice was his ideal
45. Lily of the opera
46. Met home
47. Having a stage
49. Throb
50. Sea bird
51. Unfruitful
52. Gossip's offering
53. Grain
54. Andy Gump's wife
55. Man with a horn
57. ___ Paulo
59. Wood sorrel
61. Court decrees
62. Lowell's visionary sir
66. Iranian Turk
68. Kind of nonpicnic day
69. Occasional store event
70. Stallone and others
71. Natives of: Suffix
72. Lakes or guns
73. Ireland's ___ Fail
74. A name for Jesus
76. Vamoosed
77. Norwegian saint
78. Actress Mary and others
79. Toward shelter
80. Wimpole St. monogram
82. Prickly seed coat: Var.
84. Hyson, for one
86. Actress Patricia
87. Callouslike organ
91. Sister-in-law of Ruth
93. Royal baker of verse
96. Psalm liturgy
97. Chemical suffix
98. Words before king
99. Prefix for an age
100. One giving lip service
101. Lends a hand
102. Quiet Russian river
103. Otherwise

DOWN

1. Bible book
2. Merry sounds
3. Home for 8 Across and 14 Down
4. Big leagues
5. Taj ___
6. Irish Sea isle
7. Shine brightly
8. Enoch and Eve
9. Performers
10. Scottish alder
11. ___ en scène
12. Sunday paper section
13. Undo, to poets
14. Eve
15. Yugoslavs' hero
16. Smell ___
22. Hematite, for one
23. Sierra ___
28. Goodly number
33. Kind of case or tube
34. Mutts
35. "That's ___ of hokum!"
36. Abie's friend
37. Unify
38. Pocahontas's married name
39. Immaculate
40. Spectral
41. Hamlet or Borge
43. Yugoslav river
44. Red dye
45. Indian wheat cakes
48. Prefix for angle
49. Social doing
52. Scrooge et al., for short
56. "Tempest" spirit
57. Bird-feeder item
58. Response: Abbr.
59. Bone: Prefix
60. Halcyon
61. Whet
63. Constellation
64. Inter ___
65. Frond
67. Romanov family member
69. Sponge on
72. Gather
75. Word before world or lands
76. Armadas
77. Flattened at the ends
79. Have ___ for (require)
80. One of the Allens
81. Tennis-match drawing
82. Scarves
83. Sky Bear
85. Water, to Horace
88. City of Russia
89. Fr. holy women
90. Serf
92. Exist
94. Site of the Tell legend
95. Ziegfeld

191 Typecasting by Manny Miller

Identifying people by their specialties.

ACROSS

1. V.P. under Coolidge
6. Sand or tourist
10. Economist Smith
14. Infants' mealtime wear
18. I.D. for a primitive fire maker
19. I.D. for a mountain climber
20. Group of Moslem scholars
21. Time long past
22. I.D.'s for Fidel
26. Italy's second city
27. Fields
28. Consolation, in Bonn
29. Well-armed swimmer
32. Apologies
33. Condition: Suffix
34. More intimate
35. I.D.'s for Rover
36. Constructed an Alpine shortcut
40. Two-wheelers
41. Lullabies
43. Fixed point in time
44. Retired
45. Aga ____, Moslem leader
46. Positive factor
47. Sikorsky
48. River of Poland
49. I.D. for Daniel Boone
53. Like a good cake
54. Private
56. Songs
57. Medieval merchant guilds
58. Radio part
59. Maritime: Abbr.
60. Find fault with
61. Awn
63. Neighbor of Rhodes
65. Some stage shows
68. I.D.'s for ditch diggers
69. Drill command
71. Faucet
72. Roman date
73. North American Indian
74. Respiratory sound
75. I.D. for Pavlova
76. Personality
77. I.D.'s for umpires
81. Kitchen implement
82. Pioneer in radio
84. Schisms
85. Natural endowment
86. Descartes
87. Naive ones
88. Counselors
89. Dispatch boat
91. Brings down
92. Pears, to Pedro
93. I.D.'s for Dickey or Bench
99. I.D. for an angel
100. ____ a limb
101. Similar
102. De Valera
103. Israeli statesman
104. Doyen
105. Riches' counterpart
106. I.D. for an anteater

DOWN

1. I.D. for an Air Force hero
2. Moslem caliph
3. I.D. for Dolly Parton
4. Inflamed with love
5. I.D.'s for a noncom
6. Company off.
7. Sheepskin
8. Calendar page: Abbr.
9. Rode a cycle
10. Alan and Robert
11. Lawsuit figures: Abbr.
12. Doctors' org.
13. Dull surfaces
14. Outmoded
15. Markers
16. Author Harte
17. French possessive
20. Anxiety
23. Smudge
24. Pertaining to space
25. Heatable devices
29. In scoring position
30. Large tropical trees
31. Heed
32. Has in mind
33. Time of day
35. 100 centimes
36. Indian weights
37. Government units
38. Like some leaves
39. Board game
41. Kind of loft
42. Humane gp.
45. Peninsular country
47. Type of architecture
49. Coins
50. Helen and Citizen
51. Boiling
52. Actor David
53. Song thrush
55. I.D.'s for Jumbo
57. "That old black magic ____ in . . ."
60. I.D.'s for Little Miss Marker
61. On foot, in France
62. Narrow elevation
63. I.D. for a cockatoo
64. Emit fumes
65. Feminine titles of respect
66. Undeveloped
67. Gushes forth
69. Use a lever: Var.
70. Runs lopingly
73. Goosefoot plant
75. Good-luck charm
77. Distort
78. Shameless
79. Early stringed instrument
80. I.D. for a brigadier general
81. Pompous shows
83. Prayer
85. Word after left or U
87. I.D. for Zubin Mehta
88. I.D.'s for a teen-ager
89. Captain of the Pequod
90. The Sail constellation
91. List of persons
92. Pedantic one
93. Guevara
94. Champs-Elysées, e.g.
95. Arm of the Volga
96. Spanish boss
97. Former French coin
98. Chess piece: Abbr.

192 Split-ups by Marion Moeser

Wherein some entries come in two installments.

ACROSS

1. Do art work
5. Ecce ____
9. Lederer and Burdick character, with 71 Down
13. Unchanged
17. Place for a Cuban heel
18. More of subject: Abbr.
19. Place
20. "To ____ and a bone . . ."
21. Challenge of sorts, with 45 Down
23. Ancient Asian land
24. See 85 Down
25. Toad move
26. Kind of boxing punch
28. See 47 Down
30. One of the bad guys
32. ____ Oa, Marquesas island
34. Ain't, more politely
35. "____ in the Money"
36. Showing spunk
39. One of the family
40. Sarge's words to a platoon
42. One in uniform
44. Some medicos
47. Bit of camp gear
50. Untidy person
52. Show temperament
53. Sp. lady
54. Italian greeting
56. "____ Arizona," Warner Baxter film
57. Unclear condition
58. Kennel sounds
60. Noël Coward classic, with 51 Down
62. Yucatán's Chichén ____
63. American Indian
64. Fokker or Spad
65. Stern's counterpart
68. Category
69. Flock
70. "Thereby ____ tale"
72. Conceives
74. W.W. II spy group
75. Chancy game
76. Chinese leader's creed
78. Cloth measure
79. St. ____, Loire capital
81. Racing strip
85. Rural field fixture
88. Chalcedony
89. Take for ____
90. Mrs. Bardell's tale is told here, with 49 Down
94. ERA advocate
97. Indian area on the Arabian Sea
98. Further a cause
99. Takes off
101. Stanley Kubrick film, with 55 Down
103. City of Nevada
104. Cassowary's relative
105. Aspect
106. ____ fixe
107. Shamrock land
108. See 8 Down
109. Disadvantaged state
110. He said "yup" a lot, with 3 Down

DOWN

1. Avoid
2. Seat for Victoria
3. See 110 Across
4. Men
5. Shaped with an axe
6. Nebraska Indian
7. Northeast Vineyard
8. Novel of two sisters, with 108 Across
9. Diminutive suffix
10. Coolidge Dam's river
11. Far from obese
12. City on the Colorado
13. Deities known for revelry
14. Instruction to "My lady sweet"
15. County north of S.F.
16. Cast out
22. One of the beans
27. Egg: Prefix
29. Café au ____
31. Stew ingredient
33. Italian port on the Adriatic
36. Bolivian river
37. Beating of a drum
38. French dances
39. Put in the mail
41. Private eye
43. Work of an eraser
44. ____ hammer and tongs (work hard)
45. See 21 Across
46. Entree orders
47. Couch treatment, with 28 Across
48. Spiny rats
49. See 90 Across
51. See 60 Across
52. Greek letter
55. See 101 Across
59. But, to Caesar
61. Gold or iron bars
64. Comedian Silvers
66. Miss Adams
67. French possessive
71. See 9 Across
73. Love god
75. Carried on windily
77. After black, a colorful condition
78. Former Maryland's elopers' town
80. Suffix for manor or tutor
82. Abe of TV
83. Fervent fan
84. British anthropologist
85. Fifth wheel, with 24 Across
86. River Caesar knew
87. Boadicea's people
89. Biblical boat
91. "____ a kick out of you"
92. Nonconscious state
93. Boat part
95. Be tiresome
96. Environmental unit
100. Go to court
102. Old Bailey wear

193 Name Calling by Herman Surasky

With some revisions to make things appropriate.

ACROSS

1. Building material
6. Letter addenda
9. Item on Mercury's foot
13. Lunar-solar relation
18. Toast for Nellie
19. River islet
20. Miss Massey
22. Consumer expert
23. Metal mass
24. U.N. agency
25. Pierre of France
26. Sultan's decree
27. Mauna ____
28. Esteemed
31. Military maneuvers
33. Strays
35. Ones who speak
38. Smirks
39. Kind of slicker
41. Old car
43. Miss West
44. Latin section of a city
46. Lead weight
48. Russian ruler
52. Grampus
53. Novelist Hamsun
55. Reduces again
58. Keats output
59. American writer
60. Grayish-green color
63. Fulton's Folly was one
65. Miss Kett et al.
68. Nero
69. Asian weight
70. Frédéric's favorite philosopher
72. Fugue master's meal
78. Slot-machine cheating aid
79. Stringed instrument
80. Wary
81. Moonlighting jobs
86. Salad herb
88. Free
89. Miner's quest
90. Record players
92. Violin-tuning devices
94. Neck style
95. Period
97. Itch, in Italy
98. Clamors
100. Kirghiz town
103. Of religious rites
106. Sole kitchen survivor
107. Theater districts
111. Reorganizes, in a way
113. Musical Burl
117. Composer Leroy
119. Worn by friction
121. Whitney
122. Ravel's "La ____"
123. South African province
126. Lively, in Paris
127. Stage projection
129. Growing out
130. Garbo
131. Corporate initials
132. Marsh plant
133. Believer in God
134. Legal document
135. Tray or Wednesday
136. Tests

DOWN

1. Facial expression
2. Barbershop voice
3. British composer
4. Tropical tree
5. Wood strip
6. Musical for Richard
7. TV tryout
8. Laid away
9. High old time for Oscar
10. Pier union: Abbr.
11. Election time: Abbr.
12. Eat away
13. Puzzling "Variations" by 3 Down
14. Rampart
15. "There is nothing like ____"
16. One who gives up
17. Lock
21. Sorrowful cry
29. Excursion
30. Present, in Soho
32. Edge
34. Movie text: Abbr.
36. Part
37. Shirt ornaments
40. Vex
42. Neglect
44. Soup for convalescents
45. Vinegar: Prefix
47. Quaff for Ludwig
49. Famous canals
50. Oklahoma city
51. Soak
52. Oil cartel
54. Mississippi Indian
56. Chinese pagodas
57. Rose feature
61. Slithery fish: Var.
62. Former Berlin govt.
64. Melancholy
66. Church recess
67. Beverly of the opera
71. Paris night
72. Big ____
73. City official: Abbr.
74. Rapid gait
75. Pluck
76. Weeps
77. Soapbox park
79. Dish for Franck
81. Drunkard
82. Wrath
83. German article
84. Cupid
85. Tobacco item: Var.
87. Self-interested one
91. Enough, traditionally
93. Original ____
96. Annoys
99. Snow runner
101. Perry's Della
102. Merry sounds
104. Lawman: Abbr.
105. Baltic republic
107. Stormed
108. Empty
109. Stevenson
110. Ditty
112. Glazing compounds
114. Aida's creator
115. Funeral oration
116. Math ratios
118. Fragrant ointment
120. Bridge seat
124. Golf gadget
125. Ingested
128. ____ capita

194 Off Center by Diana Sessions

And tending to be subordinate.

ACROSS

1. Fanatical
6. Nickname for a newspaper
10. Calendar abbr.
13. Blame, usually bum
16. "You ___ Sunshine"
17. Counting-out word
18. Less important recording
20. Equestrienne's equipment
22. Uneven
23. Detriment
24. Subordinate event
26. Actress Samantha
27. Large area of the earth
28. Owl variety
29. Minerals
31. Stout character
32. Commanded
33. Bullet
34. Shock
36. These, in Spain
38. Plant of the parsley family
39. Showed more staying power
43. ___ fidelis
45. Puppet of note
46. Gear tooth
47. Contraction
48. Frighten
49. Pacific island
50. On an upper ship deck
52. Scene of Christ's first miracle
53. Dodges
55. Attestation: Abbr.
56. Place for a close view
58. Cautious
59. Out-of-date
60. Compass point
61. Reading matter on an urn
62. Thin coating
63. Vacation vehicle
64. Throw off course
66. Headland
67. Hostelry
68. Preliminary part
70. Oodles
71. Pier union
74. Insect
77. Addictive
78. Scapa ___
79. roman road
80. Base-running situation
82. Secondary pursuit
84. Morning ___
85. Prejudiced
87. Together
89. Brandy cocktails
90. Prophet
91. Relatives
92. Kind of day
93. Naval off.
94. Offends
95. "Ain't ___ fun!"

DOWN

1. Scamp
2. Melodic
3. Important attribute for an M.D.
4. "___ man with seven wives"
5. Impaired, Prefix
6. Wearisome
7. Football blitz
8. Small bay
9. Cricket runs
10. Corsage unit
11. Undo one's sewing
12. ___ dixit
13. Vimy or Oak
14. "___ and true industrious friend": Shak.
15. Variety of seven-up
18. Kind of wreath
19. Official seal
21. Square building stone
25. Vehemently
30. Condescends
33. Stalk
34. Glancing blow
35. Carries
37. Mine-roof prop
38. Mrs. Astin's maiden name
40. Hilarious
41. Reluctant
42. Canopy
43. Inviolate
44. Lady of Shalott
45. Chinatown purchase
46. Journalist's subject matter
49. Roomy
50. Expression
51. What "veni" means
53. Moved furtively
54. Narrative
57. French evening
59. Strokes
62. Died out
63. Part of a haunted-house scene
65. Put side by side
66. Cherubs
67. Leather finishers
69. Unsuccessful ones
70. Porch seat
72. "All roads ___ Rome"
73. Check
74. Sound of swift movement: Var.
75. First name of a markswoman
76. Rundown
78. Handbill
79. Distribute
81. Agreeable
83. Existence: Lat.
86. Fancy ___
88. Deviation

195 Sounds of Numbers by Alfio Micci

All you have to do is pronounce them.

ACROSS

1. Charges
5. Templeton
9. Roam about
12. Court proceedings
16. Wings
17. Athenian square
18. Ending for photo
20. Downcast
21. Fiercely
23. Choice meats
25. Groups of six
26. ____ Pitcher
28. Eagle's perch
29. Steep
30. Seine sight
31. Numerical prefix
32. ____ and out the other
35. ____ vincit amor
37. Tender poultry
41. Besmirches
42. O'Neill play, with "The"
44. Clock numeral
45. Clue
46. Gasp ____ (breathe with difficulty)
47. Ice, in Bonn
48. Engrossed
49. ____ rule (generally)
50. Melees
54. Brush, in Bretagne
56. One of the May days
59. Kind of attack
60. Inclined approach
61. Like some campus walls
62. Nigerian peasant
63. Hindu mystic: Var.
64. Hiatus
65. Kind of fig
67. Prince Philip and others
70. Cut down
72. Align
74. Dined at home
75. "I cannot tell ____"
76. Nautical monogram
77. French alder
78. Madrid evergreen
79. ____ Grande
80. Instructive
85. Valentino dance
86. "True love's the gift . . . given to ____": Scott
88. Neckwear
89. Marked a certain way
90. "I ____ man with . . ."
91. Decay
92. Hard to come by
93. Ear protuberances
95. Cliburn's instrument
97. Portico
101. Broth spoilers
103. Presentations
105. Deposited
106. Character of a people
107. Moslem council
108. Spin
109. City south of Palermo
110. Work on hide
111. Meets
112. Pintail duck

DOWN

1. Markings for sailors
2. Der ____
3. Scrooge expletives
4. Driver safety device
5. Nixon V.P.
6. African worms
7. "____ tu," Verdi aria
8. Soothing
9. Rock science: Abbr.
10. Gump or Capp
11. Gambling piece
12. Away from the mouth
13. Roman 152
14. Air
15. Roman bronze
17. Stella or Larry
18. Biblical city of balm
19. City on the Vistula
22. Mrs. Helmer and Mrs. Charles
24. Admit
27. Musical collection
31. Spanish gold pieces
32. Bandleader Jones
33. Din
34. Unique indeed
35. Bay window
36. ____ d'hotel
37. Energetic
38. Irritating
39. Slashes
40. Locale
42. ____ pod (tannin source)
43. Bartók
46. Nearest-lying land
48. Paris's rival
51. Author E.M.
52. Liven
53. Embankment
54. Anne, Charlotte or Emily Jane
55. Tatters
57. Plant seed
58. Anger
63. Newly formed
65. Esther, to friends
66. Thunderstorm feature: Abbr.
67. Dracula, for one
68. Trace
69. Hairnet
70. Old MacDonald's place
71. Kazan
73. Sandalwood
76. Forearm bone
78. Spectacles
80. Poem by Gray
81. Warning
82. Torment
83. "When the frost ____ the punkin . . ."
84. Devilfish
85. ____ firma
87. Peregrine Pickle's wife
89. Toscanini's birthplace
92. Turns over a new leaf
93. Govt. agent
94. Maugham story
95. Hawaiian gooseberry
96. Religious representation: Var.
97. Waste allowance
98. Impure matter
99. Parched
100. Bondsman of old
101. Peter O'____
102. Mel of baseball
104. Wallach or Whitney

196 Cons and Pros by Mel Taub

With some interpretive license involved.

ACROSS

1. Chinese peninsula
6. Gaily mischievous
10. It follows Nov. 30
14. Jimmy Dorsey's instr.
17. Add splendor to
18. Section of London or N.Y.C.
19. Thames prep
20. Feel a need to
21. De latest San Kventin style
23. Post-jailbreak headline
25. Bowlike object
26. Late actor Erwin
27. Change the décor
29. Sullen
30. Garden intruder
32. Parisian friend
34. Human-rights org.
36. Reproach
39. Hush-hush
41. Emergency reserve
43. Scamp
45. Current unit, for short
48. Flower-garden staple
49. Names on post-office circulars
51. Hot under the collar
54. Emotional tension
55. Newborn child
56. Variable star
57. Fender misfortunes
58. Prisoner's trial
61. Northern Spy
66. Shaping tools
67. Actor Mitchell
69. Noblemen of the East
74. That is, to Cicero
75. Fabulous beast
76. Identification groups
78. Tobacco residue
80. Frozen desserts
81. Naming a trump
84. Panelist Francis
86. Et ____
87. Siouan
88. Mine, on the Marne
89. Noisy aircraft
92. Use parcel post
94. Pet name
96. Calendar abbr.
98. Not fully anted
99. Nicklaus discovered
102. Onnald Pommer sputs attire
105. Whilom Mideast union
106. Suffix with angel or evangel
107. Adroitness
108. In the company of
109. Commuter's special
110. Descartes
111. Cleaner's companion
112. Target area

DOWN

1. Harsh-voiced parrot
2. Think the world of
3. Inmate's formal surrender
4. Woof
5. Change for a fiver
6. Undertake
7. Louis or Francois, e.g.
8. Odd job
9. Make keen
10. Boil down
11. D.D.E.'s milieu
12. Anti-Mussolini
13. Inside dope
14. Vinegar-to-be
15. Barley beard
16. Checked an application box
22. Aspiring Hollywood lass
24. Computer's production
28. "____ Rheingold"
31. Pour into a new bottle
33. Ending for señor or Juan
35. Move along easily
37. Pelvic bones
38. Yoke together
40. Sonoran realty listings
42. Chessmen: Abbr.
43. Sally of the fans
44. Not aweather
46. Moocher of song
47. Tom Watson experiment
50. Dry, as champagne
52. Sacred Zoroastrian writings
53. Heap, in Cannes
59. Not even
60. Fort Worth campus
61. ____ a minute
62. Nuts for pies
63. Sam Snead's giving up
64. Body of learning
65. River of Austria
68. In English
69. Robert or Alan
70. Honey: Sp.
71. Canines' neighbors
72. Word in gaspill ads
73. Latin possessive
74. "____ my turn?"
77. Sympathetic to Mussolini
79. Crash into
82. Pate
83. "____ whiz!"
85. Slate worker
88. Marshal
90. Sandal lace
91. He wrote "Riders to the Sea"
93. Black, in Brest
95. Did a takeoff
97. Anastasia's father
99. Taproom
100. Indian writer Santha Rama ____
101. Mrs. Reagan, for short
103. Suffix for verb
104. Not big, to Burns

197 Edibles by David Crosatto

Some items that might or might not be on menus.

ACROSS

1. Spring flower
6. Pickwickian delicacy
13. "____ art's sake"
19. Italian portraitist
20. Eager for
21. Shell used for money
22. Blasco ____, Spanish author
23. Big game for dessert
25. "____ but the lonely heart"
26. Imposing arrangement
28. Jai alai
29. Z at Balliol
30. Turned-off elite
32. Famed film roarer
33. Flinch
35. Chess pieces: Abbr.
36. City in Utah
37. English scholar, called Grammaticus
39. "This is ____" (my treat)
42. Fish at a fire sale
44. Croissants are served here
45. An officer, to Gunga Din
48. "The fat ____ the fire"
49. ____ crow
50. Certain teachers
51. Phosphate mineral
53. Old Scottish county
55. Minced-meat dish
56. Describing the Godhead
57. "Roberta" composer
58. Appetizer for a bird
59. Cub Scout unit
60. Goose spread for Miss Hearst
65. ____ Dai, Indochinese leader
68. ____-in-the-hole, sausage dish
69. Organic compound
70. Fancy pancakes
74. Emulating W. J. Bryan
76. Electrical unit
78. Moving with a light anchor
79. French subways
80. Shade tree
81. Singer Kirk
83. Early illustrator of Holmes stories
84. Meaty English philosopher
85. Appetizer for the ill-tempered
88. Jewish month
89. Water sport
90. Hungary's Nagy
91. Poker kitty
94. Lake near Novgorod
96. Thy, in France
97. A bivalve gets worked up
99. ____ gestae
101. Up
103. Misrepresent
104. Water buffalo
105. A hot dish that's cool
108. Fostered
110. Humble worker
111. Most profound
112. City of India
113. Smooths
114. M. Lupin and others
115. Divisions of geologic time

DOWN

1. Besides
2. Father of the Titans
3. Eremite or hermit
4. Chemical ending
5. Conqueror of the Incas
6. Coarse laceworks
7. Israelite camp in Exodus
8. Shout from the deck
9. Muscular spasm
10. Feature of a Spad or Sopwith
11. British summer mecca
12. And others, in a footnote
13. Vinegary
14. Sophia Loren is one
15. Word before "for the show"
16. Eskimo fare
17. Seine tributary
18. Walter or Willis
19. Russian city
24. Bet a horse
27. Auld ____, name for Edinburgh
31. Lock up this salad
32. Grassland
34. Paint units
37. "It's ____ and a delusion"
38. Plant disease
40. Blackbird
41. Eat, in Emden
42. Kind of exercise
43. Wined and ____
44. Mack Sennet missiles
45. Met
46. Diamond's mo.
47. "Bali ____"
50. Fencer's move
52. Sight from Jackson Hole
54. Deduce
55. Snug place for a bug
57. Elizabethan dramatist
58. It's usually avec poivre
61. Tackle in touch football
62. Like a bump
63. Containing an antiseptic
64. "Love Story" author
65. This dessert's a blast
66. Of a surface
67. Fine food for a French filly
71. Kind of iron or Latin
72. Chemical ending
73. Platoon N.C.O.
75. King in "Peer Gynt"
76. Steamroller, for one
77. Environments
78. Large Alaskan volcano
80. Pitching stat
82. Frying pans
85. Kind of math section
86. Basic rules: Abbr.
87. Soviet republic
89. Bluish greens
91. Individual
92. Haves
93. Hebrew letter
95. Former South African premier
97. To perfume, in a way
98. Slow, in Seville
99. Sgt. Preston's outfit
100. Earlier, in Germany
102. Drink mix
103. British gun
106. Noted U.N. name
107. O'Neill animal
109. French article

198 In Flight by Mary Russ

With travelers that don't need airports.

ACROSS

1. More, in Madrid
4. Junkman's purchase
9. Confuses
15. "All ___ glisters . . ."
19. Former Fed. agency
20. Southwestern plain
21. Kuybyshev, formerly
22. Sharpen
23. Kind of advised
24. Kilns
25. Model of thinness
26. Chow
27. Entree under glass
30. ___ de corps
32. Bishop's-weed genus
33. Caucasian language
34. Where Asmara is
37. Constellation Apus
42. Author Bombeck
45. Persian gazelle
46. Japanese coin
47. Stretchers
50. Pitiable
54. Roman or Arabic item
57. Italian painter
58. Scent
59. Noisy exit sound
61. Violinist Bull
62. Ammonia compounds
64. Lahore garments
66. Train
69. Kind of day at Black Rock
70. Name for Barnum's singer
77. He's Tiny
78. Row for Porgy and Bess
79. "___ a dull moment"
80. Take down a peg
83. Swiss river
84. Old-school items
86. Dread
87. Up above
88. What clam diggers await
92. Tall drinking glasses
94. Like Cornelia
96. Tolkien creature
98. Wake-robin
99. Playwright Coward
100. Words for the shortest way
106. Arm of the Antarctic
108. ___ -les-Bains
109. D-day craft
111. Dumbbell
114. Dessert, occasionally
119. Cupid
120. Mysterious
123. "No ___!" (Nix!)
124. "___ man answers . . ."
125. Entitle
126. It is sometimes shrinking
127. Hackneyed
128. Shade tree
129. Church corner
130. City on the Rio Grande
131. A Ford
132. Ottoman official

DOWN

1. Dancer Shearer
2. Self-possession
3. Sandwich meat
4. Place for a coin
5. Thunder sound
6. Allergy symptom
7. Feed the kitty
8. Spanish inns
9. Screen canine
10. Became light
11. Composer Shostakovich
12. Jet-trip woe
13. Work unit
14. Actor Leo from England
15. TV series with Shirley Jones
16. Rime
17. Against
18. Try out
28. St. Paul's was his No. 1 job
29. Lorelei, e.g.
31. Compre-hends
35. River to the Rhone
36. Honduran port
38. Buck's mate
39. Food fragments
40. Did not pass
41. Akkadian god
43. Manner
44. Skin problem
48. "I wasn't there," for one
49. Spanish assents
50. Wiley or Emily
51. Esau's wife
52. Ripped
53. Moslem judge
55. Main theme
56. Judicial writ
60. Wine grape
63. American educator
65. Actress Loretta
67. African river
68. Sluggard's model
71. Arabian ruler
72. Chinese dynasty
73. It has a long arm
74. Assert
75. Request to kindly light
76. Goes astray
80. Hoover or Aswan
81. Type of collar
82. Marquand's Mr.
83. Bottomless pit
85. Villein
89. Lesage's Gil
90. Aberdeen's river
91. In case, in Vichy
93. Brynner
95. People in a Wells novel
97. Italian port
101. Roof tile, to Caesar
102. Non-Polynesians, in Hawaii
103. Sandpiper
104. Discovered
105. Suppress
107. Kitchen item
110. Unpleasant
111. Darlings' dog
112. Islamic leader
113. "Listen ___!"
115. Combustion-engine inventor
116. Goddess of discord
117. Network
118. Lively dance
121. Brigitte's eyelash
122. ___ a plea

199 Messages by Frances Hansen

Musical postcards to be sent to the homebound.

ACROSS

1. King of the jungle
5. Soprano Lucine
10. Cutup
14. Hooky, mil. style
18. Furnish with funds
20. Plutocrat
21. Mine, in Marseille
22. Marsh bird
23. Cub pack leader
24. Legree's creator
25. Sun or moon follower
26. Do last-minute studying
27. Dixon/Wrubel card
31. Anecdote
32. Formicary occupant
33. Newfoundland airport
34. Skeleton's residence
37. Confirmation slap
40. Zounds!
41. Gehrig or Costello
42. Room fresheners
45. ____ possidetis (war principle)
46. "____ culpa!"
49. Radford/Whiting card
54. Meat of the matter
55. Painter Rockwell
56. Document certifiers: Abbr.
57. Doone
58. Composer Satie
61. Tidal bore
64. Newspaper spread
65. Leslie/Warren card
71. Singer Julius
72. Krupp works' city
73. Relative of etc.
74. "The lines go with ____": Stevenson
75. Not DNA, but close
76. Equipment
79. Up a ____
83. Kennett/Udall card
89. Little boy
90. Paul Kruger
91. Idleness
92. "But ____ on forever"
93. Abrupt
95. All in ____ work
96. Rarely
98. Warhol's specialty
101. Pirates' gold
102. Fall guy
104. Kent/Gannon/Ram/card
112. Jewish month
113. Paradise
114. Evita or Juan
115. Warehouse
116. Hoarfrost
117. Split
118. 1903 King song
119. Pick-me-up
120. Bird or hay follower
121. Tammany baiter
122. Vincent or Trini
123. Super!

DOWN

1. Table extender
2. "____ Dinka Doo"
3. Breslau's river
4. No more, ____ (fixed amount)
5. Goose genus
6. Chum, in Soho
7. "Baby, Take ____"
8. Baseball's Schoolboy
9. Eve raised Cain with him
10. Beach structure
11. Catkin
12. Horse color
13. Joltin' Joe
14. Rise upward
15. Pulitzer's paper
16. Fanon
17. Debussy favorite
19. French painter
28. "There's a Small ____"
29. Fall from grace
30. Sheepish remark
34. Trim the hedge
35. Viaud's pen name
36. Give the boot to
37. Abbr. on an envelope
38. Dillydallies
39. Sea extension
40. Numerical suffixes
43. ____-tikki-tavi
44. Copy
45. Release from confinement
46. Seder condiment
47. Boredom
48. "____ which will live . . ." (Dec. 7, 1941)
50. ____ See (papal court)
51. Letters on the cross
52. Beast of South America
53. Allegiance
59. "And ____ well know where": Bridges
60. Gershwin
62. Peer Gynt's mother
63. "Make room ahead!"
64. "____ Me Go, Lover"
65. Explosion
66. Conference site, 1945
67. Three of a kind
68. Spite
69. Birthright-seller
70. Felt sun hat
75. Peasant of India
77. Letter inserts: Abbr.
78. German composer
80. Invasion
81. Therefore
82. Land in the Bible
84. Fruity Spy
85. Get ____ (shed)
86. "____ Clear Day"
87. Rib: Prefix
88. Israeli parliament
93. Sent a wire
94. Actress Mary
95. Author Hannah
97. Britain's Bulwer-____
98. Plowman of fiction
99. Fran's friend
100. Shako feature
101. Signs
102. Ring up
103. Desi of TV
105. Ancient theaters
106. October stone
107. Gambling city
108. Jockey's adjunct
109. Pride of 1 Across
110. Samoan capital
111. Religious group

200 Energy Crunch by Henry Hook

The vehicle is supplied by Mr. Hook and Nancy Shuster. You tank up some squares with fuel.

ACROSS

1. Loft a golf ball
5. Lloyd and Teen
12. Resident: Suffix
15. Sternward
18. Philippine city
19. Kyrie ____
20. Antimacassar
21. Not in good spirits
23. Section of Quebec
25. Goose, in Grenoble
26. ____-kiri
27. D.C. thoroughfare
28. Ovens
30. Defense weaponry: Abbr.
31. Entertainment co. initials
33. Writer Rand
34. On the rocks
36. Suffix for poly or penta
38. Hits 100°C
39. Wine-cask crust
41. Like three-minute eggs
45. Watson's warning
47. Kind of duck or heat
48. Steiger, in "The Pawnbroker"
50. Court or series
53. Go on ____ (count calories)
55. Lucrezia's brother
56. Putting one's two cents in
58. Cash
59. Big Board initials
60. Eeyore's creator
62. Word that alphabetizers ignore
63. Eltanin's constellation
65. Congregation's reply
67. Hunting-lodge hatrack
70. Pass out
72. "Dadgummit!"
75. Cooper role
76. Talk-show helpers
78. "I'm ____ wits' end!"
79. Shed feathers
81. Sacred, in Soho
82. "If ____ a Rich Man"
84. Cagers' org.
85. Data in a Wallechinsky book
89. Indian Ocean island
92. Atwater-Kents
95. Author Germaine de
96. Cressida's love
97. Grass-hopper's kin
99. La ____, Calif.
100. Beasts of burden
102. Marksman
104. Winged horse of myth
105. V.I.P. of a state
107. Ill-lit
109. Singer Columbo
110. Altar affirmation
112. Globe: Abbr.
113. Ends
115. "Far above ____ waters . . ."
117. Ta-ta
120. Indiana ex-Senator
121. Kipling lad
122. "Spare ____ . . ."
127. Old woman's home
128. Placed inside: Abbr.
129. Of a mother-son complex
130. Very wide shoe
131. Neighbor of Hung.
132. Green area
133. Cathleen and Evelyn
134. Contents of a pile

DOWN

1. As ____ all outdoors
2. Mont Pelvoux, e.g.
3. Villain's closing line
4. Dandies
5. Master Aldrich
6. Martian visitors and others
7. Descartes
8. Cockney's lift
9. Baton Rouge campus
10. 1,000 mills: Abbr.
11. Medicine-show staple
12. Golden calf
13. Engaged in drudgery
14. "Five foot two, ____ blue"
15. Moslem officer
16. Dumbstruck
17. Commotion
22. Kind of media
24. Handy bit of Latin
29. The same, in a footnote
31. "Call me ____"
32. Belief
34. Mexico's Chichén ____
35. Car-radio buff, for short
37. "____ lay me . . ."
40. Zip-Dah link
42. Have ____ many (overdrink)
43. Gaining, as a clock
44. Actress Arlene
46. Howard or Ely
49. Zola novel
51. Bert's family
52. Becomes a redhead
54. No pros, they
55. Top mil. officer
57. Sold, in Somme
61. Participial suffix
64. Huxley's "____ Hay"
65. Alphonse's reply, in part drive
66. It's the word
68. Plays the snitch
69. Beatles movie
70. Modern type of power
71. "Show Boat" tune
73. Port city: Abbr.
74. Make a cameo
76. Financial official: Abbr.
77. Love-letter initials
80. Western org.
83. Time spans
84. Nests
86. West Indies waters
87. Prepare for a
88. Tire vandalism
90. ____ Cayes, Haiti
91. Talked on and on
93. Bits of activity
94. Telegraph noises
98. From one end to t'other
101. One place to see Jefferson
103. ____ zero (scoreless)
104. X-rated stuff
105. Sailors
106. City of Nebraska
108. Potato state
111. Transactions
114. Long cuts
116. Youth org.
117. Nursery need
118. Arizona tribe
119. Date for Caesar
123. ____-haw
124. Asner et al.
125. Ballpoint
126. Lubricated

Puzzle 1

```
WIEN  CAPA  CITS  PLAN
AGUE  HIES  AREA  ROBE
FORWHOMTHEBELLTOLLS
TROPES  AVID  TABLET
ORE  AMEN  LIKE
SPARE  LIEN  FINESSES
LOFT  ANDTHESEA  TAU
OLA  BUST  ARTS  LORE
PORTENT  WARM  CORNY
ERNESTHEMINGWAY
PEWIT  HESS  OUTFLOW
OLEO  SURE  MOMS  IDA
ILL  THEOLDMAN  ANDY
SELFRULE  EONS  DRESS
RATE  ANNE  SIR
ACCOST  ASST  TOARMS
DEATHINTHEAFTERNOON
DISH  NENE  NEAP  GONE
SLAY  GOON  ANDS  ETTE
```

Puzzle 2

```
TEC  TRAP  AHAB  ALAS
SARA  HOPI  TUBA  ROSE
PRINCETONTIGER  MATA
TOKYO  ASHE  HANDYMAN
OSA  TOLD  MAAM
COLUMBIALION  BRUINS
ARE  ORATE  MARY  LOCO
BOAT  ENE  BITE  TETON
OWE  BANANAS  ASS
ARIZONAWILDCATS
TOD  SEVILLE  URI
ALONE  ITIS  SAT  PALL
LIRA  ESTH  FORES  PEA
CONVEX  YALEBULLDOGS
YEAR  ISMS  YAO
WRIGGLED  TATA  SNOOT
EERO  TEXASLONGHORNS
STOA  EVIL  ERIE  RALE
TENT  DEVI  SYLT  SLY
```

Puzzle 3

```
CLARA  CALLON  BARBER
AUGUR  AMOEBA  AMELIA
SCATTERBRAIN  COBALT
CIT  EARLY  EGOS  TET
ODER  GEE  SATAN  THEE
HOLT  AMITY  TREND
DERIDE  CRATE  BOER
ELAND  PAIRS  CELESTE
COTES  RUST  BRED  KEY
APT  WISEACRES  IRE
MEL  FADE  LOIS  BETEL
PREPARE  BENET  ARETE
BRIM  PACER  CLOSET
PAROL  TACKY  DRED
LEAD  PERKY  WEE  EDOM
ERI  TUNA  SIMAR  IBO
BANTER  SIMPLEMINDED
ETERNE  ONEIDA  MOOSE
SEDATE  LENTEN  EDSEL
```

Puzzle 4

```
ABEAM  THERM  PSIS  LAST
SAMBA  HANOI  ALOE  ORTA
HIBERNATION  BEDWARMER
ILED  INEFFABLE  SIESTA
EER  STKS  TROOPS  MNO
RESPOTS  HOES  YOU  SFCS
RAY  SEPT  SHARP  MOP
CATER  HAS  SLEEPNOMORE
OLAF  RAPT  ANAP  TORME
LIKEFUN  SOUNDOFPOP
STEROID  THEDA  WRITHES
FRONTDOORS  DEEPEST
SHOED  ORTO  BEET  OUSE
LORDOFHOSTS  OUR  RISES
ART  FLAWY  OLOR  BON
BAYS  ANS  GMAN  FLATBET
WPA  DEMIES  TOAD  EVE
ARIOSO  DEGRADERS  ADIN
LANDOFNOD  SLUMBERLAND
ELKE  FIFI  ELOPE  EDUCE
FESS  ALFA  TESTS  TOBED
```

Puzzle 5

```
SUB  CARP  DELTA  BRA
NNE  ARIA  ALIEN  SEES
ILL  BEARSWALLTOWALL
PALS  ANTENNA  MARIE
ECOLE  TYPED  GRANDEE
REWIND  HOD  NOAH  ESP
PARLAY  LEOTARD
BOB  TOOT  LEA  NABES
LARGEST  SEARS  CULT
ASEA  SURPASSES  EDDA
REAP  SIEVE  PLODDER
ESKER  GEE  RAIN  YRS
ERECTED  RELETS
FOR  SOIL  PAC  RAISIN
ORBLESS  SIDED  PRIME
BARON  APLASIA  SEPT
BLOWTHEDOORSOFF  GAT
ELKS  ALERT  EDEL  ELL
DYE  MASTS  SERO  DEE
```

6

```
SMART   ARAB    AMASS
DIALER  RISE    DAVAO
INSOLE  AGHA    INEPT
NOTHINGSHORTOF
    AETA    TREASURES
AGO DOMS  ERR   LOPE
MALT  NITA   SST  CEE
PLEAS   EAVE   AWAKEN
  ASLARGEASLIFE
HONKED  ERSE   GATOR
ARD  DOP  TEXT   REDO
LEER  RIB  DIRE  DEW
FORETELLS   SELE
  FORGOODMEASURE
RANIN  RULE   TITTAT
ALONE  ISON   ONEEYE
PAWED  MESS   PERSE
```

7

```
TAPIOCA   ENCASE    AFTS
ADOLLAR   VAUNTS    IRON
MARKETTHEPLAYS    LENI
EST   CION   PIX   TEEUP
SHOWTHESTEAL    TOROSE
   HAY   TIGE   SONOF
CAPON   REDO   SPRINTER
AMRA   MILE   EPEE   SHAW
LEO  MOD   SNOCAT   ETA
ORO   KNOTTHETIDE   LIN
RIF   SATINY   MOC   AND
IGOT   STET   CBER  ANTA
COFACTOR   LOIN   ENDON
  BLOIS   RAMS   MLI
GAULIC   COOPTHEFLIES
APRIL   LAG   ORAN   ORA
OLDE   LOCUSTOFTHEDAY
LEER   ADHERE   THEWISE
SYNS   DIESIS   SERENER
```

8

```
BARB   SKIPS   VAL   BAIT
REEL   ANNAL   ONO   ANDA
ARNO   SOFIA   LILABNER
DOONESBURY   ALLEYOOP
  DRY   REST   SOL
WADIS   KID   ORC   NOMAD
ELIE   BAA   IDAHO   NATE
SIC   MUTTANDJEFF   RNA
TAKEON   ERN   STORYOF
  TAT   ASPIRES   RAW
MARTIAL   NEA   PAGODA
OCA   FLASHGORDON   REP
ARCS   ATHOS   LAX  PTAS
BOYLE   EEL   SYN  TEHEE
  ETA   MATT   ELA
WIZARDOF   BOOBMCNUTT
OLIVEOYL   ALBUM   USER
KINE   BEE   SIENA   TILE
SECS   ERE   EDDAS   SALK
```

9

```
BAND   BAND   BAND   BAND
LIEU   OVER   ODOR   ALOU
ONEO   XIII   AUTOMATIC
WURST   AMP   LINT   ARK
   RATA   KRAMER
BRAKEMEN   RATE   ABIRD
LEANTO   SAME   MILIEU
ONNO   KEEPUP   PONTIAC
WIDTH   NEUT   ALTI   ILK
  SEATED   DIETER
BRA   ILIE   BARA   RILED
LIBERIA   DIREST   PERU
OMELET   SAGE   ATOMIC
WEEMS   OTTO   ALMANACK
  SANEST   LOON
BID   EVER   MAW   ACHED
LOUISIANA   ESEL   REVU
OLAN   ETAS   OKLA   EXEC
WALK   WALK   WALK   WALK
```

10

```
AYES   ROUP   APTS   ASSI
RARE   ERNE   CROP   MAID
ALAN   DADE   COLUMBINE
BUTTERCUP   OCURI   NNE
  COLE   HUT   SCAT
PURPOSE   MENOT   ADEAL
ORIOLE   CONTRAS   ULNA
UNTIE   ROANS   POSTMAN
TAEN   AORTA   APRICOTS
  SASSES   SHEATH
BREECHES   SCARS   MATE
PUTTEES   STENS   PASHA
ODET   ROSTAND   BANTER
EYRIE   FLORA   FISSION
  NANS   ENS   SODS
PEA   ATONE   GARDENIAS
ALLAMANDA   LOGE   ERST
RILL   ALEG   ONER   WISE
RAYS   TYRE   WETS   TSAR
```

11

```
LESS   REACT   COMBO   DAMS
ALTA   OMLAH   ALIEN   AREA
TIER   AISLE   FINAL   STAR
EZWAYSTOFIXEVERYTHING
  ASCOTS   ROSES   ETC
  ERE   BOOS   IBN   USS
EZNODIETWAYTOGETSLIM
AVES   NEON   ARSON   AARE
MET   BETTE   CHAIR   ATREE
ONATEAR   AROID   ANU
ITSEZTOLIVEONEZSTREET
  RES   AMASS   ATINGLE
GOBEL   GNATS   SODAS   RLS
ANAS   TIARA   IAMA   SEAT
EZCARENOIRONGARMENTS
LAK   ADA   TSAR   ITA
  SET   HASTO   STAKES
PULLEZTABTOLIFTTHELID
ENID   ARDOR   EVERE   PESO
RIDE   RUANA   NOMAN   IMAM
ITER   FETED   TREYS   TILE
```

2

```
CAREER · EMBED · PLEADS
EMERGE · ROUTE · ROTTEN
SUNRISEATCAMPOBELLO
TRESSES · OMERS · ALB
· EWE · ALINE · PAN
RECESS · STINT · CENTUM
OPAL · NANCE · MORNING
GONE · ROTO · RANSACKS
ECON · AVION · ALII
THEAFTERNOONOFAFAUN
· ATLE · DRONE · LITE
CODICILS · AVER · ODIC
OCARINA · RATES · WELK
PARANG · LAMER · RASSES
· KEG · DIVAS · IER
STN · ROSIN · CLASSIC
THENIGHTOFTHEIGUANA
RESENT · ELOPE · CORDED
SASHES · DIRKS · SNEEZE
```

13

```
ABIB · CHEF · BOSC · LAID
NOTE · HEAL · ACTA · INTO
THEHEARTOFTHEMATTER
ARMENIA · TAOS · EPHORS
· AOR · TSIN · ALIEN
SCADS · TEAR · ADOS · YOU
ALMS · ARMSANDTHEMAN
VIA · FERN · ELDS · LSTS
ENTAILS · AXIS · DAM
SKINFLINT · BONEHEADS
· GEE · OMRI · OVERSEE
BARE · IRAE · ELAM · PAD
EYELESSINGAZA · GENE
DEL · LIMA · RUIN · LINER
· ANILS · DADO · MIV
SETOSE · CADI · DEMETER
THEHANDOFETHELBERTA
AERI · COIF · OUST · AIRY
RUST · EELY · REIS · ROES
```

14

```
ARETES · LOCAL · TAGS · POP
HEARTH · ERASE · LORAN · RAE
UPROAR · AIRTO · ELABORATE
WHISKEYONBEER · WESER
SUDS · LOON · AORT · ASPENS
IKE · LOUT · ERNE · ALTE
RUR · DENT · EIDER · STONERS
ELIDED · BRNO · STARTOUT
NEVER · FEAR · THEARM · SLO
ELEC · OLLA · SHUT · PIER
DESIROUS · PRIEST · HANDY
BUTBEERONWHISKEY
GREET · WRITES · NOISIEST
ROLL · ISME · IGOT · NATO
ABA · CRISTO · LOST · STREP
MOTORIZE · ARAN · POOLER
STERILE · PARED · SKAT · IPA
ATES · ALTO · ONER · EAT
PARTED · DREI · NAPA · ERSE
AMEER · MAKESUSFRISKY
CANDIDATE · ANAIL · ONEDAY
EST · ORDER · NITRE · LEROYS
SSE · NYES · STEED · SESTET
```

15

```
MEIR · PAULO · ASSAIL
ENNA · ESTOC · PEERCE
WEJEWSHAVEASECRET
ERI · REY · ELGIN · EFT
DOGSIT · SILOS · MARE
WEAPONIN · SORER
PLODS · OLA · ICTUSES
SOD · TALI · ACORN
ATIP · NATAL · MATES
OURSTRUGGLEWITH
SMEAR · DREAD · ENOS
CLINE · SKYS · ART
SCHISMA · HIE · ATSEA
THOSE · THEARABS
RITE · SHEAS · LIESTO
EMS · AHARD · TIN · TOZ
WEHAVENOPLACETOGO
ERODED · NIECE · OVEN
DATERS · SNITS · METE
```

16

```
SARAH   ABBE    AMPERE
SERENE  ENROLS  SMEARED
ENAMOR  MIASMA  TERRACE
TIMONOFMOSCOW   ENC
ALIT   LENS    FASHION
ESE  PATSY  AMID  ADLER
LAMS   LID    NADIR
MESSAGE  HELENOFATHENS
ONETWO  BODICE  ALOON
LOBAR  IOWAN  ALIF
TWOGENTLEMENOFSALERNO
NEST   MURRE   ETAIN
MACRO  DUENNA  GEORGE
CLIVEOFFRANCE  SADNESS
ROLEO   OEN    EELS
SCARF  BRIG  BONES  EMP
INTERIM  ONIT  NEAT
GIN   LLOYDSOFPARIS
INSTYLE  DERAIL  LAMINA
PARAPET  STERNE  OPENER
ABORTS   ONDE   PALOS
```

17

```
AHEAD   ADDS   ELECT  SHAM
RECTI   GOUT   NABOB  LALA
AIRES   OESE   ATOSS  IRAN
BLUNTINSTRUMENT  MCMIX
SIRENS  ROSY   POE
BEA  CAST  TART  POSTHOC
RALPH   AIN   SUNSHINE
ORLO  CLIPCOUPONS  ENID
ATOI  RACES  SING  TBONE
DOWNSIDE  LES  NOOSED
TEE  DULLDAY  ALL
ANTLER  NOB  ONCEOVER
DIRER  FAIT  EAGER  GORE
AXES  CUTTINGGIBE  NINA
GOASHORE  IGO  HALID
ENTRIES  DITS  LALO  EES
EDD  BIRR  FACETS
SLIME  FIVEOCLOCKSHARP
CODA  ROSIN  MOTE  HONOR
AVER  ERODE  LOSS  ONETO
DESK  DENES  IRES  TETES
```

18

```
LAHR  BASS  OSTE  APSO
IDEO  ACAT  HARM  TAOS
LILYWHITE  ALICEBLUE
IMPARTS  AGRA  EWELL
LAS  ALLA  LEIS
ABBEY  BITE  POINTSAT
CAL  REDHERRING  EWE
MIA  BORA  SING  MELS
ETCHING  AVES  HEIST
KOLA  WARPS  DARN
SPOOK  MILK  RENEGED
LAUD  RUED  BACK  RAY
ART  YELLOWJACK  EVA
TASSELED  RORY  ARDEN
AMAS  MEIN  ARE
ALBEN  BONN  ESTATES
GREENCROW  INTHEPINK
YEAR  EYRE  NATO  ERDA
MARS  DEED  GNAT  REST
```

19

```
PETER  SILOAM  SAFE
ARETE  AMERCE  PRIM
GREATEXPECTATIONS
EONS  WOUKS  IRAN
DRY  TENTS  CATERS
HORSE  CAMUS
SCANS  PARIS  ANT
SWART  SILLS  SLOE
LASTOFTHEMOHICANS
ALEE  ROADS  NOTES
BEY  POOLS  MARES
DANTE  PRONE
SPORTS  CLARE  FEE
AIRS  COATS  ERAS
THEMILLONTHEFLOSS
RITE  AERATE  AIMEE
IBAR  MEANER  GAELS
```

20

21

23

22

24

C	A	R	P	E		S	T	O	L	E			V	I	S	A	S
A	B	O	U	T		C	A	R	R	A	R	A		P	A	R	T	L	Y
S	E	C	R	E	T	A	R	Y	B	I	R	D		M	O	N	S	O	O	N
E	L	K	E		A	R	G	O		C	O	I	L	E	R		N	O	G
D	E	S		L	I	V	E	N		A	R	T	I	S	T	S	L	I	F	E
			H	A	L	E		E	L	S		F	A	S	T	E	N
T	O	L	E	D	O		G	A	L		I	T	S		R	A	G	E	D
E	L	U	D	E	R		A	R	M	A	D	A	S		W	I	S	T	E	R
R	I	N	G		S	L	U	E		W	E	N		O	R	A	T	O	R	Y
M	O	T	E		T	A	C	T	I	L	E		S	N	I	T		N	O	S
		S	W	A	T	H	E	S		P	L	A	I	T	E	D
S	M	A		E	C	H	O		E	S	S	E	N	C	E		A	B	E	T
P	A	N	C	A	K	E		U	R	E		V	E	E	R		R	O	P	E
A	S	T	O	R	S		P	L	E	A	S	E	S		S	M	I	L	E	R
S	T	E	V	E		S	E	T		A	R	T		C	A	N	T	E	R
		C	E	R	A	T	E		R	G	T		B	R	I	G
P	O	E	T	S	C	O	R	N	E	R		A	B	E	A	M		L	A	S
R	F	D		U	N	S	U	R	E		L	O	A	M		S	O	R	T
I	T	E	R	A	T	E		B	U	T	L	E	R	S	P	A	N	T	R	Y
D	E	N	U	D	E		S	N	E	E	R	A	T		T	O	T	A	L
E	N	T	R	E			S	L	O	T	H			T	B	O	N	E

25

G	A	L	L		T	R	A	C	T		S	A	D	E		F	O	R	A
E	T	U	I		R	I	D	E	R		E	D	E	N		R	E	B	E	C
N	O	M	A	N	I	S	A	N	I	S	L	A	N	D		E	R	E	C	T
U	N	P	R	O	V	E	D		F	I	F	T	Y		B	R	Y	C	E
S	E	Y		T	E	N		B	O	R	I	S		A	W	A	I	T	E	D
			B	E	T		A	R	R	A	S		S	M	I	T	C	H
O	R	L	E	S		S	T	E	M	T	H	E	T	I	D	E		A	B	A
M	E	E	D		S	U	L	A			T	A	T	E		S	T	O	P
A	N	T		S	P	E	A	K	S	O	F	T	L	Y		S	T	I	L	E
R	E	T	R	E	A	T	S		T	R	I	L	L		S	H	A	M	E	D
			H	A	I	R	Y		F	A	B	L	E		S	T	R	I	P
S	T	E	R	N	E		M	A	N	I	C		S	P	E	E	D	U	P	S
P	U	R	E	E		H	O	L	D	T	H	E	W	I	N	D		L	O	P
A	L	E	E		L	A	T	S			X	E	N	O		A	S	S	E
N	A	B		W	E	T	H	E	P	E	O	P	L	E		G	R	E	E	D
		E	R	A	S	E	S		R	E	V	O	L		P	R	Y
B	E	L	O	V	E	D		C	A	R	E	S		T	R	A		V	P	S
E	L	I	D	E		S	E	N	I	R		T	E	A	S	P	O	O	N
T	I	G	E	R		P	E	A	C	E	A	T	A	N	Y	P	R	I	C	E
E	T	H	O	S		E	A	S	E		R	O	U	S	E		A	C	H	E
L	E	T	S			A	L	E	S		M	E	T	E	R		M	E	E	R

26

S	P	O	N	D	E	E		P	A	U	L	S		B	O	S	S
R	E	G	A	I	N	S		R	U	P	E	E		I	D	E	A	S
T	A	L	K	O	F	T	H	E	T	O	W	N		T	E	R	R	A
A	T	E		R	I	R	E	S		L	I	A	S		A	J	A	X
			P	A	N	E	L		H	U	S	T	L	E		E	N	E
I	S	L	A	M		L	I	M	E			O	N	D	A
S	T	A	T	A		L	O	A	D	S		D	E	T	E	N	T	E
M	E	D	I		P	A	S	A	D	E	N	A		W	A	T	E	R
	Y	O	G	A			A	G	O	N		I	N	B	A	D
T	I	C		R	U	M	E	R	G	O	D	D	E	N		U	S	A
A	S	H	O	E		A	R	O	A		M	E	T	Z
B	E	A	S	T		P	R	O	B	A	T	E	S		A	F	A	R
S	E	T	T	E	E	S		F	L	E	E	S		P	R	U	N	E
		T	E	L	L			E	R	A	S		A	N	Z	I	O
A	Y	E		S	E	A	L	E	R		R	E	A	R	S
N	O	R	A		F	R	E	D		P	U	N	T	O		I	A	L
A	D	L	I	B		G	O	S	S	I	P	C	O	L	U	M	N	S
S	E	E	D	Y		O	N	E	R	S		E	L	E	M	E	N	T
		L	Y	S	E		S	E	L	A	H		S	E	D	A	T	E	S

27

J	O	S	H		I	H	A	D	A		P	A	W		N	E	P		F	R	O	M
A	L	T	O		S	O	P	U	P		H	E	R		O	M	O		R	E	D	O
M	I	C		M	A	N	T	L	E		I	C	E	H	O	C		G	A	M	E	S
I	V	Y		A	D	O	L	L	S			A	O	N	E			U	N	I	T	S
E	E	R		L	O	R	Y		P	A	N	T	S		E	N	A	C	T	S
			E	A	R	S		B	L	A	N	C	H	E	D		A	M	I
L	I	B	R	A		L	A	R	G	O		D	O	N	T		S	A	M	E
D	E	B	A		B	U	R	K	E			Z	O	O		S	T	O	W
O	N	I	N		S	H	O	E	R	S		T	A	M	E	R		S	C	O	R	E
N	O	D		L	E	A	K	Y		N	Y	L	O	N	S		H	O	M	E	S
O	R	E	M		E	A	R	N		O	P	E	N		E	D	I	T
R	E	M	O	T	E		D	I	S	C	J	O	C	S		I	N	T	U	N	E
			N	A	P	S		G	A	R	O		S	P	E	C			N	E	S
R	I	C	S		A	S	H	L	E	Y		S	H	A	R			D	A	T
A	L	O	S	S		B	I	T	T	E		D	O	I	N	G	S		S	O	R	E
S	L	O	E		A	R	T		T	R	U	N	K		B	A	N	E	S
H	Y	L	E		D	E	A	L		G	O	O	S	E	Y		G	O	N	E	R
			M	A	A		R	E	L	I	E	V	E	S		T	U	R
T	R	O	I	K	A		M	O	N	D	E		P	H	I	Z		T	O	D
A	H	A	N	D		B	L	O	C		A	B	U	E	L	O		E	M	U
D	O	N		S	E	R	E	N	A	D	E		T	U	R		D	I	N	N	E	R
A	R	I	D		V	A	N		L	U	G		T	R	I	T	E		I	A	G	O
M	O	N	O		A	M	O		S	E	G		A	R	M	O	R		X	M	A	S

28

DOSE · ROWS · GIST · LTD
ERIN · EPEE · ANTA · SOIREE
MINDOVERMATTER · ALSACE
USN · NONE · DERMA · TITIAN
ROE · EKE · BOLUS · RIVEN
ENDOWED · ANET · PERIDOT
WAD · BRIGHTIDEA · FRA
PATLY · POTS · ANTS · ATAN
ASHY · TORO · SALTO · APHID
RHO · THINKINGCAP · BOON
STUDIO · REI · RESULT
AGUE · FRAMEOFMIND · GOO
ABHOR · RADAR · OILS · SHAD
RUTS · TIME · VILE · OUTDO
ALP · BRAINCHILD · SCI
ARMOIRE · LACE · TATTLER
OASES · FEMUR · ILO · EVE
FACETS · GRAIN · ITUP · GAS
ARENOT · MENTALATTITUDE
TISANE · ADUE · OGLE · OMEN
LSD · NAPS · TOES · PEST

29

AQUA · CAMPI · AMAT · MIEN
BUND · ACORN · BEREA · AXLE
CARE · NADIA · ERINS · RIOS
REPONDEZSILVOUSPLAIT
STATU · RENO · STARE
TED · STANDINGROOMONLY
KRYPTON · TIROS · BEAST
USUALE · CAT · UTE · DEI
SPAR · CHELA · NIECE · PYRE
MULISH · SITED · FLAME
UNITEDSTATESOFAMERICA
AMOLE · ERODE · SASSED
ELAN · WARNS · NACHT · ITEA
GAL · ANT · ATE · STEERS
GRAIN · PIEDA · BROTHER
SIGNALOFDISTRESS · OSA
NUMEN · TESA · INSTS
REVOLUTIONSPERMINUTE
OMAR · STARY · STEAD · DILL
OISE · EERIE · ISSUE · ELLE
FRED · RDGS · SETIN · SEAT

30

MADRID · UPSET · SOG · ELSA
AVOICE · MOONY · ORE · MAID
MIDRIFFBULGE · FANDANGO
EVOE · IREFUL · FATTENING
WAIR · SALA · ESTA
HELPINGS · NUMBS · ETHER
ARIOSTO · BADGER · GREENE
TIGRE · BIN · OTO · SATS
ICHOR · POST · FEARNO · VET
NATS · BITT · BANDIED · YRS
SECRETARIALSPREAD
FIN · REMOTES · AILS · PUPA
ARA · SEAMED · URDE · SITES
TACT · DNS · AGE · HAIRS
ANKERS · UNSURE · SIENESE
LISLE · SPAIN · RECLOSES
LAMA · GRIP · AREA
THESCALES · CLINIC · ASIS
RELATION · POUNDFOOLISH
ARIL · ZOO · ARMEE · LEADTO
PEAL · ENS · SNEER · DRIEST

31

PILAF · APPAL · ADAM · ARABIC
AMINO · DRUPE · TATE · HELENA
LITTLEMISSMUFFET · AGATES
OTT · NICHE · GOOSE · ARTES
MAL · CAREY · CARET · BALMY
ATE · AMES · CANT · RILL · BRA
REBATED · HANDYSPANDY · LIN
OREL · SANTA · TANGO · FUND
PAYER · MURAL · KATIE · ELEGY
ELBA · SIMPLESIMON · ERA
ELL · TANEY · ATEN · GRASPED
LAUGHTER · LOREN · BOOTHOME
SHEARER · GOAD · SOLDO · LIB
BED · OLDKINGCOLE · ELLA
TITLE · CRAZY · ARABY · SAYER
OBOE · SAND · APERY · SURF
DAM · ELSIEMARLEY · SHELLAC
ORT · RATS · ARCED · PLOD · IRA
USAGE · FITAS · LEAVE · NIT
FACTS · LANIN · HEAVE · DEC
UPKEEP · ELIZABETHELSPETH
SIERRA · ASTA · URGER · HARTE
SEREST · PEEN · GOONY · ANSER

32

SAMBA | NOAH | PAD | DDE
SALAAM | ARMOR | TONIC | NUIT
SATCHELPAIGE | HENRYLODGE
SRO | TRIPLE | PARMA | CORES
INEE | ADOS | SLOG
ATM | AGED | LION | COMEDIE
LEADSON | GEORGEBURNS | OMA
DEREKS | CORDS | OTOE | BRAS
ESSES | MARNE | BARED | MOORE
RUHR | RING | PEPES | POUTED
SPA | DANIELBEARD | FOUGHT
LOAVES | LIETO | SLUSHY
SLATES | HARLANSTONE | PLO
SIFTED | PONDS | TOED | MAID
ARIES | LIMOS | PEERS | CARVE
BRER | CASE | HONEY | DARKEN
EEL | HOWARDBAKER | CARTERS
REDWINE | EERY | CANT | RYE
IRAS | SPAT | MARC
ARLEN | STORM | SAREES | ERA
BRAMSTOKER | ANDREWMELLON
TATA | SAINT | NEALS | AROUSE
UNE | RNS | TKOS | NEWLY

33

SCOPE | CLOGUP | SOAPS
ORNATE | RETYPE | ANDRE
NEARAT | IGOROT | LEVEE
GETSTHEBUSINESS | AFS
SPEE | ALP | ERN | GNAR
RINSE | GASSY | ECCE
AFG | OIE | AMS | STEED
BLEWUP | FATAL | AIS
IOTA | VAL | LETSLOOSE
ERAT | GANT | GEEK | VIAL
LATCHONTO | AVE | ELKE
HAP | HOMME | TUREEN
POSOL | ENS | PRR | RNA
ETTU | ABBAS | EYING
AHAT | DOR | UTA | ORAE
CEN | GONEWITHTHEWIND
OLDTO | HEARTY | ANEDGE
CLING | AZRAEL | UNSEEN
KONGO | METERS | STARS

34

CATHER | TBAR | ADDAS | CHASE
ATHOME | AERO | DAILY | OILER
PLENUM | MYSONMYSON | NADER
RACKS | PALOMA | THESISTERS
ASHE | HELEN | BRIES | STUNS
IDEATES | FOAMS | BEAS
PEL | AWES | SABRE | MIEN | OWE
ANDOVER | VALSE | SONATINAS
CARPED | SOUS | SANE | WRIST
TRETS | UNCLEVANYA | SIMONE
SENS | SLOE | EGOS | INFANTS
GRAB | SEROW | ELIE
LATERAN | CATS | SLIT | CPAS
ADELAS | FATHERTIME | TORRE
NOLAN | LOSE | AIDS | TRYOUT
GRANDPAPA | MAINE | GRANDMA
ENE | MENS | SENSE | PRIG | IST
LOLA | PHASE | SHAPING
ABATE | PLATA | ATOMS | EARS
BROTHERRAT | TANANA | ALLEN
ARNEE | AUNTIEMAME | LESSEE
LODER | SNEES | AMER | GROOVE
TWINS | PETRO | TENS | SINNER

35

OMERS | BRADS | ASSUAGE
ACADIA | TEACUP | STIRRER
LEXICOGRAPHER | TANNING
ELITE | LIST | LACING | SRO
ONO | RANT | SIWARD | BEET
TERRACE | TESLA | TAO
SERE | VICTIMSOFNERO
THEE | HAM | NAT | FADED
BOIL | JER | DAG | ASARULE
CARP | SOLDIER | ASTI | CAN
ART | SCHOOLTEACHER | ATS
UBI | CANT | LEARNER | ATEE
MELLONS | PER | NED | AMOR
ALLER | OAL | RES | ADAR
SLAININBATTLE | LIEN
LYN | EYERS | CENSURE
ALMA | BRASSY | THRU | EEL
MIS | PEANUT | OHIO | SNARE
ENTRAIN | PRIMEMINISTER
BEATING | TURNIP | EVIANS
ARRANGE | ONAIR | TASSO

36

| T | A | C | O | M | A | | | R | O | M | E | | | C | O | R | | | P | L | A | I | N | S |

```
TACOMA   ROME   COR    PLAINS
APEMAN   IMAM   SOLE   LARGOS
NEREID   TARP   AMID   UNTOST
DERRYGARYANDMOUNTAIRY
     SEER   ALOW   SCOOTS
TSP   STAT   SENOR   ETCETERA
APIS   TES   OREL   URD   VAN
NAMPAPAMPAANDTAMPA   PACE
AREOLE   PURPOSIVE   TSADES
GENTLE   TROP   EADS   WREST
ATT   ERR   MESA   BARRIE
HOUMAYUMAANDMONTEZUMA
NATALE   LYRA   ADZ   AMS
SPAIN   NOTE   INTO   ALETAP
TIRADE   SEPARATOR   CERATE
ALIT   SHERIDANANDMERIDEN
BOS   OCA   SCOP   GEO   SOUD
STELLULA   SPICK   RIMA   RRS
OILERS   TELI   RIPA
CLOVERDOVERANDHANOVER
RAISIN   EPEE   MERO   CLAROS
ASSENT   NOES   OTUS   ELINOR
HAINES   TRS   ROME   SONOMA
```

37

```
SPA   HARSH   TSPS   FRAN
HAIL   ABOMA   EQUI   LEGAL
UNCLEREMUS   AUNTIEMAME
TEASDALE   BORA   REAPED
PISE   LEROT   POTTED
OBIES   SHEAF   ESNES
PARC   GRANDFATHER   MRA
OTOE   BOAS   CHAR   DYED
PST   ELSAS   DRAW   CASED
HOVEL   PLAIN   SHROVE
PLENARY   BLOND   STERNER
HERESY   POINT   CAROM
AERIE   TACT   ECLAT   YET
STAN   SETH   RILE   PSIS
EST   INTHEFAMILY   AONE
PLIES   AVAST   MARNE
CHILDS   PLOTS   CADI
JOANNE   ETNA   POLISHED
SISTERKATE   DENMOTHERS
DRIES   AVER   ODEON   ERGO
STRS   TESS   ROUSE   SOS
```

38

```
DEBAR   SOAR   SCAB   TODD
ERODE   BOMBE   THIO   EVER
CARDI   ARABS   OILY   SEMA
ASOLDASTHEHILLS   STREP
LENE   SHEA   LID   MATURE
DATER   SAID   WATUSI
ICS   BASS   WPA   IAN   BET
TOTAL   PERCENTAGE
SHAMES   DAD   DAT   ABET
MOTA   APOGEE   IRA   BALI
ERIN   COMINGOFAGE   BANG
TOFF   WIN   ORIGEN   ISEE
SNOB   DNA   ACE   EMETIN
RIPEOLDAGE   ASIDE
AGA   ORS   APE   OBIT   CST
COLONY   PITS   NONES
SCALED   CES   KAYS   IMPS
POLAR   THEYOUNGATHEART
ORIG   POOR   SNEER   ISSUE
IDEE   ERSE   ADARS   STONE
LOSS   NEED   RODS   SANER
```

39

```
IHAVE   KEEP   AHAB   SWANS
MARIA   ILLE   ROBE   AIMEE
ALMOSTLIKEBEHANINLOVE
LIONS   PROOF   SELLER
ASCEND   FEEL   TALLIERS
SOONGOFNORWAY   LAYS
CRAT   LARS   ARAM   CAM
HET   PUTT   CRAM   LODI
LISTOFTHEREDHOTMAMAS
COMFY   VALES   EOCENE
ATEAWAY   FINER   AERATOR
LOLLED   BONER   ASHER
LOVELETTUCEINTHESAND
ALIS   EURE   ESCE   YOM
YES   FAST   BREA   ALMA
PILL   HEARTANDSEOUL
SURENESS   ASIS   ALONSO
PLEASE   PARTE   PENAL
INTHESTILLOFTHEKNIGHT
FARER   ELLA   EVIL   TAPER
FRONT   CLAP   DALY   SNOWY
```

40

| B A T C H | M O L D | B R A T | A M A Z E |

```
BATCH  MOLD  BRAT  AMAZE
ORALE  AREA  ROLE  RUPEE
ACTOR  ORAL  IOTA  OTTER
THEPETRIFIEDFOREST
EIR  HIS  YET  FLEECED
RESEDA  ORE  RHUS  RARE
DENTURE  OEIL  SERIN
OLDOAKENBUCKET  GARRET
REO  TSARINAS  OAR
LATCH  ITEM  DUPLICATE
OVER  IMPEDIMENTS  STAN
PEDIGREED  SIVA  CARLS
RAT  GENERATE  IOU
RETAIN  CASSTIMBERLANE
EMEND  COCA  ENSURES
AMAT  BANC  IDS  ASTRAY
MAKESUP  ROB  ASP  OLE
DESIREUNDERTHEELMS
MACAW  TODS  URGE  PALOS
ORATE  ASIT  SNOW  OVINE
TAPED  LETS  TETS  SENDS
```

41

```
BERT  BORG  VEAL  SPEC
AGAR  MALAR  ATLES  HARM
GOFORARIDE  GOESAROUND
LONGDISTANCERUNNER
HOTLINE  AHAB  ABA
ETHEL  STATO  SAC  SRAS
DOERS  MAIM  NOTRE  ITA
DEBS  HILO  DRAIN  ODOR
ASI  PARENT  LARD  BRENT
GROVE  ROOTS  CRATER
OPPOSED  CARVE  THENOSE
ROAMER  COMTE  HEATH
SIRED  DUMP  ROTUND  OAM
ORAS  TILES  URGE  TUNE
NOD  EVERT  STAS  HENNA
STEM  HAT  EXPOS  ELDER
ADE  ALEF  ARALSEA
WANDERINGMINSTRELS
OVERMATURE  STARTSOVER
RAMI  NADIR  EERIE  FIRE
ELOD  LETS  RPTS  FEAT
```

42

```
ORA  ANITA  TIFF  SABOT
PERIMETER  APERS  THANI
ENGROSSED  PAREE  RAGES
DEARS  MONEYINTHEBANK
INT  SEROW  ACTUP  SEE
ATTESTED  NOM  HON  ASST
III  CAR  SERAIS  GENES
MONEYEARNSMONEYAND
NEXT  IOU  FAIRCATCH
OHO  ABCS  MLI  LISA
WARDENS  SHAHS  LACUNAS
ECTO  THB  LEHR  NOS
THENTHERE  LOU  HIFI
THEMONEYMONEYEARNS
CHIEF  OGRESS  RON  ETO
AREA  ARK  ELM  TRUSTEES
TOA  TROTS  LENOS  APR
EARNSMOREMONEY  CANON
ATSEA  KOTOW  MONEYTREE
SITAR  SUAVE  ENTREATED
EASTS  TEED  ASHES  SSS
```

43

```
SEC  ARRAS  BASH  GIFTS
ADA  MIAMI  OSCAR  ORIOLE
THEFLOATINGOPERA  DENIES
RANEES  GEE  INEPT  ALES
ARISE  PRO  MARES  OMELET
MAT  BRASS  HIS  SPIDER
NESTLES  LOAN  STERE  SID
TREY  BARB  FLUKE  SOSO
BABIED  SLID  FAUNA  RIFLE
ORALS  FAUN  MITES  FALTER
ETTE  BEAR  BUNA  EARTH
RAH  BEERBARRELPOLKA  EFT
IVIES  SOAR  RISE  ASIA
LINERS  SPOOL  BASE  FEELS
EGGED  STAND  CANE  CORALS
NOBS  SCALE  CONK  BALI
ARE  PEARL  RUNG  COLDEST
ASTERS  CUR  SPOOK  PUP
TULANE  FASTS  LOB  TRIBE
BETA  DARNS  ABO  SOONER
OPINED  WATERTOWNNEWYORK
BEETLE  EMOTE  RENEW  ASI
ESSAY  ERSE  GREEN  LEN
```

44

```
BLAST   APA   DIDAH   ABBE
EARTH  BANC  EDEMA    REAR
ENURE ODDLOTOFBROKERS
REMUS   LOOM   SELEN
NIL  ORRIS  NEMATODE
PECKSOFCRITICS   SNAFUS
ALA  ILKAS  MOE   LINE
ROSSINI  SPAS   BOLDER
FITIN  TRAILL    ARNEE
AGORAS  EMOTE  DETRACT
INF HEAPOFUSEDCAR  POA
TESTONE  FATTY  DIVEAT
KELTS   LIT  HEH  AMORT
SPIREA   RACE   ELLIPSE
PEEK   EVE  EGALE   LER
ARREST PARTYOFPOOPERS
DISLOYAL  SHEAF   NOR
ARLOS   ALTO    LATHE
LOADSOFWORRIERS  OTHER
ARIA  NIECE  DEDO  NEARS
WORD  ENDOF  DST  GRIST
```

45

```
ANKARA  CREST  MORT  RELIC
WEEDED  ROMEO  ABOU  UREDO
NONAGENARIAN  SEPTENNIAL
OPENER   THOSE    LOAFED
RIDS  TEEM  DIANE   SUN
EMOTES  ANT  CRITIQUE
SPUES  SINGLEENTRIES  URN
URBAN  TOILES  ORALS  HASA
MOLLE  ANNAS  AMUSE  EDIT
EVES  SNITS  FLESH  CARNE
DEB  DECAHEDRONS  REVUES
ABELE  OER  POLYP
SORREL  TETRAHEDRAL  LAS
ORRIS  HORTE  IVIED  CELT
OPEC  TOPAY  ASIZE  SOFIA
NILE  SEROS  BATTEN  TRUMP
ENE  SEXAGENARIANS  ANGEL
REDSTATE  ORO  TRIUNE
ORB  THORN  LAVA  SETS
URANIA  SHAKE  HABITS
PENTAGONAL  TRIPLETHREAT
DETAT  RANT  TENSE  LAURIE
OSAGE  AGES  ESTER  ENTIRE
```

46

```
HAT  SCALE  TONIC  TOPER
NOPE  TATAR  EDINA  SHOVES
TWENTYFOURACROSS  PALACE
HEDDA  FEDIN  ABUTS  RYDER
ROSE  ENTS  ELIM  ATEST
ASTI  WILDGOAT  TROW  HRS
SPILLANE  NRA  OGIVE
SIN  ANETS  SATURN  TENSED
ANDES  TOO  SAO  REEVE
MEED  PELTS  RUGGED  MEW
TRIPPER  THEW  TRADUCER
COATIS  AEI  SATIRE
RETICENT  HELP  DETENTE
DOR  TARGET  TALUS  TEMP
OLAVI  PIA  GSA  TONIA
METIER  USAGES  UTICA  ELD
CRISP  ALE  EDUCATED
PET  BESS  RECORDER  ISSY
BIJOU  RUIN  ERLE  OLOR
ONERS  ARLES  EDSEL  SPARE
LACIER  GETTOTHEBOTTOMOF
ENTERO  ENTER  ADAGE  ROOT
GASSY  STAND  TANYA  TIM
```

47

```
FAINT  CASTE  MAME  OLDEN
OCCUR  ACTOR  ICON  SORTE
ROESOFSHARON  GROSS  WAITS
TOR  MISERY  EARED  TEMPUS
ELS  POISE  AGRAS  BEG
ERN  BRACT  NOLO  JAR
SIBS  DIEDINTHEWOOL  HAVE
ORATES  RENEE  ALIA  ONES
LARES  DRAG  SUDAN  PRUNE
EDEMA  HARERAISING  ARAGE
DEM  COTE  ELMO  STORED
OTTAWA  ALI  CANARY
FLURRY  ICAL  NERA  SIS
LANAI  LOSTTHECENT  LEASH
ANTIS  IDEAS  AGTS  AVILA
KUAN  APIA  ELDER  STOLEN
EGIS  FOURINSERVICE  ESTE
DON  SLIM  NOTRE  ORE
PAD  SLEEP  RANIN  ADD
IMADAM  PEALE  PENTAD  VIR
MYFARELADY  MALEDELIVERY
ATALE  INGE  MOVES  VIRGA
SHRED  BEER  IDEST  EASED
```

48

RAFT HOPI UPONA ASTORIA
UGLY EARN NABOB RIOTING
FAIR BRAVISSIMO ANDAMAN
UPROAR DINES IDLE TALE
SET LASONNAMBULA QUELLS
VAIN OSTEAL DOUR
COCA CONV SENORAS ARS
AMISH BEES ASSE ANAGRAM
PARCEL BRANDO WACO ECCE
ENCORE IVANS HUN NAIL
SEN TANA UDAL FIDEL
FACESALANGUAGEBARRIER
SURLY ZEST SEAU ROI
IRMA PAS SEANS VESTAL
GRAV AREA TANDEM ENTIRE
MODISTE SCUM AXIS DINGO
AWA WINESAP MATH LYON
ISER PANAMA AARE
IBEAMS DANSEMACABRE SUP
BOLT EWER TITHE PLINTH
EYESORE POSTERIORI MATA
REVERIE ASHEN NNES ARES
TREATED DEEDS ASST MERE

49

STOWE ABBA JAMB CRASS
HORAL HELD OLEO HANNA
ERATO STEALHERBLANKET
MENTHE ENGINE BINGLEY
MILO NIN LIEN ERR
TAKEMETOYOURWEEDER
ALOT AIM SEEN LINDY
FLIER SNUG STIES AIRA
TENREC ITISTHESCENTER
NESTED EGO ENTERTAIN
OLAV ILL TENO
CYCLOTRON TOO RIDING
HEREKITTYKITTY CEREAL
IDUN CHELA STAB DIGBY
TOXIC DONG LOO DELE
NOTHINGITJUSTWAVED
SAT CAAN SHA CHIC
PRESORT POMACE EGERIA
ITSTOOFARTOWALK GOING
FITIN UNIT ENOW LUNGE
FEARS LAGO DANS ESKER

50

CACTI ALMAS MERCI SCOT
ALLEN BEAME EXERT CALEB
PLEAS OAKUM RUGAE ENERO
AWOMANWHOLIVEDINMONTANA
SENATE ESE ELK PIANET
NITER TOR DEDUCT
MAA AHMED LAPP DOL ABCS
ECLAT AMICI AIM REA IAT
WASSEENINADIRTYBANDANNA
STOP TATES MAYOR TAGDAY
SAT CAPP NAB NALDI
WHENTHEYHOLLEREDUNCLEAN
RANEE DUE EATA TEE
ASNERS MILAN CESTA ESQS
SHEDECLAREDTHEYWEREMEAN
SEA SAO STE ERRED SUEDE
EDDY RUR AREA EDICT PIE
EASTER SRS ENOIL
RIALTO VEL ATO SMOCKS
ANDLEFTINAHUFFFORHAVANA
NADIA ALAPA ETAPE TEREK
GWENS PETAL LETIN EMILE
EDGE ADAZE TREED DEBTS

51

SATIRE TASK GAMED
TREVES OLEO PERIGEE
ARRAYS QUESTIONMARX
TARN ARUM HARI LIT
UNO SYNE ORANGEAIDE
STRIPES BUENO STEN
FARR LETBE PRIEST
AMIGAS EROS SAUD
LEROY SELF DECREPIT
AIM STREPTEAS STU
DRAWAWAY LAIR MAYAN
OLAY BAIT MUSCLE
LABRET VEINY INCH
IVES SINCE ANCHORS
MARTINETTE SHAH PUT
IRT NEUT LIAR THAR
TIRANASAURUS ETHANE
SCALERS PUNS TRENDS
EMIRS INKY SANTAS

52

53

54

55

56

PICK · SWANS · BPOE · HOHO'S
ADUE · MONTH · LARD · OPERA
TERNFORTHEWURST · MIRAK
HAT · LODE · AERIE · DENOTE
WAT · ARABS · SERENER
STORKHOLDERS · FAMISH
HOMEY · NEDDY · MALIC · OAR
AMEN · TEE · GAVOT · CUKE
WEND · BIRDOFAVON · ORNIS
ELAM · RARER · GOODTO
SECRETE · FITIN · DROWSED
KALINE · MEETS · EDOM
AGENT · HOLLYHAWKS · AWLS
TRAG · TAPIS · LOA · GAIT
EER · DOTED · AMEER · ANILE
DUELER · GROUSEPROFIT
SCENTED · FAINT · HEN
WALLET · CASED · EARN · EMU
ALOON · LARKSANDBEAGLES
GLOAT · ONCE · LODEN · IMRE
SANDE · BEET · ERATO · GOER

57

OSTIA · TRISTE · POUNDS
LEANS · EOLIAN · LINEUP
PHILHARMONIC · ALPACA
ERNA · IRAN · PEDS · APES
WARY · ARE · ETUI
RAS · SECT · BILLETDOUX
ANNAS · LOCI · EIRE · NNE
STEVEDORE · GAS · SEDAN
PIERROT · LARK · YESO
ITCH · LEI · DOVE
ETAL · GATE · ORIFICE
CROSS · GAR · VANCOUVER
CAN · TOOL · MEIN · LLANO
EMERYBOARD · LYRE · SES
ULES · END · BETA
ALES · LEES · ERRE · POLY
BONSAI · TOMFOOLERIES
ALAINS · ARIOSO · ROSSE
DAMASK · STREAK · SNEER

58

LAW · ORB · SOAP · ABCD
AUTO · AREA · ABLE · BEAR
ALONGWAYTOTIPPERARY
RUMORED · TRI · SPRINT
VIS · MEANS · END
ASTEP · BURN · PUREGOLD
LAHR · PAN · BEN · EVER
ERE · LILIMARLENE · ENE
CABRINI · ELUL · ADORED
AHAT · BRENS · GNAT
TYRONE · RIRE · AGATHAS
UAR · ARMENTIERES · ELA
ALES · ONO · GAD · DREW
MELLOWED · CHAN · GREEN
ACE · ALLEN · MAI
TESTAE · OER · SIZZLER
THEHALLSOFMONTEZUMA
IOLE · TEEN · ALIT · LAIT
MUSS · HEDY · NET · EUR

59

ETTAS · ROBERT · PAGAN
ADRIFT · OCREAE · HEAVE
WHEELERDEALER · ARMED
ESA · PEELS · SNEE · ERS
TOP · LOOSE · SYDOW
DRILLMASTERS · ERRANT
RUNSOUT · SNIP · AGREE
URGE · REFS · EMIT · ADEN
NAM · RUT · PERTNESS
ABS · SUPERSEEDER · NEE
TRAVERSE · ERR · MAB
LIFE · SIDE · ISNO · REZA
ANENT · SONS · OLEATES
SEGUES · MOTORCOACHES
USEOF · LEVEE · REE
ARA · PURO · PENNY · RAU
SERVE · OXFORDTOOTERS
EADIE · DELUDE · GAWAIN
APSES · ORATOR · ATOLL

60

```
B E S S . A S P . G A S . I S I S
E X P E D I T E . E X O C R I N E
S C R E A M E R . R E F L E X E S
T A E . M E W . M A S . P X S . .
. V A T . D E M E T E R . R E P .
R A D A R . D I X O N . S I N E S
A T O N E S . L I P . F I A C R E
P E N . D I G A T . S O X . E T A
. . O X E N . X Y S T . . . . . .
A M E . U T E . T E R S E . M A D
S A X O N Y . L A B . A E R A T E
A C T E D . S A X E S . N I X O N
. H E R . M E X I C A N . D I M .
D I R . E A R . . V I M . M I L .
A N N E X I V E . C A N O N I Z E
L E A V E N E D . O N E D O Z E N
I S L E . E S E . P T S . W E R T
```

61

```
F A U C E T . D R I P . B A K E R
I G N O R E . E A R L . A L I N E
N A T H A N . A B O U . R E L I C
I V I E S . C L I N G S . A L G A
S E E R . S L I D . G U M . E M S
. . . E A T E N . D E M O C R A T
P O P . B U R G . A R U L E . . .
T H E R A N K S . E S P A L I E R
A N E A T . . . . . S L O P E . .
S O L I T U D E . A N D S A T I N
. S E P I A . R O U E . A C T . .
P E T E R P A N . B O A S T . . .
O D E . Y E T . F I N D . H A R E
L I R A . R O T A T E . T U B E R
I T A L S . M O V E . L I M B E R
C O T E S . I G O R . I M P O S E
E R O S E . C A R S . V E S T E D
```

62

```
M O S S . A V A S T . A H E A D . W A L K
O C T A . D E L T A . M A R I A . A L E E
T H E I N V I S I B L E M A N F R I D A Y
T R A . O I L O F . O R A L . F A V O R S
S E L A H S . F A G I N . C O V E . . . .
. C I E S . E R I C . B O D E . S T E . .
T R E N T S L A S T C A S E H I S T O R Y
R A T E . A C T E . N E A L . O D E R . .
E L A . N O V O . B O R N . S P A K E . .
A P P R O V E R . P A R R . A P I . . . .
T H E E T E R N A L C I T Y S L I C K E R
. L O N . S A T E . A P P R A I S E . . .
B A S I N . A R T Y . L O S E . R T E . .
A L A S . O L O R . A L T O . T I O S . .
W A S H I N G T O N S Q U A R E D A N C E
L I S . M E A L . O P U S . S N I T . . .
. A P S E . S W E A T . R A S H E S . . .
S A N S E I . B A H T . R A T O N . O V A
T H E O L D W I V E S T A L E B E A R E R
O I N K . E I N E R . A T O N E . P A N G
A R E A . D E G R E . M E E T S . T E T E
```

63

```
C A P A N D . D R O S S . H A T I N
A P O G E E . R E N E E . I R O N I C
T U R R E T . I S T L E . T O M A T O
C R E E . A L L T H E S A M E . P W A
H E R E D I T Y . E N A T E . C E I L
. T O L D . S I W A . O T T S . . .
A B H O R S . S A P A . T R I M . .
R E I D S . A C T O N . A W E I G H
A S S I . G R O A T . S E L A S S I E
M I S S O U T O N . T A L L S T O R Y
I D E A L I S T . T O K A Y . O B A D
S E D G E S . B A T E S . S T A R E
. R O E S . E K E S . M A H R E N .
A L E E . A R T E . S A G E . . . .
D E L E . B A I T S . C R I S P I S H
A G E . F O R G E A H E A D . O S M O
L U M M O X . O R D E R . E D I S O N
E M I G R E . U T I L E . N O N E T O
. E S S E S . T O P I S . S I T T E R
```

64

Row 1: CAGY · MOAN · ECGS · AGIO
Row 2: LIRA · ABNER · SHREW · DECK
Row 3: AMAL · RETRO · CAIRO · RTES
Row 4: SEVENTYSIXTROMBONES
Row 5: HEYDAYS · AROSE · IAMAT
Row 6: APR · ITNOW · INS · LOA
Row 7: THEMUSICMAN · SINGALONG
Row 8: ROW · MEAS · SWAN · ONTO
Row 9: AGE · ATURN · SHAM · MAGOG
Row 10: GARAGES · ALAMB · SAT
Row 11: INSWEETMUSICISSUCHART
Row 12: NIS · AROCK · ADHERER
Row 13: FIFIS · BILK · GIDDY · UBI
Row 14: AMUN · HEED · FASH · BIB
Row 15: RINGABELL · DRUMUPTRADE
Row 16: MTN · LAP · PEELE · RHO
Row 17: SYBIL · SPUME · TEAMSUP
Row 18: GETDOWNTOBRASSTACKS
Row 19: FAIR · ARIES · IOWAS · IRAS
Row 20: AWRY · SALUT · EVADE · NEST
Row 21: TELL · ELMO · EYES · EWES

65

Row 1: RAJAH · ENTICE · COFFER
Row 2: EDINA · LOOSEN · AVERSE
Row 3: GOBYTHEBOARD · DENOTE
Row 4: ABE · HOVEL · ODER · MAL
Row 5: LEST · MEL · BERET · ETTE
Row 6: ADEN · CRASS · OTHER
Row 7: SIGNER · ARISE · CANE
Row 8: ANODE · SLANT · GOTAWAY
Row 9: CLAY · APING · THUS · OSA
Row 10: ROS · GOBETWEEN · RIN
Row 11: ACY · ANDI · ORANT · ADAK
Row 12: LOOKSEE · EBERT · LIGNE
Row 13: UNOS · BLESS · MOROSE
Row 14: UPPER · TOBAT · MOTE
Row 15: NILE · SILER · COO · DRAM
Row 16: ALE · STLO · SACRE · IGO
Row 17: GLANCE · GOTOTHEDEVIL
Row 18: EASEUP · NAUSEA · ADELE
Row 19: DREAMS · ARBORS · METES

66

Row 1: REED · WAAFS · LAMA · SLAGS
Row 2: AGRA · ADMIT · ICON · PALEO
Row 3: GORGONZOLA · FRANGIPANI
Row 4: WATER · RITES · UNITER
Row 5: RESORTS · CLAMS · MADNESS
Row 6: ARIOSO · SIEGE · BIRLS
Row 7: BUDD · COTTONCANDY · PAD
Row 8: ACES · SIRE · ASKS · SEMI
Row 9: TAO · CHERRYTARTS · HITON
Row 10: FREELY · EARNS · SATIRE
Row 11: ROBARDS · BARGE · SPRITES
Row 12: AGATES · METOO · BAIRNS
Row 13: PACES · ROASTTURKEY · FOG
Row 14: IGOR · PARR · SEED · COCO
Row 15: DEN · CORNDODGERS · AUTO
Row 16: PATES · MORES · TARRED
Row 17: MARINER · MESAS · DEMASTS
Row 18: AMALIE · CALEB · HIRAM
Row 19: MAYONNAISE · BLUECHEESE
Row 20: AROSE · INST · AERIE · LYON
Row 21: SONES · DEES · GUEST · SEND

67

Row 1: APITCH · BIDSUP · JEREZ · YOU
Row 2: SHOALY · ERRATA · ONETO · ARM
Row 3: HINKYDINKYPARLAYVOO · CIA
Row 4: EMERIES · VINOS · TYKES
Row 5: BATS · END · PLEBS · USUALS
Row 6: ASHIGH · SAONE · OFSUCH
Row 7: SHENSI · FUNICULIFUNICULA
Row 8: ALA · ALIENOR · AHS · TALON
Row 9: LABS · INLAWS · GALOSH · SAUD
Row 10: TRAP · LIT · IOR · NYON · HIS
Row 11: DIGIT · BOATRACE · OASIS
Row 12: SARAH · BIMBOMBEY · PRICE
Row 13: OBOLI · LOADLESS · ADARK
Row 14: HOA · ALIA · HUD · LIE · EELS
Row 15: OTHE · OSTEAL · BESIDE · NYET
Row 16: WHOLE · SAR · ALAMEDA · DNA
Row 17: EENYMEENYMINEYMO · OBTUND
Row 18: ESPRIT · OMARS · OCELOT
Row 19: SAYERS · POPES · THE · MANE
Row 20: CAMEI · BEANO · SEALSUP
Row 21: IRO · SHIMMYSHIMMYKOKOBOP
Row 22: FOO · EATUP · EUROPE · RERATE
Row 23: INN · SHESA · STAGES · ISADOR

68

C O M E T S		S T E P A T A		H O T A I R
A N E M I C		A R R A S E S		O R A N G E

COMETS · STEPATA · HOTAIR
ANEMIC · ARRASES · ORANGE
MEDICALDEGREES · RAKING
ALIT · RODEOS · PAID · EMIR
SAC · BEALL · GEYSER · UTE
SPICA · DEER · REEL · ASSET
NAST · STAGE · RICIN
DAVIES · STEAM · PANAMA
POLECATS · OTTER · REPENT
IMPI · KOLA · BERATED · DAR
KILN · EMERGENCIES · BITE
ANA · STAYOUT · ISMS · ACOW
SONNET · SMITE · EPIGRAMS
STEALS · ALERT · OVERLY
SLEEP · DROOP · ERIS
LAPSE · PAGE · SLED · MOCKS
ELL · ROARER · ETONS · HEW
SLAW · CLAN · KARATE · SORA
SENATE · MEDICALHISTORY
EGERIA · OVERATE · GOALIE
NETMEN · SAINTED · HORSED

69

SHOP · SDAK · JOG · PIPET
AARE · CEDE · EVA · INANE
CRANEOPERATOR · EDWIN
KINGTUT · CUTIE · BINDS
UAR · SHRED · SAG
KEPIS · PLIED · MOLOKAI
IRAN · RODEO · HAND · IBN
WIN · OOP · FLEERS · STUN
INTERMIT · ERIK · PITTS
ALBANIA · ARCHERY
MALLS · JEEP · SLIPSHOD
EGOS · PARSES · ADS · APO
OHO · BUYS · ENTRE · SWIM
WANTONS · SPOOK · BIKES
HUT · SKIRT · MIN
SHORN · STINT · SANGRIA
IONIC · PIDGINENGLISH
BRYCE · ELD · NERO · ELLA
SAXES · ELY · GWEN · SLAB

70

ARAM · WRIST · IRIS · SABIN
MEMO · AEGIA · NINA · PEALE
ACATONHOTBRICKS · ARTEL
SANEST · RARITIES · NASAL
SPA · LIM · REMIND · ANTIC
SONAR · TEA · STEEN
ORAE · GLASSSLIPPER · TRA
MODES · ANE · RIEN · AHIR
ADO · APIGINAPOKE · ERECT
REGALES · ALONE · ADOBES
ISTLE · PRISS · CRIME
MANTEL · LACES · RECALLS
ALTER · GETONESGOAT · FOP
LAHR · LIAT · OWS · SERVE
ESE · MUFFETSGUEST · DYED
MOUNT · EIR · NURSE
CAUSE · KARMAS · PET · AMI
PANTS · INFRAMES · POSTER
ANGLE · CATERPILLARTALK
STEEL · EVEN · UNION · ALEE
TORTS · SERE · SETTS · BLED

71

OLLAS · SHED · SAWED · DASH
VOICE · PEAR · UNAPT · ONTO
ADORN · RARE · BALES · UNIS
LINEDRIVEDOUBLE · HBARS
SEATED · DRAY · GEL
CAB · RYES · FOBS · ALLEGRO
ACADS · EER · OXYMORON
KENO · SIAMESETWIN · ROLE
ETTU · CEPES · ARES · ENOLS
DOUBLERS · LSU · ATOMS
LIN · ESTATES · RET
ABELE · TOP · HARSHEST
ALLIS · BOIL · SHONE · INTO
STUN · DOUBLEAGENT · NEON
TARDIEST · ANT · AGANA
ARTEMIS · ESSE · PARR · SEL
MIL · FLOE · ESCORT
GRAND · DOUBLEDECKERBUS
LOCI · HORDE · AGUE · SOUSE
UNIT · ALTER · RADS · TUNER
EDDY · SLEDS · PROS · START

72

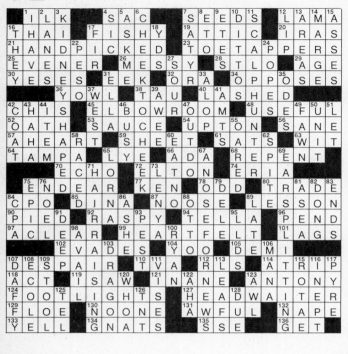

73

74

75

76

```
ADDICT  BULBS  REAM  OWN
WOODER  APIAN  EBRO  RHO
ANGORA  RICHARDBOURBON
REM  FAY  EAGER  LEA
DEANMARTINI  NOEL  PARA
ORLEANS  PEST  APSES
MONTEGO  GEORGECSCOTCH
ALAI  ALE  COE  AERATE
JOHNTRAVODKA  REP  TRON
INUSE  OVA  MEGA
DAMON  SKID  SOSO  ASSNS
BYES  ANE  RANIN
LIMB  END  JACKLEMONADE
ENOUGH  OER  LVI  IRRA
MARLONSBRANDY  ENABLED
ANOLD  DAMN  REARISE
YENI  ARRO  KARLSMALTED
STR  OLLOW  TOI  AGO
ANTHONYQUININE  ZEPHYR
REA  LIEU  DINER  ESTOPS
KEN  DENE  SAGOS  ROSETO
```

77

```
TACT  WADED  TRIAL  SACO
ALOE  INURE  RINGO  ODRA
MANNANDANN  EEKANDMEEK
SENTINEL  TANKS  DIANES
ADES  PINTA  MORT
SOCCER  SANTO  ONTARIO
URALS  RAYEANDGREY  ADD
PARE  MAGI  EMAR  NEY
ELY  LORENANDBEN  TIDAL
REASONER  DARIN  MORALE
NADER  MANAT  PEPIN
SEDLEY  MARDI  SHREDDED
ORGAN  KYLEANDPYLE  SLA
PGA  LENT  RIME  CAIN
HOR  TINAANDGENA  DANTE
STYLIST  ERASE  MONDES
OATS  AGERS  BIRD
ASPIRE  LEADA  DELAYERS
BARTANDART  GUYANDBAYH
AMIE  EERIE  ENATE  ATEE
DEER  RAKED  SODAS  RASP
```

78

```
GULAG  BLS  STABS  SEAM
ATALL  AEC  ORBUTS  URVA
GETSALLGUSSIEDUP  NOON
ASH  DAKOTA  BEATENDOWN
DRY  FATCAT  NEA
AGORA  GILL  NASTYAS
REPEGS  HERO  ITE  GREW
CLASSTEA  ETH  PAR  OMRI
SHS  ALN  SHUNS  SITARS
ISLED  ENNA  CODA
GENTLEMANSGENTLEMAN
ARGO  ELAH  DOUSE
CONFAB  DEMOB  TNT  ELA
ALAI  AGO  ERA  USESTACT
DENT  TOW  STOX  STIGMA
DITCHON  BEHN  ANSER
OAR  BESTED  ORG
SILKBOWTIE  UNARCH  OSO
ALII  BESTBIBANDTUCKER
GENL  ELATES  MAO  NORMA
AXEL  TRYST  EES  TWAIN
```

79

```
REDCAPS  COTERIE  OFFERTO
OCEANIC  EROSION  RAISERS
PLATINA  SLAKING  MUSTEES
EARS  DTS  AMES  ENOCH  NEA
STS  SATE  TAR  ANELE  CCS
SPRECHENSIEDEUTSCH
RABAT  ROAR  ODER  LIANA
IRED  PINT  PINER  TRAINER
AIR  MEND  SEMIS  BREV  TRI
TEEMING  BERIA  ERASE  EVA
ASTERN  QUEST  KRAIT  ADES
DOYOUSPEAKENGLISH
PAGE  WRITS  TRIES  FEARED
APR  LINDY  MOORS  FORSALE
NRA  ISIS  PIRNS  ERRS  GAT
DONATES  LEASE  SLAM  PETE
ANDRE  AERO  BEAN  WADER
PARLEZVOUSFRANCAIS
CAB  AMAIN  TOO  DIRT  HIT
OAR  AMENT  BARNS  SSS  NERO
CREAMER  ACETATE  CIGARET
TENDING  TANAGER  ANEMONE
ASTARTE  ENDLESS  NEMESES
```

80

```
POSSE  PAUSE  SMELT  LOPAT
ACTOR  UNPIN  COSTA  ERASE
THE AGING PROCESS HAS BEGUN
TEAR  MILES  UNTER  CAGERS
IRK  SPEED  PREEN  DONATE
ETAS  URIS  PATON
AND CERTAINLY IT AINT NO FUN
VIOLET  ANIS  TNT  ONE
ONTAP  GRATE  BLOKE  SPRIT
WEST  MOORS  GRIMY  SLIEST
MANNU  ALOE  MONGOL
AS THINGS GIVE OUT ONE BY ONE
SPRANG  BEAD  AREAS
PIERCE  CHARM  TUBER  FARM
ERNIE  SHORT  FETID  PUPAE
NED  KIP  ALEN  WERENT
SAYING IT IN STRONGER WORDS
NARES  OPEC  PIER
MAPPER  GORSE  SMITE  TAM
EUROPE  DONAT  HEATH  MULE
GROWING OLD IS FOR THE BIRDS
ARMEE  INDAN  ABATE  ARIES
DEARS  STAYS  TOLET  HENRY
```

81

```
BMT  OBIE  DALLAS  MOTOR
OAR  ALAS  UMLAUT  ADELA
THOUSAND  SEDILE  DENIM
COUNTS  RAT  CARROTTOP
HUGS  TSARIST  EONS  FUM
THE COWS IN THE CORN
ALFA  ARLO  YACINE
CAULIFLOWER EARS  AXIS
HASSO  ECARTE  USELESS
ERE  RNAS  ABJURE
RED AS A BEET  STRING BEAN
NARRAS  PARE  DRU
LETTUCE  BEGINS  HSIEN
OSAR  AS LIKE AS TWO PEAS
SQUASH  OENO  AANI
EST  CABBAGES AND KINGS
DELI  ESTHETE  AOUT
ONION SKIN  IAL  NECTAR
BOOZE  IRONIC  SLITHERY
INNER  NEWARK  OONA  RET
TEENY  IDIOTS  NIGH  AZO
```

82

```
STIRS  TABU  LUTE  SPATE
MINOAN  AMAN  ENERO  MUTED
IGNITE  SANG  APEAK  URIAH
THE LOWEST CARD IN THE DECK
TRY  DREI  LOINS  RAGE
TEAL  CLANS  KATYDIDS
OPS  RAT  URAL  PINE  NEA
BACHELORS AND DOLLAR BILLS
TRAIT  UNIT  ELAN  ANAIS
EIRE  WOMAN  BRENS  BADWAY
SAC  GARB  AURIC  GOBI
THE RED BARON RICKENBACKER
AMES  HAILS  SABA  ELI
FERVID  COSTS  DOTTY  DRAM
ALIEN  ODER  AERO  SEATO
DUPLICATES AND FACSIMILES
ODE  ACES  IDOL  ANE  ADE
SERVANTS  NACRE  THAW
ATOI  WITHE  PUER  ASS
FALLEN ARCHES OR FLAT FEET
MANIA  ALIKE  SPOT  GRIEVE
AMASS  LATEN  EINE  EARNED
BESET  SELS  DEED  PEONS
```

83

```
BEMOAN  LAUD  BACKED
AROUSE  SOPPY  ASHORE
CLOTHESHORSE  REASON
HERR  TINE  SET  ROSS
ASPIRES  ROLL
STAGPARTY  SNAKE EYES
TIN EAR  EPOS  GSUIT
ELT  TALC  TORE  ALADY
STAB  SORGHUM  STANE
APOGEE  SACHEM
BASIL  MOSELLE  BEDE
DRIER  SODA  SEAR  LET
MELBA  ENAM  TOILER
GREAT SEAL  NIGHTMARE
LEAD  TODREAM
ABEL  USA  EPEE  ESCE
GAMBIT  GREASE MONKEY
REMAKE  VAULT  INSIDE
ORATES  AMPS  BEEPED
```

84

85

86

87

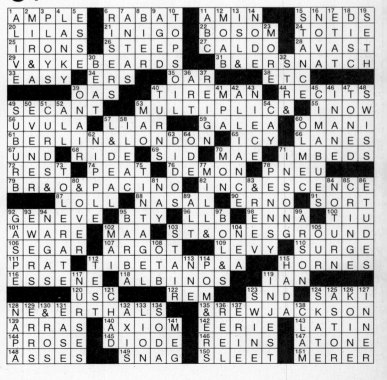

88

```
S A S S   H I C K S     T E A C H   C A M
M A T T E   L I T A N Y   A L T A I   A G A S
I N U R E   E T A P E S   R I A N T   L A R A
S T R I K E A B L O W   W O N   T R E M O R
S A N K   S P A I N   P A T O N T H E B A C K
    E A T   C A E S A R   R O R E M
D A Y B R E A K   S A P   A S T O R S   N A R
O L E A T E S     R E D S   S O O   L A D E
T A L C   H R E   D R I P S   P A N A M A S
S I L K   S L A N T S   N I T S   D A M A G E
  S H A S T A   P A R R O T   R E T I N
S T R I K E W H I L E T H E I R O N I S H O T
C E A R A   N E C K E D   R A R E E S
A R M A G H   R E A L   O S T E N D   C L E F
L E A D S I N   S L E E R   E L A   R U N E
E T T E   T O R   O R N E   I N D E N T S
S E E   A T T E S T   J A M   F L I N D E R S
  W H E E L   I O D I D E   T A I
H I T O N E S F A N C Y   S E N O R   T A L I
E G R E S S   M E A   K N O C K O N W O O D
A L I I   P R I M E   L E A D E R   C I R R I
D U E L   O O Z E D   S A M A R A   O S T E O
  S R S   T I E R S   U S E R S   S E A S
```

89

```
O P A L S   V A P O R   E L K S   S E E S T O
L E R O Y   A G A P E   L O O P   T E N T H S
G N A W S   N I N E S   M O R O   R E T O R T
A S S E T   G O O N   C O N D O R   S I R E E
    B E C   R E M O   S A K E S   A M A N
F A R R M Y R N A D E L L   W Y E T H   S T D
A M O I   R I E M   D E N T O   D E A N E
L O U D   U N S A F E   G E O L   R I A L T O
L U N G   S G T   L A B   A D I T   L O L A S
A R D E N   O L E O   E A R   P H I   M E T E
    S O D   E N R O L L   A D M I R E R
S A W   R E D D S A K A L L H O W E S   S R A
C R Y B A B Y   A B S O R B   A E S
A I N U   S E T   D Y O   U S E S   C O M E T
P A N S Y   R O W E   R L S   L T S   M A T E
E N D E A R   N I L E   A E R I A L   M O H A
    E D N A S   L E T U P   E S T A   E R I C
H E M   G R I N D   O R S O N K E I R R I C H
A C I S   E M E E R   G E N E   N E T
V O L P E   P E L I T E   E G A N   G H O S T
A L L O T S   D E V I   S W A G E   R E V U E
N E E D E D   L I E N   H A D E S   E D E M A
A S S E S S   E F T S   E Y E R S   T A R O S
```

90

```
S T I R   S I P S     B E T   C A J U N
I R M A   O N I O N   S L O E   O V U L E
T U P P E N C E T O S P E N D   W E S E R
A R E   V O I D   T E E N   C E N T S
R O L L E R S   S I D E D   L A R G O
  I R A E   T O A D   C A R E E N E D
A N T E S   P E N N Y S A V E D   E L I
D A H S   E I R   U N I T   S T L O
I S R   N I C K E L O D E O N   E P H A S
T H E P E A C E   A T E T E   M A I S
  E R A S E   D A N   S T E R N
S P A R   B A E R S   T U R N E D O N
P O E T S   P E N N Y E A R N E D   I D E
A N N E   W E E K   T O G   A M E X
T I N   H A L F A C R O W N   C L E A T
H A Y L O F T S   R E B A   G A O L
  O A S T   P A Y E R   A T L A N T A
S P I T S   B O N E R   O T T O   E A R
S W E D E   C O I N S O F T H E R E A L M
M A R I S   P O N Y   N A R E S   C L E O
S T A N S   A R T   D A R T   U S S R
```

91

```
A M P L E   R A B A T   A M I N   S N E D S
L I L A S   I N I G O   B O S O M   T O T I E
I R O N S   S T E E P   C A L D O   A V A S T
V & Y K E B E A R D S   B & E R S N A T C H
E A S Y   E R S   O A R   E T C
    O A S   T I R E M A N   R E C I T S
S E C A N T   M U L T I P L I C &   I N O W
U V U L A   L I A R   G A L E A   O M A N I
B E R L I N & L O N D O N   I C Y   L A N E S
U N D   R I D E   S I D   M A E   I M B E D S
R E S T   P E A T   D E M O N   P N E U
B R & O & P A C I N O   I N C & E S C E N C E
L O L L   N A S A L   E R N O   S O R T
G E N E V E   B T Y   L L B   E N N A   T I U
A W A R E   M A A   S T & O N E S G R O U N D
S E G A R   A R G O T   L E V Y   S U R G E
P R A T   T I B E T A N P & A   H O R N E S
E S S E N E   A L B I N O S   I A N
    U S C   R E M   S N D   S A K I
N E & E R T H A L S   & R E W J A C K S O N
A R R A S   A X I O M   E E R I E   L A T I N
P R O S E   D I O D E   R E I N S   A T O N E
A S S E S   S N A G   S L E E T   M E R E R
```

92

```
FATSO  RAFTS  CAGED  REF
ERROLS ERIAN  LIANE  EARN
PATRICKHENRYJAMESMONROE
HIE DAREONE OREL OUTLET
OSLO RIALS RUED STRAW
RESTS STA COLT APES ABC
APO STROBE GRID WRAY
LISTENS EAVE WEAR BIRLS
ANTEDATE FERVOR EARNEST
NAES AAS STIR MADONNAS
CLV OTROS RADII DOOB
ELIZABETHTAYLORCALDWELL
EELA HORTA FARGE AIL
LOWLANDS AINT NON STLO
ANODISE INPOOR SELECTLY
RANAS MIND NYET STRAYED
INDS CARD TEETHE SOL
DYE WANE LOAD AMB SEDER
ROALD SELL RIPER DINO
INLAID APSE BOLIVAR ETA
SCARLETSISTERMARYMARTIN
MANE RHONE DIANE PIKERS
ADD SORER SENDS SNORE
```

93

```
PASSE BWANA MESAS ATTAR
OREAD ARRAS AROSE PHORA
EAGLE SAINT KANIN NINTH
MOINESPLAINESANDPERES
VINO YSER HAS
INFACT MANILA BOA TSAR
MOOT CASINO SPIREA ECU
BURENCORTLANDTANDDRUTEN
ENE ORMER SEALS RAPT
POET ODA FRA CATALAN
PARSEES EMMA TIL ELI
LESSEPSKALBVRIESANDWITT
ARC SIC RIGS AMORINO
PEERAGE TAO ERA BRIG
NOSE MISSA BEAME AGO
SYDOWSTROHEIMANDKARAJAN
RUE ETHENE RENEGE NAVE
OLDE AID BINARY HATRED
RAT DOLE AUDE
MONTERIOSARTOANDNORTE
CIDER AROAR ARMED ROILS
ICOSI CONGE IDEAL NORIA
CARTA KNEED LORRE SMEAR
```

94

```
CHESS AIMS PAST SCARPED
SARAH ITEA ALPH SOMEONE
THEGANGSALLHERE EMILIAS
DURANTE ASP INA
IMMODEST STATOR NOTED
DIMWIT BAR NOGG ORE
HOLE STOPLOVINGYOU RUNS
ALI STEPSASIDE ARPA DIE
LITRE AES MINERALIZE
ASIAN SLUE CLOAK ORATED
STANDAT DRURY NESS TENS
RACED ROM ELEMI
BORI CROW NAMED ASONANT
AREOLE MOIST VEST REVUE
DISTENSION ENT ARETE
GOP ATEN CLEARSAWAY RAT
ELIS TEARSINMYEYES LATH
ETA CATO TSO LESAGE
SELAH ETCHER SALVAGED
ECU SAO ASEPSIS
SPARTAN THEOLDAPPLETREE
CONNOTE EARL ALAE BEAUX
TUTORED SNIT KELD OCHRE
```

95

```
SMART PRIM CLEW ASIS
PIPER CROCE OATH TENT
AGAPE HOVEL UNTO EDGE
THREETIMESTHREE SNARE
ETTA AMOR ESS TOTTER
TACET SOLE FISHES
ATC LODE EEL RUT OSS
PRAHA STROGANOFF
SINAIS GAT LIT ANTH
ICEL ATOLLS UNI TIRO
SELF PRIMETVTIME NAMA
PLOD ANO NOTNEW EDEN
SAFE IGN TOG ESTERS
ENGLISHMEN MYRIA
CII LEN BAR TRUE SCE
ANGLER POTS RARER
ARCHIE GAM AIDA ALPS
MOLTS ANYBASEBALLTEAM
ATOE OBOE AUGUR ETAPE
RISE PETE REINS NASAL
ADEN ETES ERSE SNELL
```

96

Across (filled grid):
SPAN · TAN · FORUM · AROMA
PANO · ANY · ATONES · HANOI
ALTA · YOUKNOWWHATIMEAN
TOEHOLD · ROSSETTI · OWNS
UMA · HOOHA · DAYTONA
LIT · ORNO · ALD · REPAYER
ANET · LACEUP · SRA · STE
SORRYSPECTACLE · SLATES
IOTA · LISTAR · SERRI
SIBONEY · EOE · YIPS · REND
ILL · GRINANDBEARIT · EAU
CLOY · ETON · IOD · ACASTLE
ABCDE · TOOTOO · NAPE
IRKSME · AUTOSUGGESTION
REB · BAD · TRUTTA · IONA
EDUCATE · OTS · SWAP · LET
SORETOE · SHAVE · ASA
ACTH · REDMAPLE · LEARNIT
FREEASSOCIATIONS · ITDO
EARNS · TREMOR · CUT · CHER
RUSSE · SEANS · ATA · HEDY

97

VALET · CLASP · RAJAH · SLAVE
AGAVE · RISER · ELATE · AIMED
PAVEDWITHGOODINTENTIONS
ONA · SECT · ADHOC · IDEE · RUE
RASH · EKE · LUISE · TEN · REEL
ADDERS · COE · SURETY
MURRE · TENSE · SANDS · RATAL
ABIDES · DAW · DUE · FINITE
SECEDES · GAP · ERG · GIE · NEA
TRANSECT · PLANE · CORSICAN
DORS · ENCASED · TEASE
NOFURYLIKEAWOMANSCORNED
ATONE · DAYSTAR · ITER
SHRAPNEL · CERES · ONETOONE
HEM · ARR · CAD · SUB · DAWDLER
URANIA · MOP · RAN · KEDGES
ASTOR · PAPER · PENAL · READE
ASHORE · EAR · CREEPS
BACH · ORT · ANGER · ROM · THAW
ILO · ANTI · GEESE · ONUS · ANI
GOODMEANINGSANDWISHINGS
ONTOP · LEVEE · GALEN · ADDLE
TESTS · STEWS · ELIDE · MAYOR

98

WAGED · TASTE · DUMBO · CIVIL
ELIDE · IDEAL · EBOLA · ONINE
BORINGPARTY · GOTOTHEDOGS
BELT · ATRIA · PRATT · AVILES
CLONE · SEATO · LIAR
RES · ALE · SATED · WALLACE
EXORCISE · MAKESWAVES · LAT
MICAH · STEN · DUELED · LOTI
ALINE · SPENDS · ESTD · VISED
PEAT · PLEAD · AEDES · WINERY
SDL · QUICKSILVER · CHEERY
COURSE · RAE · AHERNE
BLUISH · DEADRINGERS · LED
TRISTE · LASKI · MOOSE · JAPE
AIMTO · DINT · NABORS · MOTIF
EBBS · MINCES · LUNA · ALICE
LEE · TICKERTAPE · SULLIVAN
DROWSES · REEDY · NET · ELD
NITS · HEARS · EDINA
ESSENE · CANDO · HAITI · AJAX
FLOWERCHILD · RUNNINGMATE
TAMAR · MORAL · IRENE · RIVEN
STAYS · SUSIE · DADAS · ADANO

99

BONNET · CAPRA · ALCOA · BOAZ
ENOUGH · AHEAD · MAORI · ABLE
MONROE · FERMI · BOXER · LIDA
ARES · WEEMS · SPUN · CHISEL
EDAM · ISSUS · TROY · PRO
THEDEVILTAKETHEHINDMOST
EAR · SERAI · IRS · MENDED
SNEAKS · STINT · LUIGI · SACO
TACT · BASAL · ACU · ROTE · ZAP
APTERYX · NOUTURN · INJURE
OVID · PISCES · ORISON
MYFAMILYANDOTHERANIMALS
CAESAR · SLOANE · ALEC
CHIANG · POTOROO · ADONAIS
OWN · SINE · KEN · SHEEN · IDOL
YETI · NOSES · REHAN · ILLINI
GUILTY · SOI · ROUGE · EIN
WHENFATHERCARVESTHEDUCK
HEX · EWES · HOSEA · ETSI
ARCARO · MITT · CHASM · GATH
MEET · OLEAN · PSHAW · AMECHE
MAST · LARGO · ISERE · RASHER
OTSU · FINIS · GELID · EXTEND

100

```
TABUS ACERB PACER SATAN
ADELA ROLEO LLANO ALAMO
PODAL ANGLO AORTA BOBBY
IREMEMBERABOYFROMTRALEE
REWARD YET LATI RIDERS
      NCO CORD EATEN
AMAPOLA ORO PARSE ASSAD
SAME ITS MILS IRS HOLE
WHODEVELOPEDAHATREDOFME
ADREM RUHR LION EQUATED
TINEAR IWO ETTA NULLAHS
     NEATH EHS STEEL
LOSTALL ELLA MAE LISSOM
APPETIT NOON IZAR SHIRE
WHATEVERIDIDTOIRETHEKID
NIRO ERA ESSO SUA BABE
SCENT EVASE RIB NIGERIA
      RODIN MIMI ELA
VASSAR DAMA PTA ELDERS
IENTIRELYFORGETSODOESSHE
ASIAN SEATO IDEAL OFTEN
LODGE CANED VERNE TOOTS
SPEED ANGRY EDNAS SEPTA
```

101

```
LABS WAGE SOGS SIMP
EQUI OXEN AGRI IDEA
TURNOVERS BEATSDOWN
TANGLED LOREN WELLS
     EIN WADE TWOS
MACRO DIVES LAR DEL
ALAS JUTES HANDFULS
AIL LOCHS ZONE ACID
MILDOATH MOLD ILKAS
     DAWN OILED BOSC
ABUTS LLDS STONEAGE
LECT WADS SWISS LED
DAKOTANS SPINS CLOG
OKS HID SPATE POSSE
     BUNG EACH CON
ASSAM RINSE TUESDAY
DOWNBEATS OVERTURNS
DRAG SNEE UELE MUTE
SAPS STAD TEED EMIR
```

102

```
COVEN BBL PSI RATS
OLIVE PROA RON ERIE
ALLIGATORCLIPS FINE
TILLAGE NEIGH ARDEN
SEA TORPEDO IAGO
   PER LOUNGELIZARD
CODA ARI PEP UNEVEN
APART AGT LOAM ADA
RACER CHOU GNAT
THENIGHTOFTHEIGUANA
   TORE OVEN EMBER
ASA ELSA AID EBOLI
DILATE IMP GAG LULL
DRAGONSTEETH ETE
   ERST BRETONS UNO
DIALS ALIGN WIELDER
ROBE CROCODILETEARS
UTES ORD LOSS SALVO
BATS DYE ANT ELLEN
```

103

```
ESTA ORCA AGO
LEHI AVERSE BLEU
AFTERONESOWNHEART
WITH DON WATUSIS
ENLIVEN BENET
ELIS BRDS TASS
SHALE TRI BOTHER
PAS LOADS INTONE
ARC CARDGAMES WAN
SLOVEN YENAN OTT
MORALE ADD ACNES
WELL LACY AIRE
ABELE ENLISTS
TEAROSE IWO SHOT
CALLSASPADEASPADE
APSE TOPPER TENA
BEE NOTE ANDY
```

104

S	A	B	R	E		S	H	O	A	L		M	A	W	
A	R	E	E	L		H	O	R	A	L		A	D	H	O	C
W	E	F	E	L	T	A	G	A	R	D	E	N	E	A	S	Y
E	N	I	D		I	N	A	N	E		W	A	L	L	I	S
D	A	T		P	L	A	N	T		C	A	G	I	E	S	T
			B	E	E	N			A	L	E	N				
A	H	O	E	A	R	A	K	E	A	N	D	S	E	E	D	S
R	A	C	E	R	S		I	L	L	E			B	I	T	
D	I	T	T	Y		S	T	I	E	S		S	M	O	T	E
E	K	E			T	E	A	R		C	H	O	A	T	E	
B	U	T	W	E	D	I	D	N	T	C	O	U	N	T	O	N
		A	V	O	N				O	T	T	O				
S	E	L	L	O	U	T		S	P	O	T	S		C	B	I
S	P	I	L	L	S		S	C	A	L	E		C	L	A	N
T	H	E	E	V	E	R	L	O	V	I	N	W	E	E	D	S
S	A	N	T	E		P	U	R	E	E		A	D	A	G	E
			S	S	S		M	E	N	D	S		G	E	N	E	T

105

A	P	S	O		B	E	R	G		G	E	E		A	C	T	E
N	E	I	L		E	N	O	L		H	O	O	T		E	L	A	N
D	A	M	E	N	G	A	I	O	M	A	R	S	H		D	E	N	Y
E	L	I		E	S	S		I	A	N	S		A	I	M	T	O
S	E	L	M	A			R	U	D	Y	V	A	L	L	E	E
		S	E	A	T		A	B	E	L	L		A	R	L	E	N
			T	H	E	R	A			E	S	S	I	E		T	I	S
F	U	J	I		M	E	R	V	S			E	E	L	Y		M	O	T
A	R	A	N		M	E	N	A	C	E	D			S	T	O	N	E
K	A	Y	E		A	L	A	N	A	D	A	L	E		R	O	I	L
I	N	N	E	R		B	E	R	A	T	E	S		I	R	A	E
R	U	E		E	L	L	A		P	R	I	A	M		E	E	N	S
S	S	M		F	O	I	S	T			O	V	E	N	S
			E	L	I	R	E		H	E	I	N	E		I	T	S	A
		S	A	L	L	Y	F	I	E	L	D			T	E	T	R	A
M	E	D	A	L			D	E	A	L		E	A	R		A	I	R
A	T	O	M		J	O	E	Y	H	E	A	T	H	E	R	T	O	N
T	A	W	A		A	N	S	E		R	I	T	A		H	O	S	E
T	E	S	S		G	E	T			S	T	U	B		O	R	E	S

106

O	N	E	T	O		S	O	D	A	P	O	P		P	A	T	T	I
P	E	A	R	L		O	V	E	R	A	T	E		O	R	R	I	S
E	G	G	E	D		R	E	G	A	L	I	A		S	K	E	E	T
R	E	L		C	O	T	T	A	G	E	C	H	E	E	S	E
A	V	E	M	A	R	I	A	S			E	R	S		H	U	G
			O	M	N	E	S		D	I	A	N	A		L	O	P	E
S	E	R	A	P	E			B	O	D	E			M	O	U	S	E
A	L	O	N	G		S	T	A	T	I	O	N	H	O	U	S	E	S
M	I	N	E	R		A	H	A	S		L	I	E	U		E	T	E
			R	O	M	M	E	L		S	I	L	E	N	T
O	P	T		U	M	B	O		A	L	A	E		D	O	R	A	S
G	R	E	E	N	M	A	N	S	I	O	N	S		B	H	A	M	O
L	I	N	E	D		L	A	D	E			C	U	E	B	I	D
E	S	T	S		S	T	Y	L	E		B	L	A	I	R
S	E	A		P	O	H		P	R	E	E	L	E	C	T	S
		C	H	A	T	E	A	U	B	R	I	A	N	D		L	E	W
P	A	L	O	S		R	E	R	E	A	D	S		I	N	A	N	E
A	D	E	P	T		A	R	I	S	T	A	E		N	O	R	S	E
N	O	S	E	S		M	O	S	T	E	L	S		G	R	E	E	T

107

J	A	W		C	C	C		I	S	I	T		S	I	G	N	O	N
O	N	E		O	H	O		S	E	M	I		U	N	R	I	P	E
S	T	I	G	M	A	S		T	R	U	M	A	N	K	A	P	U	T
H	A	R	E	M	S		R	E	S	E	L	L			T	A	S	S
			O	U	T	G	A	I	N			L	E	V	I
C	O	R	N	E	L	I	A	O	T	I	S	S	I	N	N	E	R
L	A	R	G	E		U	R	N		O	B	E	S	E		A	G	E
I	R	A	E		D	E	Y		L	A	S	T			E	R	G	O
A	N	N	A	T	E	S		F	E	T	E			A	C	D	C
R	E	G	I	O	N		M	A	V	E	N		H	O	W	O	L	D
		E	D	G	Y		A	L	E	E		D	E	B	A	T	E	R
F	A	M	E		R	O	L	L		M	U	M		R	I	V	E
O	D	A		I	S	E	R	E		S	I	C		A	D	Z	E	D
E	D	N	A	S	T	V	I	N	C	E	N	T	M	E	L	E	E
			T	H	A	I			L	E	I	S	U	R	E
S	A	L	T		M	E	A	D	O	W		S	I	E	S	T	A
P	H	I	L	I	P	W	R	O	T	H		S	C	A	R	L	E	T
A	M	P	E	R	E		A	G	H	A		I	L	L		A	C	T
R	E	S	E	E	D		N	Y	E	T		X	E	S		W	H	Y

108

LOPER · SHEBA · RELAY
AGORA · TOVAR · EDEMA
HENRY JAMES MADISON
RED · SATIRE · DETER
PELT · ODES
SAC · VERY · SHIM · CUR
ABATERS · PEAS · ANE
MANET · AERO · OLLA
ULYSSES S GRANT WOOD
ROOT · MAKE · SERAI
ANN · PIED · SEASIDE
IES · BALE · SPAR · ESS
TUNS · SHIV
BARGE · SHARES · BAH
LOWELL THOMAS HARDY
ALONE · HORAL · OREAD
COLTS · OPENS · TORME

109

PARTY · AGCY · SMU · CLAD
ASOKA · MERE · MAS · HAGI
WHOOPS IT UP · IN HEAVEN
EOM · ANAS · SLO · IPASS
DRESSED TO THE NINES
EROS · AERO · BER
IMPULSE · III · OAHU
SOAR · INK · WING DINGER
ONME · PSI · SAFEST · RAG
FLEET · TNT · MIT · SHAVE
FIB · A MAGIC · NYE · ADEN
IN A TWITTER · EOS · NEST
TEER · NEO · EFFUSES
IHS · PELE · LETS
LOOKS LIKE A MILLION
BROMO · OIE · ATON · NCO
CHOPPERS · IN HIGH GEAR
DASH · ART · ACER · ORAGE
EPEE · TYS · NERA · GOREN

110

TITLE · MAAMS · SHEBA
RACIAL · ARRET · PAVANE
TINY TIM · READE · AVERAGE
ACT · ORIBI · MINUTES · TOT
SHAG · DRIED · ADLER · GOIN
SERA · ANTIC · HAS · BALSA
ORALES · STAYMAN · MOTETS
OLOR · ALDOL · CAROF
REJOICED · SCP · CATARRHS
OVETA · FOX · HECATES · AIT
LENS · JUDY GARLAND · ANKA
ERN · HANDLER · UNA · RICER
STIPENDS · NIB · SPEARERS
FIFES · PESOS · SAKI
AGENTS · LESSONS · REESES
SORTS · JAG · EBOLI · SECT
TOJO · MEIGS · SWOON · TALE
EDO · CARRYON · LENIN · GAL
RANSACK · LOOSE · ITERATE
SEE THE · ETTES · ARMETS
STOOD · EYERS · NOOSE

111

AHAB · BOZ · LOKI · SCAB
DODO · LIMA · ANUT · TALL
DOOR · EGAN · NELL · ASIA
SPRING AHEAD FALL BACK
ULE · EMMA · IMOK · ALBEE
PARKWAY · ADAR · AREAS
AYN · STAR · ABA
LALO · MEW · KALE · CABS
SEVER · YEA · TIA · OMOO
THANKS FOR · THE MEMORY
LAND · OAF · EEN · XENIA
ORTS · DIFF · ENS · TOGS
JAR · OPUS · ARF
APSOS · QUIP · PREFACE
IRATE · SUNS · POEM · MUR
30 DAYS HATH SEPTEMBER
RUNT · LAVA · KOPH · ALDA
UNAU · ONEI · INEE · NEUT
EDGE · BERN · PYR · ARPA

112

```
OGLE  ARTA  DACE  GALOP
LAIC  LEON  OLAS  OVOLO
BERMUDATRIANGLE  EATER
EARP  INRE  LUAU  ISNTIT
STEERS  ORBIT  MONOTONE
ETTU  ADORE  SNIFF  SSS
NAB  ENJOYLIFE
CIRCULARSAW  SNAFFLE
CANOE  ANS  BEL  ITSALL
TARTU  AVA  LORETTA  BAA
INTONATE  SOT  PRETEENS
ANO  DETRACT  STE  ATROT
RENOIR  STR  CRO  SNAGS
ARSENIC  HAVEANANGLE
SCALLOPED  SAE
CAS  ILIES  LATCH  NAPA
ASTARLIT  AVRIL  STRIDE
CHANCY  FINE  NICE  SLOW
HOTEL  BACKTOSQUAREONE
EROSE  OLEA  PEUR  ANTI
SERTS  OLDS  SLED  MESS
```

113

```
TAFT  CHAIR  SCALAR  PST
IDIO  HORNE  PIGINAPOKE
LEST  EROSE  ITOLDYOUIT
EPHAH  NAE  SLY  UTES
STOLE  ERRANT  IMTIRED
USEIT  TRA  ONEPAIR
EST  HASP  SKINFLINT  ASP
THO  AGNEW  ENSUE  WAR
ARF  WOETOHIM  SEMI
LAWS  SERENADE  INSOLE
PARENT  MATTE  CASTLE
INTONE  BYTHESEA  AFAR
SEE  DOSE  HESNOTIN  ABA
TLR  IRREG  ANISE  TLC
BLUEBERRY  SNAG  TEA
BRAGGED  AAR  TRASH
CRASHER  ASMUCH  TIERS
ROAN  ATS  DRE  EMDEN
IDIDNTCARE  ADOBE  POMI
CANOFWORMS  RENAL  LOAD
OSS  LOWEST  TREGA  ERNE
```

114

```
EMBAY  MAMA  ATA  ASLANT
LAURA  ENID  NAG  SCOTIA
BLOCKANDTACKLE  PACINO
ELYSEE  REPLACED  ROPES
TRIESTE  ROAM
STAYIN  ATOMICBOMBE
PUSSYFOOT  VERONA  TIES
INAWAY  PIMENTO  MIDAS
KODAK  BABA  DAREDEVIL
LIEN  ALLEGE  RISE
ELS  SHOOTINGSTARS  BAS
ROMA  ARIOSE  CANT
SPARETIRE  ANTE  BONGO
CURIE  MELANGE  PASTOR
IRIS  HOTDOG  SMALLTALK
SEEEYETOEYE  MADAMA
DEMI  IMITATE
MARCO  SERENELY  EASTER
DREAMT  PIDGEONENGLISH
XAVIER  ICE  TSAR  LOTTE
VIENNA  CON  SENN  EPODE
```

115

```
QUAHOG  THAW  SINGE
UPSALA  HOWE  TREAD
IFTHEREWERE  RICIN
TORA  VARY  PESETA
SRO  BEER  BLAHS
HEARTBREAK  SAO
DREAMS  SEEDY  MINN
REPLAYS  DELA  ATIE
ETHOS  HEDDA  DRAMA
WARE  MOTO  MARITAL
UPAS  OTHER  TOSELL
PEI  POINSETTIA
MOURN  WHAT  RUB
MATURE  BLEU  ROSA
ACUTE  WOULDYOUBUY
METRE  HOLD  ASHORE
ESTES  OPUS  MARTYR
```

116

```
SALT    MAENAD    TWAIN     COR
AMAH    ASSIZE    EAGRE     OCH
GIVETHATBUCHAREST           LEE
ONEHOUR      CIAO      BLAT
  1MATTHEBERLINPOINT
SCAPE    AUNE      ENEMIES
THISSHOWMALAYANEGG
OER    AINU    LAGER        PUP
PAL  LILYS    ILLUS    BUALS
STERILE     ANOTE    SURREY
  THATDANCEWASVOLGA
HETERO   CATES     ANGELAS
IDEAS    MAINS   ARRAY   LIT
TOR    SERAO     BEET     ESC
  BOYDIDWEPICCADILLY
SIBERIA      NOLA      ISSER
MEKONGANDYOUAPEMAN
AWAY        YOUR     LINTIER
GAR   YOUDIDNOTKALAHARI
ORI   AUDEN    CURATE    OSIS
ODA   PRONG    ETITES    TINE
```

117

```
   GUMMY      HENS     ACH   AMI
SENORA     FELON     TRAPPIST
WALLAWALLAWA       LOVERSLA
ARIAN    CAPP    PLANER     SAP
PST   DARKISH    ASEA    ARMS
   AMMO    TEACHES     ORB
   ARREST    SLURS    OFNOTE
EMITS    SOL   FTS   FREEAND
GAMINS     LAMPS    MRED    TSE
ORTS     COEDIT     SOUSE
SCOTLANDYD       MANMTNDEAN
   OLEOS     SCRAPE     RAVE
HOT    NERO    PRIAM    SLAVES
MAHLERS    ALP   HQS    BIERS
STEELS     FLORA    BATONS
   LOY    HOOTOWL     YAFS
ALAN   DORN    MEANSOF    DCV
SIS    AIMEES     SWAN   LEROI
PVTLIVES       PTOFNORETURN
SEMINOLE    CAMUS    ASTINS
RIB    TYE    ABEL     SHADY
```

118

```
AMLA    MINOR    AMESS    OBIT
ROOM    ADANA    ROSIE    BORE
CABBAGESANDKINGS          ENOS
ASSIGNAT    RISE    TALENT
  TARES    SCENT    LILIS
BENET    BORA     ONESTEP
FORCE    ANIMALCRACKERS
LOPE   GAINS   LILA    SAGA
INO   HASTYPUDDING      KOL
TETHERS     NEON     ROAST
   EMITS   LIN   TROUT
  BRASS   ASIA   ASCENTS
NEO   HAMILTONFISH     OOP
ELLA    DORA    HORNE   MODE
WILDGOOSECHASE        SODAS
SEEMING      IRED     NOBLY
  DIVAS    ETNAS    PURSE
BOOTES    AMID    MARECHAL
ALAS   LEGOMUTTONSLEEVE
MITT    ORATE    OVINE   NAIL
SOSO    WARES    WALES   EDDY
```

119

```
BETAS    SHOP    OVAL    CLODS
ALAMP    PARR    VIDA    HOPEH
SAMUELANDOPERASFIGARO
ETERNA     DECORUM     OMELET
DER    DYE    RESTS     PRES
   ELENA    EEL    SOU    OPA
SAWYERSBUDDYANDMICKEY
CARESS     ILS    RES    CAINE
ALORS     ADE    TOTE   TOKENS
LETS    AVENGED        ARNE
ENE    BERTANDHYDE       MAT
   STES    RESEEDS     FADO
CAPPED     FRET    VAS   SAGOS
ALLAN    TIE    SER    THRONE
LEANDERSLOVEANDHOAGIE
LEN    XAT    VAR    SNERD
   ESPY    MEDEA    ALT   SOB
AMERCE    CORINNE    MENTAL
DANIELJAMESANDVANDYKE
ALTEN    ULUA    DIDO   DALIS
GEESE    GIST    EVAN   SKEET
```

120

B	A	D	G	E			F	R	E	E		R	A	T	A	L
E	R	I	E	S		D	O	I	N	G		E	L	E	N	A
F	I	V	E	P	O	U	N	D	S	O	F	C	A	N	D	Y
I	T	E	R		S	E	D	G	E		O	T	I	O	S	E
T	A	R		S	P	L	A	Y		A	R	O		N	O	R
		B	I	R	L			F	U	R	S					
T	O	G	I	V	E	O	U	T	A	T	M	Y	D	O	O	R
O	N	E	D	A	Y		N	A	R	E	S		L	U	X	E
K	I	N			V	I	S	O	R				T	I	B	
A	C	E	D		R	I	F	T	S		O	V	E	R	D	O
Y	E	T	E	V	E	R	Y	Y	E	A	R	I	W	E	E	P
		B	E	N	T				G	A	L	E				
G	E	M		T	A	U		P	O	N	C	E		S	A	D
O	N	E	A	C	T		H	O	R	A	L		A	L	M	A
F	O	R	I	H	A	V	E	E	A	T	E	N	F	O	U	R
E	L	I	D	E		M	A	T	T	E		E	R	O	S	E
R	A	T	E	S		I	P	S	E		T	O	P	E	R	

121

H	E	A	T		C	H	I	C		A	N	A	K		S	H	O	V	E	S
O	T	T	O		I	A	T	A		R	O	P	E		T	A	H	I	T	I
P	U	T	O	N	T	H	E	R	M	A	L	U	N	D	E	R	W	E	A	R
S	I	N	K	E	R	S		L	A	W	E	S		R	A	R	E	S	T	
			I	R	O		F	O	R	A	N		S	O	L	I				
P	U	L	L	O	N	S	L	A	C	K	S		L	O	S	S		H	E	L
A	N	I	L	L		H	I	D			H	I	L	O		T	O	R	O	
N	U	B			B	O	P		S	C	R	A	P		N	I	O	B	I	C
O	S	E	A		U	N	O		C	O	A	T	I		S	M	O	O	C	H
V	E	R	B	O	T	E	N		A	M	M	O	N			S	A	W		
		D	A	U	N	T		S	E	R	P	E	N	T		O	R	I	B	I
			R	T	O		C	A	R	I	S		O	C	C	I	D	E	N	T
H	E	A	D	O	N		A	D	E	L	E		B	O	K		E	D	N	A
I	L	L	E	P	U		R	I	D	E	S		O	M	S			E	A	R
E	L	A	N		P	A	V	E			B	O	B		F	A	C	T	O	
D	A	S		A	T	M	E		R	A	C	E	T	O	M	A	R	K	E	T
			L	O	I	S		O	D	O	R	S		A	G	E				
	S	C	A	L	P	S		A	G	O	R	A		F	R	O	L	I	C	S
G	A	L	L	O	P	H	O	M	E	R	E	T	U	R	N	T	O	B	E	D
E	L	A	I	N	E		I	M	R	E		E	L	E	E		S	A	D	A
T	E	N	T	E	R		L	O	S	E		D	E	E	R		T	R	E	K

122

C	A	S	H		C	H	I	D	E		S	H	O	T		D	A	T	A
O	S	L	O		H	E	R	O	N		R	H	I	N	E		I	L	E	S
S	T	I	M		A	R	A	N	G	L	E	A	D	E	R		M	A	R	K
T	O	M	E	L	T	O	N			L	A	D	D	E	R		W	O	R	M	S
			P	O	E	T	S		P	A	T	S	Y		O	L	E	U	M
S	P	O	N	G	E		P	E	N	C	E		A	M	O	R	T	I	Z	E
A	L	S		A	R	N	O	L	D	H	A	T	R	A	D	E		E	A	T
R	A	T	E	L		O	R	E	S		N	I	N	E		A	S	N	O
A	T	E	N		A	U	T		A	T	O	N		P	R	E	E	N	
S	E	A	S	O	N	S		C	A	N	N	E	S		S	O	T	
		L	I	S	T	E	R	R	A	I	N	S	E	T	T	O	R	E
		L	T	S		H	A	R	L	O	T		R	E	L	I	N	E	S
T	H	R	E	E		R	I	T	E			R	A	M		P	O	L	O
H	O	O	D		D	O	N	E		S	E	A	L		A	E	S	I	R
E	N	D		A	R	M	O	R	E	D	E	N	T	A	L	C		A	D	E
N	E	A	R	L	Y	E	S		L	O	A	N	S		E	E	R	I	E	R
	R	O	O	S	T		C	I	R	C	A		O	A	R	E	D	
M	A	T	T	E		E	D	I	T	I	O		O	F	F	S	T	A	G	E
O	M	I	T		T	R	A	D	E	C	A	R	M	E	L		A	N	A	T
P	I	L	E		H	E	R	E	S		S	T	E	V	E		I	D	L	E
S	E	E	R		O	D	E	R		T	E	N	E	T		N	Y	E	S

123

	I	D	L	E		P	R	O		H	U	T	S			R	F	D
I	D	I	O	M		L	I	N		O	C	H	E			M	E	L	A
W	E	A	R	E		A	G	E		M	U	R	R		E	N	C	Y	C	S
W	O	M	E	N		T	H	R	E	E	T	O	E	D	S	L	O	T	H	S
		O	L	D	S	E	T		A	R	S	E	N	I	C		A	H	A	B
N	N	E		S	N	E	A	K	S			E	N	A	B	L	E	
S	A	D	I	S	T		D	R	E	W		P	R	E	P	S		C	U	E
L	I	M		O	S	S		T	R	I	B	E		E	S	C	O	R	T
A	V	A	I	L		E	T	O		T	A	R	E		A	O	N	E	
P	E	N	N	A	M	E	O	F	H	H	M	U	N	R	O		M	P	S
			P	R	O	T	O		A	B	B		A	E	R	I	E	
	P	G	A		M	O	U	N	T	A	I	N	C	A	N	A	R	I	E	S
C	A	R	R		R	I	I	S			O	T	T		M	A	N	T	O
O	N	A	T	A	B		K	N	E	L	T		A	L	B		A	H	A
Y	E	N		G	U	I	L	E		S	E	A	R		A	S	I	S	A	Y
	D	E	A	R	T	O		L	A	T	E	P	M		L	M	N	
A	S	S	N		R	E	A	L	T	O	R		B	A	B	A	L	U	
C	A	L	I	F	O	R	N	I	A	A	N	G	E	L		R	U	C	H	E
S	T	A	G	E	S		L	A	N	D		A	C	E		A	S	H	E	N
	I	M	M	Y		A	N	T	E			I	C	S		G	E	A	R	S
N	S	A		W	E	E	D		T	A	T		O	S	S	A

124

```
S P R A T   E A V E     L A B O R
S P R U C E   A L G E R   C I M A B U E
M O U N T C A V A L R Y   I N E D I B L E
E O N S   S C O P E S   A S E A   E S S
A N E T   H I S T O R I C A L   S L I T
R E R O B   E D E   E N O L   G Y L E S
S R S   E A S E   P A C T   D U M A S
  I N G O D   O S A   L A M P
  C A M D E N   A U S P I C E S   A Q U A
M A I M E D   L U T E   N O A H   T U R N
A R M O R   T I D Y   E G O S   S H A G S
L E E R   S E M I   T R O T   S O I R E E
E D D A   E X P O N E N T   B E R E T S
  L U N T   E R I   P A T E S
G R I N D   C O M E   I R A S   D B S
E R A T O   S O O N   F R O   T R O U T
T O D Y   I M P O S I T I O N   E N N A
A T I   D O I N   C O N G E S   N A I F
S T A L L I O N   T H E A U T O M A T O F
O N E V O T E   V O I L E   B A T O N S
  T E E T H   A R N E   S E A R S
```

125

```
A P A R   M E G A   B A L F E     W O E
D E L I   I R A N   O P E R A   E G E S T
S I L V E R A N D S L I V E R   F R E S H
  E L A S T I C   S E T   U T O P I A
P E E R A G E   A C H E S O N   A Y E N
O C T A N E   P A P A   P E E N
O L A   P A T A N D A P T   R A K E D
N A P U   G O N E   E R M A S   A N I M E
  T E N   R I T E   D U E T   D O M E
    T E E N   F A I N T   S L O W E R
A S P I R A T E D A N D D I S P A R A T E
F L U E N T   L O R D S   T R I G
R A R A   E N I D   A S E A   A C T
O V E N S   A M A N A   S O R T   N A H A
S O R D O   N I T A N D T I N   P R N
  U S E D   C E I L   P E D R O S
S E I N   S A R A C E N   A R A R I B A
C A N I N E   A I L   S C E N E R Y
O V A T E   S T R I P E A N D S P R I T E
T E N E T   T E E M S   P O E T   O D E R
T S E   A S S E T   E S S O   T A X I
```

126

```
  P R I S M   H U M U S     B A D H O P
S E A N C E   T E N A N T S   O R I O L E
T E N N I S C H A M P I O N   W I N C E S
A R T S   H O R D E S   M E W E D   K I T
B A H   M O R T   S P E E D   B E N E
S T E M   B O B O   S U E R S   S A Y E R
  M E M O   S O C C E R S T A R S
M A D E O F   M O A T   C L A U S E S
F I R E T R A P   P T Y   T O O   T U L A
E R A S E   K A R A T   O R A N   O M A N
T A T   S T E E P L E C H A S E S   M I T
I C H U   A D A M   R E M I T   A R E N A
S L O P   B A N   M S L   L E C T U R E S
H E N C O O P   A H E M   R H I N O S
  A R O U N D R O B I N   I T A L
C L O S E   N E W A T   G O A T   T Y P O
H I N T   A C R E S   A R G O   M O B
A M E   E T H E L   A V A U N T   S P U E
S P I R A L   I L L G O T T E N G A I N S
M E D U S A   D E A R I E S   T E N A C E
S T A G E S   D Y A D S   S L I D E
```

127

```
  D I S H   B A R B   A S P S   N O A H
M I N C E   P Y X I E   S L A P   O S S A
A T T A R   A L O N E   H A R A   P I P S
T H E B E A N A N D T H E C O D   L E E T
Z E N S   D E W   A N K L E   A R N O
O R D   S O L   B E T S   E D U C
  C A R   V E L I T E S   L E W I S
H O M E S I C K N E S S   S E L E C T
C R A M P   A D A   P T A H   I D Y L
S O R E L   C E L L O S   N E C K
T I T H E   H O M E S T E A D   R E D A N
  O S T E   S U N D R Y   O H A R E
S T E M   O M A R   I R E   T O T S Y
R A R E S T   B E G I N S A T H O M E
A M A T I   E L A T I O N   E N E
  O R T S   B E E N   M A S   S S B
H E R R   A P P A L   P O T   S A I L
O L I O   B E I T E V E R S O H U M B L E
M I S O   L E T O   I L I A D   S I R E N
E T E S   E D O M   S U R L Y   E L A N D
R E N T   D Y N S   E L E M   R E S T
```

128

T	A	R	I	F	F			B	R	I	E			B	E	T	A	
A	B	A	S	E	R		L	E	A	D	S			M	A	N	O	R
G	A	S	T	R	O	L	O	G	I	S	T		S	U	R	G	E	O	N
S	A	R	A		I	C	E	S		R	E	S	T			M	I	A
	I	L	L	F	A	T	E	D		A	T	H	E	N	I	A	N	S
A	P	I	A		A	T	T	S		O	D	D	S		R	I	N	S	E	S
U	R	N		A	T	E	E		T	A	I			S	T	D
R	E	T	I	R	E	D		O	N	E	F	O	O	T		O	C	H	S
A	M	E	N	D		P	O	R	T	L	I	E	R		O	L	E	O
	A	R	G	O	T		S	T	R	S		O	L	L	A		R	I	A	L
C	T	N		R	A	T	I	O		G	E	L	I	D		N	R	S
L	U	I	S		N	O	R	M		S	T	I	R		L	I	C	I	T
E	R	S	E		S	T	E	E	P	L	E	S		T	A	C	I	T
F	E	T	E		E	N	T	R	A	N	T		P	E	T	T	I	E	R
	D	I	P		R	O	T		A	L	S	O		A	S	E
A	P	P	E	A	R		L	I	M	E		B	R	A	T		A	N	T	E
H	E	A	D	L	I	N	E	S		S	A	R	A	C	E	N	S
A	N	C		C	E	N	T		R	A	R	E		A	H	A	B
	D	E	N	T	I	S	T		P	E	D	I	A	T	R	I	C	I	A	N
R	A	I	N	S		E	V	E	N	T		E	V	A	D	E	R
S	M	O	G		P	A	N	S		G	E	N	E	R	A

129

E	L	F			P	A	P			T	H	A	I		E	G	A	D	S
A	R	E	O		O	L	I	O		G	H	A	T	S		A	L	L	E	R
U	N	C	L	E	T	O	M	S		R	E	D	H	O	T	M	A	M	A	S
F	E	T	I	S	H		T	I	A	R	A		W	O	D	E	N
	A	T	E		P	E	O	N	Y		W	I	N	E
S	I	S	T	E	R	C	A	R	R	I	E		S	I	N		M	A	S
O	S	I	E	R		I	T	S		S	I	T	S		C	Y	S	T
A	S	S		S	I	D	E		S	H	A	S		O	L	A	T	H	E
P	U	T		M	E	R		S	C	A	N	T		N	E	P	H	E	W
S	E	E	D		A	R	P		P	O	S	T	E		S	E	E	R
	D	R	I	P		A	M	O	T	H	E	R		S	T	E	P
		H	A	R	M		T	A	N	T	E		E	S	S		S	E	R	S
T	H	E	D	A	Y		R	I	G	I	D		I	T	O		S	E	A
R	I	L	E	Y	S		I	N	E	E		L	E	N	S		O	S	T
I	D	E	M		I	R	A	E		C	E	E		U	I	N	T	A
M	E	N		S	H	E		F	A	T	H	E	R	A	N	D	S	O	N
	M	O	T	O		A	L	I	E	N		T	D	Y
S	I	E	V	E		G	L	A	N	D		T	A	L	E	N	T
S	I	S	T	E	R	C	A	L	L	S		D	A	N	I	E	L	S	O	N
A	L	L	E	N		A	L	O	E	S		A	V	E	C		I	T	I	S
G	L	A	S	S		D	A	W	N		R	A	W		C	O	R

130

S	I	B	S		U	B	O	L	T		I	N	D		P	A	L	E
C	L	O	T		R	E	F	E	R	E	N	C	E		E	N	I	D
O	L	O	R		G	O	T	H	I	C	R	O	M	A	N	C	E	S
W	A	K	E	N	E	R		I	N	T	O		E	N	N	I	S
S	T	R	A	N	D		A	G	I	O		P	R	Y		E	L	I
		E	K	E		E	D	H		G	A	I		E	N	O	S
L	I	V	Y		A	N	A		C	H	A	P	T	E	R	T	W	O
I	F	I		F	B	I		H	E	N		S	D	R
N	E	E	D	L	E	S	S		E	M	E	R		W	A	L	D	O
D	E	W	E	Y	C	L	A	S	S	I	F	I	C	A	T	I	O	N
E	L	S	I	E		E	D	I	T		S	T	O	R	A	B	L	E
		S	R	S		D	D	E		U	N	D		R	O	N
B	E	S	T	S	E	L	L	E	R		O	A	K		L	A	R	D
A	M	A	S		M	O	E		M	I	L		F	O	R
S	O	L		L	I	T		B	A	A	L		M	A	G	Y	A	R
	T	A	C	I	T		A	R	M	Y		A	U	R	I	C	L	E
B	I	B	L	I	O	G	R	A	P	H	E	R	S		C	A	T	S
R	O	L	E		N	O	V	E	L	E	T	T	E		A	R	A	T
A	N	E	W		E	D	A		E	M	E	E	R		L	D	R	S

131

A	S	O		B	A	S	E	S		C	A	R		R	O	B	E	D
C	H	I	A		O	G	I	V	E		S	A	B	E		A	R	E	T	E
H	O	L	D	Y	O	U	R	E	Q	U	I	N	E	S		D	E	L	T	A
E	R	E	M	I	T	E		U	N	L	I	T		D	I	L	L	E	R
S	T	R	I	P	E	S		R	E	S	E	T		L	E	A	S	E
		R	E	D		G	A	L	E	N		B	A	L	L	E	D	U	P
C	O	P	E	S		S	U	B	S	T	I	T	U	T	E	S		T	K	O
H	O	U	R		A	H	A	B		O	C	H	S		S	H	A	W
I	N	T		B	O	V	I	N	E	P	O	K	E		T	H	E	S	E
C	A	S	A	N	O	V	A		I	D	O	L	S		L	O	A	F	E	R
	O	L	I	V	E		T	S	P		S	A	L	L	E
I	G	N	A	C	E		C	R	E	E	P		A	P	P	A	L	L	E	D
B	U	T	T	E		W	H	I	R	L	Y	A	V	E	S		I	T	A
A	S	H	E		C	O	I	F		L	E	N	E		S	N	U	B
R	T	E		W	O	R	D	F	O	R	W	O	R	D		G	W	E	N	S
S	O	C	I	A	B	L	E		C	A	R	E	S		P	R	O
	A	C	R	I	D		O	T	R	A	S		O	R	I	O	L	E	S
G	E	N	E	R	A		S	W	E	E	P		C	A	N	N	U	L	A
A	L	I	C	E		W	H	I	T	E	P	A	C	H	Y	D	E	R	M	S
R	E	N	A	N		E	O	N	S		E	N	U	R	E		D	I	E	S
B	E	E	P	S		B	E	G		D	A	T	E	D		D	R	Y

132

C	A	F	E		A	S	P	I	E			I	D	E	A	S		F	I	B
A	P	I	N		S	C	U	L	L		O	N	E	I	L	L		I	M	A
G	I	V	E		T	H	R	E	E	I	F	B	Y	S	E	A		V	A	N
E	S	E		D	E	E	R		V	O	T	E	S			S	T	E	M	S
		A	F	A	R	M		F	E	T	E	D			S	H	O	P	S	
G	E	N	U	I	N	E		O	N	A	N		B	O	L	E	R	O		
A	N	D	E	S			D	U	O	S		T	I	M	I	D		S	H	A
O	A	L		B	A	I	R	N		A	W	A	I	T		P	T	A	S	
E	L	F		M	O	S	E	S		C	R	O	S	S		T	A	E	L	S
		S	T	R	A	I	T		I	C	E	N	I		S	A	R	T	R	E
	H	U	S	H		S	E	R	I	F			I	N	I	T				
S	P	I	D	E	R		T	R	O	M	B			O	N	E	I	D	A	
M	O	A	N	S		E	P	E	E	S		Y	A	N	A	S		E	N	A
P	O	L	O		W	E	I	R	S		B	L	I	S	S		T	S	A	R
S	T	E		P	A	T	E	S		C	R	A	M		M	U	S	I	C	
		A	L	A	T	E	D		S	H	U	N		M	O	M	B	A	S	A
K	N	E	L	T		V	I	A	N	D		I	D	E	A	L				
I	N	D	I	A		S	A	D	I	E		A	N	D	S		I	S	O	
D	E	T		C	H	A	P	T	E	R	T	H	R	E	E		K	N	O	T
L	A	W		E	A	S	I	E	R		T	E	A	R	S		A	E	R	O
E	D	O		S	T	A	T	S		E	R	N	S	T			S	S	T	S

133

I	L	E	F	T		A	R	A	P		S	O	B	S		A	C	C	S	
S	E	M	I	S		C	A	R	R	S		A	L	O	U		R	H	E	O
R	O	U	L	E	T	T	E	B	E	T		I	D	L	E		E	E	L	S
			M	T	N	S		U	F	O		L	I	S	T	E	N	S	T	O
A	S	S	I	S	T		S	T	A	R	F	I	S	H		T	O	T		
C	A	Y	C	E		C	H	I	C	K	E	N	H	E	A	R	T	E	D	
M	U	M		S	C	A	R		E	S	T			V	I	E		R	E	B
E	L	B	E		O	P	U	S		A	M	B	I	T		S	T	I	R	
S	T	O	W		R	O	B	I	N	S		I	R	K		L	O	O	S	E
		L	E	N	I	N		M	E	T	T	L	E		H	A	U	N	T	S
C	O	O		I	N	E	X	P	E	R	I	E	N	C	E	D		S	S	T
O	F	F	I	N	G		M	E	D	I	N	A		R	I	D	O	F		
A	F	I	R	E		B	A	R		P	E	G	G	E	R		R	A	S	P
T	E	N	S		F	E	S	S	E			E	A	S	T		O	T	T	O
I	N	N		I	R	A		D	A	G		S	T	O	P		H	E	L	
D	O	W	N	I	N	T	H	E	D	U	M	P	S		A	P	E	E	K	
			C	Y	S		G	R	A	N	D	P	A	S		S	I	E	R	R	A
S	W	E	E	T	M	E	A	T		U	P	I		C	O	D	A			
P	A	N	T		A	R	U	T		C	I	T	R	U	S	F	R	U	I	T
A	R	C	H		M	E	M	E		E	E	R	I	E		O	L	S	O	N
D	Y	E	S		A	D	A	R		S	E	N	D		R	Y	A	N	S	

134

A	C	H		J	A	N	U	S		T	O	P	S		B	A	S	I	E	
L	A	Y		A	L	I	N	E		A	T	I	T		A	B	A	C	U	S
E	L	D	E	R	B	E	R	R	Y	W	I	N	E		R	O	P	E	R	S
G	I	R	L	S		R	E	T	E		S	T	I	R	R	U	P	C	U	P
A	P	O	D		A	S	S	A	M	S		S	N	E	E		I	R	S	
R	E	M		M	I	T	T		E	H	S		S	E	N	D	E	E		
		R	E	C	E	D	E		I	N	E	P	T		S	E	R	R	A	T	E
S	L	I	D		I	S	T		R	E	E	K	E	R	S		M	A	S	
G	I	A	N	T	S		R	E	N	I	S			I	S	I	S			
J	A	G		A	S	E	A		R	Y	D	E	R		C	A	R	O	L	E
A	B	U	T	T	E	R	S		E	V	E		S	C	O	R	E	D	O	N
E	R	N	I	E	S		H	E	M	A	D		T	A	H	R		A	R	E
G	A	P	E			B	E	V	E	L		L	E	R	N	E	R			
E	D	O		B	A	R	D	E	L	L		I	N	C		S	E	R	F	
R	E	W	R	O	T	E		S	T	I	E	S		A	N	T	H	E	R	
		D	E	L	T	A	S		S	E	M		E	V	A	S		F	U	M
C	E	T		A	T	T	S		S	E	C	R	E	T		E	R	I	O	
M	A	R	A	S	C	H	I	N	O		S	O	U	L		A	M	A	T	I
A	M	T	R	A	K		P	I	N	E	A	P	P	L	E	J	U	I	C	E
N	E	E	D	L	E		E	D	E	N		S	T	O	M	A		N	U	T
	L	A	S	E	R		S	E	R	E		E	S	S	E	X		S	P	Y

135

B	O	T	H		O	B	O	E		C	H	O	P			G	A	P	E	
A	C	H	E	S		F	I	V	E		A	I	N	O		S	A	X	O	N
T	T	E	R	T	O	T	T	E	R		V	N	U	S	D	E	M	I	L	O
H	O	P		A	M	E	E	R		D	O	G	S		E	D	I	S	O	N
			T	A	K	E	N		S	U	C	R	E		G	M	A	N		
S	T	E	V	E	N		G	E	N	E	T		G	A	I	N	E	R		
T	I	R	E	D		N	E	I	N		C	O	L	T	S		A	S	S	
E	M	P	S		B	A	E	R		T	S	A	D	E	S		C	L	A	N
N	E	R		D	A	M	A	S		R	I	P	E			P	A	P	P	I
O	R	I	G	I	N	A	L		F	A	Z	E	S		C	A	R	H	O	P
		N	A	V	A	H	O		I	L	E		I	N	A	R	O	W		
S	A	C	R	A	L		G	E	L	I	D		C	E	L	I	B	A	T	E
A	L	I	E	N		I	N	E	Z		I	D	O	L	S		L	E	S	
R	I	P	S		R	O	S	T	R	A		S	O	N	S		S	D	A	K
A	T	L		L	E	N	T	O		T	O	O	M			C	H	O	S	E
		E	M	O	T	E	S		W	I	N	C	E		R	O	O	M	E	R
	A	V	I	S		S	H	O	A	L		P	E	L	E	E				
S	A	D	D	E	N		P	A	I	N		I	L	I	A	D		R	B	I
C	D	A	R	R	A	P	I	D	S		U	N	X	P	R	E	S	S	E	D
A	R	R	I	S		T	E	A	K		P	A	V	E		R	H	O	N	E
D	Y	E	D			A	R	T	Y		S	L	I	D		O	N	Z	A	

136

RIOT · BABAS · SEAT
ISOLDE · SEVILLA · COLLAR
LAMODE · THETEARSOFLOVE
KIEV · NERO · SEGMENT · NEB
ALOE · ROLF · ARE · EZRA
SAL · HILDEGARDE · ASON
NODEAL · DELLA · LES
PADUAN · NONES · IDEATE
FIJIS · CORIA · REGENCIA
CRUS · DELTAOFVENUS · IER
FLA · ONOR · EMIR · ISR
TAI · ILOVEAPARADE · TACO
VIENNESE · DORAN · ASNER
ARTIER · FINNS · RIDDLE
ERE · TUTTI · NUTMEG
PACT · BESSIELOVE · LAC
MATE · SRA · SOBE · OLAF
OTT · OCARINA · ALAS · VARI
THEFLAMEISLOVE · TEETER
HOSIER · DIRTIER · AGLETS
STNS · IBARS · GOYA

137

TALCUM · EKE · ARCS · OPTIC
ARIOSO · NOR · POLO · PERDU
TENLOSTTRIBESOFISRAEL
ENDO · TERESA · TSAR · CYST
STARS · LEA · YORE · IRA
APPLE · PARADISELOST
PRUNER · FERAL · DECENCY
LOSTWEEKEND · DESK · DEL
AMES · SLIDE · GHEE · LAINE
TED · BALD · LIARS · TENTER
LEGENDOFTHELOST
POMADE · ASPIE · ROTS · ORB
ERICS · BPOE · FEEDA · APAR
TON · TAUS · LOSTINSPACE
ANISEED · THOLE · GOPHER
LOSTANDFOUND · PROWL
SORB · AIRS · LOWEST · ASEA
THELOSTCITYOFTHEINCAS
AIDED · TELE · PUT · ENCASE
GOOSE · OSSA · SLY · SCENTS

138

BOARD · SAP · TRES · CABLE
ANNEE · TWIT · HEAP · ANEAR
TAKEFRENCHLEAVE · RETRO
HILLIER · TRAMPED · ALOES
ERE · ASEA · AMASS · EVENS
ANTON · LEK · BRASA
WRIST · GOLDENMEAN · SOB
EONS · STER · EINS · CURE
ETH · THELASTWORD · LORES
DIEHARDS · LORNE · BAREST
ROPES · CANIS · ARMET
GAITED · MANET · SLIPSHOD
ALTER · TANGLEDWEBS · ILE
TEAL · HALO · OISE · SNIP
OFF · SETONESCAP · BIGOT
ORCAS · SPA · ESSES
BREAD · EATER · SELF · NBA
RETAR · IMPALES · TEAROOM
ELUDE · LITTLEKNOWLEDGE
LINER · ELLE · RIEN · LEDIN
SEERS · DEYS · PES · SKYES

139

ABED · ASMARA · WAC · PST
CALEB · REATAS · ELI · HOR
THEROCKETTES · AIRMILES
ANGOLA · SENSUAL · CALIPH
AGAR · ARTHUR · DIE
ARNA · ROCKINGCHAIR · ADD
DICTA · RONNIE · STEPS
AGEES · ERECT · EAT · DIAL
STONEHEARTED · PRIM
PARSEE · RISE · OPPOSE
AMOUNT · ARE · MEN · ORACLE
RECITE · LENS · RISKED
INKS · STONEOFSCONE
DASH · RED · BELEM · SCAPE
BEANO · SIMONE · TARTS
COY · ROLLINGSTONE · MIAS
ORE · MILACA · ROIS
BABIES · REPROOF · INSIDE
STANDING · PEBBLESTONES
OBE · LEO · EVADER · OLGAS
RYE · YES · RENTER · ESNE

140

SALAD · SPADE · BARA · CPA
ILONA · STALIN · AVIS · AIR
STUTZBEARCAT · TELEGRAM
SET · ZORBA · MEA · LAUDS
YRS · LIES · CORNERS · TITO
VETS · JUNONIA · DEARS
SPHERE · CORD · ENSCONCES
PEARS · SLEEPS · CURB
YARD · BOA · SIMILAR · EBRO
PICASSO · NODAL · ARROW
PREACH · HRS · GAS · ENGINE
ECRUS · RECAP · SCARABS
PAST · SEDATES · ARR · ITEM
OLEG · INHALE · ABOVE
MARGARITA · NIPA · SELLER
EXERT · LOBBYER · PERE
GILA · ADSORBS · FERO · APE
SAPOR · SOL · OLEAN · DOS
AMPHORAE · WAGNERIANMSS
DAS · NAST · SCREES · UNITE
OPE · ASHE · EKERS · TETES

141

CASTOFF · SPLAT · CROAKER
ANTONIO · ALIVE · HAWKEYE
SOONERORLATER · ALLAYED
IMP · SPLUTTER · WILY · SRO
NAPS · OSTLER · POSY · STOA
GLENS · HEN · GALE · SHOOK
SYRIA · ESS · GALV · SHUNTS
PLAN · SHOWMESTATE
RESPOND · ELK · ROAM · SIA
ORIENT · BEAD · KING · HANS
LILTS · GARDENING · DOCKS
LEVY · SODA · NOME · TINKLE
OSE · APIG · ALI · HARDSET
ROMANEMPIRE · EMEU
GASPER · RASP · DIX · CROUP
OCCUR · CIRE · CIN · TAUPE
OARS · CANE · BUTLER · STAR
DDE · RING · VITIATES · STU
BEEHIVE · YELLOWHAMMERS
AMNESIA · ALLEN · ICEDTEA
RESPECT · POSTS · CHESSEL

142

ELIAS · FRET · SMA · MAE
SIDLE · REDO · PALOALTO
SMELLSOMETHINGFISHY
ANEW · ELAN · ANO · FLOSSES
ASTIR · OVERSEE · TIO
HOLYMACKEREL · END · TERN
ALOSA · ALA · PAD · PER
GAG · RETHROW · ELS · LASTS
STREET · HOT · CUSTER
UFO · MIRAMAR · LOOM · ELI
LIVEINAGOLDFISHBOWL
SAD · ANTS · PENANCE · ESS
OLDAGE · REO · GEARED
SALLE · THY · FLANNEL · AGA
EAR · HUE · AYR · EGRET
BARS · LIL · STEAMEDCLAMS
TLC · ARACHIS · EMOTE
UPROOTS · LAM · ARES · ERAS
APRETTYKETTLEOFFISH
BURNSIDE · STIR · OUTTO
SAT · DES · PANS · PLEAD

143

ROAMS · TOPO · UPDO · EBERT
APPAL · IMAM · PREC · LAMAS
FERIA · GALA · PERT · ACUTE
FROMTHEHORSESMOUTH
IAN · ERA · IDA · BREEDER
ASSERT · SRS · GWEN · LIRA
ROMANCE · BEAR · DORIC
ALLIGATORPEARS · TURKEY
MOI · ENTREATS · ROC
BOOST · MESH · FRANKNESS
ESNE · PLANTATIONS · ELIE
RESTRAINS · NELL · LEASE
IRE · CONCLUDE · NAP
WOMBAT · WHOLEHEARTEDLY
OLIOS · COIL · TERRAIN
LENA · PANG · ASS · GNEISS
FOXTROT · HEN · ISO · SEE
RAININGCATSANDDOGS
COPAL · ANOA · BULL · EILAT
ONICE · PROD · BEET · ADDLE
WAGES · SENS · ESTS · DOEST

144

OHMIC · OMSK · SWAB · HARP
NAURU · RAYE · AHEY · ASEA
SERDAB · SINGAPORESLING
LIVS · AVOTE · CHOO · EFFIE
ALE · PLENA · STES · OUT
PLY · AIL · ISAIAH · CROSSE
WARBLE · PLOD · SCANTER
BLACKRUSSIAN · SAUTERNE
WILE · EMOTE · ERR · SAT
ALLYE · ALEC · CATO · WIN
NAB · ORANGEBLOSSOM · BEA
ACA · NEMO · DOOR · SCENT
ENT · CAR · OSIER · ARCA
TOGOLAND · PINKSQUIRREL
RUEDELA · SIDE · HUMBLY
ISREAL · MCCOYS · ARI · BRA
SDS · AURA · OTTOS · LAG
AGAPE · ANTI · GLUEY · ZONE
FLYINGDUTCHMAN · AVENGE
RUES · ORAL · MACE · LAUDE
OGRE · PYLE · SNED · ELSES

145

ROTAS · STELES · SMEW
SECRET · PARANA · OATHS
FIFTYFOURFORTY · BRAINS
ARIA · PLATS · RIDES · TAP
RIND · SPOT · SANER · HEIR
CUE · CHESS · PANGS · LISLE
ESS · HARE · WANTS · MOROSE
BOGS · CARD · GANEF
EMBERS · BAREST · INERTLY
SALLE · CORES · RIPER · HEP
KNOT · BRAES · TIROS · BEAR
EGO · GUEST · TRAIN · RAISE
RODENTS · SHREDS · MITRES
SWATS · EYES · CITE
SAWERS · AMASS · SALE · PAT
ICERS · SMART · GAGES · ALA
CHAS · TEARS · RBIS · CROP
EAT · LATHE · STAIN · ASHE
SEAPORT · NOTHINGTOFEAR
ANYONE · GREENE · APERS
DENSE · OBSESS · MESS

146

PENCE · AHEM · STOA · AKRON
IDIOM · SOLI · IESI · READY
COPPERHEAD · GLAMORPUSS
TREED · SONAR · BIT
ARF · GEN · CHLOE · SLEIGH
TOOTED · CHIEF · CARTOOL
OGRES · SHIPOFSTATE · IMA
LUTE · SOON · AONE · ANEW
LEU · SHOWOFHANDS · ANGST
SNIPERS · ROMEO · ONETWO
GENIES · SITAR · THETOE
VACANT · OWLET · EARLOBE
ILONA · SPELLINGBEE · ATL
SLOE · HEED · EGON · OTHO
EEK · HOUSEKEEPER · DEFOE
DRIVERS · ARPAD · CAROMS
YEARNS · SPOIL · SOS · RES
SSE · TWIST · ANITA
DUTCHTREAT · OUTONALIMB
ASHOE · EMMA · MAYO · RADIO
WEENY · BAIL · ERST · DRESS

147

PRIMES · KOJAK · AGHAST
RESOLES · BATTLE · BROGUE
IADMITIWONTSEE21AGAIN
ADO · STARTS · POEM · KTS
MINOT · MES · CLEOS · SHOE
STEGOSAUR · CHERI · STARR
ORALS · HAIGS · HANS
AKA · OKS · PERC · PTER
DIVANS · ALAE · KOREAGATE
AMOST · FLARE · ITIN · AMAN
YOUWOULDNTRECOGNIZEIT
INCH · PEEK · WAKES · WELLI
NOHITTERS · ODES · GORIER
TOOT · AMIR · TAJ · ADE
HEER · EMCEE · CHRIS
RELAY · AXMEN · SHOEMAKER
EXES · BLUES · CHA · ALINE
GAG · KEEL · SEARCH · TAM
AGAINAFTERALLTHISTIME
LONDON · ENABLE · INTONED
ENTITY · DAWES · TANGLY

148

S C A L A ■ C O P S ■ V E R A ■ F O R E
M I A M I S ■ O V A L ■ O L I N ■ E R A L
A G L O V E ■ L I R A ■ T A C T ■ I B I S
T H E R E A S O N A B L E T H I N G I S
T I N E A ■ M R E D ■ I R E ■ U N T I E
E N D ■ N R A ■ E D S ■ D A M ■ E N G
R G S ■ D O R I A ■ E L E G I Z E ■ D S O
■ A L I T T L E L E A R N I N G ■
M U L E ■ S T A G ■ T O O M ■ A V E S
P E N T A D ■ A L S E A ■ U L T I M A
E N C O R E ■ T O L E A R N ■ T E E T E R
T A L O N S ■ A N E N D ■ H A L T E D
S T E N ■ C A N S ■ H O S P ■ R E A R
■ A D A N G E R O U S T H I N G ■
A P T ■ E L A S T I C ■ M A O R I ■ U T A
U R U ■ N E T ■ L A I ■ B A N ■ S I L
F E R M I ■ Y A K ■ T H A I ■ G R E E T
■ F R O M T H O S E W H O C A N T E A C H
C A E N ■ R O U T ■ H A L O ■ D I B B L E
A C T E ■ I N R E ■ I C E R ■ A M E L I A
B E S T ■ P E E R ■ T A R N ■ K E L E P

149

I L K ■ M A I M ■ E A M ■ P R A M
R A U ■ P E R S I A ■ T H A I ■ L O P E S
M I R R O R M I R R O R O N T H E W A L L
A R D O R ■ S T A T U E O F L I B E R T Y
■ I T S O ■ G I T ■ T U A N ■ T S E
A N D ■ R A F ■ E S S A ■ L Y D D A
M O R T A L ■ R S T ■ G E L S ■ U R B A N
P H A R I S E E ■ H O L Y ■ S P A R S E
S P I T A N D I M A G E ■ B I L L E T S
E G O ■ D A D D Y ■ G A R N I ■ W I T
■ O F F I C E S ■ F I N A N C E ■
L A W ■ J U N T A ■ R E A D D ■ A T E
I C E B E R G ■ T W I N C R Y S T A L S
A R L E N S ■ W E E K ■ E S T E L L E S
R E D A N ■ C I S T ■ U B I ■ O B S E S S
■ T Y P E D ■ S I N E ■ I R R ■ N E T
U F O ■ A R E O ■ C C L ■ S K I T
P I C T U R E O F H E A L T H ■ D O Z E S
A U T O G R A P H E D P H O T O G R A P H
S M A L L ■ L E E R ■ S O L A C E ■ N E E
■ E D D Y ■ N R A ■ P E R T ■ Y E A

150

C O W E D ■ C A P E ■ C A M E L ■ S W E D
A B A T E ■ U N I V ■ O V A T E ■ I H A D
D E N O M ■ P A L E ■ L I G H T ■ P I S A
E A D I E ■ I B A R S ■ A N O S E ■ T E Y
T H E L A N D O F T H E R I S I N G ☀
■ R E N E S ■ S O L I ■ N O R T H ☆
A L I ■ S A B E R ■ T M E N ■ A I L E
D I N G ■ L O N E ★ ■ S O A K ■ I D E R
D A G O N ■ W A N T A ■ ■ D O W N E R S
U N ☆ V E D ■ M E L L ■ ■ A R E
P A S T I E S ■ W E L L S ■ H E A D ★ T S
■ G N U ■ ☆ S K Y ■ A R I S E N
U N Ⓞ G H E R O ■ S T E A M ■ S A C R O
R I S E ■ B E A L ■ S I N U S ■ Z A S U
S E P T ■ R A S H ■ N A S A L ■ T E T
A T O A S T ■ N E A R ■ T R A C T ■
T H E ☾ ☀ A N D T H E ☾ A N D T H E ★ S
C O Z ■ L A M A S ■ A S T R E ■ E A R L E
O M O O ■ M A K E Ⓞ S H I N E ■ E N D I N
☆ A N D ■ I R E N E ■ I D I D ■ N E O N S
S N E E ■ C A D D Y ■ P E M S ■ S Y N G E

151

B L O W ■ S W A B ■ M A G U S ■
A E R O ■ P I N E D ■ E L A N C E
S P A R ■ I N T E R ■ R E D D O G
H O L D O N E S P E A C E ■ E R G
■ L I E D ■ W R Y ■ O R E O
A C C E S S ■ O B I E ■ A D O R N
P U L S E ■ A K I N ■ A B O N ■
O T O S ■ F L A G ■ O V E R E A T
R E S ■ T O P S E C R E T ■ S H Y
T R E M O R S ■ A L E C ■ C H O P
■ M A R E ■ C R A M ■ W H A L E
S C O R N ■ N O S Y ■ H E A T E D
H A U T ■ L I V ■ S E A S ■
A P T ■ S I L E N T P A R T N E R
M O H A I R ■ R O Y A L ■ I O N A
S T E L L A ■ T E R R E ■ S T O P
■ E D I T S ■ L E E R ■ E A S E

152

W C T U	■	M A F I A	■	■	F R A	■	A R A B
A L I A	■	E N U R E	■	R I S	■	S I R E
R U M R U N N E R S	■	A L C A P O N E
D E E	■	N A I L	■	N E O N	■	T O R
■	V I C E	■	A M O K	■	T A B
C A P O T E	■	S T O O L S	■	S O B E R
A G I L E	■	J A L O P I E S	■	O O N A
M E N S	■	O M E N	■	N E E	■	T I T I
P E S T S	■	T O A S T	■	S T I L L E D
■	E G G	■	A S H U R	■	A D E
R A T A T A T	■	T I R E D	■	O G R E S
A P O D	■	R A H	■	N I N E	■	G I R L
Z E T A	■	P R O T E S T S	■	K E E N E
E R E C T	■	S M A R T S	■	P A R S E D
■	T O Y	■	E L S A	■	D R Y S
E W E	■	W O M B	■	A R I A	■	B O A
R E V E N U E R	■	H I J A C K I N G S
S T E R	■	T R E	■	I C A M E	■	S A L K
E S N E	■	H E W	■	T E X A S	■	T I E S

153

| S E T O F F | ■ | B A R B U D A | ■ | A R C A N E |
| E L O P E R | ■ | E L E A N O R | ■ | L A U R E L |
| E M O T E I N N O B Y M K C A B G N I R B |
S K I L L E T	■	R A E	■	R E G A L I A
■	M I L D	■	C L U N Y	■	T R Y
Z U B I N S	■	B O O M S	■	A F T	■	H A H A
E N O S	■	S O R E	■	E Q U I	■	E N O L
N W O T N I K C A B S U L U L	■	L M N O P
D I T	■	O N E A L	■	I T S A	■	E O L I T H
A S H A N T I	■	G A I L	■	C O O
E E S S E N N E T N I E M O H K C A B
■	S U N	■	A X I S	■	S O A K S U P
J E S U I T	■	P A T U	■	K R A I T	■	S S A
E X E R T	■	A K L O P Y A B K C A B E H T
T O M E	■	G R I T	■	A R I A	■	E R E S
E N I D	■	L I N	■	A R L E S	■	V A S T L Y
■	F A S	■	K N E E L	■	W I S P
A D A M A N T	■	I S M	■	S E A F O O D
D R A Y K C A B N W O R U O Y N I K C A B
M E R R I E	■	A D E L I N A	■	D R E A M Y
S W E A R S	■	L A R D N E R	■	S E N S E S

154

B I B B S	■	I T S A	■	L A I C	■	S U T R A
E N O L A	■	A H E M	■	A N N A	■	U N H I T
C R O A T	■	L E M A	■	P I T T S B U R G H
K I T S C H	■	M I S S	■	M E S A	■	E G O
■	T H E B E S S E M E R P R O C E S S
A S O F	■	M A N T E A U	■	P A I N E
L O C U S	■	B O E R	■	S C O W	■	E L B O W
S A T R A P	■	M E S	■	C A L	■	S A T A R A
O R A N G E O I L	■	B U R	■	S A R	■	S A I
■	A A R O N	■	R O L L I N G M I L L S
B O S C	■	M M E	■	E R A	■	R E E	■	R E S T
L A K E S U P E R I O R	■	O R O N O
A K A	■	E T H	■	O M S	■	I N D I A N I A N
R E L A T E	■	P U P	■	O R O	■	L O A T H E
E N A C T	■	C A T O	■	L O R E	■	S N O O T
■	A L I A S	■	S A D N E S S	■	D R Y S
U N I T E D S T E E L W O R K E R S
B O S	■	E C O N	■	S I X A	■	W A T S O N
O P E N H E A R T H	■	V I N Y	■	B E I G E
A A R A U	■	D A R E	■	E D G E	■	B E L L A
T R E N T	■	E L Y S	■	S E E P	■	I L L E R

155

L O G I C	■	S E R A C	■	R S V P	■	A D A M
A V I S O	■	A D A N A	■	O P A L	■	D O R E
C A T I N T H E H A T	■	C A T A L O N I A
■	S T E I N	■	B E S O T	■	C O R M
P O T	■	A L B	■	M A N I C	■	C A T N A P S
U R A N I A	■	C A T A B O L I T E	■	R O M
B I S O N	■	S A T I E	■	A T E S	■	Q U A
L A S T	■	C O L I C	■	T I G E R	■	P U R R
I N E	■	P O U L E	■	B A L E S	■	Q U I L T
C A T A L I N A	■	L O B A R	■	M U S S E S
■	W A N D	■	B O O B Y	■	S E I S
D O C A T S	■	G O U T Y	■	A L L E Y C A T
A R A K E	■	S E U S S	■	S N O O T	■	A L A
K I T E	■	P E S T E	■	C A T O N	■	S T I B
O S A	■	S L A T	■	S A R I P	■	P A N E L
T O L	■	C A T E C H E T I C	■	F E L I N E
A N E Y E T O	■	C O D A S	■	S I R	■	P S S
■	C E N O	■	O C C U R	■	P O S S E
C A T A T O N I A	■	C A T E R C O R N E R
A T I S	■	N A S T	■	E C O L E	■	N I T R E
T A C T	■	S T E T	■	S T E E R	■	A S H E S

156

```
YANG█TOYOU█OPAL█SHEDS
AROO█ABORN█REMO█CORAL
LAUGHLINES█DROPSALINE
UNSEALED█HEELS█PRICED
█NYES█CADRE█LIVE█
HITTER█CAVIL█METERMAN
EDELS█SAFETYLINES█ADO
MINE█WREN█OATS█EGIS
SOY█ACADS█AHOME█GRIME
█MARTENS█CLOSINGLINES
ROES█GOOSE█WACO█
ENDOFTHELINE█PREDATE
TALKS█ASONG█SEANS█LST
AVIS█FUSS█ALAR█CITE
PAN█LINESOFFIRE█BANES
ELEMENTS█NIFTY█MEREST
█UTES█WALES█NATO█
COASTS█MAGIC█LISTLESS
PICKETLINE█TOETHELINE
ASTER█ICER█ENTRE█ENOW
SEATS█PADS█DETER█DEBS
```

157

```
HOSTED█CHAS█STAGE█
ONTIME█CHEWS█LAIDON
LEADUPTHEGARDENPATH
FEMME█LOOMER█RYE█ROAR
LOOP█SOWWILDOATS█SNA
OUR█ARNS█NYET█SECT
STEEPLE█ACCA█SHEET
PAT█ALIBABA█CRUDDY
THROWCOLDWATERON
SPOOK█HEWS█STONE█BAA
SOPRANO█REFRAIN
ADS█COAST█THEO█LARRY
REAPTHEWHIRLWIND
ROWENA█TARRIES█ANI
OVINE█MAYS█BIGNESS
TELE█APRA█CRES█SPA
ARD█PLANTADOUBT█PTAS
SGTS█RAG█OPIATE█BRERS
RAKEONEOVERTHECOALS
ORIONS█BERGS█RONDLE
WEANS█ESSE█UNDOER
```

158

```
SIB█SCADS█SMOCK█DUALS
ADE█ARDOR█CALLA█AGGIE
GOLDGOODSHOPEANDSHEEP
ALLEGORY█INLAYER█HIT
█RENE█STEEN█ORLONS
TAPERS█AMOS█APPEAR
REEKS█LOON█CAPA█CUD
USNA█PUNT█SLAPS█AREAS
MINN█AGEE█TARES█MIAMI
PREDATE█BARON█WIENER
RICESUGARANDBREAD
OHARAS█BESTS█EARNEST
VINED█POSSE█THAT█DATE
ADDLE█EATER█ROTH█OGEE
CAM█ETES█VINS█BALER
ONIONS█SONE█COKERS
COLDAS█EMOTE█PAUL
ALL█LAPROBE█LAUREATE
SEEROODORDERSANDSYNOD
TIGON█AROAR█ANILE█ODE
SCENE█YELLS█PACES█NON
```

159

```
MERL█MEDIC█AMIS█AZAN
ARIA█ASIDO█LESE█BANAL
LOOKOUTMOUNTAIN█LITRE
ESTELLES█NEONS█LAREDO
█EDS█ATEST█HAZE
AGARS█ARID█SADE█PAR
LODI█PAREE█SCARE█PEDI
SOME█ALANS█ARLEN█ETES
ASA█PRIMA█ABEAM█STILE
BENARES█ROAM█STATEN
MONTSAINTMICHEL
SPRINT█CONI█HOTSPOT
TRADE█FARCE█STIRS█INO
RAZE█MALTA█MAINE█CAID
ADOS█IDEAS█OLEOS█ANOA
POR█FLED█ANTS█EBONY
█ALAS█MALTS█AFL█
GROTON█PACER█PESTERED
BATOR█ATTHEEARTHSCORE
STONE█DATE█ALINE█APIN
SEES█SHED█LAMAS█RENT
```

160

LAPS · STIRCRAZY · ATTIRE
ECRU · PARAPETED · CHIMES
SHERLOCKHOLMES · TEMPTS
SESTET · GEM · ERE
ION · MPS · THREAD · CDIX
URDU · SOOT · HAILS · CRIB
NYET · CHEAPERBY · MUUMUU
TEN · DISTRUSTS · CORSETS
OSTEO · TRI · GARDENIA
SOFA · REG · PARR · TOR
ASTRANGEENIGMAISMAN
NCO · KOOK · ORR · TSAR
EQUATING · FRA · REFER
RUNNERS · CAFETERIA · RAE
DIDOES · ILLOGICAL · GERM
STUD · ADIEU · NOME · OENO
KIRK · VESPER · GNP · DES
ATA · HIS · EASTON
FICHUS · SIRACONANDOYLE
KOKOMO · SONNABEND · FLEA
ANSWER · AUDITIONS · FEST

161

TACOS · SHOW · RABBI · THAT
IRISH · PERI · ADORN · HERR
TOSSASALAD · SARAH · RITE
LATISH · PLEA · PINECONES
ERSE · ALFS · INT · TROWELS
SHOU · URE · SETS
ANNAL · CLIPSOFF · STATES
LEASEHOLDS · NOEL · AFORE
LASSIE · YEAH · GRID · INGE
SPANGLE · ALAE · AVIATION
HIGHLANDFLING
TINCTURE · SOUR · ANIMATE
OLEO · MELS · ICES · ETAGES
REACT · TORO · ASPIRATORS
EXTORT · TOGETHER · TENNE
NAIF · ROE · COMO
ESQUIRE · TEA · ETNA · AHAB
STUTTERER · NOLA · CHROMO
TUES · DURAL · PITCHESWOO
OKEH · LLAMA · ATOP · MOERS
CARY · YELPS · HERO · INSET

162

KRONEN · LASTED · APSES
GRENADE · ASHORE · FLAME
HOUSEGUESTHOUSE · LAGER
RAPID · CDII · PREDACIOUS
SLANG · ALONG · PIN
EATEN · OFFSHOOTOFF
PARDONED · ELUTED · GOA
LEARNS · DOSAGES · AARON
ISNO · ABSOLUTES · EDSELS
COUPE · LEMON · SLOT
APPLEPIEORDERAPPLEPIE
ERIN · ELENA · FRONT
ARCTIC · BEFRIENDS · INFO
VERSE · MANAGED · LISTEN
ENA · CENTRO · CLINKERS
COMEOUTCOME · SHAMS
MPO · SHEAF · TAMER
COMPENSATE · AGRI · ENARE
AMAIN · PIANOFORTEPIANO
NACRE · ENLIST · ETOILES
GREED · SUEDES · DENNED

163

SARAH · SISTER · CRABBE
ADANO · ENTREE · HARRIS
BEVYOFQUAILS · ALCOTT
OLE · FAUST · OSTE · OTE
TEND · NEE · SMUTS · DEE
AWOL · SWINE · STORM
RAGLAN · STAND · DEAF
ORALS · MAORI · TRENCH
SAGA · ALIM · PAAR · HET
ERGS · ANTCOLONY · SIRE
SAL · AMOY · FORT · ACME
TEUTON · ABONE · ARKIN
ORES · TIETO · PIGSTY
AWFUL · ARLES · CITE
RAG · APASS · SOL · SLAT
ILE · ATOM · ATLAS · OSA
STEAMS · PRIDEOFLIONS
TESTAE · LENDER · ASSET
ARETHA · ESKARS · BEERY

164

1S	2T	3E	4M		5B	6S	7T	8A	9R		10A	11C	12D	13C		14M	15C	16L
17A	R	E	A		18L	E	A	V	E		19A	C	H	A	T	20A	H	IT
22W	I	N	D	23S	A	N	D	A	N	24D	S	T	A	R	S	25L	A	NE
	26E	L	I	A	S		27D	A	H	O	O	N		28D	I	R	G	E
29A	T	L	A	S	T		31L	E	V	I	N	S		32A	I	G	L	ON
33A	T	H	O	M	E		34S	E	R	I	E		35A	L	O	N	E	
36S	T	E	N		37T	H	E	S	T	R	A	N	G	E	R	40S	O	T
43P	A	C	S		44B	E	O	R		45P	I	E	R		46A	B	B	A
47S	R	O		48M	A	R	C	E	L	P	R	O	U	S	T	52L	A	OS
	53U	N	M	A	S	K		55E	R	O	D	E		56E	L	U	L	S
57G	E	N	O	E	S	E		59N	E	S		60C	O	M	E	D	I	E
62A	L	T	O	S		63L	U	T	E	S		65S	H	R	I	N	E	
66P	I	E	S		67S	E	A	S	O	N	I	N	H	E	L	L	70L	AE
73E	T	R	E		74A	L	T	E		75U	R	S	A		76F	A	S	T
77D	E	F		78A	L	B	E	R	T	C	A	M	U	S		82L	I	ST
	83E	L	I	S	E		85H	O	R	E	B		86S	P	A	R	T	A
88T	R	I	O	D	E		90B	A	R	M	E	N		92L	A	R	U	ES
93R	E	T	I	E		94C	A	S	A	B	A		95C	A	B	O	B	
96A	B	E	T		97T	H	E	F	L	O	W	E	R	S	O	F	E	VIL
102P	U	R	E		103H	O	R	A	L		104A	V	A	S	T	105R	I	CE
	106S	S	R		107M	U	S	T		108Y	E	S	E	S		109T	E	EM

165

1T	2S	3A	4R	5S		6F	7A	8L	9A		10A	11B	12B	13O	14T		15R	16O	17M	18P
19E	N	N	U	I		20I	B	I	S		21P	E	R	I	S		26E	V	I	L
23E	A	T	E	N		24E	A	S	T		25A	C	A	S	E		26V	A	C	A
27S	P	I	R	A	L	S	T	A	I	R	C	A	S	E		30G	O	L	A	N
			31S	T	A	T	E	S		32O	H	M	S		33E	E	L			
34T	35A	36M		37R	O	A	D		38S	M	E	E		39S	L	O	V	40E	41N	42E
43E	R	I	C	A		45S	I	E			46F	E	L	L	I	N	I	S		
47M	I	N	I		48T	W	I	S	T	O	F	F	A	T	E		53N	U	N	S
54P	E	A	R		55R	O	S	E	S		56O	R	T	S		57A	G	R	E	E
58E	L	E	C	T	I	O	N			60F	O	E		61L	U	C	E	S		
			62L	I	E		63T	64W	65I	R	L	E	D	67I	R	R				
68B	69L	E	N	D		70H	A	Y			71A	S	N	I	E	R	73E	74S	75
76G	O	O	D	Y		77S	78W	I	G		79A	N	N	I	E		81D	O	L	T
82A	L	O	T		83O	N	E	G	O	O	D	T	U	R	N		85I	T	E	R
86B	O	T	H	E	R	E	D			88N	A	H			89A	T	O	N	E	
90E	S	S	E	N	C	E		91S	H	E	M		93D	94E	95M	S		96R	A	P
			97B	O	A		98W	H	O	A		99S	O	N	A	T	A			
101S	102T	103R	A	W		104W	H	I	R	L	I	N	G	D	E	R	V	106I	107S	H
109T	E	A	S		110G	A	I	N	S		111S	A	G	E		112I	R	A	T	E
113L	A	C	E		114A	L	L	E	E		115T	I	E	R		116D	I	N	A	R
117O	R	E	S		118B	E	E	R	S		119O	L	D	S		120E	L	A	N	D

166

1B	2R	3A	4H	5E		6P	7O	8I		9S	10O	11S		12E	13T	14A	15H
16I	S	L	A	N	D	E	R	S		18A	M	A	H	19D	E	T	A	CH
22D	O	N	T	T	A	K	E	M	23Y	B	I	K	24I	N	I	S	A	WAY
	25E	R	I	E		26S	O	L	L	E	R	E	T	S		27A	R	S
28N	O	R	M	A	L		31K	E	E	N	E	R		32S	I	L	O	
33A	H	E	A	P		34A	V	I	E	W		37S	O	L	U	T	I	ON
40M	A	N	I	S	A	N	I	S	L	A	N	D		44S	O	N	O	F
45B	R	E	L		46G	A	L	L		47S	U	I	48S		49W	A	P	ITI
52Y	A	W		53M	E	D	E	A		54I	T	A	L		58G	I	V	EME
		56F	I	N	E			57E	T	L	E		58G	59I	V	E	M	E
60W	I	L	D	M	A	N	61F	R	O	M	B	O	R	N	E	O		
65S	P	A	R	T	A		67D	E	L	E			68P	A	R	R		
69H	A	K	E		70Z	W	E	I		71C	R	E	T	E		73H	A	M
76E	D	E	S	77S	A		79E	T	A	S		80I	O	L	E	81S	A	BU
	82F	A	T	E	S		84S	M	A	R	T	B	E	R	M	U	D	AS
87I	N	U	L	A	S	E	S		90W	E	E	S	T		91I	Z	O	TE
92R	O	L	E		93P	A	L	94L	95E	T			96S	C	E	N	E	S
97A	R	N		98B	E	A	L	I	L	L	I	E		100R	U	E	R	
102Q	U	E	E	N	E	L	I	Z	A	B	E	T	H	I	S	L	A	NDS
108I	N	S	T	A	R		109N	A	N	A		110C	U	B	A	L	I	BRE
	111S	C	I	O		112E	S	O		113H	E	S		114E	N	C	Y	C

167

1B	2E	3T	4T	5O	6R		7I	8N	9U	10R	11E	12D		13A	14N	15A	16T	17T	18O
19A	T	H	O	M	E		20N	E	R	O	L	I		21S	L	A	T	H	ER
22T	H	E	P	A	T	H	F	I	N	D	E	R		24E	L	E	M	E	NT
25E	A	S	E	R		26O	L	G	A	S		27E	28D	N	A	S		29R	OW
30A	N	I	S		31B	R	A	H	E		32S	C	I	O	N		33B	O	NO
34U	S	S		35S	L	A	T	S		36O	T	T	E	R		37T	A	U	
		38A	P	A	C	E		39G	L	O	O	M		40T	H	I	G	H	S
43S	44T	L	U	K	E		45C	E	D	A	R		46C	H	A	T	H	A	M
47C	O	H	E	R	E		48F	R	E	R	E		49B	O	O	N		50R	IO
51O	N	E	R	S		52A	R	I	S	E		53L	O	I	R	E		54I	RK
55D	A	F	T		56R	E	B	E	L	L	I	O	N			58I	D	L	E
59I	T	O		60B	O	R	E	S		62I	A	M	B	S		63O	N	E	IR
64C	I	O		65A	M	I	D		66C	A	D	I	S		67C	A	I	R	NS
68I	N	T	A	K	E	S		69T	E	B	E	T		70S	E	T	O	S	E
72L	A	C	I	E	R		73P	E	A	L	S		74W	O	D	E	N		
	75A	R	R		76N	O	R	S	E		77G	A	L	E	N		78M	79O	W
81R	E	V	E		83M	O	O	R	E		84C	O	R	E	S		85S	E	RI
86E	T	A		87S	E	R	R	A		88R	E	A	L	M		89A	N	N	AS
90C	A	L	D	E	R	A		92C	93L	I	N	T	O	N	S	94D	I	T	CH
95A	P	R	O	P	O	S		96E	A	S	T	E	R			97D	I	P	OLE
98P	E	Y	O	T	E			99S	T	A	R	E	D			100S	T	E	RES

168

P	I	E	R	C	E		A	M	A	S	S		C	H	A	I	R	M	A	N
A	G	R	E	E	D		L	O	N	E	R		R	O	M	A	N	I	Z	E
C	O	N	T	E	M	P	L	A	T	E	S		E	V	A	N	S	T	O	N
T	R	E	E			A	S	T	I	R			W	E	T			E	V	E
			N	E	O	N		S	C	E	N	T			L	E	A	D	S	
C	H	E	E	T	A	H		S	A	R	G		U	N	E					
A	I	R		E	R	A	T	O		S	P	O	O	N	R	I	V	E	R	
G	L	A	S	S	S	N	A	K	E		S	O	H	O		O	R	A	L	
E	L	S	E		D	R	A	M	S		P	O	T	P	O	U	R	R	I	
	S	E	R	V	A	L		S	C	H	I	S	M		O	U	T	S	E	T
			A	C	E	S		E	O	N			E	C	U	S				
C	H	A	I	S	E		A	H	E	R	N	E		A	T	T	L	E	E	
C	O	N	S	T	A	B	L	E		N	E	G	E	V		A	L	B	A	
C	O	N	N		L	A	N	D		R	O	S	E	B	O	W	L	E	R	
K	E	T	T	L	E	D	R	U	M		S	E	N	O	R		E	R	E	
I	V	A		S	I	N	O		D	O	C	E	N	T	S					
S	T	A	N	D		S	E	N	N	A		I	M	A	M					
F	R	A		T	A	P		T	O	R	A	S		E	L	A	S			
L	E	M	O	N	A	D	E		M	A	C	K	T	H	E	K	N	I	F	E
A	N	A	C	O	N	D	A		O	N	A	I	R		M	A	D	C	A	P
P	O	R	T	R	A	Y	S		T	A	N	E	Y		A	S	S	E	R	T

169

I	N	L	A	N	D		A	C	T	E	S		G	U	M	B	O	S
M	O	O	N	E	R		D	R	A	P	E		O	N	I	O	N	Y
P	E	N	N	S	Y	L	V	A	N	I	A		A	L	S	A	C	E
S	L	E	E	T		I	A	G	O		E	L	I			R	E	S
			S	E	N	N		S	K	I	T			T	A	D		
A	L	L	S		N	E	C	K		I	N	R	E		S	W	A	G
P	E	A	C	H	T	R	E	E		E	S	E	L		T	A	L	E
E	N	T	R	E	E		L	E	V	I		S	P	I	L	L	S	
S	O	E	U	R		O	A	S	T		S	O	I	R		K	A	T
		B	O	U	R	B	O	N	S	T	R	E	E	T				
R	A	H		I	N	C	A		A	L	S	O		S	H	A	M	A
A	R	O	U	N	D		N	I	S	I		A	T	A	B	A	L	
Y	E	L	P		E	D	D	O		T	H	E	B	O	W	E	R	Y
S	A	L	T		R	I	O	T		S	O	D	A		S	T	O	A
			Y	O	M		G	N	A	T		O	S	S	A			
U	A	W		O	H	S		O	L	P	E		T	E	N	T	S	
G	R	O	O	V	Y		P	O	W	E	L	L	S	T	R	E	E	T
H	O	O	P	E	D		E	D	I	N	A		P	A	L	A	T	E
S	E	D	E	R	E		G	A	T	E	S		A	R	E	T	E	S

170

C	A	S	P	A	R		T	U	S	A	R		M	A	S	O	N
A	M	A	L	I	E		E	N	C	R	E		S	E	M	I	N	A	R
L	E	M	O	N	C	U	S	T	A	R	D		P	R	O	N	A	T	O	R
G	N	U		T	A	N	T	A	R	A		O	R	I	N	G		I	B	O
A	T	E	N		P	L	U	M	P	U	D	D	I	N	G		O	V	I	D
R	I	L	E		I	D	E	S		O	E	N	O		I	R	E	N	E	
Y	A	S	S		A	N	O	D		S	W	A	G		B	R	A	S	S	
	S	A	L	E	S		S	H	E			M	E	A	N					
S	T	E	E	P	E	D		T	H	O	L	E	P	I	N		G	A	S	H
T	A	L	L	I	N		S	H	O	R		V	E	S	T		E	C	H	O
A	M	I	R	S		S	W	E	E	T	M	E	A	T		A	S	I	A	N
F	I	D	O		P	I	E	T		C	A	N	T		S	C	H	E	M	E
F	L	E	D		A	N	D	A	M	A	N	S		S	P	H	E	R	E	S
			E	D	I	E			O	K	S		S	H	E	E	R			
R	A	P	I	D		E	R	N	E		S	L	I	D		B	A	N	K	
R	E	S	I	N		H	S	I	A		C	H	A	R		E	L	O	N	
A	L	A	E		B	A	K	E	D	A	L	A	S	K	A		T	I	T	I
M	I	S		E	R	V	I	N		B	O	T	H	E	R	S		T	I	G
I	C	E	C	R	E	A	M		B	U	T	T	E	R	S	C	O	T	C	H
		S	A	R	O	N	N	O		U	S	H	E	R		E	A	R	L	E	T
		L	Y	S	S	A		S	E	E	R	S		S	T	R	E	S	S

171

C	A	R	E	E	N		A	L	O	H	A		E	A	G	L	E
E	N	I	S	L	E		G	A	P	E	D		T	U	R	R	E	T
T	I	T	T	L	E	T	A	T	T	L	E		O	R	I	E	N	T
A	L	A	R		D	O	R	I	S		S	A	P		S	E	T	A
			O	U	T	R	A	N		S	T	A	S	S	E	N		
P	I	N	G	P	O	N	G		A	Y	E	A	Y	E		L	I	P
F	R	I	E	R		S	A	B	E	R		T	A	M	A	L	E	
C	A	N	N	O		R	U	R		P	L	U	T	O	N	I	C	
S	E	E		A	W	S		R	O	T	T	E	R		N	D	A	K
			R	I	L	L	S		H	E	A	V	E					
A	S	P	S		L	O	I	T	E	R		S	Y	N		R	I	A
S	P	A	N	G	L	E	D		P	O	P		A	M	O	N	G	
S	A	L	A	R	Y		G	I	B	E	D		M	A	N	S	E	
E	N	L		A	N	I	S	E	S		L	A	C	E	R	A	T	E
			M	O	D	I	S	T	E		A	L	K	A	L	I		
A	H	A	B		L	E	O		A	L	M	A	S		E	A	S	T
F	I	L	I	A	L		P	I	T	T	E	R	P	A	T	T	E	R
E	L	L	E	R	Y		A	R	T	A	L		E	N	T	I	R	E
R	O	S	S	I		T	R	A	I	L		R	O	A	S	T	S

172

```
KEPI  ALPH  SERB  LOAF
ICON  SILO  LIEU  ILLE
THESCHOOLFORSCANDAL
HOMERUN  LOPE  ODDEST
    RUR  BARE  PLIE
BUTTS  DENT  SLIMNESS
OCHS  FRED  SPACE  TAU
ALE  LIAR  AIRY  UELE
TACTISM  ASKEW  ARRAS
  RICHARDSHERIDAN
SHIRK  TOMES  ISOLATE
TOTE  IBIS  AGES  LES
ALI  ASSET  ACHE  CLAM
RECRUITS  KNIT  RHYME
  ODES  DUAD  SOO
SHADES  WARP  SOPRANO
COVENTGARDENTHEATER
OMEN  AONE  SOLO  LAME
WERT  SOTS  TROT  ENOS
```

173

```
LPS  DEN  HANG  BREL
BOLT  BALE  OLOR  ROVE
BLUEBELLS  BLUEWATER
CASPARY  TEA  SWIVEL
  PET  BLAND  USU
SOBER  SUER  UPPERBAY
ALAS  MUM  BRA  ALVA
NIB  DEEPBLUESEA  UAR
SOYLENT  LETS  STEELE
  BIND  PUNTS  TOMS
VALLEE  ORTO  PASSKEY
EMU  BLUEBONNETS  IRE
LIED  STS  ORE  TENN
DESIGNER  ESTE  LOSES
  ALE  YALTA  SEM
ALLOWS  IMA  CHATTEL
BLUEBEARD  BLUENOSES
EMIR  SLOE  ATTA  MALT
LASS  TEES  TSE  SRS
```

174

```
SLAV  IWONT  IMP  MSTS
RENO  REFER  NEO  MACACA
ATALEOF2CITIES  AGREAT
STACCATO  BUTTERFIELD8
  AAMS  SUNI  EINE
TO2ND  PINEAL  MOODIER
AT40  17YEARLOCUST  NCO
HAHS  SULU  THEO  1700
AGO  10PERCENTER  ROTLS
SOURPUSS  AVIEW  TOWHEE
  REAR  FREDS  OPAH
ASSESS  ARENA  SANENESS
TOADS  3LITTLEPIGS  AHA
RUDY  ABLE  GURU  OVAL
ATA  THE3RDDEGREE  PEKE
PHYSICA  SEEDER  GENES
  OLER  BRED  BARN
1STCLASSMAIL  LENINIST
SPACES  10COMMANDMENTS
REVERE  ATL  ANGIE  STOP
  DIRS  MOE  NOONS  SOWN
```

175

```
BLIP  UTAH  CATS  TERN
AARE  RACE  AMAH  ABEE
LIAR  GREEKFIRE  TONS
DRESDEN  DEED  ELANET
  IUS  BINS  SPAR
ALGAE  HUNT  MAIN  JAB
DARN  TANG  PULSE  EPI
DIE  DENT  TORAH  TWIT
ACADIA  ELAM  CAINE
  TURKISHDELIGHTS
CADET  SHAD  RUSHED
ORAL  ALARY  SHIM  DEO
INN  PIAVE  HOOD  PALM
FOE  ERNE  CELT  SAYSO
  HARD  CHAD  BUN
SAFARI  FAIT  GONDOLA
EBEN  FRENCHFRY  EPIC
REED  LEAD  ERIN  RASH
```

176

```
BEMA  TOADS  MARC
DARED  RAMIE  IDIOT
CONSTITUTION  LOOMED
ANTE  PASS  CEDES  MAO
SEA  DORS  SECTS  WISE
TEMPEST  MESAS  ROTES
  INE  TONES  TORT
ESCES  PITAS  ARMLETS
ETHS  MINOT  PLEADERS
LOA  CONGRESSMEN  MUG
EMIGRATE  FLOES  PACT
DERAINS  ALIAS  PANES
  MUSS  RIOTS  MAR
SLANT  CEROS  PATTERS
HUNT  LONER  MINE  LIP
ONS  SEWED  SARA  DANE
RAHWAY  WASHINGTONDC
RIANT  ELTON  EASES
```

177

CLAW TALC APR CPA
AURORA ABOO IRE ORBS
STAGESTRUCK DUMDDORAS
SIDE PATTIES DARE INK
ELLS LAS POIRE EDDY
TEE BEN KRISSKRINGLE
AMON EARTH ATEO
ELEGANT LEVE ALMOST
ROMAN TILES CRIB
GRETNAGREEN MAINSAIL
SNEE GRAND BURSE IDEA
ARSENICS BUSTERBROWN
VEST TARTS OGLES
BETISE ONLY ENMASSE
OTEA CARTA NUBS
JOHNNYJUMPUP ATT MAA
OKIE SANTO FLA RATE
AMO MERE RECLAIM ASTO
DAPPERDAN CHARLIECHAN
NIPS ITA HARI STEERS
ASS NEB OPEC TASS

178

ELAN ROOST PRAM
TOLEDO ENNUI AERATE
INSEAM FETED RATTAN
BRAE MOLAR TONAL ENDS
RAG LACS LID GEE
ODES BODE SPOKEN FLAT
SEROLOGY STAGE OSIERS
LINY FERRY SVEN
NAPERY CARAT CHEMISTS
ASIDE RANGY SAIL SLIT
OKE GORGE CORNS OLE
MECH OURS SUAVE TOPEE
IDEOLOGY BARRE TAVERN
NENE ARLES ZERO
ACCORD FRIED PYROLOGY
POOR ASLEEP DAMN OPAL
EAR WIT DECO ILE
XRAY BEMAS OCALA BALM
SLEWED INANE ORNATE
ESTATE COVEN GEARED
IRAN SWEET YALE

179

FOHN PILAF GETAT TSPS
ANYA ADAMI APURE RHEA
DEPRESSION LABORPAINS
EDIT READE AIRLINES
SHR LUG BLUNT DOING
WITHDRAWALPAIN REELIN
IDEO EGO YESSIR SEETO
TENOR ARK SPED SSTS
ASKED NERVOUSTIC
TWISTED LOAM YEAR WCF
IAO ULU POLAR SLA ROI
AYN SUNK KENO TENCENT
EXHAUSTION RIANT
ASHE EARN TAG ARCED
AMASS MISSED BRA OHSO
RUNSAT MOTIONSICKNESS
GEMOF NANNO DHU DAS
MANNERED BEERS ERIK
CRACKEDRIB GALLSTONES
ILIE RUADE ACUTO TEAK
VOLS OPTED LEMAN AERY

180

SLOAN SLED MACED
PORNO SCONE SODAPOP
BOYANDTHESEA POLLIWOG
ORAL SOONER MIDI ELA
ORLE DETROITCUB PRIG
BALSA DTS TRES GRETA
SNY BALI IDAS SNIDE
MELEE COL FAUN
WHALER HOLYCALF COCO
HIDES ZANE ABIE EXAM
LIRAS TONS BRAT MAINE
ITEM LOON JUTS PINDAR
PERE IMMATURE MENDEL
PAVE HAS CENCI
CRUDE RENT HATE QUO
SEEPS EDAM RAN SOUND
ELSA TROJANCOLT RIDE
ALT ORRA EOSINS ATRO
LOEUFDOR CALICOKITTEN
SENIORS IRENE ALOES
LOESS OSSA TERRS

181

```
REPAST   SERF   BOA   MANOR
ERASER   TRAITORS   OLONA
INTHEEYEOFTHEBEHOLDER
GIE  SMART  SERICIN   ARE
NEST  OGEE   TORSELS
    ISLE  MADEA  NEER
SWAPHORSESINMIDSTREAM
LASSO   ASCARID    IDO
UKE  ODIN  ORO  EASE  RAP
REACTING  TYL  STINTERS
    PINT        OTTO
SPOONERS LAW  INERRANT
TAP  GROW  ORA  MESA  LAY
ERA   ANTESUP   IODIN
WALLSDONOTAPRISONMAKE
   ALOP  WORST  ANSE
BEDAZED   INCA   SCAM
MEL  TEREDOS  CORNS  OBI
ALLMENARECREATEDEQUAL
SLIER  TERTIATE  ORELSE
TESTA  EKE  SUED  NODDER
```

182

```
SAPS   HUS   GOO   ILLE
LIRA   ENT   ERA   NOOK
ADEN   RHODAGRAVURE
GAYDSEAVER    SPIKED
     YAWNER   AMATI
MAJ  BIDS   DECENCY
IGOROTS   STONE   GOA
BREATH   BURR    GAP
  IKES   GALEN  MILS
OPE    LILY   BERATE
APR  BOOTY   CLASSED
FARCEUR   POOL   SRO
   WARTY   HEROIC
TRILLS  PUNSDELEON
BELLEEDANCER   ACHE
ALDA   LAG ITE   CHIC
RYES    LYE  LSD  KOOK
```

183

```
SADA   METS   PITH   HAP
ODIN   AXEL   ALIA   DESI
FINGERPAINTING    OATS
ANTONIO  VOTE   GLORIA
   LEE   DELI   CLINT
ABBA    KURT   SHINESUP
COL  BONESETTING   IRA
IOO  IRIS   RUNG   SCAR
DROPLET  GOUDA   ANKLE
   DOLL  PANSY   FLOE
SAPPY  VALET  CROWNED
OBOE  VISE   SHAN   IDA
ALI  HANDSHAKING   NIP
RESOURCE   ATIP   SGTS
   OMNIA   ARTS   ALA
SONATA   ASEA   BRASSIE
AKIN   BACKSCRATCHING
MINI   LIAM   HALE  ANGE
PEG    ETTE   EMIL  YEAR
```

184

```
SIMAR   OCAT   SENOR   TEAM
ALENE   VANE   LEONE   ADUE
REGISTEREDNURSES    KITS
ADA   THROW   AMIES   TETRA
NET   SEAL   JIBED   JOSHES
ALOE   ICEDOVER   COLIC
CANDYSTRIPER   SOLITARY
    ISS   SEL   UKASE   VEE
ACTE   TIN  NATO   RENT
FLORENCENIGHTINGALE
LIAR   DOER   PRO   NILE
ERR   BIRDS   ART OAS
SEAHORSE   JESSIEBREWER
   BOONE   JUMPEDAT   SAXE
PLATTE   JONES   ERAS  SPA
HARDY   BURKE   DORIA  TIM
INTO   TENDERLOVINGCARE
AGOG   DETAT   OVEN   EAGER
LENS   STANS   BERG   SLEDS
```

185

COBRA · SHAPES · TARTAN
ARIOT · HOMELY · EMERGE
RABBLEINARMS · ROMANS
ALL · ERNES · TUSK · MAT
TEED · RED · THESE · UPTO
· AMOR · SHAME · ANSER
SAVIOR · CHEWS · CHIT
APART · DRAWN · POETESS
LOGY · TIARA · GRIM · APT
ALA · INTENTION · MAA
ALB · FLEE · DEANS · PERT
MOODIER · TENNE · HORTA
· NARD · LEROT · VASSAL
SIDLE · VOTER · PETE
UGLY · LAVER · IAN · SALT
ENO · OONA · AMITY · DOR
DIVERS · BEGGARSOPERA
ETERNE · LINAGE · LILAC
SERGES · ENURED · KEENE

186

FORTWO · DIRT · AMBS · PAPA
ANTHRA · MOOR · LALO · RIEL
MYHEARTINSANFRANCISCO
EMORY · ATEE · ERIN · ANNAN
SNA · FER · STREAK · SCENE
IRONIE · HOD · IRAE
OSTLER · SIR · ANI · TREE
THERE · THEWORLDGOROUND
RUNOFTHE · ABEAM · ONION
ANNA · HALAS · SPIELS · NSA
DARWIN · STREAM
SOE · SUSANS · MESNE · YAWS
CAPRI · CUETO · TIROLEAN
ATHINGCALLEDJOE · MURRE
THAT · SAL · SEE · SECOND
USAR · AST · EMBANK
MARAT · DESPOT · ERY · YOD
ARULE · RAKE · ABRI · ASHES
COMINROUNDTHEMOUNTAIN
ASES · BODO · IOTA · BEARSA
WENT · IMET · MEAN · ATRAMP

187

SHAKEUP · OTTOS · DEALOUT
LUCERNE · BUHLS · INCONNU
INTROIT · ERROR · ONEPAIR
PEU · STRS · NOR · GNU · BAN
OKAS · SEESAW · RENIG · OTO
NETTY · ARARA · ENE · ROUEN
RELIC · BLOWOUT · BASTS
OPAH · TUANS · FENS
PAT · DAR · NYE · CLII · MOI
ANITA · DEAD · COUNTDOWN
STRIKEOFF · SINGALONG
CROSSOVER · SARG · SYCEE
HAS · USER · ART · SAN · HDS
EMIR · SAURO · TAPS
DARIN · REUNITE · BALED
RESET · MAN · AKING · LILAC
UFO · EBERT · RESALE · PARA
NAC · ARA · ZOO · MAMO · PER
OLIVINE · MAUVE · IMPASSE
FLAUNTS · ANNES · REPLETE
FALLOUT · PEDRO · STOPSON

188

SHARE · STAG · KIM · SOFT
HOREB · TONE · ONE · INURED
RASPBERRYTARTS · MATURE
EROS · ROY · LEO · RAISINS
DYN · FAD · CATAWBA · LET
ERSE · ODA · ELM · TSAR
PAWNEE · SOURGRAPES · OPE
ELATE · HILL · REDHOT · FED
ROTE · RAN · THAN · RETRO
TOE · CALF · ESTA · WITH
FRUITFULEXPERIENCES
MANE · LODE · CRAG · VOW
WHERE · OISE · AIR · GIBE
AIL · MAOIST · LIDS · PINES
SRO · APPLESAUCE · DESERT
PEND · TIE · ODE · LEST
POE · EXPIRES · AFT · BRA
ORANGES · ENT · HIE · SEEP
DOTAGE · STRAWBERRYPIES
DOCTOR · TEE · HARD · EAGLE
THEN · ARM · ORES · TREES

189

Row 1: FACILE · BAYARD · JINNI
Row 2: EXODUS · AGORAE · ADAIR
Row 3: REGINA · TRUISM · WYNNE
Row 4: CUSTARDPIEBLUES
Row 5: WATCH · LIME · VOL
Row 6: ICHU · DIE · NEA · ENIGMA
Row 7: THEICECREAMCONECOOT
Row 8: HEYRUBE · EPEUS · DOL
Row 9: ART · PRO · MAA · BORA
Row 10: MOOSEONROLLERSKATES
Row 11: ARPS · ROI · EEN · HAL
Row 12: CAT · RECON · HANDLES
Row 13: ELIJOHNSONSCAKEWALK
Row 14: SECEDE · TUB · RUE · ILKA
Row 15: FDR · REEL · SNOOT
Row 16: HALFBAKEDALASKA
Row 17: AMARA · ICINGS · ERRANT
Row 18: RATEL · SUNDAE · MAHLER
Row 19: ETHYL · SATYRS · PHOEBE

190

Row 1: AHEM · MME · ADAM · COTTA
Row 2: CODA · AAR · RORI · OPHIR
Row 3: THEJOHNALDENS · MEETA
Row 4: SONORA · DEER · EPI · MOT
Row 5: REL · IONS · ACTO
Row 6: CARS · IANS · RUSSETED
Row 7: ULO · DANTE · PONS · SHEA
Row 8: ROSTRATE · PULSE · TERN
Row 9: STERILE · EARFUL · RYE
Row 10: MIN · GABRIEL · SAO
Row 11: OCA · ARRETS · LAUNFAL
Row 12: SART · RAINY · FIRESALE
Row 13: SLYS · OTES · GREAT · LIA
Row 14: EMMANUEL · FLED · OLAF
Row 15: URES · ALEE · EBB
Row 16: BUR · TEA · NEAL · TYLOSE
Row 17: ORPAH · QUEENOFHEARTS
Row 18: ASHRE · URET · ALA · TEEN
Row 19: SAYER · AIDS · DON · ELSE

191

Row 1: DAWES · TRAP · ADAM · BIBS
Row 2: FLINT · ROPE · ULEMA · YORE
Row 3: CIGARBEARDANDFATIGUES
Row 4: MILAN · AREAS · TROST
Row 5: OCTOPUS · PLEAS · SION
Row 6: NEARER · FLEAS · TUNNELED
Row 7: BIKES · CRADLESONGS · ERA
Row 8: ABED · KHAN · PLUS · IGOR
Row 9: SAN · COONSKINCAP · MOIST
Row 10: ESOTERIC · ARIAS · HANSES
Row 11: TUNER · NAV · CAVIL
Row 12: ARISTA · CRETE · MUSICALS
Row 13: PICKS · PRESENTARMS · TAP
Row 14: IDES · CREE · RALE · TUTU
Row 15: EGO · WHISKBROOMS · PARER
Row 16: DEFOREST · RENTS · TALENT
Row 17: RENE · BABES · JURISTS
Row 18: AVISO · RAZES · PERAS
Row 19: CHESTPROTECTORANDMASK
Row 20: HALO · OUTON · AKIN · EAMON
Row 21: EBAN · DEAN · RAGS · SNOUT

192

Row 1: ETCH · HOMO · UGLY · SAME
Row 2: SHOE · ETAL · LIEU · ARAG
Row 3: CROSSWORD · ELAM · TIRE
Row 4: HOP · ONETWO · ANALYSIS
Row 5: ENEMY · HIVA · ARENT
Row 6: WERE · BRAVING · SIS
Row 7: ATEASE · CADET · GPS
Row 8: PUPTENT · SLOVEN · POUT
Row 9: SRA · CIAO · INOLD · HAZE
Row 10: YAPS · PRIVATE · ITZA
Row 11: CREE · PLANE · STEM · ILK
Row 12: HERD · HANGSA · IDEATES
Row 13: OSS · BINGO · MAOISM
Row 14: ELL · ETIENNE · OVAL
Row 15: STILE · SARD · ARIDE
Row 16: PICKWICK · LIBBER · GOA
Row 17: ABET · GOES · CLOCKWORK
Row 18: RENO · EMEU · AURA · IDEE
Row 19: ERIN · TALE · NEED · GARY

193

```
S T E E L . . P P S . . W I N G . . E P A C T
M E L B A . A I T . I L O N A . N A D E R
I N G O T . I L O . L A V A L . I R A D E
L O A . H O N O R E D . W A R G A M E S
E R R S . U T T R R E R S . S I M P E R S
. . C I T Y . D E S O T O . M A E
B A R R I O . P L U M B . T S A R
O R C . K N U T . R E D I E T S . O D E
P O E . G R I E G E . S T E A M B O A T
E T T A S . W O L F E . T A E L
C H O P I N A U E R . B A C H S L U N C H
S L U G . C E L L O . L E E R Y
S I D E L I N E S . E N D I V E . R I D
O R E . S T E R E O S . P E G S . V E E
T E R M . R O G N A . N O I S E S
O S H . S A C R A L . S I N K
R I A L T O S . R E S T A F F S . I V E S
A N D E R S O N . A T T R I T E . E L I
V A L S E . N A T A L . V I F . A P R O N
E N A T E . G R E T A . I T T . S E D G E
D E I S T . D E E D . A S H . T R I E S
```

194

```
R A B I D . T R I B . F R I . R A P
A R E M Y . E E N Y . F L I P S I D E
S I D E S A D D L E . L O P S I D E D
C O S T . S I D E S H O W . E G G A R
A S I A . H O O T . O R E S . N E R O
L E D . S L U G . S T A R T L E
. E S T A S . D I L L . O U T S A T
S E M P E R . J U D Y . C O B . I V E
A L A R M . W A K E . T O P S I D E S
C A N A . S I D E S T E P S . C E R T
R I N G S I D E . W A R Y . P A S S E
E N E . O D E . F I L M . C A M P E R
D E R A I L . C A P E . M O T E L
. P R E L U D E . G O B S . I L A
W A S P . D O P E . F L O W . I T E R
O N E O N . S I D E L I N E . S T A R
O N E S I D E D . S I D E B Y S I D E
S I D E C A R S . S E E R . A U N T S
H E Y . E N S . E R R S . W E G O T
```

195

```
T A B S . A L E C . G A D . A C T A
A L A E . A G O R A . G E N I C . B L U E
2 T H A N D N A I L . 1 0 D E R L O I N S
S E S T O L E S . M O L L Y . A E R I E
B R E W . I L E . O C T A
I N I E A R . O M N I A . B R O I L E R S
S O I L S . G R 8 G O D B R O W N . X I I
H I N T . 4 A I R . E I S . R A P T
A S A . F R E E 4 A L L S . B R O S S E
M E M O R I A L . S N E A K . R A M P
I V I E D . T I V . Y O G E E
L U L L . E L E M E . C O N S O R T S
F E L L E D . S T R 8 E N O U T . I N
A L I E . U S N . A U N E . P I N O
R I O . E N L I G H 1 0 I N G . T A N G O
M A N A L O N E . A S C O T . P E G G E D
M E T A . R O T . R A R E
T R A G I . P I A N O . T E R R A S S E
M A N Y C O O K S . P E R 4 M A N C E S
L A I D . E T H O S . U L E M A . T U R N
E N N A . T A N . S I T S . S M E E
```

196

```
M A C A O . A R C H . D E C I . S A X
A D O R N . S O H O . E T O N . O W E
C O N F E S S I O N . C O N F O U N D
A R C . S T U . R E D O . D O U R
W E E D . A M I E . A C L U . T W I T
S E C R E T . S T O C K P I L E
R A S C A L . A M P . P E T U N I A
A L I A S E S . I R A T E . S T E A M
N E O N A T E . N O V A
D E N T S . C O N T E S T . A P P L E
D I E S . C A M E R O N
A M I R S . I D E S T . U N I C O R N
L I N E U P S . T A R . G L A C E S
D E C L A R I N G . A R L E N E
A L I I . O T O E . A M O I . S S T S
S E N D . D E A R . O C T . S H Y
P R O F O U N D . P R O F E S S I O N
U A R . I C A L . E A S E . A M O N G
B U S . R E N E . D Y E R . R A N G E
```

197

TULIP MEATPIE ARTFOR
MORONI ATHIRST COWRIE
IBANEZ CHOCOLATEMOOSE
NONE ARRAY PELOTA ZED
SOURCREAM LEO WINCE
KTS OREM AELFRIC ONME
SMOKEDSALMON CAFES
SAHIB ISIN EAT TUTORS
APATITE NAIRN RISSOLE
TRIUNE KERN SUET DEN
PATTYDEFOIEGRAS
BAO TOAD ENOL CREPES
ORATING FARAD KEDGING
METROS ELM LISA PAGET
BACON CRABCOCKTAIL
ELUL BOATING IMRE POT
ILMEN TES CLAMSTEWS
RES ARISEN BELIE ARNA
CHILLYCONCARNE NURSED
MENIAL DEEPEST INDORE
PREENS ARSENES AEONS

198

MAS SCRAP ADDLES THAT
OPA LLANO SAMARA HONE
ILL OASTS TWIGGY EATS
ROASTPHEASANT ESPRIT
AMMI UDI ERITREA
BIRDOFPARADISE ERMA
CORA SEN ELASTICS
PATHETIC NUMERAL RENI
ODOR SLAM OLE IMINES
SARIS EDUCATE BAD
THESWEDISHNIGHTINGALE
TIM CATFISH NEVER
DEMOTE AAR TIES FEAR
ATOP EBBTIDE ALEYARDS
MOTHERLY ENT ARUM
NOEL ASTHECROWFLIES
ROSSSEA AIX LSTS
NITWIT GOOSEBERRYPIE
AMOR OCCULT SIREE IFA
NAME VIOLET TRITE ELM
AMEN ELPASO EDSEL DEY

199

LION AMARA CARD AWOL
ENDOW NABOB AMOI SORA
AKELA STOWE BEAM CRAM
FARETHEEWELLANNABELLE
STORY ANT GANDER
CLOSET ALAPA EGAD
LOU AERATORS UTI MEA
ITSTULIPTIMEINHOLLAND
PITH KENT NPS LORNA
ERIK EAGRE LAYOUT
BYTHERIVERSAINTEMARIE
LAROSA ESSEN ETAL
ALILT RNA GEAR TREE
STAYINYOUROWNBACKYARD
TAD OOM INACTION IGO
CURT ADAYS SELDOM
POPART ORO PATSY
ILLBEHOMEFORCHRISTMAS
ELUL EDEN PERON ETAPE
RIME REND ANONA TONIC
SEED NAST LOPEZ NEAT

200

BAFF HAROLDS ITE AFT
ILO ELEISON DY GLUM
PEPENINSULA OIE HARA
DSTREET KILNS ABMS
MCA AYN ICED GON S
ARGAL SOFTBOILED FORE
DEAD NAZERMAN WORLD
ADIET CESARE HAVINGAY
MONEY ITT MILNE THE
DRACO AMEN ANTLERS
SWOON OHFUDGE DEEDS
COHOSTS ATMY MOULT
OLY IWERE NBA LISTS
MADA CAR RADIOS STAEL
TRUS KATYDIDS BREA
OXEN SHOOTIST PEUS
GOV DIM RUSS IDO SPH
OME CAYU CHEERIO
BAYH KIM THERODANDSP
SHOE ENC OEDIPAL EEEE
AUS LEA NESBITS SAND